Charles Alan Fyffe

A history of modern Europe

Vol. II

Charles Alan Fyffe

A history of modern Europe
Vol. II

ISBN/EAN: 9783742842565

Manufactured in Europe, USA, Canada, Australia, Japa

Cover: Foto ©Andreas Hilbeck / pixelio.de

Manufactured and distributed by brebook publishing software (www.brebook.com)

Charles Alan Fyffe

A history of modern Europe

OF

MODERN EUROPE.

BY

C. A. FYFFE, M.A.,

BARRISTER-AT-LAW; FELLOW OF UNIVERSITY COLLEGE, OXFORD; VICE-PRESIDENT
OF THE ROYAL HISTORICAL SOCIETY.

VOL. II.

FROM 1814 TO 1848.

CASSELL & COMPANY, LIMITED:
LONDON, PARIS & MELBOURNE.
1892.

[ALL RIGHTS RESERVED.]

PREFACE.

In writing this volume I have not had the advantage of consulting the English Foreign Office Records for a later period than the end of 1815. A rule not found necessary at Berlin and some other foreign capitals still closes to historical inquirers the English documents of the last seventy years. Restrictions are no doubt necessary in the case of transactions of recent date, but the period of seventy years is surely unnecessarily long. Public interests could not be prejudiced, nor could individuals be even remotely affected, by the freest examination of the papers of 1820 or 1830.

The London documents of 1814—1815 are of various degrees of interest and importance. Those relating to the Congress of Vienna are somewhat disappointing. Taken all together they add less to our knowledge on the one or two points still requiring elucidation than the recently-published correspondence of Talleyrand with Louis XVIII. The despatches from Italy are on the other hand of great value, proving, what I believe was not established before, that the Secret Treaty of 1815, whereby Austria gained a legal right to prevent any departure from absolute Government at Naples, was communicated to the British Ministry and received its sanction. This sanction explains the obscure and embarrassed language of Castlereagh in 1820, which in its turn gave rise to the belief in Italy that England was more deeply committed to Austria than it actually was, and probably occasioned the forgery of the pretended Treaty of July 27, 1813, exposed in vol. i. of this work, p. 538, 2nd edit. The papers from France and Spain are also interesting, though not establishing any new conclusions.

While regretting that I have not been able to use the London Archives later than 1815, I believe that it is nevertheless possible, without recourse to unpublished papers, to write the history of the succeeding thirty years with substantial correctness. There exist in a published form, apart from documents printed officially, masses of first-hand material of undoubtedly authentic character, such as the great English collection known by the somewhat misleading name of Wellington Despatches, New Series; or again, the collection printed as an appendix to Prokesch von Osten's History of the Greek Rebellion, or the many volumes of Gentz' Correspondence belonging to the period about 1820, when Gentz was really at the centre of affairs. The Metternich papers, interesting as far as they go, are a mere selection. The omissions are glaring, and scarcely accidental. Many minor collections bearing on particular events might be named, such as those in Guizot's Mémoires. Frequent references will show my obligation to the German series of historical works constituting the Leipzig Staatengeschichte, as well as to French authors who, like Viel-Castel, have worked with original sources of information before them. There exist in English literature singularly few works on this period of Continental history.

A greater publicity was introduced into political affairs on the Continent by the establishment of Parliamentary Government in France in 1815, and even by the attempts made to introduce it in other States. In England we have always had freedom of discussion, but the amount of information made public by the executive in recent times has been enormously greater than it was at the end of the last century. The only documents published at the outbreak of the war of 1793 were, so far as I can ascertain, the well-known letters of Chauvelin and Lord Grenville. During the twenty years' struggle with France next to nothing was known of the diplomatic transactions between England and the Continental Powers. But from the time of the Reform Bill onwards the amount of information given to the public has been constantly increasing, and the reader of Parliamentary Papers in our own day is likely to complain of diffusiveness rather than of reticence. Nevertheless the perusal of published papers can never be quite the same thing as an examination of the originals; and the writer who first has access to the English archives after 1815 will have an advantage over those who have gone before him.

The completion of this volume has been delayed by almost every circumstance adverse to historical study and production, including a severe Parliamentary contest. I trust, however, that no trace of partizanship or unrest appears in the work, which I have valued for the sake of the mental discipline which it demanded. With quieter times the third volume will, I trust, advance more rapidly.

LONDON, *October*, 1886.

CONTENTS.

CHAPTER I.

THE RESTORATION.

PAGE

The Restoration of 1814 — Norway — Naples — Westphalia — Spain — The Spanish Constitution overthrown: victory of the clergy—Restoration in France—The Charta—Encroachments of the nobles and clergy—Growing hostility to the Bourbons—Congress of Vienna—Talleyrand and the Four Powers—The Polish question—The Saxon question—Theory of Legitimacy—Secret alliance against Russia and Prussia—Compromise—The Rhenish Provinces—Napoleon leaves Elba and lands in France—His declarations—Napoleon at Grenoble, at Lyons, at Paris—The Congress of Vienna unites Europe against France—Murat's action in Italy—The Acte Additionnel—The Champ de Mai—Napoleon takes up the offensive—Battles of Ligny, Quatre Bras, Waterloo—Affairs at Paris—Napoleon sent to St. Helena—Wellington and Fouché—Arguments on the proposed cession of French territory—Treaty of Holy Alliance—Second Treaty of Paris—Conclusion of the work of the Congress of Vienna—Federation of Germany—Estimate of the Congress of Vienna and of the Treaties of 1815—The Slave Trade . . 1

CHAPTER II.

THE PROGRESS OF REACTION.

Concert of Europe after 1815—Spirit of the Foreign Policy of Alexander, of Metternich, and of the English Ministry—Metternich's action in Italy, England's in Sicily and Spain—The Reaction in France—Richelieu and the New Chamber—Execution of Ney—Imprisonments and persecutions—Conduct of the Ultra-Royalists in Parliament—Contests on the Electoral Bill and the Budget—The Chamber prorogued—Affair of Grenoble—Dissolution of the Chamber—Electoral Law and Financial Settlement of 1817—Character of the first years of peace in Europe generally—Promise of a Constitution in Prussia—Hardenburg opposed by the partisans of autocracy and privilege — Schmalz' Pamphlet—Delay of Constitutional Reform in Germany at large—The Wartburg Festival—Progress of Reaction—The Czar now inclines to repression — Congress of Aix-la-Chapelle — Evacuation of France— Growing influence of Metternich in Europe—His action on Prussia—Murder of Kotzebue—The Carlsbad Conference and measures of repression in Germany—Richelieu and Decazes—Murder of the Duke of Berry—Progress of the reaction in France—General causes of the victory of reaction in Europe 78

CHAPTER III.

THE MEDITERRANEAN MOVEMENTS OF 1820.

Movements in the Mediterranean States beginning in 1820—Spain from 1814 to 1820—The South American Colonies—The Army at Cadiz: Action of Quiroga and Riego — Movement at Corunna — Ferdinand accepts the Constitution of 1812—Naples from 1815 to 1820—The Court-party, the Muratists, the Carbonari—The Spanish Constitution proclaimed at Naples — Constitutional movement in Portugal — Alexander's proposal with regard to Spain—The Conference and Declaration of Troppau—Protest of England—Conference of Laibach—The Austrians invade Naples and restore absolute Monarchy—Insurrection in Piedmont, which fails—Spain from 1820 to 1822—Death of Castlereagh—The Congress of Verona—Policy of England—The French invade Spain—Restoration of absolute Monarchy, and violence of the reaction—England prohibits the conquest of the Spanish Colonies by France, and subsequently recognises their independence—Affairs in Portugal—Canning sends troops to Lisbon—The Policy of Canning—Estimate of his place in the history of Europe 166

CHAPTER IV.

GREECE AND EASTERN AFFAIRS.

Condition of Greece: its Races and Institutions—The Greek Church—Communal System—The Ægean Islands—The Phanariots—Greek intellectual revival: Koraes—Beginning of Greek National Movement; Contact of Greece with the French Revolution and Napoleon—The Hetæria Philike—Hypsilanti's Attempt in the Danubian Provinces: its failure—Revolt of the Morea: Massacres: Execution of Gregorius, and Terrorism at Constantinople — Attitude of Russia, Austria, and England—Extension of the Revolt: Affairs at Hydra—The Greek Leaders—Fall of Tripolitza—The Massacre of Chios—Failure of the Turks in the Campaign of 1822—Dissensions of the Greeks—Mahmud calls upon Mehemet Ali for Aid—Ibrahim conquers Crete and invades the Morea—Siege of Missolonghi—Philhellenism in Europe—Russian proposal for Intervention—Conspiracies in Russia: Death of Alexander: Accession of Nicholas—Military Insurrection at St. Petersburg—Anglo-Russian Protocol—Treaty between England,

Russia, and France—Death of Canning—Navarino—War between Russia and Turkey—Campaigns of 1828 and 1829—Treaty of Adrianople—Capodistrias President of Greece—Leopold accepts and then declines the Greek Crown—Murder of Capodistrias—Otho, King of Greece 237

CHAPTER V.
THE MOVEMENTS OF 1830.

France before 1830 — Reign of Charles X. — Ministry of Martignac — Ministry of Polignac—The Duke of Orleans—War in Algiers—The July Ordinances—Revolution of July—Louis Philippe King—Nature and effects of the July Revolution—Affairs in Belgium—The Belgian Revolution—The Great Powers—Intervention, and establishment of the Kingdom of Belgium—Affairs of Poland—Insurrection at Warsaw—War between Russia and Poland—Overthrow of the Poles: End of the Polish Constitution—Affairs of Italy—Insurrection in the Papal States—France and Austria—Austrian Intervention—Ancona occupied by the French — Affairs of Germany — Prussia; the Zollverein — Brunswick, Hanover, Saxony—The Palatinate—Reaction in Germany—The exiles in Switzerland; Incursion into Savoy—Dispersion of the Exiles—France under Louis Philippe: Successive risings—Period of Parliamentary activity—England after 1830: The Reform Bill . . 356

CHAPTER VI.
SPANISH AND EASTERN AFFAIRS.

France and England after 1830—Affairs of Portugal—Don Miguel—Don Pedro invades Portugal—Ferdinand of Spain—The Pragmatic Sanction—Death of Ferdinand: Regency of Christina—The Constitution—Quadruple Alliance—Miguel and Carlos expelled from Portugal—Carlos enters Spain—The Basque Provinces—Carlist War: Zumalacarregui—The Spanish Government seeks French assistance, which is refused—Constitution of 1837—End of the War—Regency of Espartero—Isabella Queen—Affairs of the Ottoman Empire—Ibrahim invades Syria; his victories—Rivalry of France and Russia at Constantinople—Peace of Kutaya and Treaty of Unkiar Skelessi—Effect of this Treaty—France and Mehemet Ali—Commerce of the Levant—Second War between Mehemet and the Porte—Ottoman disasters—The Policy of the Great Powers—Quadruple Treaty without France—Ibrahim expelled from Syria—Final Settlement—Turkey after 1840—Attempted reforms of Reschid Pasha 422

CHAPTER VII.
EUROPE BEFORE 1848.

Europe during the Thirty-years' Peace—Italy and Austria—Mazzini—The House of Savoy—Gioberti—Election of Pius IX.—Reforms expected—

CONTENTS.

Revolution at Palermo—Agitation in Northern Italy—Lombardy—State of the Austrian Empire—Growth of Hungarian national spirit—The Magyars and Slavs—Transylvania—Parties among the Magyars—Kossuth—The Slavic national movements in Austria—The government enters on reforms in Hungary—Policy of the Opposition—The Rural system of Austria—Insurrection in Galicia: the nobles and the peasants—Agrarian edict—Public opinion in Vienna—Prussia—Accession and character of King Frederick William IV.—Convocation of the United Diet—Its debates and dissolution—France—The Spanish Marriages—Reform movement—Socialism—Revolution of February—End of the Orleanist Monarchy 405

LIST OF ILLUSTRATIONS.

		PAGE
Surrender of Napoleon		*Frontis.*
Execution of Marshal Ney	*To face*	99
Wartburg Festival	,,	127
Rising at Oporto	,,	187
The Siege of Cadiz	,,	222
The Hanging of the Greek Patriarch	,,	275
The Sortie from Missolonghi	,,	310
Lafayette and Louis Philippe	,,	376
Russian Fleet in the Bosphorus	,,	444
Pius IX. driving through the Streets of Rome . .	,,	472
The Erection of Barricades in Paris	,,	511

MODERN EUROPE.

CHAPTER I.

The Restoration of 1814—Norway—Naples—Westphalia—Spain—The Spanish Constitution overthrown: victory of the clergy—Restoration in France—The Charta—Encroachments of the nobles and clergy—Growing hostility to the Bourbons—Congress of Vienna—Talleyrand and the Four Powers—The Polish question—The Saxon question—Theory of Legitimacy—Secret alliance against Russia and Prussia—Compromise—The Rhenish Provinces—Napoleon leaves Elba and lands in France—His declarations—Napoleon at Grenoble, at Lyons, at Paris—The Congress of Vienna unites Europe against France—Murat's action in Italy—The Acte Additionnel—The Champ de Mai—Napoleon takes up the offensive—Battles of Ligny, Quatre Bras, Waterloo—Affairs at Paris—Napoleon sent to St. Helena—Wellington and Fouché—Arguments on the proposed cession of French territory—Treaty of Holy Alliance—Second Treaty of Paris—Conclusion of the work of the Congress of Vienna—Federation of Germany—Estimate of the Congress of Vienna and of the Treaties of 1815—The Slave Trade.

OF all the events which, in the more recent history of mankind, have struck the minds of nations with awe, and appeared to reveal in its direct operation a power overruling the highest human effort, there is none equal in grandeur and terror to the annihilation of Napoleon's army in the invasion of Russia. It was natural that a generation which had seen State after State overthrown, and each new violation of right followed by an apparent consolidation of the conqueror's strength, should view in the catastrophe of 1812 the hand of Providence visibly outstretched for the deliverance of Europe.* Since that time seventy years have passed. Perils which then seemed to envelop the future of mankind now appear in part illusory; sacrifices then counted cheap have proved of heavy cost. The history of the two last generations shows that not everything was lost to Europe in passing subjection to a usurper, nor everything gained by the victory of his opponents. It is now not easy to suppress the doubt whether the permanent interests of mankind would not have been best served by Napoleon's success in 1812. His empire had already attained dimensions that rendered its ultimate disruption certain: less depended upon the postponement or the acceleration of its downfall than on the order of things ready to take its place. The victory of Napoleon in 1812 would have been followed by the establishment of a Polish kingdom in the provinces taken from Russia. From no generosity in the conqueror, from no sympathy on his part with a fallen people, but from the necessities of his political situation, Poland must have been so organised as to render it the bulwark of French supremacy in the East. The serf would have been emancipated. The just hatred of the peasant to the noble, which made the partition of 1772 easy, and has proved fatal to every Polish uprising from that time to the present, would have been appeased by an agrarian reform executed with Napoleon's own unrivalled energy and intelligence, and ushered in with brighter hopes than have at any time in the history of Poland lit the dark shades of peasant-life.

* As Arndt, Schriften, ii. 311, Fünf oder sechs Wunder Gottes.

The motives which in 1807 had led Napoleon to stay his hand, and to content himself with half-measures of emancipation in the Duchy of Warsaw,* could have had no place after 1812, when Russia remained by his side, a mutilated but inexorable enemy, ever on the watch to turn to its own advantage the first murmurs of popular discontent beyond the border. Political independence, the heritage of the Polish noble, might have been withheld, but the blessing of landed independence would have been bestowed on the mass of the Polish people. In the course of some years this restored kingdom, though governed by a member of the house of Bonaparte, would probably have gained sufficient internal strength to survive the downfall of Napoleon's Empire or his own decease. England, Austria, and Turkey would have found it no impossible task to prevent its absorption by Alexander at the re-settlement of Europe, if indeed the collapse of Russia had not been followed by the overthrow of the Porte, and the establishment of a Greek, a Bulgarian, and a Roumanian Kingdom under the supremacy of France. By the side of the three absolute monarchs of Central and Eastern Europe there would have remained, upon Napoleon's downfall, at least one people in possession of the tradition of liberty: and from the example of Poland, raised from the deep but not incurable degradation of its social life, the rulers of Russia might have gained courage to emancipate the serf, without waiting for the lapse of

* Bernhardi, Geschichte Russlands, iii. 26.

K K 2

another half-century and the occurrence of a second ruinous war. To compare a possible sequence of events with the real course of history, to estimate the good lost and evil got through events which at the time seemed to vindicate the moral governance of the world, is no idle exercise of the imagination. It may serve to give caution to the judgment: it may guard us against an arbitrary and fanciful interpretation of the actual. The generation which witnessed the fall of Napoleon is not the only one which has seen Providence in the fulfilment of its own desire, and in the storm-cloud of nature and history has traced with too sanguine gaze the sacred lineaments of human equity and love.

The Empire of Napoleon had indeed passed away. The conquests won by the first soldiers of the Republic were lost to France along with all the latest spoils of its Emperor; but the restoration which was effected in 1814 was no restoration of the political order which had existed on the Continent before the outbreak of the Revolutionary War. The Powers which had overthrown Napoleon had been partakers, each in its own season, in the system of aggrandisement which had obliterated the old frontiers of Europe. Russia had gained Finland, Bessarabia, and the greater part of Poland; Austria had won Venice, Dalmatia, and Salzburg; Prussia had received between the years 1792 and 1806 an extension of territory in Poland and Northern Germany that more than doubled its area. It was now no part of the policy of the victorious Courts to reinstate the governments which they had

Settlement of 1814.

themselves dispossessed: the settlement of 1814, in so far as it deserved the name of a restoration, was confined to the territory taken from Napoleon and from princes of his house. Here, though the claims of Republics and Ecclesiastical Princes were forgotten, the titles of the old dynasties were freely recognised. In France itself, in the Spanish Peninsula, in Holland, Westphalia, Piedmont, and Tuscany, the banished houses resumed their sovereignty. It cost the Allies nothing to restore these countries to their hereditary rulers, and it enabled them to describe the work of 1814 in general terms as the restoration of lawful government and national independence. But the claims of legitimacy, as well as of national right, were, as a matter of fact, only remembered where there existed no motive to disregard them; where they conflicted with arrangements of policy, they received small consideration. Norway, which formed part of the Danish monarchy, had been promised by Alexander to Bernadotte, Crown Prince of Sweden, in 1812, in return for his support against Napoleon, and the bargain had been ratified by the Allies. As soon as Napoleon was overthrown, Bernadotte claimed his reward. It was in vain that the Norwegians, abandoned by their king, declared themselves independent, and protested against being handed over like a flock of sheep by the liberators of Europe. The Allies held to their contract; a British fleet was sent to assist Bernadotte in overpowering his new subjects, and after a brief resistance the Norwegians

Norway.

found themselves compelled to submit to their fate (April—Aug., 1814).* At the other extremity of Europe a second of Napoleon's generals still held his throne among the restored legitimate monarchs. Murat, King of Naples, had forsaken Napoleon in time to make peace and alliance with Austria. Great Britain, though entering into a military convention, had not been a party to this treaty; and it had declared that its own subsequent support of Murat would depend upon the condition that he should honourably exert himself in Italy against Napoleon's forces. This condition Murat had not fulfilled. The British Government was, however, but gradually supplied with proofs of his treachery; nor was Lord Liverpool, the Prime Minister, inclined to raise new difficulties at Vienna by pressing the claim of Ferdinand of Sicily to his territories on the mainland.† Talleyrand, on behalf of the restored Bourbons of Paris, intended to throw all his strength into a diplomatic attack upon Murat before the end of the Congress; but for the present Murat's chances seemed to be superior to those of his rival. Southern Italy thus continued in the hands of a soldier of fortune, who, unlike Bernadotte, was secretly the friend of Napoleon, and ready to support him in any attempt to regain his throne.

<small>Naples.</small>

The engagement of the Allies towards Bernadotte,

* Parl. Debates, xxvii. 634, 834.
† Wellington, Sup. Des., x. 468; Castlereagh, x. 145. Records, Sicily, vol. 97. The future King Louis Philippe was sent by his father-in-law, Ferdinand, to England, to intrigue against Murat among the Sovereigns

added to the stipulations of the Peace of Paris, left little to be decided by the Congress of Vienna beyond the fate of Poland, Saxony, and Naples, and the form of political union to be established in Germany. It had been agreed that the Congress should assemble within two months after the signature of the Peace of Paris: this interval, however, proved to be insufficient, and the autumn had set in before the first diplomatists arrived at Vienna, and began the conferences which preceded the formal opening of the Congress. In the meantime a singular spectacle was offered to Europe by the Courts whose restoration was the subject of so much official thanksgiving. Before King Louis XVIII. returned to Paris, the exiled dynasties had regained their thrones in Northern Germany and in Spain. The process of reaction had begun in Hanover and in Hesse as soon as the battle of Leipzig had dissolved the Kingdom of Westphalia and driven Napoleon across the Rhine. Hanover indeed did not enjoy the bodily presence of its Sovereign: its character was oligarchical, and the reaction here was more the affair of the privileged classes than of the Government. In Hesse a prince returned who was the very embodiment of divine right, a prince who had sturdily fought against French demagogues in 1792, and over whose stubborn despotic nature the revolutions of a whole generation and the loss of his own dominions since the battle of Jena had passed without leaving a

Restoration in Westphalia.

and Ministers then visiting England. His own curious account of his proceedings, with the secret sign for the Prince Regent, given him by Louis XVIII, who was afraid to write anything, is in *id.*, vol. 99.

trace. The Elector was seventy years old when, at the end of the year 1813, his faithful subjects dragged his carriage in triumph into the streets of Cassel. On the day after his arrival he gave orders that the Hessian soldiery who had been sent on furlough after the battle of Jena should present themselves, every man in the garrison-town where he had stood on the 1st of November, 1806. A few weeks later all the reforms of the last seven years were swept away together. The Code Napoléon ceased to be the law of the land; the old oppressive distinctions of caste, with the special courts for the privileged orders, came again into force, in defiance of the spirit of the age. The feudal burdens of the peasantry were revived, the purchasers of State-lands compelled to relinquish the land without receiving back any of their purchase-money. The decimal coinage was driven out of the country. The old system of taxation, with its iniquitous exemptions, was renewed. All promotions, all grants of rank made by Jerome's Government were annulled: every officer, every public servant resumed the station which he had occupied on the 1st of November, 1806. The very pigtails and powder of the common soldier under the old régime were revived.*

The Hessians and their neighbours in North-Western Germany had from of old been treated with very little ceremony by their rulers; and if they welcomed back a

---

* Wippermann, Kurhessen, pp. 9—13. In Hanover torture was restored, and occasionally practised till the end of 1818: also the punishment of death by breaking on the wheel. See Hodgskin, Travels, ii. 51, 69.

family which had been accustomed to hire them out at so much a head to fight against the Hindoos or by the side of the North American Indians, it only proved that they preferred their native taskmasters to Jerome Bonaparte and his French crew of revellers and usurers. The next scene in the European reaction was a far more mournful one. Ferdinand of Spain had no sooner re-crossed the Pyrenees in the spring of 1814, than, convinced of his power by the transports of popular en-thusiasm that attended his progress through Northern Spain, he determined to overthrow the Constitution of 1812, and to re-establish the absolute monarchy which had existed before the war. The courtiers and ecclesiastics who gathered round the King dispelled any scruples that he might have felt in lifting his hand against a settlement accepted by the nation. They represented to him that the Cortes of 1812—which, whatever their faults, had been recognised as the legitimate Government of Spain by both England and Russia—consisted of a handful of desperate men, collected from the streets of Cadiz, who had taken upon themselves to insult the Crown, to rob the Church, and to imperil the existence of the Catholic Faith. On the entry of the King into Valencia, the cathedral clergy expressed the wishes of their order in the address of homage which they offered to Ferdinand. "We beg your Majesty," their spokesman concluded, "to take the most vigorous measures for the restoration of the Inquisition, and of the ecclesiastical system that existed in Spain before your Majesty's departure." "These," replied the King, "are my own wishes, and I will not rest until they are fulfilled." *

The victory of the clergy was soon declared. On the 11th of May the King issued a manifesto at Valencia, proclaiming the Constitution of 1812 and every decree of the Cortes null and void, and denouncing the penalties of high treason against everyone who should defend the Constitution by act, word, or writing. A variety of promises, made only to be broken, accompanied this assertion of the rights of the Crown. The King pledged himself to summon new Cortes, as soon as public order should be restored, to submit the expenditure to the control of the nation, and to maintain inviolate the security of person and property. It was a significant comment upon Ferdinand's professions of Liberalism that on the very day on which the proclamation was issued the censorship of the Press was restored. But the King had not miscalculated his power over the Spanish people. The same storm of wild unreasoning loyalty which had followed Ferdinand's re-appearance in Spain followed the overthrow of the Constitution. The mass of the Spaniards were ignorant of the very meaning of political liberty: they adored the King as a savage adores his fetish: their passions were at the call of a priesthood as brutish and unscrupulous as that which in 1798 had excited the Lazzaroni of Naples against the Republicans of Southern Italy. No sooner had

Spanish Constitution overthrown.

* Baumgarton, Geschichte Spaniens, ii. 30. Wellington, D., xii. 27; S. D., ix. 17.

Ferdinand set the example by arresting thirty of the most distinguished of the Liberals, than tumults broke out in every part of the country against Constitutionalist magistrates and citizens. Mobs, headed by priests bearing the standard of the Inquisition, destroyed the tablets erected in honour of the Constitution of 1812, and burned Liberal writings in bonfires in the market-places. The prisons were filled with men who, but a short time before, had been the objects of popular adulation.

Whatever pledges of allegiance had been given to the Constitution of 1812, it was clear that this Constitution had no real hold on the nation, and that Ferdinand fulfilled the wish of the majority of Spaniards in overthrowing it. A wise and energetic sovereign would perhaps have allowed himself to use this outburst of religious fanaticism for the purpose of substituting some better order for the imprudent arrangements of 1812. Ferdinand, an ignorant, hypocritical buffoon, with no more notion of political justice or generosity than the beasts of the field, could only substitute for the fallen Cortes a government by palace-favourites and confessors. It was in vain that the representatives of Great Britain urged the King to fulfil his constitutional promises, and to liberate the persons who had unjustly been thrown into prison.* The clergy were masters of Spain and of the King: their influence daily outweighed even that of Ferdinand's own Ministers, when, under the pressure of

<small>The clergy in power.</small>

* Wellington, S. D., ix. 328.

financial necessity, the Ministers began to offer some resistance to the exorbitant demands of the priesthood. On the 23rd of May the King signed an edict restoring all monasteries throughout Spain, and reinstating them in their lands. On the 24th of June the clergy were declared exempt from taxation. On the 21st of July the Church won its crowning triumph in the re-establishment of the Inquisition. In the meantime the army was left without pay, in some places actually without food. The country was at the mercy of bands of guerillas, who, since the disappearance of the enemy, had turned into common brigands, and preyed upon their own countrymen. Commerce was extinct; agriculture abandoned; innumerable villages were lying in ruins; the population was barbarised by the savage warfare with which for years' past it had avenged its own sufferings upon the invader. Of all the countries of Europe, Spain was the one in which the events of the Revolutionary epoch seemed to have left an effect most nearly approaching to unmixed evil.

In comparison with the reaction in the Spanish Peninsula the reaction in France was sober and dignified. Louis XVIII. was at least a scholar and a man of the world. In the old days, among companions whose names were now almost forgotten, he had revelled in Voltaire, and dallied with the fashionable Liberalism of the time. In his exile he had played the king with some dignity; he was even believed to have learnt some political wisdom by his six years' residence in England. If he had not

Restoration in France.

character,* he had at least some tact and some sense of humour; and if not a profound philosopher, he was at least an accomplished epicurean. He hated the zealotry of his brother, the Count of Artois. He was more inclined to quiz the emigrants than to sacrifice anything on their behalf; and the whole bent of his mind made him but an insincere ally of the priesthood, who indeed could hardly expect to enjoy such an orgy in France as their brethren were celebrating in Spain. The King, however, was unable to impart his own indifference to the emigrants who returned with him, nor had he imagination enough to identify himself, as King of France, with the military glories of the nation and with the democratic army that had won them. Louis held high notions of the royal prerogative: this would not in itself have prevented him from being a successful ruler, if he had been capable of governing in the interest of the nation at large. There were few Republicans remaining in France; the centralised institutions of the Empire remained in full vigour; and although the last months of Napoleon's rule had excited among the educated classes a strong spirit of constitutional opposition, an able and patriotic Bourbon accepting his new position, and wielding power for the benefit of the people and not of a class, might perhaps have exercised an authority not much inferior to that possessed by the Crown before 1789. But Louis, though rational, was inexperienced and supine. He was ready enough to

* Compare his cringing letter to Pichegru in Manuscrit de Louis XVIII., p. 463, with his answer in 1797 to the Venetian Senate, in Thiers.

admit into his Ministry and to retain in administrative posts throughout the country men who had served under Napoleon; but when the emigrants and the nobles, led by the Count of Artois, pushed themselves to the front of the public service, and treated the restoration of the Bourbons as the victory of their own order, the King offered but a faint resistance, and allowed the narrowest class-interests to discredit a monarchy whose own better traditions identified it not with an aristocracy but with the State.

The Constitution promulgated by King Louis XVIII. on the 4th of June, 1814, and known as the Charta,* was well received by the French nation. Though far less liberal than the Constitution accepted by Louis XVI. in 1791, it gave to the French a measure of representative government to which they had been strangers under Napoleon. It created two legislative chambers, the Upper House consisting of peers who were nominated by the Crown at its pleasure, whether for life-peerages or hereditary dignity; the Lower House formed by national election, but by election restricted by so high a property-qualification† that not one person in two hundred possessed a vote. The Crown reserved to itself the sole power of proposing laws. In spite of this serious

The Charta.

---

* *Moniteur*, 5 Juin. British and Foreign State Papers, 1812—14, ii. 960.

† The payment of £13 per annum in direct taxes. No one could be elected who did not pay £40 per annum in direct taxes,—so large a sum, that the Charta provided for the case of there not being fifty persons in a department eligible.

limitation of the competence of the two houses, the Lower Chamber possessed, in its right of refusing taxes and of discussing and rejecting all measures laid before it, a reality of power such as no representative body had possessed in France since the beginning of the Consulate. The Napoleonic nobility was placed on an equality with the old noblesse of France, though neither enjoyed, as nobles, anything more than a titular distinction.* Purchasers of landed property sold by the State since the beginning of the Revolution were guaranteed in their possessions. The principles of religious freedom, of equality before the law, and of the admissibility of all classes to public employment, which had taken such deep root during the Republic and the Empire, were declared to form part of the public law of France; and by the side of these deeply-cherished rights the Charta of King Louis XVIII. placed, though in a qualified form, the long-forgotten principle of the freedom of the Press.

Under such a Constitution there was little room for the old noblesse to arrogate to itself any legal superiority over the mass of the French nation. What was wanting in law might, however, in the opinion of the Count of Artois and his friends, be effected by administration. Of all the institutions of France the most thoroughly national and the most thoroughly democratic was the army; it

<small>*Encroachments of Nobles.*</small>

---

* Fourteen out of Napoleon's twenty marshals and three-fifths of his Senators were called to the Chamber of Peers. The names of the excluded Senators will be found in Vaulabelle, ii. 100; but the reader must not take Vaulabelle's history for more than a collection of party-legends.

was accordingly against the army that the noblesse directed its first efforts. Financial difficulties made a large reduction in the forces necessary. Fourteen thousand officers and sergeants were accordingly dismissed on half-pay; but no sooner had this measure of economy been effected than a multitude of emigrants who had served against the Republic in the army of the Prince of Condé or in La Vendée were rewarded with all degrees of military rank. Naval officers who had quitted the service of France and entered that of its enemies were reinstated with the rank which they had held in foreign navies.* The tricolor, under which every battle of France had been fought from Jemappes to Montmartre, was superseded by the white flag of the House of Bourbon, under which no living soldier had marched to victory. General Dupont, known only by his capitulation at Baylen in 1808, was appointed Minister of War. The Imperial Guard was removed from service at the Palace, and the so-called Military Household of the old Bourbon monarchy revived, with the privileges and the insignia belonging to the period before 1775. Young nobles, who had never seen a shot fired, crowded into this favoured corps, where the musketeer and the trooper held the rank and the pay of a lieutenant in the army. While in every village of France some battered soldier of Napoleon cursed the Government that had driven him from his comrades, the Court revived at Paris all the details of military ceremonial that could be gathered from old almanacks,

* Ordonnance, in *Moniteur*, 26 Mai.

from the records of court-tailors, and from the memories of decayed gallants. As if to convince the public that nothing had happened during the last twenty-two years, the aged Marquis de Chansenets, who had been Governor of the Tuileries on the 10th of August, 1792, and had then escaped by hiding among the bodies of the dead,* resumed his place at the head of the officers of the Palace.

These were but petty triumphs for the emigrants and nobles, but they were sufficient to make the restored monarchy unpopular. Equally injurious was their behaviour in insulting the families of Napoleon's generals, in persecuting men who had taken part in the great movement of 1789, and in intimidating the peasant-owners of land that had been confiscated and sold by the State. Nor were the priesthood backward in discrediting the Government of Louis XVIII. in the service of their own order. It might be vain to think of recovering the Church-lands, or of introducing the Inquisition into France, but the Court might at least be brought to invest itself with the odour of sanctity, and the parish-priest might be made as formidable a person within his own village as the mayor or the agent of the police-minister. Louis XVIII. was himself sceptical and self-indulgent. This, however, did not prevent him from publishing a letter to the Bishops placing his kingdom under

<small>Encroachments of the clergy.</small>

---

* This poor creature owed his life, as he owes a shabby immortality, to the beautiful and courageous Grace Dalrymple Elliott. Journal of Mrs. G. D. Elliott, p. 79.

the especial protection of the Virgin Mary, and from escorting the image of the patron-saint through the streets of Paris in a procession in which Marshal Soult and other regenerate Jacobins of the Court braved the ridicule of the populace by acting as candle-bearers. Another sign of the King's submission to the clergy was the publication of an edict which forbade buying and selling on Sundays and festivals. Whatever the benefits of a freely-observed day of rest, this enactment, which was not submitted to the Chambers, passed for an arrogant piece of interference on the part of the clergy with national habits; and while it caused no inconvenience to the rich, it inflicted substantial loss upon a numerous and voluble class of petty traders. The wrongs done to the French nation by the priests and emigrants who rose to power in 1814 were indeed the merest trifle in comparison with the wrongs which it had uncomplainingly borne at the hands of Napoleon. But the glory of the Empire, the strength and genius of its absolute rule, were gone. In its place there was a family which had been dissociated from France during twenty years, which had returned only to ally itself with an unpopular and dreaded caste, and to prove that even the unexpected warmth with which it had been welcomed home could not prevent it from becoming, at the end of a few months, utterly alien and uninteresting. The indifference of the nation would not have endangered the Bourbon monarchy if the army had been won over by the King. But here

Growing hostility to the Bourbons.

the Court had excited the bitterest enmity. The accord which for a moment had seemed possible even to Republicans of the type of Carnot had vanished at a touch.* Rumours of military conspiracies grew stronger with every month. Wellington, now British Ambassador at Paris, warned his Government of the changed feeling of the capital, of the gatherings of disbanded officers, of possible attacks upon the Tuileries. "The truth is," he wrote, "that the King of France without the army is no King." Wellington saw the more immediate danger: † he failed to see the depth and universality of the movement passing over France, which, before the end of the year 1814, had destroyed the hold of the Bourbon monarchy except in those provinces where it had always found support, and prepared the nation at large to welcome back the ruler who so lately seemed to have fallen for ever.

Paris and Madrid divided for some months after the conclusion of peace the attention of the political

* Carnot, Mémoire adressé au Roi, p. 20.
† Wellington Despatches, xii. 248. On the ground of his ready-money dealings, it has been supposed that Wellington understood the French people. On the contrary, he often showed great want of insight, both in his acts and in his opinions, when the finer, and therefore more statesmanlike, sympathies were in question. Thus, in the delicate position of ambassador of a victorious Power and counsellor of a restored dynasty, he bitterly offended the French country-population by behaving like a *grand seigneur* before 1789, and hunting with a pack of hounds over their young corn. The matter was so serious that the Government of Louis XVIII. had to insist on Wellington stopping his hunts. (Talleyrand et Louis XVIII, p. 141.) This want of insight into popular feeling necessarily resulted in some portentous blunders: *e.g.*, all that Wellington could make of Napoleon's return from Elba was the following:—" He has acted upon false or no information, and the King will destroy him without difficulty and in a short time." Despatches, xii. 268.

world. At the end of September the centre of European interest passed to Vienna. The great council of the Powers, so long delayed, was at length assembled. The Czar of Russia, the Kings of Prussia, Denmark, Bavaria, and Würtemberg, and nearly all the statesmen of eminence in Europe, gathered round the Emperor Francis and his Minister, Metternich, to whom by common consent the presidency of the Congress was offered. Lord Castlereagh represented England, and Talleyrand France. Rasumoffsky and other Russian diplomatists acted under the immediate directions of their master, who on some occasions even entered into personal correspondence with the Ministers of the other Powers. Hardenberg stood in a somewhat freer relation to King Frederick William: Stein was present, but without official place. The subordinate envoys and *attachés* of the greater Courts, added to a host of petty princes and the representatives who came from the minor Powers, or from communities which had ceased to possess any political existence at all, crowded Vienna. In order to relieve the antagonisms which had already come too clearly into view, Metternich determined to entertain his visitors in the most magnificent fashion; and although the Austrian State was bankrupt, and in some districts the people were severely suffering, a sum of about £10,000 a day was for some time devoted to this purpose. The splendour and the gaieties of Metternich were emulated by his guests; and the guardians of Europe enjoyed or endured for months together a succession of fêtes, banquets, dances, and excursions, varied, through the zeal of Talleyrand to ingratiate himself with his new master, by a Mass of great solemnity on the anniversary of the execution of Louis XVI.* One incident lights the faded and insipid record of vanished pageants and defunct gallantries. Beethoven was in Vienna. The Government placed the great Assembly-rooms at his disposal, and enabled the composer to gratify a harmless humour by sending invitations in his own name to each of the Sovereigns and grandees then in Vienna. Much personal homage, some substantial kindness from these gaudy creatures of the hour, made the period of the Congress a bright page in that wayward and afflicted life whose poverty has enriched mankind with such immortal gifts.

The Congress had need of its distractions, for the difficulties which faced it were so great that, even after the arrival of the Sovereigns, it was found necessary to postpone the opening of the regular sittings until November. By the secret articles of the Peace of Paris, the Allies had reserved to themselves the disposal of all vacant territory, although their conclusions required to be formally sanctioned by the Congress at large. The Ministers of Austria, England, Prussia, and Russia accordingly determined at the outset to decide upon all territorial

<small>Talleyrand and the four Powers.</small>

* A good English account of Vienna during the Congress will be found in "Travels in Hungary," by Dr. R. Bright, the eminent physician. His visit to Napoleon's son, then a child five years old, is described in a passage of singular beauty and pathos.

questions among themselves, and only after their decisions were completely formed to submit them to France and the other Powers.* Talleyrand, on hearing of this arrangement, protested that France itself was now one of the Allies, and demanded that the whole body of European States should at once meet in open Congress. The four Courts held to their determination, and began their preliminary sittings without Talleyrand. But the French statesman had, under the form of a paradox, really stated the true political situation. The greater Powers were so deeply divided in their aims that their old bond of common interest, the interest of union against France, was now less powerful than the impulse that made them seek the support of France against one another. Two men had come to the Congress with a definite aim: Alexander had resolved to gain the Duchy of Warsaw, and to form it, with or without some part of Russian Poland, into a Polish kingdom, attached to his own crown: Talleyrand had determined, either on the question of Poland, or on the question of Saxony, which arose out of it, to break allied Europe into halves, and to range France by the side of two of the great Powers against the two others. The course of events favoured for a while the design of the Minister: Talleyrand himself prosecuted his plan with an ability which, but for the untimely return of Napoleon from Elba, would have left France, without a war, the arbiter and the leading Power of Europe.

* British and Foreign State Papers, 1814—15, p. 554, *seq.* Talleyrand et Louis XVIII., p. 13. Klüber, ix. 167. Seeley's Stein, iii. 248. Gentz, Dépêches Inédites, i. 107. Records: Continent, vol. 7, Oct. 2.

Since the Russian victories of 1812, the Emperor Alexander had made no secret of his intention to restore a Polish Kingdom and a Polish nationality.* Like many other designs of this prince, the project combined a keen desire for personal glorification with a real generosity of feeling. Alexander was thoroughly sincere in his wish not only to make the Poles again a people, but to give them a Parliament and a free Constitution. The King of Poland, however, was to be no independent prince, but Alexander himself: although the Duchy of Warsaw, the chief if not the sole component of the proposed new kingdom, had belonged to Austria and Prussia after the last partition of Poland, and extended into the heart of the Prussian monarchy. Alexander insisted on his anxiety to atone for the crime of Catherine in dismembering Poland: the atonement, however, was to be made at the sole cost of those whom Catherine had allowed to share the booty. Among the other Governments, the Ministry of Great Britain would gladly have seen a Polish State established in a really independent form; † failing this, it desired that the Duchy of Warsaw should be divided, as formerly, between Austria and Prussia. Metternich was anxious that the fortress of Cracow at any rate should not fall into the hands of the Czar. Stein and Hardenberg, and even Alexander's own Russian counsellors, earnestly opposed the Czar's project, not only on account of the claims of Prussia on Warsaw, but from

<small>Polish question.</small>

* Bernhardi, i. 2; ii. 2, 661.   † Wellington, S. D., ix. 335.

dread of the agitation likely to be produced by a Polish Parliament among all Poles outside the new State. King Frederick William, however, was unaccustomed to dispute the wishes of his ally; and the Czar's offer of Saxony in substitution for Warsaw gave to the Prussian Ministers, who were more in earnest than their master, at least the prospect of receiving a valuable equivalent for what they might surrender.

By the Treaty of Kalisch, made when Prussia united its arms with those of Russia against Napoleon (Feb. 27th, 1813), the Czar had undertaken to restore the Prussian monarchy to an extent equal to that which it had possessed in 1805. It was known before the opening of the Congress that the Czar proposed to do this by handing over to King Frederick William the whole of Saxony, whose Sovereign, unlike his colleagues in the Rhenish Confederacy, had supported Napoleon up to his final overthrow at Leipzig. Since that time the King of Saxony had been held a prisoner, and his dominions had been occupied by the Allies. The Saxon question had thus already gained the attention of all the European Governments, and each of the Ministers now at Vienna brought with him some more or less distinct view upon the subject. Castlereagh, who was instructed to foster the union of Prussia and Austria against Alexander's threatening ambition, was willing that Prussia should annex Saxony if in return it would assist him in keeping Russia out of Warsaw:* Metternich disliked the

Saxon question.

* Wellington, S. D., ix. 340. Records: Continent, vol. 7, Oct. 9, 14.

annexation, but offered no serious objection, provided that in Western Germany Prussia would keep to the north of the Main: Talleyrand alone made the defence of the King of Saxony the very centre of his policy, and subordinated all other aims to this. His instructions, like those of Castlereagh, gave priority to the Polish question;* but Talleyrand saw that Saxony, not Poland, was the lever by which he could throw half of Europe on to the side of France; and before the four Allied Courts had come to any single conclusion, the French statesman had succeeded, on what at first passed for a subordinate point, in breaking up their concert.

For a while the Ministers of Austria, Prussia, and England appeared to be acting in harmony; and throughout the month of October all three endeavoured to shake the purpose of Alexander regarding Warsaw.† Talleyrand, however, foresaw that the efforts of Prussia in this direction would not last very long, and he wrote to Louis XVIII. asking for his permission to make a definite offer of armed assistance to Austria in case of need. Events took the turn which Talleyrand expected. Early in November the King of Prussia completely yielded to Alexander, and ordered Hardenberg to withdraw his opposition to the Russian project. Metternich thus found himself abandoned on the Polish question by Prussia; and at the same moment the answer of King

<small>Talleyrand's action on Saxony.</small>

---

* Talleyrand, p. 74. Records, *id.*, Oct. 24, 25.
† Wellington, S. D., ix. 331. Talleyrand, pp. 59, 82, 85, 109. Klüber, vii. 21.

Louis XVIII. arrived, and enabled Talleyrand to assure the Austrian Minister that, if resistance to Russia and Prussia should become necessary, he might count on the support of a French army. Metternich now completely changed his position on the Saxon question, and wrote to Hardenberg (Dec. 10) stating that, inasmuch as Prussia had chosen to sacrifice Warsaw, the Emperor Francis absolutely forbade the annexation of more than a fifth part of the kingdom of Saxony. Castlereagh, disgusted with the obstinacy of Russia and the subserviency of King Frederick William, forgave Talleyrand for not supporting him earlier, and cordially entered into this new plan for thwarting the Northern Powers. The leading member of the late Rhenish Confederacy, the King of Bavaria, threw himself with eagerness into the struggle against Prussia and against German unity. In proportion as Stein and the patriots of 1813 urged the claims of German nationality under Prussian leadership against the forfeited rights of a Court which had always served on Napoleon's side, the politicians of the Rhenish Confederacy declaimed against the ambition and the Jacobinism of Prussia, and called upon Europe to defend the united principles of hereditary right and of national independence in the person of the King of Saxony.

<small>Theory of Legitimacy.</small> Talleyrand's object was attained. He had isolated Russia and Prussia, and had drawn to his own side not only England and Austria but the whole body of the minor German States. Nothing was wanting but a phrase, or an idea, which should

consecrate the new league in the opinion of Europe as a league of principle, and bind the Allies, in matters still remaining open, to the support of the interests of the House of Bourbon. Talleyrand had made his theory ready. In notes to Castlereagh and Metternich,* he declared that the whole drama of the last twenty years had been one great struggle between revolution and established right, a struggle at first between Republicanism and Monarchy, afterwards between usurping dynasties and legitimate dynasties. The overthrow of Napoleon had been the victory of the principle of legitimacy; the task of England and Austria was now to extend the work of restitution to all Europe, and to defend the principle against new threatened aggressions. In the note to Castlereagh, Talleyrand added a practical corollary. "To finish the revolution, the principle of legitimacy must triumph without exception. The kingdom of Saxony must be preserved; the kingdom of Naples must return to its legitimate king."

As an historical summary of the Napoleonic wars, Talleyrand's doctrine was baseless. No one but Pitt had cared about the fate of the Bourbons; no one would have hesitated to make peace with Napoleon, if Napoleon would have accepted terms of peace. The manifesto was not, however, intended to meet a scientific criticism. In the English Foreign Office it was correctly described as a piece of drollery; and Metternich was too familiar with the language of principles himself to attach much

<small>Alliance against Russia and Prussia, Jan. 3, 1815.</small>

* British and Foreign State Papers, 1814—15, p. 814. Klüber, vii. 61.

meaning to it in the mouth of any one else. Talleyrand, however, kept a grave countenance. With inimitable composure the old Minister of the Directory wrote to Louis XVIII. lamenting that Castlereagh did not appear to care much about the principle of legitimacy, and in fact did not quite comprehend it;* and he added his fear that this moral dimness on the part of the English Minister arose from the dealing of his countrymen with Tippoo Sahib. But for Europe at large, —for the English Liberal party, who looked upon the Saxons and the Prussians as two distinct nations, and for the Tories, who forgot that Napoleon had made the Elector of Saxony a king; for the Emperor of Austria, who had no wish to see the Prussian frontier brought nearer to Prague; above all, for the minor German courts who dreaded every approach towards German unity,—Talleyrand's watchword was the best that could have been invented. His counsel prospered. On the 3rd of January, 1815, after a rash threat of war uttered by Hardenberg, a secret treaty† was signed by the representatives of France, England, and Austria, pledging these Powers to take the field, if necessary, against Russia and Prussia in defence of the principles of the Peace of Paris. The plan of the campaign was drawn up, the number of the forces fixed. Bavaria had already armed; Piedmont, Hanover, and even the Ottoman Porte, were named as future members of the alliance.

It would perhaps be unfair to the French Minister

* Talleyrand, p. 281.   † B. and F. State Papers, 1814—15, ii. 1001.

to believe that he actually desired to kindle a war on this gigantic scale. Talleyrand had not, like Napoleon, a love for war for its own sake. His object was rather to raise France from its position as a conquered and isolated Power; to surround it with allies; to make the House of Bourbon the representatives of a policy interesting to a great part of Europe; and, having thus undone the worst results of Napoleon's rule, to trust to some future complication for the recovery of Belgium and the frontier of the Rhine. Nor was Talleyrand's German policy adopted solely as the instrument of a passing intrigue. He appears to have had a true sense of the capacity of Prussia to transform Germany into a great military nation; and the policy of alliance with Austria and protection of the minor States which he pursued in 1814 was that which he had advocated throughout his career. The conclusion of the secret treaty of January 3rd marked the definite success of his plans. France was forthwith admitted into the council hitherto known as that of the Four Courts, and from this time its influence visibly affected the action of Russia and Prussia, reports of the secret treaty having reached the Czar immediately after its signature.* The spirit of compromise now began to animate the Congress. Alexander had already won a virtual decision in his favour on the Polish question, but he abated something of his claims, and while gaining the lion's share of the Duchy of Warsaw, he ulti-

Compromise on Polish and Saxon questions.

* Castlereagh did not contradict them. Records: Cont., vol. 10, Jan. 8.

mately consented that Cracow, which threatened the Austrian frontier, should be formed into an independent Republic, and that Prussia should receive the fortresses of Dantzic and Thorn on the Vistula, with the district lying between Thorn and the border of Silesia.* This was little for Alexander to abandon; on the Saxon question the allies of Talleyrand gained most that they demanded. The King of Saxony was restored to his throne, and permitted to retain Dresden and about half of his dominions. Prussia received the remainder. In lieu of a further expansion in Saxony, Prussia was awarded territory on the left bank of the Rhine, which, with its recovered West-phalian provinces, restored the monarchy to an area and population equal to that which it had possessed in 1805. But the dominion given to Prussia beyond the Rhine, though considered at the time to be a poor equivalent for the second half of Saxony, was in reality a gift of far greater value. It made Prussia, in defence of its own soil, the guardian and bulwark of Germany against France. It brought an element into the life of the State in striking contrast with the aristocratic and Protestant type predominant in the older Prussian provinces,—a Catholic population, liberal in its political opinions, and habituated by twenty years' union with France to the democratic tendencies of French social life. It gave to Prussia something more in common with Bavaria and

Marginal note: Prussia gains Rhenish Provinces.

---

* British and Foreign State Papers, 1814—15, p. 642. Seeley's Stein, iii. 303. Talleyrand, Preface, p. 18.

the South, and qualified it, as it had not been qualified before, for its future task of uniting Germany under its own leadership.

The Polish and Saxon difficulties, which had threatened the peace of Europe, were virtually settled before the end of the month of January. Early in February Lord Castlereagh left Vienna, to give an account of his labours and to justify his policy before the English House of Commons. His place at the Congress was taken by the Duke of Wellington. There remained the question of Naples, the formation of a Federal Constitution for Germany, and several matters of minor political importance, none of which endangered the good understanding of the Powers. Suddenly the action of the Congress was interrupted by the most startling intelligence. On the night of March 6th Metternich was roused from sleep to receive a despatch informing him that Napoleon had quitted Elba. The news had taken eight days to reach Vienna. Napoleon had set sail on the 26th of February. In the silence of his exile he had watched the progress of events in France : he had convinced himself of the strength of the popular reaction against the priests and emigrants ; and the latest intelligence which he had received from Vienna led him to believe that the Congress itself was on the point of breaking up. There was at least some chance of success in an attempt to regain his throne ; and, the decision once formed, Napoleon executed it with characteristic audacity and despatch. Talleyrand, on hearing that Napoleon had left Elba,

Napoleon leaves Elba, Feb. 26.

declared that he would only cross into Italy and there raise the standard of Italian independence: instead of doing this, Napoleon made straight for France, with the whole of his guard, eleven hundred in number, embarked on a little flotilla of seven ships. The voyage lasted three days: no French or English vessels capable of offering resistance met the squadron. On the 1st of March Napoleon landed at the bay of Jouan, three miles to the west of Antibes. A detachment of his guards called upon the commandant of Antibes to deliver up the town to the Emperor; the commandant refused, and the troops bivouacked that evening, with Napoleon among them, in the olive-woods by the shore of the Mediterranean.

Lands in France, March 1.

Before daybreak began the march that was to end in Paris. Instead of following the coast road of Provence, which would have brought him to Toulon and Marseilles, where most of the population were fiercely Royalist,* and where Massena and other great officers might have offered resistance, Napoleon struck northwards into the mountains, intending to descend upon Lyons by way of Grenoble. There were few troops in this district, and no generals capable of influencing them. The peasantry of Dauphiné were in great part holders of land that had been taken from the Church and the nobles: they were exasperated

Moves on Grenoble.

---

* Chiefly, but not altogether, because Napoleon's war with England had ruined the trade of the ports. See the report of Marshal Brune, in Dandet, La Terreur Blanche, p. 173, and the striking picture of Marseilles in Thiers, xviii. 340, drawn from his own early recollections. Bordeaux was Royalist for the same reason.

against the Bourbons, and, like the peasantry of France generally, they identified the glory of the country which they loved with the name and the person of Napoleon. As the little band penetrated into the mountains the villagers thronged around them, and by offering their carts and horses enabled Napoleon to march continuously over steep and snowy roads at the rate of forty miles a day. No troops appeared to dispute these mountain passages: it was not until the close of the fifth day's march that Napoleon's mounted guard, pressing on in front of the marching column, encountered, in the village of La Mure, twenty miles south of Grenoble, a regiment of infantry wearing the white cockade of the House of Bourbon. *Troops at La Mure.* The two bodies of troops mingled and conversed in the street: the officer commanding the royal infantry fearing the effect on his men, led them back on the road towards Grenoble. Napoleon's lancers also retired, and the night passed without further communication. At noon on the following day the lancers, again advancing towards Grenoble, found the infantry drawn up to defend the road. They called out that Napoleon was at hand, and begged the infantry not to fire. Presently Napoleon's column came in sight; one of his *aides-de-camp* rode to the front of the royal troops, addressed them, and pointed out Napoleon. The regiment was already wavering, the officer commanding had already given the order of retreat, when the men saw their Emperor advancing towards them. They saw his face, they heard his voice: in another moment the ranks were broken, and the soldiers were pressing with shouts and tears round the leader whom nature had created with such transcendent capacity for evil, and endowed with such surpassing power of attracting love.

Everything was decided by this first encounter. "In six days," said Napoleon, "we shall be in the Tuileries." The next pledge of victory came swiftly. Colonel Labédoyère, commander of the 7th Regiment of the Line, had openly declared for Napoleon in Grenoble, and appeared on the road at the head of his men a few hours after the meeting at La Mure. Napoleon reached Grenoble the same evening. The town had been in tumult all day. The Préfet fled: the general in command sent part of his troops away, and closed the gates. On Napoleon's approach the population thronged the ramparts with torches; the gates were burst open; Napoleon was borne through the town in triumph by a wild and intermingled crowd of soldiers and workpeople. The whole mass of the poorer classes of the town welcomed him with enthusiasm: the middle classes, though hostile to the Church and the Bourbons, saw too clearly the dangers to France involved in Napoleon's return to feel the same joy.* They remained in the background, neither welcoming Napoleon nor interfering with the welcome offered him by others. Thus the night passed. On the morning of the next day Napoleon received the magistrates and principal inhabitants of the town, and addressed them in terms which formed the substance of every subsequent

Enters Grenoble, March 7.

---

* Berriat-St. Prix, Napoléon à Grenoble, p. 10.

declaration of his policy. "He had come," he said, "to save France from the outrages of the returning nobles; to secure to the peasant the possession of his land; to uphold the rights won in 1789 against a minority which sought to re-establish the privileges of caste and the feudal burdens of the last century. France had made trial of the Bourbons: it had done well to do so; but the experiment had failed. The Bourbon monarchy had proved incapable of detaching itself from its worst supports, the priests and nobles: only the dynasty which owed its throne to the Revolution could maintain the social work of the Revolution. As for himself, he had learnt wisdom by misfortune. He renounced conquest. He should give France peace without and liberty within. He accepted the Treaty of Paris and the frontiers of 1792. Freed from the necessities which had forced him in earlier days to found a military Empire, he recognised and bowed to the desire of the French nation for constitutional government. He should henceforth govern only as a constitutional sovereign, and seek only to leave a constitutional crown to his son."

Declaration of his purpose.

This language was excellently chosen. It satisfied the peasants and the workmen, who wished to see the nobles crushed, and it showed at least a comprehension of the feelings uppermost in the minds of the wealthier and more educated middle classes, the longing for peace, and the aspiration towards political liberty. It was also calculated to temper the unwelcome impression that an exiled

Feeling of the various classes.

ruler was being forced upon France by the soldiery. The military movement was indeed overwhelmingly decisive, yet the popular movement was scarcely less so. The Royalists were furious, but impotent to act; thoughtful men in all classes held back, with sad apprehensions of returning war and calamity;* but from the time when Napoleon left Grenoble, the nation at large was on his side. There was nowhere an effective centre of resistance. The Préfets and other civil officers appointed under the Empire still for the most part held their posts; they knew themselves to be threatened by the Bourbonist reaction, but they had not yet been displaced; their professions of loyalty to Louis XVIII. were forced, their instincts of obedience to their old master, even if they wished to have done with him, profound. From this class, whose cowardice and servility find too many parallels in history,† Napoleon had little to fear. Among the marshals and higher officers charged with the defence of the monarchy, those who sincerely desired to serve the Bourbons found themselves powerless in the midst of their troops. Macdonald, who commanded at Lyons, had to fly from his men, in order to escape being made a prisoner. The Count of Artois, who had come to join him, discovered that the only service he could render to the cause of his family was to take himself out of sight. Napoleon

* Béranger, Biographie, p. 373, ed. duod.

† See their contemptible addresses, as well as those of the army, in the *Moniteur*, from the 10th to the 19th of March to Louis XVIII., from the 27th onwards to Napoleon.

entered Lyons on the 10th of March, and now formally resumed his rank and functions as Emperor. His first edicts renewed that appeal to the ideas and passions of the Revolution which had been the key-note of every one of his public utterances since leaving Elba. Treating the episode of Bourbon restoration as null and void, the edicts of Lyons expelled from France every emigrant who had returned without the permission of the Republic or the Emperor; they drove from the army the whole mass of officers intruded by the Government of Louis XVIII.; they invalidated every appointment and every dismissal made in the magistracy since the 1st of April, 1814; and, reverting to the law of the Constituent Assembly of 1789, abolished all nobility except that which had been conferred by the Emperor himself. *[margin: Napoleon enters Lyons, March 10.]*

From this time all was over. Marshal Ney, who had set out from Paris protesting that Napoleon deserved to be confined in an iron cage,* found, when at some distance from Lyons, that the nation and army were on the side of the Emperor, and proclaimed his own adherence to him in an address to his troops. The two Chambers of Legislature, which had been prorogued, were summoned by King Louis XVIII. as soon as the news of Napoleon's landing reached the capital. The Chambers met on the 13th of March. The constitutionalist party, though they had opposed various measures of King *[margin: Marshal Ney.]* *[margin: The Chambers in Paris.]*

---

* *I.e.*, Because he had abused his liberty. On Ney's trial two courtiers alleged that Ney said he "would bring back Napoleon in an iron cage." Ney contradicted them. Procès de Ney, ii. 105, 113.

Louis' Government as reactionary, were sincerely loyal to the Charta, and hastened, in the cause of constitutional liberty, to offer to the King their cordial support in resisting Bonaparte's military despotism. The King came down to the Legislative Chamber, and, in a scene concerted with his brother, the Count of Artois, made, with great dramatic effect, a declaration of fidelity to the Constitution. Lafayette and the chiefs of the Parliamentary Liberals hoped to raise a sufficient force from the National Guard of Paris to hold Napoleon in check. The project, however, came to nought. The National Guard, which represented the middle classes of Paris, was decidedly in favour of the Charta and Constitutional Government; but it had no leaders, no fighting-organisation, and no military spirit. The regular troops who were sent out against Napoleon mounted the tricolor as soon as they were out of sight of Paris, and joined their comrades. The courtiers passed from threats to consternation and helplessness. On the night of March 19th King Louis fled from the Tuileries. Napoleon entered the capital the next evening, welcomed with acclamations by the soldiers and populace, but not with that general rejoicing which had met him at Lyons, and at many of the smaller towns through which he had passed.

<small>Napoleon enters Paris, March 20.</small>

France was won: Europe remained behind. On the 13th of March the Ministers of all the Great Powers, assembled at Vienna, published a manifesto denouncing Napoleon Bonaparte as the common enemy of mankind, and declaring

<small>Congress of Vienna outlaws Napoleon.</small>

him an outlaw. The whole political structure which had been reared with so much skill by Talleyrand vanished away. France was again alone, with all Europe combined against it. Affairs reverted to the position in which they had stood in the month of March, 1814, when the Treaty of Chaumont was signed, which bound the Powers to sustain their armed concert against France, if necessary, for a period of twenty years. That treaty was now formally renewed.* The four great Powers undertook to employ their whole available resources against Bonaparte until he should be absolutely unable to create disturbance, and each pledged itself to keep permanently in the field a force of at least a hundred and fifty thousand men. The presence of the Duke of Wellington at Vienna enabled the Allies to decide without delay upon the general plan for their invasion of France. It was resolved to group the allied troops in three masses; one, composed of the English and the Prussians under Wellington and Blücher, to enter France by the Netherlands; the two others, commanded by the Czar and Prince Schwarzenberg, to advance from the middle and upper Rhine. Nowhere was there the least sign of political indecision. The couriers sent by Napoleon with messages of amity to the various Courts were turned back at the frontiers with their despatches undelivered. It was in vain for the Emperor to attempt to keep up any illusion that peace was possible. After a brief interval he himself acquainted France with the

* British and Foreign State Papers, 1814—15, ii. 448.

true resolution of his enemies. The most strenuous efforts were made for defence. The old soldiers were called from their homes. Factories of arms and ammunition began their hurried work in the principal towns. The Emperor organised with an energy and a command of detail never surpassed at any period of his life; the nature of the situation lent a new character to his genius, and evoked in the organisation of systematic defence all that imagination and resource which had dazzled the world in his schemes of invasion and surprise. Nor, as hitherto, was the nation to be the mere spectator of his exploits. The population of France, its National Guard, its *levée en masse*, as well as its armies and its Emperor, was to drive the foreigner from French soil. Every operation of defensive warfare, from the accumulation of artillery round the capital to the gathering of forest-guards and free-shooters in the thickets of the Vosges and the Ardennes, occupied in its turn the thoughts of Napoleon.* Had France shared his resolution or his madness, had the Allies found at the outset no chief superior to their Austrian leader in 1814, the war on which they were now about to enter would have been one of immense difficulty and risk, its ultimate issue perhaps doubtful.

Napoleon's preparations for defence.

Before Napoleon or his adversaries were ready to move, hostilities broke out in Italy. Murat, King of Naples, had during the winter of 1814 been represented at Vienna by an envoy: he was aware of the efforts made

* Correspondance de Napoléon, xxviii. 171, 267, &c.

by Talleyrand to expel him from his throne, and knew that the Government of Great Britain, convinced of his own treachery during the pretended combination with the Allies in 1814, now inclined to act with France.* The instinct of self-preservation led him to risk everything in raising the standard of Italian independence, rather than await the loss of his kingdom; and the return of Napoleon precipitated his fall. At the moment when Napoleon was about to leave Elba, Murat, who knew his intention, asked the permission of Austria to move a body of troops through Northern Italy for the alleged purpose of attacking the French Bourbons, who were preparing to restore his rival, Ferdinand. Austria declared that it should treat the entry either of French or of Neapolitan troops into Northern Italy as an act of war. Murat, as soon as Napoleon's landing in France became known, protested to the Allies that he intended to remain faithful to them, but he also sent assurances of friendship to Napoleon, and forthwith invaded the Papal States. He acted without waiting for Napoleon's instructions, and probably with the intention of winning all Italy for himself even if Napoleon should victoriously re-establish his Empire. On the 10th of April, Austria declared war against him. Murat pressed forward and entered Bologna, now openly proclaiming the unity and independence of Italy. The feeling of the towns and of the educated classes generally seemed to be in his

Campaign and fall of Murat, April, 1815.

---

* British and Foreign State Papers, 1814—15, ii. 275. Castlereagh, ix. 512. Wellington, S. D., ix. 244. Records: Continent, vol. 12, Feb. 26.

favour, but no national rising took place. After some indecisive encounters with the Austrians, Murat retreated. As he fell back towards the Neapolitan frontier, his troops melted away. The enterprise ended in swift and total ruin; and on the 22nd of May an English and Austrian force took possession of the city of Naples in the name of King Ferdinand. Murat, leaving his family behind him, fled to France, and sought in vain to gain a place by the side of Napoleon in his last great struggle, and to retrieve as a soldier the honour which he had lost as a king.*

In the midst of his preparations for war with all Europe, Napoleon found it necessary to give some satisfaction to that desire for liberty which was again so strong in France. He would gladly have deferred all political change until victory over the foreigner had restored his own undisputed ascendancy over men's minds; he was resolved at any rate not to be harassed by a Constituent Assembly, like that of 1789, at the moment of his greatest peril; and the action of King Louis XVIII. in granting liberty by Charta gave him a precedent for creating a Constitution by an Edict supplementary to the existing laws of the Empire. Among the Liberal politicians who had declared for King Louis XVIII. while Napoleon was approaching Paris, one of the most

The Acte Additionnel, April 23, 1815.

---

* Correspondance de Napoléon, xxviii. 111, 127. The order forbidding him to come to Paris is wrongly dated April 19; probably for May 29. The English documents relating to Ferdinand's return to Naples, with the originals of many proclamations, &c., are in Records: Sicily, vols. 103, 104. They are interesting chiefly as showing the deep impression made on England by Ferdinand's cruelties in 1799.

eminent was Benjamin Constant, who had published an article attacking the Emperor with great severity on the very day when he entered the capital. Napoleon now invited Constant to the Tuileries, assured him that he no longer either desired or considered it possible to maintain an absolute rule in France, and requested Constant himself to undertake the task of drawing up a Constitution. Constant, believing the Emperor to be in some degree sincère, accepted the proposals made to him, and, at the cost of some personal consistency, entered upon the work, in which Napoleon by no means allowed him entire freedom.* The result of Constant's labours was the Decree known as the Acte Additionnel of 1815. The leading provisions of this Act resembled those of the Charta: both professed to establish a representative Government and the responsibility of Ministers; both contained the usual phrases guaranteeing freedom of religion and security of person and property. The principal differences were that the Chamber of Peers was now made wholly hereditary, and that the Emperor absolutely refused to admit the clause of the Charta abolishing confiscation as a penalty for political offences. On the other hand, Constant definitely extinguished the censorship of the Press, and provided some real guarantee for the free èxpression of opinion by enacting that Press-offences should be judged only in the ordinary Jury-courts. Constant was sanguine enough to believe that the document which he had composed would reduce Napoleon to the condition of

* Benjamin Constant, Mémoire sur les Cent Jours.

a constitutional king. As a Liberal statesman, he pressed the Emperor to submit the scheme to a Representative Assembly, where it could be examined and amended. This Napoleon refused to do, preferring to resort to the fiction of a Plébiscite for the purpose of procuring some kind of national sanction for his Edict. The Act was published on the 23rd of April, 1815. Voting lists were then opened in all the Departments, and the population of France, most of whom were unable to read or write, were invited to answer Yes or No to the question whether they approved of Napoleon's plan for giving his subjects Parliamentary government.

There would have been no difficulty in obtaining some millions of votes for any absurdity that the Emperor might be pleased to lay before the French people; but among the educated minority who had political theories of their own, the publication of this reform by Edict produced the worst possible impression. No stronger evidence, it was said, could have been given of the Emperor's insincerity than the dictatorial form in which he affected to bestow liberty upon France. Scarcely a voice was raised in favour of the new Constitution. The measure had in fact failed of its effect. Napoleon's object was to excite an enthusiasm that should lead the entire nation, the educated classes as well as the peasantry, to rally round him in a struggle with the foreigner for life or death: he found, on the contrary, that he had actually injured his cause. The hostility of public opinion was so serious that Napoleon judged it

The Chambers summoned for June.

wise to make advances to the Liberal party, and sent his brother Joseph to Lafayette, to ascertain on what terms he might gain his support.* Lafayette, strongly condemning the form of the Acte Additionnel, stated that the Emperor could only restore public confidence by immediately convoking the Chambers. This was exactly what Napoleon desired to avoid, until he had defeated the English and Prussians; nor in fact had the vote of the nation accepting the new Constitution yet been given. But the urgency of the need overcame the Emperor's inclinations and the forms of law. Lafayette's demand was granted: orders were issued for an immediate election, and the meeting of the Chambers fixed for the beginning of June, a few days earlier than the probable departure of the Emperor to open hostilities on the northern frontier.

Lafayette's counsel had been given in sincerity, but Napoleon gained little by following it. The nation at large had nothing of the faith in the elections which was felt by Lafayette and his friends. In some places not a single person appeared at the poll: in most, the candidates were elected by a few scores of voters. The Royalists absented themselves on principle: the population generally thought only of the coming war, and let the professed politicians conduct the business of the day by themselves. Among the deputies chosen there were several who had sat in the earlier Assemblies of the Revolution; and, mingled with placemen and soldiers

Elections.

* Lafayette, Mémoires, v. 414.

of the Empire, a considerable body of men whose known object was to reduce Napoleon's power. One interest alone was unrepresented—that of the Bourbon family, which so lately seemed to have been called to the task of uniting the old and the new France around itself.

Napoleon, troubling himself little about the elections, laboured incessantly at his preparations for war, and by the end of May two hundred thousand men were ready to take the field. The delay of the Allies, though necessary, enabled their adversary to take up the offensive. It was the intention of the Emperor to leave a comparatively small force to watch the eastern frontier, and himself, at the head of a hundred and twenty-five thousand men, to fall upon Wellington and Blücher in the Netherlands, and crush them before they could unite their forces. With this object the greater part of the army was gradually massed on the northern roads at points between Paris, Lille, and Maubeuge. Two acts of State remained to be performed by the Emperor before he quitted the capital; the inauguration of the new Constitution and the opening of the Chambers of Legislature. The first, which had been fixed for the 26th of May, and announced as a revival of the old Frankish Champ de Mai, was postponed till the beginning of the following month. On the 1st of June the solemnity was performed with extraordinary pomp and splendour, on that same Champ de Mars where, twenty-five years before, the grandest and most affecting of all the festivals of the Revolution, the Act

Champ de Mai.

of Federation, had been celebrated by King Louis XVI. and his people. Deputations from each of the constituencies of France, from the army, and from every public body, surrounded the Emperor in a great amphitheatre enclosed at the southern end of the plain: outside there were ranged twenty thousand soldiers of the Guard and other regiments; and behind them spread the dense crowd of Paris. When the total of the votes given in the Plébiscite had been summed up and declared, the Emperor took the oath to the Constitution, and delivered one of his masterpieces of political rhetoric. The great officers of State took the oath in their turn: mass was celebrated, and Napoleon, leaving the enclosed space, then presented their standards to the soldiery in the Champ de Mars, addressing some brief, soul-stirring word to each regiment as it passed. The spectacle was magnificent, but except among the soldiers themselves a sense of sadness and disappointment passed over the whole assembly. The speech of the Emperor showed that he was still the despot at heart: the applause was forced: all was felt to be ridiculous, all unreal.*

The opening of the Legislative Chambers took place a few days later, and on the night of the 11th of June Napoleon started for the northern frontier. The situation of the forces opposed to him in this his last campaign strikingly resembled that which had given him his first Italian victory in 1796. Then the Austrians and Sardinians, resting on

Plan of Napoleon.

* Miot de Melito, iii. 484.

opposite bases, covered the approaches to the Sardinian capital, and invited the assailant to break through their centre and drive the two defeated wings along diverging and severed paths of retreat. Now the English and the Prussians covered Brussels, the English resting westward on Ostend, the Prussians eastward on Cologne, and barely joining hands in the middle of a series of posts nearly eighty miles long. The Emperor followed the strategy of 1796. He determined to enter Belgium by the central road of Charleroi, and to throw his main force upon Blücher, whose retreat, if once he should be severed from his colleague, would carry him eastwards towards Liége, and place him outside the area of hostilities round Brussels. Blücher driven eastwards, Napoleon believed that he might not only push the English commander out of Brussels, but possibly, by a movement westwards, intercept him from the sea and cut off his communication with Great Britain.*

On the night of the 13th of June, the French army, numbering a hundred and twenty-nine thousand men, had completed its concentration, and lay gathered round Beaumont and Philippeville. Wellington was at Brussels; his troops, which consisted of thirty-five thousand English and about sixty thousand Dutch, Germans, and Belgians,† guarded the country west of the

Situation of the armies.

---

* Napoleon to Ney; Correspondance, xxviii. 334.

† "I have got an infamous army, very weak and ill-equipped, and a very inexperienced staff." (Despatches, xii. 358.) So, even after his victory, he writes:—"I really believe that, with the exception of my old

Charleroi road as far as Oudenarde on the Scheldt. Blücher's headquarters were at Namur; he had a hundred and twenty thousand Prussians under his command, who were posted between Charleroi, Namur, and Liége. Both the English and Prussian generals were aware that very large French forces had been brought close to the frontier, but Wellington imagined Napoleon to be still in Paris, and believed that the war would be opened by a forward movement of Prince Schwarzenberg into Alsace. It was also his fixed conviction that if Napoleon entered Belgium he would throw himself not upon the Allied centre, but upon the extreme right of the English towards the sea.* In the course of the 14th, the Prussian outposts reported that the French were massed round Beaumont: later in the same day there were clear signs of an advance upon Charleroi. Early next morning the attack on Charleroi began. The Prussians were driven out of it, and retreated in the direction of Ligny, whither Blücher now brought up all the forces within his reach. It was unknown to Wellington until the afternoon of the 15th that the French had made any movement whatever: on receiving the news

Spanish infantry, I have got not only the worst troops but the worst-equipped army, with the worst staff, that was ever brought together." (Despatches, xii. 509.)

* Therefore he kept his forces more westwards, and further from Blücher, than if he had known Napoleon's actual plan. But the severance of the English from the sea required to be guarded against as much as a defeat of Blücher. The Duke never ceased to regard it as an open question whether Napoleon ought not to have thrown his whole force between Brussels and the sea. (*Vide* Memoir written in 1842; Wellington, S.D., ix. 530.)

of their advance, he ordered a concentrating movement of all his forces eastward, in order to cover the road to Brussels and to co-operate with the Prussian general. A small division of the British army took post at Quatre Bras that night, and on the morning of the 16th Wellington himself rode to Ligny, and promised his assistance to Blücher, whose troops were already drawn up and awaiting the attack of the French.

But the march of the invader was too rapid for the English to reach the field of battle. Already, on returning to Quatre Bras in the afternoon, Wellington found his own troops hotly engaged. Napoleon had sent Ney along the road to Brussels to hold the English in check and, if possible, to enter the capital, while he himself, with seventy thousand men, attacked Blücher. The Prussian general had succeeded in bringing up a force superior in number to his assailants; but the French army, which consisted in a great part of veterans recalled to the ranks, was of finer quality than any that Napoleon had led since the campaign of Moscow, and it was in vain that Blücher and his soldiers met them with all the gallantry and even more than the fury of 1813. There was murderous hand-to-hand fighting in the villages where the Prussians had taken up their position: now the defenders, now the assailants gave way: but at last the Prussians, with a loss of thirteen thousand men, withdrew from the combat, and left the battle-field in possession of the enemy. If the conquerors had followed up the pursuit that night, the cause

Ligny, June 16.

of the Allies would have been ruined. The effort of battle had, however, been too great, or the estimate which Napoleon made of his adversary's rallying power was too low. He seems to have assumed that Blücher must necessarily retreat eastwards towards Namur; while in reality the Prussian was straining every nerve to escape northwards, and to restore his severed communication with his ally.

At Quatre Bras the issue of the day was unfavourable to the French. Ney missed his opportunity of seizing this important point before it was occupied by the British in any force; and when the battle began the British infantry-squares unflinchingly bore the attack of Ney's cavalry, and drove them back again and again with their volleys, until successive reinforcements had made the numbers on both sides even. At the close of the day the French marshal, baffled and disheartened, drew back his troops to their original position. The army-corps of General d'Erlon, which Napoleon had placed between himself and Ney in order that it might act wherever there was the greatest need, was first withdrawn from Ney to assist at Ligny, and then, as it was entering into action at Ligny, recalled to Quatre Bras, where it arrived only after the battle was over. Its presence in either field would probably have altered the issue of the campaign.

Quatre Bras, June 16.

Blücher, on the night of the 16th, lay disabled and almost senseless; his lieutenant, Gneisenau, not only saved the army, but repaired, and more than repaired, all its losses by a memorable movement northwards that brought the Prussians again into communication with the British.

Prussian movement.

Napoleon, after an unexplained inaction during the night of the 16th and the morning of the 17th, committed the pursuit of the Prussians to Marshal Grouchy, ordering him never to let the enemy out of his sight; but Blücher and Gneisenau had already made their escape, and had concentrated so large a body in the neighbourhood of Wavre, that Grouchy could not now have prevented a force superior to his own from uniting with the English, even if he had known the exact movements of each of the three armies, and, with a true presentiment of his master's danger, had attempted to rejoin him on the morrow.

Wellington, who had both anticipated that Blücher would be beaten at Ligny, and assured himself that the Prussian would make good his retreat northwards, moved on the 17th from Quatre Bras to Waterloo, now followed by Napoleon and the mass of the French army. At Waterloo he drew up for battle, trusting to the promise of the gallant Prussian that he would advance in that direction on the following day. Blücher, in so doing, exposed himself to the risk of having his communications severed and half his army captured, if Napoleon should either change the direction of his main attack and bend eastwards, or should crush Wellington before the arrival of the Prussians, and seize the road from Brussels to Louvain with a victorious force. Such considerations would have driven a commander like Schwarzenberg back to Liége, but they were thrown to the winds by Blücher and Gneisenau. In just reliance on his colleague's energy, Wellington, with thirty thousand English and forty thousand Dutch, Germans, and Belgians, awaited the attack of Napoleon, at the head of seventy-four thousand veteran soldiers. The English position extended two miles along the brow of a gentle slope of corn-fields, and crossed at right angles the great road from Charleroi to Brussels; the château of Hugomont, some way down the slope on the right, and the farmhouse of La Haye Sainte, on the high-road in front of the left centre, served as fortified outposts. The French formed on the opposite and corresponding slope; the country was so open that, but for the heavy rain on the evening of the 17th, artillery could have moved over almost any part of the field with perfect freedom.

At eleven o'clock on Sunday, the 18th of June, the battle began. Napoleon, unconscious of the gathering of the Prussians on his right, and unacquainted with the obstinacy of English troops, believed the victory already thrown into his hands by Wellington's hardihood. His plan was to burst through the left of the English line near La Haye Sainte, and thus to drive Wellington westwards and place the whole French army between its two defeated enemies. The first movement was an assault on the buildings of Hugomont, made for the purpose of diverting Wellington from the true point of attack. The English commander sent detachments to

Waterloo, June 18.

this outpost sufficient to defend it, but no more. After two hours' indecisive fighting and a heavy cannonade, Ney ordered D'Erlon's corps forward to the great onslaught on the centre and left. As the French column pressed up the slope, General Picton charged at the head of a brigade. The English leader was among the first to fall, but his men drove the enemy back, and at the same time the Scots Greys, sweeping down from the left, cut right through both the French infantry and their cavalry supports, and, charging far up the opposite slope, reached and disabled forty of Ney's guns, before they were in their turn overpowered and driven back by the French dragoons. The English lost heavily, but the onslaught of the enemy had totally failed, and thousands of prisoners remained behind. There was a pause in the infantry combat; and again the artillery of Napoleon battered the English centre, while Ney marshalled fresh troops for a new and greater effort. About two o'clock the attack was renewed on the left. La Haye Sainte was carried, and vast masses of cavalry pressed up the English slope, and rode over the plateau to the very front of the English line. Wellington sent no cavalry to meet them, but trusted, and trusted justly, to the patience and endurance of the infantry themselves, who, hour after hour, held their ground, unmoved by the rush of the enemy's horse and the terrible spectacle of havoc and death in their own ranks; for all through the afternoon the artillery of Napoleon poured its fire wherever the line was left open, or the assault of the French cavalry rolled back.

At last the approach of the Prussians visibly told. Napoleon had seen their vanguard early in the day, and had detached Count Lobau with seven thousand men to hold them in check; but the little Prussian corps gradually swelled to an army, and as the day wore on it was found necessary to reinforce Count Lobau with some of the finest divisions of the French infantry. Still reports came in of new Prussian columns approaching. At six o'clock Napoleon prepared to throw his utmost strength into one grand final attack upon the British, and to sweep them away before the battle became general with their allies. Two columns of the Imperial Guard, supported by every available regiment, moved from the right and left towards the English centre. The column on the right, unchecked by the storm of Wellington's cannon-shot from front and flank, pushed to the very ridge of the British slope, and came within forty yards of the cross-road where the English Guard lay hidden. Then Wellington gave the order to fire. The French recoiled; the English advanced at the charge, and drove the enemy down the hill, returning themselves for a while to their own position. The left column of the French Guard attacked with equal bravery, and met with the same fate. Then, while the French were seeking to re-form at the bottom of the hill, Wellington commanded a general advance. The whole line of the British infantry and cavalry swept down into the valley; before them the baffled and sorely-stricken host of the enemy broke into a confused mass; only the battalions of the old Guard, which had halted in the rear of the attacking columns, remained firm together. Blücher, from the east, dealt the death-blow, and, pressing on to the road by which the French were escaping, turned the defeat into utter ruin and dispersion. The pursuit, which Wellington's troops were too exhausted to attempt, was carried on throughout the night by the Prussian cavalry with memorable ardour and terrible success. Before the morning the French army was no more than a rabble of fugitives.

Napoleon fled to Philippeville, and made some ineffectual attempts both there and at Laon to fix a rallying point for his vanished forces. From Laon he hastened to Paris, which he reached at sunrise on the 21st. His bulletin describing the defeat of Waterloo was read to the Chambers on the same morning. The Lower House immediately declared against the Emperor, and demanded his abdication. Unless Napoleon seized the dictatorship his cause was lost. Carnot and Lucien Bonaparte urged him to dismiss the Chambers and to stake all on his own strong will; but they found no support among the Emperor's counsellors. On the next day Napoleon abdicated in favour of his son. But it was in vain that he attempted to impose an absent successor upon France, and to maintain his own Ministers in power. It was equally in vain that Carnot, filled with the memories of 1793, called upon the Assembly to continue the war and to provide for the defence of Paris. A Provisional Government entered upon office.

Napoleon at Paris.

Days were spent in inaction and debate while the Allies advanced through France. On the 28th of June, the Prussians appeared on the north of the capital; and, as the English followed, they moved to the south of the Seine, out of the range of the fortifications with which Napoleon had covered the side of St. Denis and Montmartre. Davoust, with almost all the generals in Paris, declared defence to be impossible. On the 3rd of July, a capitulation was signed. The remnants of the French army were required to withdraw beyond the Loire. The Provisional Government dissolved itself; the Allied troops entered the capital; and on the following day the Members of the Chamber of Deputies, on arriving at their Hall of Assembly, found the gates closed, and a detachment of soldiers in possession. France was not, even as a matter of form, consulted as to its future government. Louis XVIII. was summarily restored to his throne. Napoleon, who had gone to Rochefort with the intention of sailing to the United States, lingered at Rochefort until escape was no longer possible, and then embarked on the British ship *Bellerophon*, commending himself, as a second Themistocles, to the generosity of the Prince Regent of England. He who had declared that the lives of a million men were nothing to him * trusted to the folly or the impotence of the English nation to provide him with some agreeable asylum until he could again break loose and deluge Europe with blood. But the lesson of 1814 had been learnt. Some island

Allies enter Paris, July 7.

---

* Metternich, i., p. 155.

in the ocean far beyond the equator formed the only prison for a man whom no European sovereign could venture to guard, and whom no fortress-walls could have withdrawn from the attention of mankind. Napoleon was conveyed to St. Helena. There, until at the end of six years death removed him, he experienced some trifling share of the human misery that he had despised.

Victory had come so swiftly that the Allied Governments were unprepared with terms of peace. The Czar and the Emperor of Austria were still at Heidelberg when the battle of Waterloo was fought; they had advanced no further than Nancy when the news reached them that Paris had surrendered. Both now hastened to the capital, where Wellington was already exercising the authority to which his extraordinary successes as well as his great political superiority over all the representatives of the Allies then present, entitled him. Before the entry of the English and Prussian troops into Paris he had persuaded Louis XVIII. to sever himself from the party of reaction by calling to office the regicide Fouché, head of the existing Provisional Government. Fouché had been guilty of the most atrocious crimes at Lyons in 1793; he had done some of the worst work of each succeeding government in France; and, after returning to his old place as Napoleon's Minister of Police during the Hundred Days, he had intrigued as early as possible for the restoration of Louis XVIII., if indeed he had not held treasonable communication with the enemy during the campaign. His sole claim to power was

Wellington and Fouché.

that every gendarme and every informer in France had at some time acted as his agent, and that, as a regicide in office, he might possibly reconcile Jacobins and Bonapartists to the second return of the Bourbon family. Such was the man whom, in association with Talleyrand, the Duke of Wellington found himself compelled to propose as Minister to Louis XVIII. The appointment, it was said, was humiliating, but it was necessary; and with the approval of the Count of Artois the King invited this blood-stained eavesdropper to an interview and placed him in office. Need subdued the scruples of the courtiers: it could not subdue the resentment of that grief-hardened daughter of Louis XVI. whom Napoleon termed the only man of her family. The Duchess of Angoulême might have forgiven the Jacobin Fouché the massacres at Lyons: she refused to speak to a Minister whom she termed one of the murderers of her father.

Fouché had entered into a private negotiation with Wellington while the English were on the outskirts of Paris, and while the authorised envoys of the Assembly were engaged elsewhere. Wellington's motive for recommending him to the King was the indifference or hostility felt by some of the Allies to Louis XVIII. personally, which led the Duke to believe that if Louis did not regain his throne before the arrival of the sovereigns he might never regain it at all.* Fouché was the one man who could at that moment throw open the road to the Tuileries. If his overtures were rejected,

* Wellington Despatches, xii. 649.

he might either permit Carnot to offer some desperate resistance outside Paris, or might retire himself with the army and the Assembly beyond the Loire, and there set up a Republican Government. With Fouché and Talleyrand united in office under Louis XVIII., there was no fear either of a continuance of the war or of the suggestion of a change of dynasty on the part of any of the Allies. By means of the Duke's independent action Louis XVIII. was already in possession when the Czar arrived at Paris, and nothing now prevented the definite conclusion of peace but the disagreement of the Allies themselves as to the terms to be exacted. Prussia, which had suffered so bitterly from Napoleon, demanded that Europe should not a second time deceive itself with the hollow guarantee of a Bourbon restoration, but should gain a real security for peace by detaching Alsace and Lorraine, as well as a line of northern fortresses, from the French monarchy. Lord Liverpool, Prime Minister of England, stated it to be the prevailing opinion in this country that France might fairly be stripped of the principal conquests made by Louis XIV.; but he added that if Napoleon, who was then at large, should become a prisoner, England would waive a permanent cession of territory, on condition that France should be occupied by foreign armies until it had, at its own cost, restored the barrier-fortresses of the Netherlands.* Metternich for a while held much the same language as the

Disagreement on terms of peace.

---

* Wellington, S. D., xi. 24, 32. Maps of projected frontiers, Records: Cont., vol. 23.

Prussian Minister: Alexander alone declared from the first against any reduction of the territory of France, and appealed to the declarations of the Powers that the sole object of the war was the destruction of Napoleon and the maintenance of the order established by the Peace of Paris.

The arguments for and against the severance of the border-provinces from France were drawn at great length by diplomatists, but all that was essential in them was capable of being very briefly put. On the one side, it was urged by Stein and Hardenberg that the restoration of the Bourbons in 1814 with an undiminished territory had not prevented France from placing itself at the end of a few months under the rule of the military despot whose life was one series of attacks on his neighbours: that the expectation of long-continued peace, under whatever dynasty, was a vain one so long as the French possessed a chain of fortresses enabling them at any moment to throw large armies into Germany or the Netherlands: and finally, that inasmuch as Germany, and not England or Russia, was exposed to these irruptions, Germany had the first right to have its interests consulted in providing for the public security. On the other side, it was argued by the Emperor Alexander, and with far greater force by the Duke of Wellington,* that the position of the Bourbons would be absolutely hopeless if their restoration, besides being the work of foreign armies, was accompanied by the loss

Arguments for and against cessions.

---
* Despatches, xii. 596. Seeley's Stein, iii. 332.

of French provinces: that the French nation, although it had submitted to Napoleon, had not as a matter of fact offered the resistance to the Allies which it was perfectly capable of offering: and that the danger of any new aggressive or revolutionary movement might be effectually averted by keeping part of France occupied by the Allied forces until the nation had settled down into tranquillity under an efficient government. Notes embodying these arguments were exchanged between the Ministers of the great Powers during the months of July and August. The British Cabinet, which had at first inclined to the Prussian view, accepted the calm judgment of Wellington, and transferred itself to the side of the Czar. Metternich went with the majority. Hardenberg, thus left alone, abandoned point after point in his demands, and consented at last that France should cede little more than the border-strips which had been added by the Peace of 1814 to its frontier of 1791. Chambéry and the rest of French Savoy, Landau and Saarlouis on the German side, Philippeville and some other posts on the Belgian frontier, were fixed upon as the territory to be surrendered. The resolution of the Allied Governments was made known to Louis XVIII. towards the end of September. Negotiation on details dragged on for two months more, while France itself underwent a change of Ministry; and the definitive Treaty of Peace, known as the second Treaty of Paris, was not signed until November the 20th. France escaped without substantial loss of

Prussia isolated.

Second Treaty of Paris, Nov. 20.

territory; it was, however, compelled to pay indemnities amounting in all to about £40,000,000; to consent to the occupation of its northern provinces by an Allied force of 150,000 men for a period not exceeding five years; and to defray the cost of this occupation out of its own revenues. The works of art taken from other nations, which the Allies had allowed France to retain in 1814, had already been restored to their rightful owners. No act of the conquerors in 1815 excited more bitter or more unreasonable complaint.

It was in the interval between the entry of the Allies into Paris and the definitive conclusion of peace that a treaty was signed which has gained a celebrity in singular contrast with its real insignificance, the Treaty of Holy Alliance. Since the terrible events of 1812 the Czar's mind had taken a strongly religious tinge. His private life continued loose as before; his devotion was both very well satisfied with itself and a prey to mysticism and imposture in others; but, if alloyed with many weaknesses, it was at least sincere, and, like Alexander's other feelings, it naturally sought expression in forms which seemed theatrical to stronger natures. Alexander had rendered many public acts of homage to religion in the intervals of diplomatic and military success in the year 1814; and after the second capture of Paris he drew up a profession of religious and political faith, embodying, as he thought, those high principles by which the Sovereigns of Europe, delivered from the iniquities of Napoleon, were henceforth to maintain the reign of peace

Treaty of Holy Alliance, Sept. 26.

and righteousness on earth.* This document, which resembled the pledge of a religious brotherhood, formed the draft of the Treaty of the Holy Alliance. The engagement, as one binding on the conscience, was for the consideration of the Sovereigns alone, not of their Ministers; and in presenting it to the Emperor Francis and King Frederick William, the Czar is said to have acted with an air of great mystery. The King of Prussia, a pious man, signed the treaty in seriousness; the Emperor of Austria, who possessed a matter-of-fact humour, said that if the paper related to doctrines of religion, he must refer it to his confessor, if to secrets of State, to Prince Metternich. What the confessor may have thought of the Czar's political evangel is not known: the opinion delivered by the Minister was not a sympathetic one. "It is verbiage," said Metternich; and his master, though unwillingly, signed the treaty. With England the case was still worse. As the Prince Regent was not in Paris, Alexander had to confide the articles of the Holy Alliance to Lord Castlereagh. Of all things in the world the most incomprehensible to Castlereagh was religious enthusiasm. "The fact is," he wrote home to the English Premier, "that the Emperor's mind is not completely

---

* B. and F. State Papers, 1815—16, iii. 211. The second article is the most characteristic:—" Les trois Princes . . . confessant que la nation Chrétienne dont eux et leurs peuples font partie n'a réellement d'autre Souverain que celui à qui seul appartient en propriété la puissance . . . c'est-à-dire Dieu notre Divin Sauveur Jésus-Christ, le Verbe du Très Haut, la parole de vie : leurs Majestés recommandent . . . à leurs peuples . . . de se fortifier chaque jour davantage dans les principes et l'exercice des devoirs que le Divin Sauveur a enseignés aux hommes."

sound."* Apart, however, from the Czar's sanity or insanity, it was impossible for the Prince Regent, or for any person except the responsible Minister, to sign a treaty, whether it meant anything or nothing, in the name of Great Britain. Castlereagh was in great perplexity. On the one hand, he feared to wound a powerful ally; on the other, he dared not violate the forms of the Constitution. A compromise was invented. The Treaty of the Holy Alliance was not graced with the name of the Prince Regent, but the Czar received a letter declaring that his principles had the personal approval of this great authority on religion and morality. The Kings of Naples and Sardinia were the next to subscribe, and in due time the names of the witty glutton, Louis XVIII., and of the abject Ferdinand of Spain were added. Two potentates alone received no invitation from the Czar to enter the League: the Pope, because he possessed too much authority within the Christian Church, and the Sultan, because he possessed none at all.

Such was the history of the Treaty of Holy Alliance, of which, it may be safely said, no single person connected with it, except the Czar and the King of Prussia, thought without a smile. The common

---

* Wellington, S. D., xi. 175. The account which Castlereagh gives of the Czar's longing for universal peace appears to refute the theory that Alexander had some idea of an attack upon Turkey in thus uniting Christendom. According to Castlereagh, Metternich also thought that "it was quite clear that the Czar's mind was affected," but for the singular reason that "peace and goodwill engrossed all his thoughts, and that he had found him of late friendly and reasonable on all points." (*Id.*) There was, however, a strong popular impression at this time that Alexander was on the point of invading Turkey. (Gentz, D. I., i. 197.)

belief that this Treaty formed the basis of a great monarchical combination against Liberal principles is erroneous; for, in the first place, no such combination existed before the year 1818; and, in the second place, the Czar, who was the author of the Treaty, was at this time the zealous friend of Liberalism both in his own and in other countries. The concert of the Powers was indeed provided for by articles signed on the same day as the Peace of Paris; but this concert, which, unlike the Holy Alliance, included England, was directed towards the perpetual exclusion of Napoleon from power, and the maintenance of the established Government in France. The Allies pledged themselves to act in union if revolution or usurpation should again convulse France and endanger the repose of other States, and undertook to resist with their whole force any attack that might be made upon the army of occupation. The federative unity which for a moment Europe seemed to have gained from the struggle against Napoleon, and the belief existing in some quarters in its long continuance, were strikingly shown in the last article of this Quadruple Treaty, which provided that, after the holding of a Congress at the end of three or more years, the Sovereigns or Ministers of all the four great Powers should renew their meetings at fixed intervals, for the purpose of consulting upon their common interests, and considering the measures best fitted to secure the repose and prosperity of nations, and the continuance of the peace of Europe.*

Treaty between the Four Powers, Nov. 20.

* B. and F. State Papers, 1815—16, iii. 273. Records: Continent, vol. 30.

Thus terminated, certainly without any undue severity, yet not without some loss to the conquered nation, the work of 1815 in France. In the meantime the Congress of Vienna, though interrupted by the renewal of war, had resumed and completed its labours. One subject of the first importance remained unsettled when Napoleon returned, the federal organisation of Germany. This work had been referred by the Powers in the autumn of 1814 to a purely German committee, composed of the representatives of Austria and Prussia and of three of the Minor States; but the first meetings of the committee only showed how difficult was the problem, and how little the inclination in most quarters to solve it. The objects with which statesmen like Stein demanded an effective federation were thoroughly plain and practical. They sought, in the first place, that Germany should be rendered capable of defending itself against the foreigner; and in the second place, that the subjects of the minor princes, who had been made absolute rulers by Napoleon, should now be guaranteed against despotic oppression. To secure Germany from being again conquered by France, it was necessary that the members of the League, great and small, should abandon something of their separate sovereignty, and create a central authority with the sole right of making war and alliances. To protect the subjects of the minor princes from the abuse of power, it was necessary that certain definite civil rights and a measure of representative government should be assured by Federal Law to the inhabitants of

German Federation.

every German State, and enforced by the central authority on the appeal of subjects against their Sovereigns. There was a moment when some such form of German union had seemed to be close at hand, the moment when Prussia began its final struggle with Napoleon, and the commander of the Czar's army threatened the German vassals of France with the loss of their thrones (Feb., 1813). But even then no statesman had satisfied himself how Prussia and Austria were to unite in submission to a Federal Government; and from the time when Austria made terms with the vassal princes little hope of establishing a really effective authority at the centre of Germany remained. Stein, at the Congress of Vienna, once more proposed to restore the title and the long-vanished powers of the Emperor; but he found no inclination on the part of Metternich to promote his schemes for German unity, while some of the minor princes flatly refused to abandon any fraction of their sovereignty over their own subjects. The difficulties in the way of establishing a Federal State were great, perhaps insuperable; the statesmen anxious for it few in number; the interests opposed to it all but universal. Stein saw that the work was intended to be unsubstantial, and withdrew himself from it before its completion. The Act of Federation,* which was signed on the 8th of June, created a Federal Diet, forbade the members of the League to enter into alliances against the common interest, and declared that in each State, Constitutions should be established. But it left the

* Klüber, ii. 598.

various Sovereigns virtually independent of the League; it gave the nomination of members of the Diet to the Governments absolutely, without a vestige of popular election; and it contained no provision for enforcing in any individual State, whose ruler might choose to disregard it, the principle of constitutional rule. Whether the Federation would in any degree have protected Germany in case of attack by France or Russia is matter for conjecture, since a long period of peace followed the year 1815; but so far was it from securing liberty to the Minor States, that in the hands of Metternich the Diet, impotent for every other purpose, became an instrument for the persecution of liberal opinion and for the suppression of the freedom of the press.

German affairs, as usual, were the last to be settled at the Congress; when these were at length disposed of, the Congress embodied the entire mass of its resolutions in one great Final Act* of a hundred and twenty-one articles, which was signed a few days before the battle of Waterloo was fought. This Act, together with the second Treaty of Paris, formed the public law with which Europe emerged from the warfare of a quarter of a century, and entered upon a period which proved, even more than it was expected to prove, one of long-lasting peace. Standing on the boundary-line between two ages, the legislation of Vienna forms a landmark in history. The provisions of the Congress have sometimes been

Final Act of the Congress, June 10.

---

* Klüber, vi. 12. It covers, with its appendices, 205 pages.

criticised as if that body had been an assemblage of philosophers, bent only on advancing the course of human progress, and endowed with the power of subduing the selfish impulses of every Government in Europe. As a matter of fact the Congress was an arena where national and dynastic interests struggled for satisfaction by every means short of actual war. To inquire whether the Congress accomplished all that it was possible to accomplish for Europe is to inquire whether Governments at that moment forgot all their own ambitions and opportunities, and thought only of the welfare of mankind. Russia would not have given up Poland without war; Austria would not have given up Lombardy and Venice without war. The only measures of 1814—15 in which the common interest was really the dominant motive were those adopted either with the view of strengthening the States immediately exposed to attack by France, or in the hope of sparing France itself the occasion for new conflicts. The union of Holland and Belgium, and the annexation of the Genoese Republic to Sardinia, were the means adopted for the former end; for the latter, the relinquishment of all claims to Alsace and Lorraine. These were the measures in which the statesmen of 1814—15 acted with their hands free, and by these their foresight may fairly be judged. Of the union of Belgium to Holland it is not too much to say that, although planned by Pitt, and treasured by every succeeding Ministry as one of his wisest schemes, it was wholly useless and inexpedient. The tranquillity of Western Europe was preserved during fifteen years, not by yoking together discordant nationalities, but by the general desire to avoid war; and as soon as France seriously demanded the liberation of Belgium from Holland, it had to be granted. Nor can it be believed that the addition of the hostile and discontented population of Genoa to the kingdom of Piedmont would have saved that monarchy from invasion if war had again arisen. The annexation of Genoa was indeed fruitful of results, but not of results which Pitt and his successors had anticipated. It was intended to strengthen the House of Savoy for the purpose of resistance to France:* it did strengthen the House of Savoy, but as the champion of Italy against Austria. It was intended to withdraw the busy trading city Genoa from the influences of French democracy: in reality it brought a strong element of innovation into the Piedmontese State itself, giving, on the one hand, a bolder and more national spirit to its Government, and, on the other hand, elevating to the ideal of a united Italy those who, like the Genoese Mazzini, were now no longer born to be the citizens of a free Republic. In sacrificing the ancient liberty of Genoa, the Congress itself unwittingly began the series of changes which was to refute the famous saying of Metternich, that Italy was but a geographical expression.

* In the first draft of the secret clauses of the Treaty of June 14, 1800, between England and Austria (see vol. i., p. 223), Austria was to have had Genoa. But the fear arising that Russia would not permit Austria's extension to the Mediterranean, an alteration was made, whereby Austria was promised half of Piedmont, Genoa to go to the King of Sardinia in compensation.

But if the policy of 1814—15 in the affairs of Belgium and Piedmont only proves how little an average collection of statesmen can see into the future, the policy which, in spite of Waterloo, left France in possession of an undiminished territory, does no discredit to the foresight, as it certainly does the highest honour to the justice and forbearance of Wellington, whose counsels then turned the scale. The wisdom of the resolution has indeed been frequently impugned. German statesmen held then, and have held ever since, that the opportunity of disarming France once for all of its weapons of attack was wantonly thrown away. Hardenberg, when his arguments for annexation of the frontier-fortresses were set aside, predicted that streams of blood would hereafter flow for the conquest of Alsace and Lorraine,* and his prediction has been fulfilled. Yet no one perhaps would have been more astonished than Hardenberg himself, could he have known that fifty-five years of peace between France and Prussia would precede the next great struggle. When the same period of peace shall have followed the acquisition of Metz and Strasburg by Prussia, it will be time to condemn the settlement of 1815 as containing the germ of future wars; till then, the effects of that settlement in maintaining peace are entitled to recognition. It is impossible to deny that the Allies, in leaving to France the whole of its territory in 1815, avoided inflicting the most galling of all tokens of defeat upon a

<small>Alsace and Lorraine.</small>

* Portz, Leben Steins, iv. 524.

spirited and still most powerful nation. The loss of Belgium and the frontier of the Rhine was keenly enough felt for thirty years to come, and made no insignificant part of the French people ready at any moment to rush into war: how much greater the power of the war-cry, how hopeless the task of restraint, if to the other motives for war there had been added the liberation of two of the most valued provinces of France. Without this the danger was great enough. Thrice at least in the next thirty years the balance seemed to be turning against the continuance of peace. An offensive alliance between France and Russia was within view when the Bourbon monarchy fell; the first years of Louis Philippe all but saw the revolutionary party plunge France into war for Belgium and for Italy; ten years later the dismissal of a Ministry alone prevented the outbreak of hostilities on the distant affairs of Syria. Had Alsace and Lorraine at this time been in the hands of disunited Germany, it is hard to believe that the Bourbon dynasty would not have averted, or sought to avert, its fall by a popular war, or that the victory of Louis Philippe over the war-party, difficult even when there was no French soil to reconquer, would have been possible. The time indeed came when a new Bonaparte turned to enterprises of aggression the resources which Europe had left unimpaired to his country: but to assume that the cessions proposed in 1815 would have made France unable to move, with or without allies, half a century afterwards, is to make a confident guess in a doubtful matter; and, with Germany in the condition in which it remained after 1815, it is at least as likely that the annexation of Alsace and Lorraine would have led to the early reconquest of the Rhenish provinces by France, or to a war between Austria and Prussia, as that it would have prolonged the period of European peace beyond that distant limit which it actually reached.

Among the subjects which were pressed upon the Congress of Vienna there was one in which the pursuit of national interests and calculations of policy bore no part, the abolition of the African slave-trade. The British people, who, after twenty years of combat in the cause of Europe, had earned so good a right to ask something of their allies, probably attached a deeper importance to this question than to any in the whole range of European affairs, with the single exception of the personal overthrow of Napoleon. Since the triumph of Wilberforce's cause in the Parliament of 1807, and the extinction of English slave-traffic, the anger with which the nation viewed this detestable cruelty, too long tolerated by itself, had become more and more vehement and widespread. By the year 1814 the utterances of public opinion were so loud and urgent that the Government, though free from enthusiasm itself, was forced to place the international prohibition of the slave-trade in the front rank of its demands. There were politicians on the Continent credulous enough to believe that this outcry of the heart and the conscience of the nation

English efforts at the Congress to abolish the slave-trade.

was but a piece of commercial hypocrisy. Talleyrand, with far different insight, but not with more sympathy, spoke of the state of the English people as one of frenzy.* Something had already been effected at foreign courts. Sweden had been led to prohibit slave-traffic in 1813, Holland in the following year. Portugal had been restrained by treaty from trading north of the line. France had pledged itself in the first Treaty of Paris to abolish the commerce within five years. Spain alone remained unfettered, and it was indeed intolerable that the English slavers should have been forced to abandon their execrable gains only that they should fall into the hands of the subjects of King Ferdinand. It might be true that the Spanish colonies required a larger supply of slaves than they possessed; but Spain had at any rate not the excuse that it was asked to surrender an old and profitable branch of commerce. It was solely through the abolition of the English slave-trade that Spain possessed any slave-trade whatever. Before the year 1807 no Spanish ship had been seen on the coast of Africa for a century, except one in 1798 fitted out by Godoy.† As for the French trade, that had been extinguished by the capture of Senegal and Goree; and along the two thousand miles of coast from Cape Blanco to Cape Formosa a legitimate commerce with the natives was gradually springing up in place of the desolating traffic in flesh and blood. It was hoped by the English people that Castlereagh would succeed in

* Talleyrand, p. 277.
† B. and F. State Papers, 1815—16, p. 928.

obtaining a universal and immediate prohibition of the slave-trade by all the Powers assembled at Vienna. The Minister was not wanting in perseverance, but he failed to achieve this result. France, while claiming a short delay elsewhere, professed itself willing, like Portugal, to abolish at once the traffic north of the line; but the Government on which England had perhaps the greatest claim, that of Spain, absolutely refused to accept this restriction, or to bind itself to a final prohibition before the end of eight years. Castlereagh then proposed that a Council of Ambassadors at London and Paris should be charged with the international duty of expediting the close of the slave-trade; the measure which he had in view being the punishment of slave-dealing States by a general exclusion of their exports. Against this Spain and Portugal made a formal protest, treating the threat as almost equivalent to one of war. The project dropped, and the Minister of England had to content himself with obtaining from the Congress a solemn condemnation of the slave-trade, as contrary to the principles of civilisation and human right (Feb., 1815).

The work was carried a step further by Napoleon's return from Elba. Napoleon understood the impatience of the English people, and believed that he could make no higher bid for its friendship than by abandoning the reserves made by Talleyrand at the Congress, and abolishing the French slave-trade at once and for all. This was accomplished; and the Bourbon ally of England, on his second restoration, could not undo what had been done by the usurper. Spain and Portugal alone continued to pursue—the former country without restriction, the latter on the south of the line—a commerce branded by the united voice of Europe as infamous. The Governments of these countries alleged in their justification that Great Britain itself had resisted the passing of the prohibitory law until its colonies were far better supplied with slaves than those of its rivals now were. This was true, but it was not the whole truth. The whole truth was not known, the sincerity of English feeling was not appreciated, until, twenty years later, the nation devoted a part of its wealth to release the slave from servitude, and the English race from the reproach of slave-holding. Judged by the West Indian Emancipation of 1833, the Spanish appeal to English history sounds almost ludicrous. But the remembrance of the long years throughout which the advocates of justice encountered opposition in England should temper the severity of our condemnation of the countries which still defended a bad interest. The light broke late upon ourselves: the darkness that still lingered elsewhere had too long been our own.

CHAPTER II.

Concert of Europe after 1815—Spirit of the Foreign Policy of Alexander, of Metternich, and of the English Ministry—Metternich's action in Italy, England's in Sicily and Spain—The Reaction in France—Richelieu and the New Chamber—Execution of Ney—Imprisonments and persecutions—Conduct of the Ultra-Royalists in Parliament—Contests on the Electoral Bill and the Budget—The Chamber prorogued—Affair of Grenoble—Dissolution of the Chamber—Electoral Law and Financial Settlement of 1817—Character of the first years of peace in Europe generally—Promise of a Constitution in Prussia—Hardenberg opposed by the partisans of autocracy and privilege—Schmalz's Pamphlet—Delay of Constitutional Reform in Germany at large—The Wartburg Festival—Progress of Reaction—The Czar now inclines to repression—Congress of Aix-la-Chapelle—Evacuation of France—Growing influence of Metternich in Europe—His action on Prussia—Murder of Kotzebue—The Carlsbad Conference and measures of repression in Germany—Richelieu and Decazes—Murder of the Duke of Berry—Progress of the reaction in France—General causes of the victory of reaction in Europe.

FOR nearly twenty years the career of Bonaparte had given to European history the unity of interest which belongs to a single life. This unity does not immediately disappear on the disappearance of his mighty figure. The Powers of Europe had been too closely involved in the common struggle, their interests were too deeply concerned in the maintenance of the newly-established order, for the thoughts of Governments to be withdrawn from foreign affairs, and the currents of national policy to fall at once apart into separate channels. The Allied army continued to occupy France; the defence of the Bourbon monarchy had been declared the cause of Europe at large; the conditions under which the numbers of the army of occupation might be reduced, or the period of occupation shortened, remained to be fixed by the Allies themselves. France thus formed the object of a common European deliberation; nor was the concert of the Powers without its peculiar organ. An International Council was created at Paris, consisting of the Ambassadors of the four great Courts. The forms of a coalition were, for the first time, preserved after the conclusion of peace. Communications were addressed to the Government of Louis XVIII., in the name of all the Powers together. The Council of Ambassadors met at regular intervals, and not only transacted business relating to the army of occupation and the payment of indemnities, but discussed the domestic policy of the French Government, and the situation of parties or the signs of political opinion in the Assembly and the nation.

Concert of Europe regarding France.

In thus watching over the restored Bourbon monarchy, the Courts of Europe were doing no more than they had bound themselves to do by treaty. Paris, however, was not the only field for a busy diplomacy. In most of the minor capitals of Europe each of the Great Powers had its own supposed interests to pursue, or its own principles of government to inculcate. An age of transition seemed to have begun. Constitutions had been promised in many States, and created in some; in Spain and in Sicily they had reached the third stage, that of suppression. It was not likely that the statesmen who had succeeded to Napoleon's power in Europe

Action of the Powers outside France.

should hold themselves entirely aloof from the affairs of their weaker neighbours, least of all when a neighbouring agitation might endanger themselves. In one respect the intentions of the British, the Austrian, and the Russian Governments were identical, and continued to be so, namely, in the determination to countenance no revolutionary movement. Revolution, owing to the experience of 1793, had come to be regarded as synonymous with aggressive warfare. Jacobins, anarchists, disturbers of the public peace, were only different names for one and the same class of international criminals, who were indeed indigenous to France, but might equally endanger the peace of mankind in other countries. Against these fomenters of mischief all the Courts were at one.

Here, however, agreement ceased. It was admitted that between revolutionary disturbance and the enjoyment of constitutional liberty a wide interval existed, and the statesmen of the leading Powers held by no means the same views as to the true relation between nations and their rulers. The most liberal in theory among the Sovereigns of 1815 was the Emperor Alexander. Already in the summer of 1815 he had declared the Duchy of Warsaw to be restored to independence and nationality, under the title of the Kingdom of Poland; and before the end of the year he had granted it a Constitution, which created certain representative assemblies, and provided the new kingdom with an army and an administration of its own, into which no person not a Pole could enter. The promised

Alexander.

introduction of Parliamentary life into Poland was but the first of a series of reforms dimly planned by Alexander, which was to culminate in the bestowal of a Constitution upon Russia itself, and the emancipation of the serf.* Animated by hopes like these for his own people, hopes which, while they lasted, were not merely sincere but ardent, Alexander was also friendly to the cause of constitutional government in other countries. Ambition mingled with disinterested impulses in the foreign policy of the Czar. It was impossible that Alexander should forget the league into which England and Austria had so lately entered against him. He was anxious to keep France on his side; he was not inclined to forego the satisfaction of weakening Austria by supporting national hopes in Italy; † and he hoped to create some counterpoise to England's maritime power by allying Russia with a strengthened and better-administered Spain. Agents of the Czar abounded in Italy and in Germany, but in no capital was the Ambassador of Russia more active than in Madrid. General Tatistcheff, who was appointed to this post in 1814, became the terror of all his colleagues and of the Cabinet of London from his extraordinary activity in intrigue; but in relation to the internal affairs of Spain his influence was

* Bernhardi, iii. 2, 10, 666.
† "We are now inundated with Russian agents of various descriptions, some public and some secret, but all holding the same language, all preaching 'Constitution and liberal principles,' and all endeavouring to direct the eyes of the independents towards the North. . . . A copy of the instructions sent to the Russian Minister here has fallen into the hands of the Austrians." A'Court (Ambassador at Naples) to Castlereagh, Dec. 7, 1815. Records: Sicily, 104.

beneficial; and it was frequently directed towards the support of reforming Ministers, whom King Ferdinand, if free from foreign pressure, would speedily have sacrificed to the pleasure of his favourites and confessors.

In the eyes of Prince Metternich, the all-powerful Minister of Austria, Alexander was little better than a Jacobin. The Austrian State, though its frontiers had been five times changed since 1792, had continued in a remarkable degree free from the impulse to internal change. The Emperor Francis was the personification of resistance to progress; the Minister owed his unrivalled position not more to his own skilful statesmanship in the great crisis of 1813 than to a genuine accord with the feelings of his master. If Francis was not a man of intellect, Metternich was certainly a man of character; and for a considerable period they succeeded in impressing the stamp of their own strongly-marked Austrian policy upon Europe. The force of their influence sprang from no remote source; it was due mainly to a steady intolerance of all principles not their own. Metternich described his system with equal simplicity and precision as an attempt neither to innovate nor to go back to the past, but to keep things as they were. In the old Austrian dominions this was not difficult to do, for things had no tendency to move and remained fixed of themselves;* but on the

Metternich.

---

* A profound reason has been ascribed to Metternich's conservatism by some of his English apologists in high place, namely the fear that if ideas of nationality should spring up, the non-German components of the Austrian monarchy, viz., Bohemia, Hungary, Croatia, &c., would break off and become independent States. But there is not a word in outside, both on the north and on the south, ideas were at work which, according to Metternich, ought never to have entered the world, but, having unfortunately gained admittance, made it the task of Governments to resist their influence by all available means. Stein and the leaders of the Prussian War of Liberation had agitated Germany with hopes of national unity, of Parliaments, and of the impulsion of the executive powers of State by public opinion. Against these northern innovators, Metternich had already won an important victory in the formation of the Federal Constitution. The weakness and timidity of the King of Prussia made it probable that, although he was now promising his subjects a Constitution, he might at no distant date be led to unite with other German Governments in a system of repression, and in placing Liberalism under the ban of the Diet. In Italy, according to the conservative statesman, the same dangers existed and the same remedies were required. Austria, through the acquisition of Venice, now possessed four times as large a territory beyond the Alps as it had possessed before 1792; but the population was no longer the quiescent and contented folk that it had been in the days of Maria Theresa. Napoleon's kingdom and army of Italy had taught the people warfare, and given them political aims and a more masculine spirit.

Metternich's policy in Germany.

In Italy.

Metternich's writings which shows that this apprehension had at this time entered his mind. To generalise his Italian policy of 1815 into a great prophetic statesmanship, is to interpret the ideas of one age by the history of the next.

Metternich's own generals had promised the Italians independence when they entered the country in 1814; Murat's raid a year later had actually been undertaken in the name of Italian unity. These were disagreeable incidents, and signs were not wanting of the existence of a revolutionary spirit in the Italian provinces of Austria, especially among the officers who had served under Napoleon. Metternich was perfectly clear as to the duties of his Government. The Italians might have a Viceroy to keep Court at Milan, a body of native officials to conduct their minor affairs, and a mock Congregation or Council, without any rights, powers, or functions whatever; if this did not satisfy them, they were a rebellious people, and government must be conducted by means of spies, police, and the dungeons of the Spielberg.*

On this system, backed by great military force, there was nothing to fear from the malcontents of Lombardy and Venice: it remained for Metternich to extend the same security to the rest of the peninsula, and by a series of treaties to effect the double end of exterminating constitutional government and of establishing an Austrian Protectorate over the entire country, from the Alps to the Sicilian Straits. The design was so ambitious that Metternich had not dared to disclose it at the Congress of Vienna; it was in fact a direct violation of the Treaty

Scheme of an Austrian Protectorate over Italy.

---

* In Moravia. For the system of espionage, see the book called "Carte segrete della polizia Austriaca," consisting of police-reports which fell into the hands of the Italians at Milan in 1848.

of Paris, and of the resolution of the Congress, that Italy, outside the possessions of Austria, should consist of independent States. The first Sovereign over whom the net was cast was Ferdinand of Naples. On the 15th of June, 1815, immediately after the overthrow of Murat, King Ferdinand signed a Treaty of Alliance with Austria, which contained a secret clause, pledging the King to introduce no change into his recovered kingdom inconsistent with its own old monarchical principles, or with the principles which had been adopted by the Emperor of Austria for the government of his Italian provinces.* Ferdinand, two years before, had been compelled by Great Britain to grant Sicily a Constitution, and was at this very moment promising one to Naples. The Sicilian Constitution was now tacitly condemned; the Neapolitans were duped. By a further secret clause, the two contracting Sovereigns undertook to communicate to one another everything that should come to their knowledge affecting the security and tranquillity of the Italian peninsula; in other words, the spies and the police of Ferdinand were now added to Metternich's staff in Lombardy. Tuscany, Modena, and Parma entered into much the same condition of vassalage; but the scheme for a universal federation of Italy under Austria's leadership failed through the resistance of Piedmont

---

* Bianchi, Storia Documentata, i. 208. The substance of this secret clause was communicated to A'Court, the English Ambassador at Naples. "I had no hesitation in saying that anything which contributed to the good understanding now prevailing between Austria and Naples, could not but prove extremely satisfactory to the British Government." A'Court to Castlereagh, July 18, 1815. Records: Sicily, vol. 104.

and of the Pope. Pius VII. resented the attempts of Austria, begun in 1797 and repeated at the Congress of Vienna, to deprive the Holy See of Bologna and Ravenna. The King of Sardinia, though pressed by England to accept Metternich's offer of alliance, maintained with great decision the independence of his country, and found in the support of the Czar a more potent argument than any that he could have drawn from treaties.*

<small>Spirit of England's foreign policy.</small>
The part played by the British Government at this epoch has been severely judged not only by the later opinion of England itself, but by the historical writers of almost every nation in Europe. It is perhaps fortunate for the fame of Pitt that he did not live to witness the accomplishment of the work in which he had laboured for thirteen years. The glory of a just and courageous struggle against Napoleon's tyranny remains with Pitt; the opprobrium of a settlement hostile to liberty has fallen on his successors. Yet there is no good ground for believing that Pitt would have attached a higher value to the rights or inclinations of individual communities than his successors did in re-adjusting the balance of power; on the contrary, he himself first proposed to destroy the Republic of Genoa, and to place Catholic Belgium under the Protestant Crown of Holland; nor

* Letters in Reuchlin, Geschichte Italiens, i. 71. The Holy Alliance was turned to better account by the Sardinian statesmen than by the Neapolitans. "Après s'être allié," wrote the Sardinian Ambassador at St. Petersburg, "en Jésus-Christ notre Sauveur, parole de vie, pourquoi et à quel propos s'allier en Metternich?"

was any principle dearer to him than that of aggrandising the House of Austria as a counterpoise to the power of France.* The Ministry of 1815 was indeed but too faithfully walking in the path into which Pitt had been driven by the King and the nation in 1793. Resistance to France had become the one absorbing care, the beginning and end of English statesmanship. Government at home had sunk to a narrow and unfeeling opposition to the attempts made from time to time to humanise the mass of the people, to reform an atrocious criminal law, to mitigate the civil wrongs inflicted in the name and the interest of a State-religion. No one in the Cabinet doubted that authority, as such, must be wiser than inexperienced popular desire, least of all the statesman who now, in conjunction with the Duke of Wellington, controlled the policy of Great Britain upon the Continent. Lord Castlereagh had no sympathy with cruelty or oppression in Continental rulers; he had just as little belief in the value of free institutions to their subjects.† The nature of his influence, which has been drawn sometimes in too dark colours, may be fairly gathered from the course of action which he followed in regard to Sicily and to Spain.

In Sicily the representative of Great Britain, Lord William Bentinck, had forced King Ferdinand, who could

---

* See the passages from Grenville's letters quoted in vol. i, p. 186 of this work.

† Castlereagh, x. 18. "The danger is that the transition" (to liberty) "may be too sudden to ripen into anything likely to make the world better or happier. . . . . I am sure it is better to retard than accelerate the operation of this most hazardous principle which is abroad."

not have maintained himself for an hour without the arms and money of England, to establish in 1813 a Parliament framed on the model of our own. The Parliament had not proved a wise or a capable body, but its faults were certainly not equal to those of King Ferdinand, and its re-construction under England's auspices would have been an affair of no great difficulty. Ferdinand, however, had always detested free institutions, and as soon as he regained the throne of Naples he determined to have done with the Sicilian Parliament. A correspondence on the intended change took place between Lord Castlereagh and A'Court, the Ambassador who had now succeeded Lord William Bentinck.* That the British Government, which had protected the Sicilian Crown against Napoleon at the height of his power, could have protected the Sicilian Constitution against King Ferdinand's edicts without detaching a single man-of-war's boat, is not open to doubt. Castlereagh, however, who for years past had been paying, stimulating, or rebuking every Government in Europe, and who had actually sent the British fleet to make the Norwegians submit to Bernadotte, now suddenly adopted the principle of non-intervention, and declared that, so long as Ferdinand did not persecute the Sicilians who at the

_{In Sicily.}

---

* B. and F. State Papers, 1816—17, p. 553. Metternich, iii. 80. Castlereagh had at first desired that the Constitution should be modified under the influence of the English Ambassador. Instructions to A'Court, March 14, 1814, marked "Most Secret;" Records: Sicily, vol. 99. A'Court himself detested the Constitution. "I conceive the Sicilian people to be totally and radically unfit to be entrusted with political power." July 23, 1814, id.

invitation of England had taken part in political life, or reduce the privileges of Sicily below those which had existed prior to 1813, Great Britain would not interfere with his action. These stipulations were inserted in order to satisfy the House of Commons, and to avert the charge that England had not only abandoned the Sicilian Constitution, but consented to a change which left the Sicilians in a worse condition than if England had never intervened in their affairs. Lord Castlereagh shut his eyes to the confession involved, that he was leaving the Sicilians to a ruler who, but for such restraint, might be expected to destroy every vestige of public right, and to take the same bloody and unscrupulous revenge upon his subjects which he had taken when Nelson restored him to power in 1799.

The action of the British Government in Spain showed an equal readiness to commit the future to the wisdom of Courts. Lord Castlereagh was made acquainted with the Spanish Ferdinand's design of abolishing the Constitution on his return in the year 1814. "So far," he replied, "as the mere existence of the Constitution is at stake, it is impossible to believe that any change tranquilly effected can well be worse."* In this case the interposition of England would perhaps not have availed against a reactionary clergy and nation: Castlereagh was, moreover, deceived by Ferdinand's professions that he had no desire to restore absolute government. He

* Castlereagh, x. 25.

credited the King with the same kind of moderation which had led Louis XVIII. to accept the Charta in France, and looked forward to the maintenance of a constitutional régime, though under conditions more favourable to the executive power and to the influence of the great landed proprietors and clergy.* Events soon proved what value was to be attached to the word of the King; the flood of reaction and vengeance broke over the country; and from this time the British Government, half confessing and half excusing Ferdinand's misdeeds, exerted itself to check the outrages of despotism, and to mitigate the lot of those who were now its victims. In the interest of the restored monarchies themselves, as much as from a regard to the public opinion of Great Britain, the Ambassadors of England urged moderation upon all the Bourbon Courts. This, however, was also done by Metternich, who neither took pleasure in cruelty, nor desired to see new revolutions produced by the extravagances of priests and emigrants. It was not altogether without cause that the belief arose that there was little to choose, in reference to the constitutional liberties of other States, between the sentiments of Austria and those of the Ministers of free England. A difference, however, did exist. Metternich actually prohibited the Sovereigns

---

* "If his Majesty announces his determination to give effect to the main principles of a constitutional régime, it is possible that he may extinguish the existing arrangement with impunity, and re-establish one more consistent with the efficiency of the executive power, and which may restore the great landed proprietors and the clergy to a due share of authority." Castlereagh, *id.*

over whom his influence extended from granting their subjects liberty: England, believing the Sovereigns to be more liberal than they were, did not interfere to preserve constitutions from destruction.

Such was the general character of the influence now exercised by the three leading Powers of Europe. Prussia, which had neither a fleet like England, an Italian connection like Austria, nor an ambitious Sovereign like Russia, concerned itself little with distant States, and limited its direct action to the affairs of France, in which it possessed a substantial interest, inasmuch as the indemnities due from Louis XVIII. had yet to be paid. The possibility of recovering these sums depended upon the maintenance of peace and order in France; and from the first it was recognised by every Government in Europe that the principal danger to peace and order arose from the conduct of the Count of Artois and his friends, the party of reaction. The counter-revolutionary movement began in mere riot and outrage. No sooner had the news of the battle of Waterloo reached the south of France than the Royalist mob of Marseilles drove the garrison out of the town, and attacked the quarter inhabited by the Mameluke families whom Napoleon had brought from Egypt. Thirteen of these unfortunate persons, and about as many Bonapartist citizens, were murdered.* A few weeks later Nismes

<small>Outrages of the Royalists in the south of France, June—August.</small>

<small>* Daudet, La Terreur Blanche, p. 186. The loss of the troops was a hundred. The stories of wholesale massacres at Marseilles and other places are fictions.</small>

was given over to anarchy and pillage. Religious fanaticism here stimulated the passion of political revenge. The middle class in Nismes itself and a portion of the surrounding population were Protestant, and had hailed Napoleon's return from Elba as a deliverance from the ascendancy of priests, and from the threatened revival of the persecutions which they had suffered under the old Bourbon monarchy. The Catholics, who were much more numerous, included the lowest class in the town, the larger landed proprietors of the district, and above half of the peasantry. Bands of volunteers had been formed by the Duke of Angoulême at the beginning of the Hundred Days, in the hope of sustaining a civil war against Napoleon. After capitulating to the Emperor's generals, some companies had been attacked by villagers and hunted down like wild beasts. The bands now reassembled and entered Nismes. The garrison, after firing upon them, were forced to give up their arms, and in this defenceless state a considerable number of the soldiers were shot down (July 17). On the next day the leaders of the armed mob began to use their victory. For several weeks murder and outrage, deliberately planned and publicly announced, kept not only Nismes itself, but a wide extent of the surrounding country in constant terror. The Government acted slowly and feebly; the local authorities were intimidated; and, in spite of the remonstrances of Wellington and the Russian Ambassador, security was not restored until the Allies took the matter into their own hands, and a detachment of Austrian troops occupied the

Department of the Gard. Other districts in the south of France witnessed the same outbreaks of Royalist ferocity. Avignon was disgraced by the murder of Marshal Brune, conqueror of the Russians and English in the Dutch campaign of 1799, an honest soldier, who after suffering Napoleon's neglect in the time of prosperity, had undertaken the heavy task of governing Marseilles during the Hundred Days. At Toulouse, General Ramel, himself a Royalist, was mortally wounded by a band of assassins, and savagely mutilated while lying disabled and expiring.

Crimes like these were the counterpart of the September massacres of 1792; and the terrorism exercised by the Royalists in 1815 has been compared, as a whole, with the Republican Reign of Terror twenty-two years earlier. But the comparison does little credit to the historical sense of those who suggested it. The barbarities of 1815 were strictly local: shocking as they were, they scarcely amounted in all to an average day's work of Carrier or Fouché in 1794; and the action of the established Government, though culpably weak, was not itself criminal. A second and more dangerous stage of reaction began, however, when the work of popular vengeance closed. Elections for a new Chamber of Deputies were held at the end of August. The Liberals and the adherents of Napoleon, paralysed by the disasters of France and the invaders' presence, gave up all as lost: the Ministers of Louis XVIII. abstained from the usual electoral manœuvres, Talleyrand through carelessness,

Elections of 1815.

Fouché from a desire to see parties evenly balanced: the ultra-Royalists alone had extended their organisation over France, and threw themselves into the contest with the utmost passion and energy. Numerically weak, they had the immense forces of the local administration on their side. The Préfets had gone over heart and soul to the cause of the Count of Artois, who indeed represented to them that he was acting under the King's own directions. The result was that an Assembly was elected to which France has seen only one parallel since, namely in the Parliament of 1871, elected when invaders again occupied the country, and the despotism of a second Bonaparte had ended in the same immeasurable calamity. The bulk of the candidates returned were country gentlemen whose names had never been heard of in public life since 1789, men who had resigned themselves to inaction and obscurity under the Republic and the Empire, and whose one political idea was to reverse the injuries done by the Revolution to their caste and to their Church. They were Royalists because a Bourbon monarchy alone could satisfy their claims: they called themselves ultra-Royalists, but they were so only in the sense that they required the monarchy to recognise no ally but themselves. They had already shown before Napoleon's return that their real chief was the Count of Artois, not the King; in what form their ultra-Royalism would exhibit itself in case the King should not submit to be their instrument remained to be proved.

The first result of the elections was the downfall of

Talleyrand's Liberal Ministry. The Count of Artois and the courtiers, who had been glad enough to secure Fouché's services while their own triumph was doubtful, now joined in the outcry of the country gentlemen against this monster of iniquity. Talleyrand promptly disencumbered himself of his old friend, and prepared to meet the new Parliament as an ultra-Royalist; but in the eyes of the victorious party Talleyrand himself, the married priest and the reputed accomplice in the murder of the Duke of Enghien, was little better than his regicide colleague; and before the Assembly met he was forced to retire from power. His successor, the Duc de Richelieu, was recommended to Louis XVIII. by the Czar. Richelieu had quitted France early in the Revolution, and, unlike most of the emigrants, had played a distinguished part in the country which gave him refuge. Winning his first laurels in the siege of Ismail under Suvaroff, he had subsequently been made Governor of the Euxine provinces of Russia, and the flourishing town of Odessa had sprung up under his rule. His reputation as an administrator was high; his personal character singularly noble and disinterested. Though the English Government looked at first with apprehension upon a Minister so closely connected with the Czar of Russia, Richelieu's honesty and truthfulness soon gained him the respect of every foreign Court. His relation to Alexander proved of great service to France in lightening the burden of the army of occupation; his equity, his acquaintance with the real ends of monarchical

Fall of Talleyrand and Fouché.

Richelieu's Ministry, Sept., 1815.

government, made him, though no lover of liberty, a valuable Minister in face of an Assembly which represented nothing but the passions and the ideas of a reactionary class. But Richelieu had been too long absent from France to grasp the details of administration with a steady hand. The men, the parties of 1815, were new to him: it is said that he was not acquainted by sight with most of his colleagues when he appointed them to their posts. The Ministry in consequence was not at unity within itself. Some of its members, like Decazes, were more liberal than their chief; others, like Clarke and Vaublanc, old servants of Napoleon now turned ultra-Royalists, were eager to make themselves the instruments of the Count of Artois, and to carry into the work of government the enthusiasm of revenge which had already found voice in the elections.

The session opened on the 7th of October. Twenty-nine of the peers, who had joined Napoleon during the Hundred Days, were excluded from the House, and replaced by adherents of the Bourbons; nevertheless the peers as a body opposed themselves to extreme reaction, and, in spite of Chateaubriand's sanguinary harangues, supported the moderate policy of Richelieu against the majority of the Lower House. The first demand of the Chamber of Deputies was for retribution upon traitors;* their first

<small>Violence of the Chamber of 1815.</small>

* See the Address, in *Journal des Débats*, 15 Octobre: "Nous oserons solliciter humblement la rétribution nécessaire," &c. For the general history of the Session, see Duvergier de Hauranne, iii. 257; Viel-Castel, iv. 139; Castlereagh's severe judgment of Artois. Records: Cont., 28, Sep. 21.

conflict with the Government of Louis XVIII. arose upon the measures which were brought forward by the Ministry for the preservation of public security and the punishment of seditious acts. The Ministers were attacked, not because their measures were too severe, but because they were not severe enough. While taking power to imprison all suspected persons without trial, or to expel them from their homes, Decazes, the Police-Minister, proposed to punish incitements to sedition by fines and terms of imprisonment varying according to the gravity of the offence. So mild a penalty excited the wrath of men whose fathers and brothers had perished on the guillotine. Some cried out for death, others for banishment to Cayenne. When it was pointed out that the infliction of capital punishment for the mere attempt at sedition would place this on a level with armed rebellion, it was answered that a distinction might be maintained by adding in the latter case the ancient punishment of parricide, the amputation of the hand. Extravagances like this belonged rather to the individuals than to a party; but the vehemence of the Chamber forced the Government to submit to a revision of its measure. Transportation to Cayenne, but not death, was ultimately included among the penalties for seditious acts. The Minister of Justice, M. Barbé-Marbois, who had himself been transported to Cayenne by the Jacobins in 1797, was able to satisfy the Chamber from his own experience that they were not erring on the side of mercy.*

* *Journal des Débats*, 29 October.

It was in the midst of these heated debates that Marshal Ney was brought to trial for high treason. A so-called Edict of Amnesty had been published by the King on the 24th of July, containing the names of nineteen persons who were to be tried by courts-martial on capital charges, and of thirty-eight others who were to be either exiled or brought to justice, as the Chamber might determine. Ney was included in the first category. Opportunities for escape had been given to him by the Government, as indeed they had to almost every other person on the list. King Louis XVIII. well understood that his Government was not likely to be permanently strengthened by the execution of some of the most distinguished men in France; the emigrants, however, and especially the Duchess of Angoulême, were merciless, and the English Government acted a deplorable part. "One can never feel that the King is secure on his throne," wrote Lord Liverpool, "until he has dared to spill traitors' blood. It is not that many examples would be necessary; but the daring to make a few will alone manifest any strength in the Government."* Labédoyère had already been executed. On the 9th of November Ney was brought before a court-martial, at which Castlereagh and his wife had the bad taste to be present. The court-martial, headed by Ney's old comrade Jourdan, declared itself incompetent to judge a peer of France accused of high treason.† Ney was accordingly tried before the

marginal note: Ney executed, Dec. 7.

---

* Wellington, S. D., xi. 95. This self-confident folly is repeated in many of Lord Liverpool's letters. † Procès du Maréchal Ney, i. 212.

EXECUTION OF MARSHAL NEY.

House of Peers. The verdict was a foregone conclusion, and indeed the legal guilt of the Marshal could hardly be denied. Had the men who sat in judgment upon him been a body of Vendean peasants who had braved fire and sword for the Bourbon cause, the sentence of death might have been pronounced with pure, though stern lips : it remains a deep disgrace to France that among the peers who voted not only for Ney's condemnation but for his death, there were some who had themselves accepted office and pay from Napoleon during the Hundred Days. A word from Wellington would still have saved the Marshal's life, but in interceding for Ney the Duke would have placed himself in direct opposition to the action of his own Government. When the Premier had dug the grave, it was not for Wellington to rescue the prisoner. It is permissible to hope that he, who had so vehemently reproached Blücher for his intention to put Napoleon to death if he should fall into his hands, would have asked clemency for Ney, had he considered himself at liberty to obey the promptings of his own nature. The responsibility for Marshal Ney's death rests, more than upon any other individual, upon Lord Liverpool.

On the 7th of December the sentence was executed. Ney was shot at early morning in an unfrequented spot, and the Government congratulated itself that it had escaped the dangers of a popular demonstration, and heard the last of a disagreeable business. Never was there a greater mistake. No crime committed in the Reign of Terror attached a deeper popular opprobrium to its authors than the execution of Ney did to the Bourbon family. The victim, a brave but rough half-German soldier,* rose in popular legend almost to the height of the Emperor himself. His heroism in the retreat from Moscow became, and with justice, a more glorious memory than Davoust's victory at Jena or Moreau's at Hohenlinden. Side by side with the thought that the Bourbons had been brought back by foreign arms, the remembrance sank deep into the heart of the French people that this family had put to death "the bravest of the brave." It would have been no common good fortune for Louis XVIII. to have pardoned or visited with light punishment a great soldier whose political feebleness had led him to an act of treason, condoned by the nation at large. Exile would not have made the transgressor a martyr. But the common sense of mankind condemns Ney's execution: the public opinion of France has never forgiven it.

On the day after the great example was made, Richelieu brought forward the Amnesty Bill of the

* Ney was not, however, a mere fighting general. The Military Studies published in English in 1833 from his manuscripts prove this. They abound in acute remarks, and his estimate of the quality of the German soldier, at a time when the Germans were habitually beaten and despised, is very striking. He urges that when French infantry fight in three ranks, the charge should be made after the two front ranks have fired, without waiting for the third to fire. "The German soldier, formed by the severest discipline, is cooler than any other. He would in the end obtain the advantage in this kind of firing if it lasted long." (P. 100.) Ney's parents appear to have been Würtemberg people who had settled in Alsace. The name was really Neu (New).

NAPOLEON'S TRENDER.

Government in the House of Representatives. The King, while claiming full right of pardon, desired that the Chamber should be associated with him in its exercise, and submitted a project of law securing from prosecution all persons not included in the list published on July 24th. Measures of a very different character had already been introduced under the same title into the Chamber. Though the initiative in legislation belonged by virtue of the Charta to the Crown, resolutions might be moved by members in the shape of petition or address, and under this form the leaders of the majority had drawn up schemes for the wholesale proscription of Napoleon's adherents. It was proposed by M. la Bourdonnaye to bring to trial all the great civil and military officers who, during the Hundred Days, had constituted the Government of the usurper; all generals, préfets, and commanders of garrisons, who had obeyed Napoleon before a certain day, to be named by the Assembly; and all voters for the death of Louis XVI. who had recognised Napoleon by signing the Acte Additionnel. The language in which these prosecutions were urged was the echo of that which had justified the bloodshed of 1793; its violence was due partly to the fancy that Napoleon's return was no sudden and unexpected act, but the work of a set of conspirators in high places, who were still plotting the overthrow of the monarchy.* It

Amnesty Bill, Dec. 8.

---

* See the extracts from La Bourdonnaye's printed speech in *Journal des Débats*, 19 Novembre. "Pour arrêter leurs trames criminelles, il faut des fers, des bourreaux, des supplices. La mort, la mort seule peut

was in vain that Richelieu intervened with the expression of the King's own wishes, and recalled the example of forgiveness shown in the testament of Louis XVI. The committee which was appointed to report on the projects of amnesty brought up a scheme little different from that of La Bourdonnaye, and added to it the iniquitous proposal that civil actions should be brought against all condemned persons for the damages sustained by the State through Napoleon's return. This was to make a mock of the clause in the Charta which abolished confiscation. The report of the committee caused the utmost dismay both in France itself and among the representatives of foreign Powers at Paris. The conflict between the men of reaction and the Government had openly broken out; Richelieu's Ministry, the guarantee of peace, seemed to be on the point of falling. On the 2nd of January, 1816, the Chamber proceeded to discuss the Bill of the Government and the amendments of the committee. The debate lasted four days; it was only by the repeated use of the King's own name that the Ministers succeeded in gaining a majority of nine votes against the two principal categories of exception appended to the amnesty by their opponents. The proposal to restore confiscation under the form of civil actions was rejected by a much greater majority, but on the vote affecting the regicides the Government was defeated. This indeed was considered of no great moment. Richelieu, content

effrayer leurs complices et mettre fin à leurs complots," &c. The journals abound with similar speeches.

with having averted measures which would have exposed several hundred persons to death, exile, or pecuniary ruin, consented to banish from France the regicides who had acknowledged Napoleon, along with the thirty-eight persons named in the second list of July 24th. Among other well-known men, Carnot, who had rendered such great services to his country, went to die in exile. Of the seventeen companions of Ney and Labédoyère in the first list of July 24th, most had escaped from France; one alone suffered death.* But the persons originally excluded from the amnesty and the regicides exiled by the Assembly formed but a small part of those on whom the vengeance of the Royalists fell; for it was provided that the amnesty-law should apply to no one against whom proceedings had been taken before the formal promulgation of the law. The prisons were already crowded with accused persons, who thus remained exposed to punishment; and after the law had actually passed the Chamber, telegraph-signals were sent over the country by Clarke, the Minister of War, ordering the immediate accusation of several others. One distinguished soldier at least, General Travot, was sentenced to death on proceedings thus instituted between the passing and the promulgation of the law of amnesty.† Executions, however, were

---

* General Mouton-Duvernet. Several were sentenced to death in their absence; some were acquitted on the singular plea that they had become subjects of the Empire of Elba, and so could not be guilty of treason to the King of France.
† The sentence was commuted by the King to twelve years' imprisonment. General Chartran was actually shot. It is stated, though it appears

not numerous except in the south of France, but an enormous number of persons were imprisoned or driven from their homes, some by judgment of the law-courts, some by the exercise of the powers conferred on the administration by the law of Public Security.* The central government indeed had less part in this species of persecution than the Préfets and other local authorities, though within their own departments Clarke and Vaublanc set an example which others were not slow to follow. Royalist committees were formed all over the country, and assumed the same kind of irregular control over the officials of their districts as had been practised by the Jacobin committees of 1793. Thousands of persons employed in all grades of the public service, in schools and colleges as well as in the civil administration, in the law-courts as well as in the army and navy, were dismissed from their posts. The new-comers were professed agents of the reaction; those who were permitted to retain their offices strove to outdo their colleagues in their renegade

<small>Persecution of suspected persons over all France.</small>

---

not to be clear, that his prosecution began at the same late date. Duvergier de Hauranne, iii. 335.

* The highest number admitted by the Government to have been imprisoned at any one time under the Law of Public Security was 319, in addition to 750 banished from their homes or placed under surveillance. No one has collected statistics of the imprisonments by legal sentence. The old story that there were 70,000 persons in prison is undoubtedly an absurd exaggeration; but the numbers given by the Government, even if true at any one moment, afford no clue to the whole number of imprisonments, for as fast as one person gets out of prison in France in a time of political excitement, another is put in. The writer speaks from personal experience, having been imprisoned in 1871. Any one who has seen how these affairs are conducted will know how ridiculous it would be to suppose that the central government has information of every case.

zeal for the new order. It was seen again, as it had been seen under the Republic and under the Empire, that if virtue has limits, servility has none. The same men who had hunted down the peasant for sheltering his children from Napoleon's conscription now hunted down those who were stigmatised as Bonapartists. The clergy threw in their lot with the victorious party, and denounced to the magistrates their parishioners who treated them with disrespect.* Darker pages exist in French history than the reaction of 1815, none more contemptible. It is the deepest condemnation of the violence of the Republic and the despotism of the Empire that the generation formed by it should have produced the class who could exhibit, and the public who could tolerate, the prodigies of baseness which attended the second Bourbon restoration.

Within the Chamber of Deputies the Ultra-Royalist majority had gained Parliamentary experience in the debates on the Amnesty Bill and the Law of Public Security: their own policy now took a definite shape, and to outbursts of passion there succeeded the attempt to realise ideas. Hatred of the Revolution and all its works was still the dominant impulse of the Assembly; but whatever may have been the earlier desire of the Ultra-Royalist noblesse, it was no longer their intention to restore the political system that existed before 1789. They would in that case have desired to restore absolute monarchy,

The reactionists adopt Parliamentary theory.

---

* See, *e.g.*, the Pétition aux Deux Chambres, 1816, at the beginning of P. L. Courier's works.

and to surrender the power which seemed at length to have fallen into the hands of their own class. With Artois on the throne this might have been possible, for Artois, though heir to the crown, was still what he had been in his youth, the chief of a party: with Louis XVIII. and Richelieu at the head of the State, the Ultra-Royalists became the adversaries of royal prerogative and the champions of the rights of Parliament. Before the Revolution the noblesse had possessed privileges; it had not possessed political power. The Constitution of 1814 had unexpectedly given it, under representative forms, the influence denied to it under the old monarchy. New political vistas opened; and the men who had hitherto made St. Louis and Henry IV. the subject of their declamations, now sought to extend the rights of Parliament to the utmost, and to perpetuate in succeeding assemblies the rule of the present majority. An electoral law favourable to the great landed proprietors was the first necessity. This indeed was but a means to an end: another and a greater end might be attained directly, the restoration of a landed Church, and of the civil and social ascendancy of the clergy.

It had been admitted by King Louis XVIII. that the clause in the Charta relating to elections required modification, and on this point the Ultra-Royalists in the Chamber were content to wait for the proposals of the Government. In their ecclesiastical policy they did not maintain the same reserve. Resolutions in favour of the State-Church

Ecclesiastical schemes of the reaction.

were discussed in the form of petitions to be presented to the Crown. It was proposed to make the clergy, as they had been before the Revolution, the sole keepers of registers of birth and marriage; to double the annual payment made to them by the State; to permit property of all kinds to be acquired by the Church by gift or will; to restore all Church-lands not yet sold by the State; and finally, to abolish the University of France, and to place all schools and colleges throughout the country under the control of the Bishops. One central postulate not only passed the Chamber, but was accepted by the Government and became law. Divorce was absolutely abolished; and for nearly seventy years from that time no possible aggravation of wrong sufficed in France to release either husband or wife from the mockery of a marriage-tie. The power to accept donations or legacies was granted to the clergy, subject, however, in every case to the approval of the Crown. The allowance made to them out of the revenues of the State was increased by the amount of certain pensions as they should fall in, a concession which fell very far short of the demands of the Chamber. In all, the advantages won for the Church were scarcely proportioned to the zeal displayed in its cause. The most important question, the disposal of the unsold Church-lands, remained to be determined when the Chamber should enter upon the discussion of the Budget.

The Electoral Bill of the Government, from which the Ultra-Royalists expected so much, was introduced

at the end of the year 1815. It showed in a singular manner the confusion of ideas existing within the Ministry as to the nature of the Parliamentary liberty now supposed to belong to France. The ex-préfet Vaublanc, to whom the framing of the measure was entrusted, though he imagined himself purged from the traditions of Napoleonism, could conceive of no relation between the executive and the legislative power but that which exists between a substance and its shadow. It never entered his mind that the representative institutions granted by the Charta were intended to bring an independent force to bear upon the Government, or that the nation should be treated as more than a fringe round the compact and lasting body of the administration. The language in which Vaublanc introduced his measure was grotesquely candid. Montesquieu, he said, had pointed out that powers must be subordinate; therefore the electoral power must be controlled by the King's Government.*
By the side of the electors in the Canton and the Department there was accordingly placed, in the Ministerial scheme, an array of officials numerous enough to carry the elections, if indeed they did not actually outnumber the private voters. The franchise was confined to the sixty richest persons in each Canton: these, with the officials of the district, were to elect the voters of the Department, who, with a similar contingent of officials, were to choose the Deputies. Re-affirming the principle laid down in the Constitution of 1795 and repeated in

Electoral Bill, Dec. 18, 1815.

* *Journal des Débats*, 19 Decembre, 1815.

the Charta, Vaublanc proposed that a fifth part of the Assembly should retire each year.

If the Minister had intended to give the Ultra-Royalists the best possible means of exalting the peculiar policy of their class into something like a real defence of liberty, he could not have framed a more fitting measure. The creation of constituent bodies out of mayors, crown-advocates, and justices of the peace, was described, and with truth, as a mere Napoleonic juggle. The limitation of the franchise to a fixed number of rich persons was condemned as illiberal and contrary to the spirit of the Charta: the system of yearly renovation by fifths, which threatened to curtail the reign of the present majority, was attributed to the dread of any complete expression of public opinion. It was evident that the Bill of the Government would either be rejected or altered in such a manner as to give it a totally different character. In the Committee of the Chamber which undertook the task of drawing up amendments, the influence was first felt of a man who was soon to become the chief and guiding spirit of the Ultra-Royalist party. M. de Villèle, spokesman of the Committee, had in his youth been an officer in the navy of Louis XVI. On the dethronement of the King he had quitted the service, and settled in the Isle of Bourbon, where he gained some wealth and an acquaintance with details of business and finance rare among the French landed gentry. Returning to France under the Empire, he took up his abode near Toulouse,

Counter-project of Villèle.

his native place, and was made Mayor of that city on Napoleon's second downfall. Villèle's politics gained a strong and original colour from his personal experience and the character of the province in which he lived. The south was the only part of France known to him. There the reactionary movement of 1815 had been a really popular one, and the chief difficulty of the Government, at the end of the Hundred Days, had been to protect the Bonapartists from violence. Villèle believed that throughout France the wealthier men among the peasantry were as ready to follow the priests and nobles as they were in Provence and La Vendée. His conception of the government of the future was the rule of a landed aristocracy, resting, in its struggle against monarchical centralisation and against the Liberalism of the middle class, on the conservative and religious instincts of the peasantry. Instead of excluding popular forces, Villèle welcomed them as allies. He proposed to lower the franchise to one-sixth of the sum named in the Charta, and, while retaining a system of double-election, to give a vote in the primary assemblies to every Frenchman paying annual taxes to the amount of fifty francs. In constituencies so large as to include all the more substantial peasantry, while sufficiently limited to exclude the ill-paid populace in towns, Villèle believed that the Church and the noblesse would on the whole control the elections. In the interest of the present majority he rejected the system of renovation by fifths proposed by the Government, and demanded that the present Chamber should continue unchanged until its dissolution, and the succeeding Chamber be elected entire.

Villèle's scheme, if carried, would in all probability have failed at the first trial. The districts in which the reaction of 1815 was popular were not so large as he supposed: in the greater part of France the peasantry would not have obeyed the nobles except under intimidation. This was suspected by the majority, in spite of the confident language in which they spoke of the will of the nation as identical with their own. Villèle's boldness alarmed them: they anticipated that these great constituencies of peasants, if really left masters of the elections, would be more likely to return a body of Jacobins and Bonapartists than one of hereditary landlords. It was not necessary, however, to sacrifice the well-sounding principle of a low franchise, for the democratic vote at the first stage of the elections might effectively be neutralised by putting the second stage into the hands of the chief proprietors. The Assembly had in fact only to imitate the example of the Government, and to appoint a body of persons who should vote, as of right, by the side of the electors chosen in the primary assemblies. The Government in its own interest had designated a troop of officials as electors: the Assembly, on the contrary, resolved that in the Electoral College of each Department, numbering in all about 150 persons, the fifty principal landowners of the Department should be entitled to vote, whether they had been nominated by the primary constituencies or

Result of debates on Electoral Bill.

not. Modified by this proviso, the project of Villèle passed the Assembly. The Government saw that under the disguise of a series of amendments a measure directly antagonistic to their own had been carried. The franchise had been altered; the real control of the elections placed in the hands of the very party which was now in open opposition to the King and his Ministers. No compromise was possible between the law proposed by the Government and that passed by the Assembly. The Government appealed to the Chamber of Peers. The Peers threw out the amendments of the Lower House. A provisional measure was then introduced by Richelieu for the sake of providing France with at least some temporary rule for the conduct of elections. It failed; and the constitutional legislation of the country came to a dead-lock, while the Government and the Assembly stood face to face, and it became evident that one or the other must fall. The Ministers of the Great Powers at Paris, who watched over the restored dynasty, debated whether or not they should recommend the King to resort to the extreme measure of a dissolution.

The Electoral Bill was not the only object of conflict between Richelieu's Ministry and the Chamber, nor indeed the principal one. The Budget excited fiercer passions, and raised greater issues. It was for no mere scheme of finance that the Government had to

<small>Contest on the Budget.</small>   fight, but against a violation of public faith which would have left France insolvent and creditless in the face of the Powers who still

held its territory in pledge. The debt incurred by the nation since 1813 was still unfunded. That part of it which had been raised before the summer of 1814 had been secured by law upon the unsold forests formerly belonging to the Church, and upon the Communal lands which Napoleon had made the property of the State: the remainder, which included the loans made during the Hundred Days, had no specified security. It was now proposed by the Government to place the whole of the unfunded debt upon the same level, and to provide for its payment by selling the so-called Church-forests. The project excited the bitterest opposition on the side of Count of Artois and his friends. If there was one object which the clerical and reactionary party pursued with religious fervour, it was the restoration of the Church-lands: if there was one class which they had no scruple in impoverishing, it was the class that had lent money to Napoleon. Instead of paying the debts of the State, the Committee of the Chamber proposed to repeal the law of September, 1814, which pledged the Church-forests, and to compel both the earlier and the later holders of the unfunded debt to accept stock in satisfaction of their claims, though the stock was worth less than two-thirds of its nominal value. The resolution was in fact one for the repudiation of a third part of the unfunded debt. Richelieu, seeing in what fashion his measure was about to be transformed, determined upon withdrawing it altogether: the majority in the Chamber, intent on executing its own policy and that of the Count of Artois, refused to recognise the withdrawal. Such a step was at once an insult and a usurpation of power. So great was the scandal and alarm caused by the scenes in the Chamber, that the Duke of Wellington, at the instance of the Ambassadors, presented a note to King Louis XVIII. requiring him in plain terms to put a stop to the machinations of his brother.* The interference of the foreigner provoked the Ultra-Royalists, and failed to excite energetic action on the part of King Louis, who dreaded the sour countenance of the Duchess of Angoulême more than he did Wellington's reproofs. In the end the question of a settlement of the unfunded debt was allowed to remain open. The Government was unable to carry the sale of the Church-forests, the Chamber did not succeed in its project of confiscation. The Budget for the year, greatly altered in the interest of the landed proprietors, was at length brought into shape. A resolution of the Lower House restoring the unsold forests to the Church was ignored by the Crown; and the Government, having obtained the means of carrying on the public services, gladly abstained from further legislation, and on the 29th of April ended the turmoil which surrounded it by proroguing the Chambers.

The Chambers prorogued, April 29.

It was hoped that with the close of the Session the system of imprisonment and surveillance which prevailed in the Departments would be brought to an end. Vaublanc, the Minister of coercion, was removed from

* Wellington, S. D., xi. 309.

office. But the troubles of France were not yet over. On the 6th of May, a rising of peasants took place at Grenoble. According to the report of General Donnadieu, commander of the garrison, which brought the news to the Government, the revolt had only been put down after the most desperate fighting. "The corpses of the King's enemies," said the General in his despatch, "cover all the roads for a league round Grenoble." * It was soon known that twenty-four prisoners had been condemned to death by court-martial, and sixteen of these actually executed: the court-martial recommended the other eight to the clemency of the Government. But the despatches of Donnadieu had thrown the Cabinet into a panic. Decazes, the most liberal of the Ministers, himself signed the hasty order requiring the remaining prisoners to be put to death. They perished; and when it was too late the Government learnt that Donnadieu's narrative was a mass of the grossest exaggerations, and that the affair which he had represented as an insurrection of the whole Department was conducted by about 300 peasants, half of whom were unarmed. The violence and illegality with which the General proceeded to establish a régime of military law soon brought him into collision with the Government. He became the hero of the Ultra-Royalists; but the Ministry, which was unwilling to make a public confession that it had needlessly put eight persons to death, had to bear the odium of an act of cruelty for which

Rising at Grenoble, May 6th. Executions.

* Despatch in Duvergier de Hauranne, iii. 442.

Donnadieu was really responsible. The part into which Decazes had been entrapped probably strengthened the determination of this Minister, who was now gaining great influence over the King, to strike with energy against the Ultra-Royalist faction. From this time he steadily led the King towards the only measure which could free the country from the rule of the Count of Artois and the reactionists—the dissolution of Parliament.

Louis XVIII. depended much on the society of some personal favourite. Decazes was young and an agreeable companion; his business as Police-Minister gave him the opportunity of amusing the King with anecdotes and gossip much more congenial to the old man's taste than discussions on finance or constitutional law. Louis came to regard Decazes almost as a son, and gratified his own studious inclination by teaching him English. The Minister's enemies said that he won the King's heart by taking private lessons from some obscure Briton, and attributing his extraordinary progress to the skill of his royal master. But Decazes had a more effective retort than witticism. He opened the letters of the Ultra-Royalists and laid them before the King. Louis found that these loyal subjects jested upon his infirmities, called him a dupe in the hands of Jacobins, and grumbled at him for so long delaying the happy hour when Artois should ascend the throne. Humorous as Louis was, he was not altogether pleased to read that he "ought either to open his eyes or to close them for ever." At the same time the reports of Decazes' local agents proved that the Ultra-

Decazes.

Royalist party were in reality weak in numbers and unpopular throughout the greater part of the country. The project of a dissolution was laid before the Ministers and some of the King's confidants. Though the Ambassadors were not consulted on the measure, it was certain that they would not resist it. No word of the Ministerial plot reached the rival camp of Artois. The King gained courage, and on the 5th of September signed the Ordonnance which appealed from the Parliament to the nation, and, to the anger and consternation of the Ultra-Royalists, made an end of the intractable Chamber a few weeks before the time which had been fixed for its re-assembling.

<small>Dissolution of the Chamber, Sept. 5, 1816.</small>

France was well rid of a body of men who had been elected at a moment of despair, and who would either have prolonged the occupation of the country by foreign armies, or have plunged the nation into civil war. The elections which followed were favourable to the Government. The questions fruitlessly agitated in the Assembly of 1815 were settled to the satisfaction of the public in the new Parliament. An electoral law was passed, which, while it retained the high franchise fixed by the Charta, and the rule of renewing the Chamber by fifths, gave life and value to the representative system by making the elections direct. Though the constituent body of all France scarcely numbered under this arrangement a hundred thousand persons, it was extensive enough to contain a majority hostile to the reactionary policy of the Church

<small>Electoral law, 1817.</small>

and the noblesse. The men who had made wealth by banking, commerce, or manufactures, the so-called higher bourgeoisie, greatly exceeded in number the larger landed proprietors; and although they were not usually democratic in their opinions, they were liberal, and keenly attached to the modern as against the old institutions of France, inasmuch as their industrial interests and their own personal importance depended upon the maintenance of the victory won in 1789 against aristocratic privilege and monopoly. So strong was the hostility between the civic middle class and the landed noblesse, that the Ultra-Royalists in the Chamber sought, as they had done in the year before, to extend the franchise to the peasantry, in the hope of overpowering wealth with numbers. The electoral law, however, passed both Houses in the form in which it had been drawn up by the Government. Though deemed narrow and oligarchical by the next generation, it was considered, and with justice, as a great victory won by liberalism at the time. The middle class of Great Britain had to wait for fifteen years before it obtained anything like the weight in the representation given to the middle class of France by the law of 1817.

Not many of the persons who had been imprisoned under the provisional acts of the last year now remained in confinement. It was considered necessary to prolong the Laws of Public Security, and they were re-enacted, but under a much softened form.

Establishment of financial credit.

It remained for the new Chamber to restore the financial credit of the country by making some equitable arrangement for securing the capital and paying the interest of the unfunded debt. Projects of repudiation now gained no hearing. Richelieu consented to make an annual allowance to the Church, equivalent to the rental of the Church-forests; but the forests themselves were made security for the debt, and the power of sale was granted to the Government. Pending such repayment of the capital, the holders of unfunded debt received stock, calculated at its real, not at its titular, value. The effect of this measure was at once evident. The Government was enabled to enter into negotiations for a loan, which promised it the means of paying the indemnities due to the foreign Powers. On this payment depended the possibility of withdrawing the army of occupation. Though Wellington at first offered some resistance, thirty thousand men were removed in the spring of 1817; and the Czar allowed Richelieu to hope that, if no further difficulties should arise, the complete evacuation of French territory might take place in the following year.

Thus the dangers with which reactionary passion had threatened France appeared to be passing away. The partial renovation of the Chamber which took place in the autumn of 1817 still further strengthened the Ministry of Richelieu and weakened the Ultra-Royalist opposition. A few more months passed, and before the third anniversary of Waterloo, the Czar was ready to advise the entire withdrawal of foreign armies from France. An invitation was issued to the Powers to meet in Conference at Aix-

Character of the years 1816–18.

la-Chapelle. There was no longer any doubt that the five years' occupation, contemplated when the second Treaty of Paris was made, would be abandoned. The good will of Alexander, the friendliness of his Ambassador, Pozzo di Borgo, who, as a native of Corsica, had himself been a French subject, and who now aspired to become Minister of France, were powerful influences in favour of Louis XVIII. and his kingdom: much, however, of the speedy restoration of confidence was due to the temperate rule of Richelieu. The nation itself, far from suffering from Napoleon's fall, regained something of the spontaneous energy so rich in 1789, so wanting at a later period. The cloud of military disaster lifted; new mental and political life began; and under the dynasty forced back by foreign arms France awoke to an activity unknown to it while its chief gave laws to Europe. Parliamentary debate offered the means of legal opposition to those who bore no friendship to the Court: conspiracy, though it alarmed at the moment, had become the resort only of the obscure and the powerless. Groups of able men were gathering around recognised leaders, or uniting in defence of a common political creed. The Press, dumb under Napoleon except for purposes of sycophancy, gradually became a power in the land. Even the dishonest eloquence of Chateaubriand, enforcing the principles of legal and constitutional liberty on behalf of a party which would fain have used every weapon of despotism in its own interest, proved that the leaden weight that had so long crushed thought and expression existed no more.

But if the years between 1815 and 1819 were in France years of hope and progress, it was not so with Europe generally. In England they were years of almost unparalleled suffering and discontent; in Italy the rule of Austria grew more and more anti-national; in Prussia, though a vigorous local and financial administration hastened the recovery of the impoverished land, the hopes of liberty declined beneath the reviving energy of the nobles and the resistance of the friends of absolutism. [sidenote: Prussia after 1815.] When Stein had summoned the Prussian people to take up arms for their Fatherland, he had believed that neither Frederick William nor Alexander would allow Prussia to remain without free institutions after the battle was won. The keener spirits in the War of Liberation had scarcely distinguished between the cause of national independence and that of internal liberty. They returned from the battle-fields of Saxony and France, knowing that the Prussian nation had unsparingly offered up life and wealth at the call of patriotism, and believing that a patriot-king would rejoice to crown his triumph by inaugurating German freedom. For a while the hope seemed near fulfilment. On the 22nd of May, 1815, Frederick William published an ordinance, declaring that a Representation of the People should be established.* [sidenote: Edict promising a Constitution, May 22, 1815.] For this end the King stated that the existing Provincial Estates should be re-organised, and new ones founded where none existed, and that out of the Provincial

* Pertz, Leben Steins, iv. 428.

Estates the Assembly of Representatives of the country should be chosen. It was added that a commission would be appointed, to organise under Hardenberg's presidency the system of representation, and to draw up a written Constitution. The right of discussing all legislative measures affecting person or property was promised to the Assembly. Though foreign affairs seemed to be directly excluded from parliamentary debate, and the language of the Edict suggested that the representative body would only have a consultative voice, without the power either of originating or of rejecting laws, these reservations only showed the caution natural on the part of a Government divesting itself for the first time of absolute power. Guarded as it was, the scheme laid down by the King would hardly have displeased the men who had done the most to make constitutional rule in Prussia possible.

But the promise of Frederick William was destined to remain unfulfilled. It was no good omen for Prussia that Stein, who had rendered such glorious services to his country and to all Europe, was suffered to retire from public life.

Resistance of the feudal and autocratic parties.

The old court-party at Berlin, politicians who had been forced to make way for more popular men, landowners who had never pardoned the liberation of the serf, all the interests of absolutism and class-privilege which had disappeared for a moment in the great struggle for national existence, gradually re-asserted their influence over the King, and undermined the authority of

Hardenberg, himself sinking into old age amid circumstances of private life that left to old age little of its honour. To decide even in principle upon the basis to be given to the new Prussian Constitution would have taxed all the foresight and all the constructive skill of the most experienced statesman; for by the side of the ancient dominion of the Hohenzollerns there were now the Rhenish and the Saxon Provinces, alien in spirit and of doubtful loyalty, in addition to Polish territory and smaller German districts acquired at intervals between 1792 and 1815. Hardenberg was right in endeavouring to link the Constitution with something that had come down from the past; but the decision that the General Assembly should be formed out of the Provincial Estates was probably an injudicious one; for these Estates, in their present form, were mainly corporations of nobles, and the spirit which animated them was at once the spirit of class-privilege and of an intensely strong localism. Hardenberg had not only occasioned an unnecessary delay by basing the representative system upon a reform of the Provincial Estates, but had exposed himself to sharp attacks from these very bodies, to whom nothing was more odious than the absorption of their own dignity by a General Assembly. It became evident that the process of forming a Constitution would be a tedious one; and in the meantime the opponents of the popular movement opened their attack upon the men and the ideas whose influence in the war of Liberation appeared to have made so great a break between the German present and the past.

The first public utterance of the reaction was a pamphlet issued in July, 1815, by Schmalz, a jurist of some eminence, and brother-in-law of Scharnhorst, the re-organiser of the army. Schmalz, contradicting a statement which attributed to him a highly honourable part in the patriotic movement of 1808, attacked the Tugendbund, and other political associations dating from that epoch, in language of extreme violence. In the stiff and peremptory manner of the old Prussian bureaucracy, he denied that popular enthusiasm had anything whatever to do with the victory of 1813,* attributing the recovery of the nation firstly to its submission to the French alliance in 1812, and secondly to the quiet sense of duty with which, when the time came, it took up arms in obedience to the King. Then, passing on to the present aims of the political societies, he accused them of intending to overthrow all established governments, and to force unity upon Germany by means of revolution, murder, and pillage. Stein was not mentioned by name, but the warning was given to men of eminence who encouraged Jacobinical societies, that in such combinations the giants end by serving the dwarfs. Schmalz's pamphlet, which was written with a strength and terseness of style very unusual in Germany, made a deep impression, and excited great indignation in Liberal circles. It was answered, among other writers, by Niebuhr; and the controversy thickened until King Frederick William, in the interest of public tranquillity, ordered that no more should be

margin: Schmalz's pamphlet, 1815.

* Schmalz. Berichtigung, &c., p. 14.

said on either side. It was in accordance with Prussian feeling that the King should thus interfere to stop the quarrels of his subjects. There would have been nothing unseemly in an act of impartial repression. But the King made it impossible to regard his act as of this character. Without consulting Hardenberg, he conferred a decoration upon the author of the controversy. Far-sighted men saw the true bearing of the act. They warned Hardenberg that, if he passed over this slight, he would soon have to pass over others more serious, and urged him to insist upon the removal of the counsellors on whose advice the King had acted.* But the Minister disliked painful measures. He probably believed that no influence could ever supplant his own with the King, and looked too lightly upon the growth of a body of opponents, who, whether in open or in concealed hostility to himself, were bent upon hindering the fulfilment of the constitutional reforms which he had at heart.

In the Edict of the 22nd of May, 1815, the King had ordered that the work of framing a Constitution should be begun in the following September. Delays, however, arose; and when the commission was at length appointed, its leading members were directed to travel over the country in order to collect opinions upon the form of representation required. Two years passed before even this preliminary operation began. In the meantime very little progress had been made towards the establishment

The promised Constitutions delayed in Germany.

* Pertz, Leben Steins, v. 23.

of constitutional government in Germany at large. One prince alone, the Grand Duke of Weimar, already eminent in Europe from his connection with Goethe and Schiller, loyally accepted the idea of a free State, and brought representative institutions into actual working. In Hesse, the Elector summoned the Estates, only to dismiss them with contumely when they resisted his extortions. In most of the minor States contests or negotiations took place between the Sovereigns and the ancient Orders, which led to little or no result. The Federal Diet, which ought to have applied itself to the determination of certain principles of public right common to all Germany, remained inactive. Though hope had not yet fallen, a sense of discontent arose, especially among the literary class which had shown such enthusiasm in the War of Liberation. It was characteristic of Germany that the demand for free government came not from a group of soldiers, as in Spain, not from merchants and men of business, as in England, but from professors and students, and from journalists, who were but professors in another form. The middle class generally were indifferent: the higher nobility, and the knights who had lost their semi-independence in 1803, sought for the restoration of privileges which were really incompatible with any state-government whatever. The advocacy of constitutional rule and of German unity was left, in default of Prussian initiative, to the ardent spirits of the Universities and the Press, who naturally exhibited in the treatment of political problems more fluency than knowledge, and more zeal

THE WARTBURG FESTIVAL.

than discretion. Jena, in the dominion of the Duke of Weimar, became, on account of the freedom of printing which existed there, the centre of the new Liberal journalism. Its University took the lead in the Teutonising movement which had been inaugurated by Fichte twelve years before in the days of Germany's humiliation, and which had now received so vigorous an impulse from the victory won over the foreigner.

On the 18th of October, 1817, the students of Jena, with deputations from all the Protestant Universities of Germany, held a festival at Eisenach, to celebrate the double anniversary of the Reformation and of the battle of Leipzig. Five hundred young patriots, among them scholars who had been decorated for bravery at Waterloo, bound their brows with oak-leaves, and assembled within the venerable hall of Luther's Wartburg Castle; sang, prayed, preached, and were preached to; dined; drank to German liberty, the jewel of life, to Dr. Martin Luther, the man of God, and to the Grand Duke of Saxe-Weimar; then descended to Eisenach, fraternised with the Landsturm in the market-place, and attended divine service in the parish church without mishap. In the evening they edified the townspeople with gymnastics, which were now the recognised symbol of German vigour, and lighted a great bonfire on the hill opposite the castle. Throughout the official part of the ceremony a reverential spirit prevailed; a few rash words were, however, uttered against promise-breaking kings, and some of the hardier spirits took advantage of the bonfire to consign to the flames, in imitation of Luther's dealing with the Pope's Bull, a quantity of what they deemed un-German and illiberal writings. Among these was Schmalz's pamphlet. They also burnt a soldier's strait-jacket, a pigtail, and a corporal's cane, emblems of the military brutalism of past times which was now being revived in Westphalia.* Insignificant as the whole affair was, it excited a singular alarm not only in Germany but at foreign Courts. Richelieu wrote from Paris to inquire whether revolution was breaking out. The King of Prussia sent Hardenberg to Weimar to make investigations on the spot. Metternich, who saw conspiracy and

* A curious account of the festival remains, written by Kieser, one of the Professors who took part in it (Kieser, Das Wartburgfest, 1818). It is so silly that it is hard to believe it to have been written by a grown-up man. He says of the procession to the Wartburg, "There have indeed been processions that surpassed this in outward glory and show; but in inner significant value it cannot yield to any." But making allowance for the author's personal weakness of head, his book is a singular and instructive picture of the mental condition of "Young Germany" and its teachers at that time—a subject that caused such extravagant anxiety to Governments, and so seriously affected the course of political history. It requires some effort to get behind the ridiculous side of the students' Teutonism; but there were elements of reality there. Persons familiar with Wales will be struck by the resemblance, both in language and spirit, between the scenes of 1817 and the religious meetings or the Eisteddfodau of the Welsh, a resemblance not accidental, but resulting from similarity of conditions, viz., a real susceptibility to religious, patriotic, and literary ideas among a people unacquainted with public or practical life on a large scale. But the vigorous political action of the Welsh in 1880, when the landed interest throughout the Principality lost seats which it had held for centuries, surprised only those who had seen nothing but extravagance in the chapel and the field-meeting. Welsh ardour, hitherto in great part undirected, then had a practical effect because English organisation afforded it a model: German ardour in 1817 proved sterile because it had no such example at hand.

revolution everywhere and in everything, congratulated himself that his less sagacious neighbours were at length awakening to their danger. The first result of the Wartburg scandal was that the Duke of Weimar had to curtail the liberties of his subjects. Its further effects became only too evident as time went on. It left behind it throughout Germany the impression that there were forces of disorder at work in the Press and in the Universities which must be crushed at all cost by the firm hand of Government; and it deepened the anxiety with which King Frederick William was already regarding the promises of liberty which he had made to the Prussian people two years before.

Twelve months passed between the Wartburg festival and the beginning of the Conferences at Aix-la-Chapelle. In the interval a more important person than the King of Prussia went over to the side of reaction. Up to the summer of 1818, the Czar appeared to have abated nothing of his zeal for constitutional government. In the spring of that year, he summoned the Polish Diet; addressed them in a speech so enthusiastic as to alarm not only the Court of Vienna but all his own counsellors; and stated in the clearest possible language his intention of extending the benefits of a representative system to the whole Russian Empire.* At the close of the brief session he thanked the Polish Deputies for their boldness in throwing out a measure proposed by himself. Alexander's popular rhetoric at Warsaw might perhaps

Alexander in 1818.

* See the speech in Bernhardi, iii. 669.

be not incompatible with a settled purpose to permit no encroachment on authority either there or elsewhere; but the change in his tone was so great when he appeared at Aix-la-Chapelle a few months afterwards, that some strange and sudden cause has been thought necessary to explain it. It is said that during the Czar's residence at Moscow, in June, 1818, the revelation was made to him of the existence of a mass of secret societies in the army, whose aim was the overthrow of his own Government. Alexander's father had died by the hands of murderers: his own temperament, sanguine and emotional, would make the effects of such a discovery, in the midst of all his benevolent hopes for Russia, poignant to the last degree. It is not inconsistent either with his character or with earlier events in his personal history that the Czar should have yielded to a single shock of feeling, and have changed in a moment from the liberator to the despot. But the evidence of what passed in his mind is wanting. Hearsay, conjecture, gossip, abound;* the one man who could have told all has left no word. This only is certain, that from the close of the year 1818, the future, hitherto bright with dreams of peaceful progress, became in Alexander's view a battle-field between the forces of order and anarchy. The task imposed by Providence on himself and other kings was no longer to spread knowledge and liberty among mankind, but to defend existing authority, and even authority that

---

* Gentz, D.I., ii. 87, iii. 72.

was oppressive and un-Christian, against the madness that was known as popular right.

At the end of September, 1818, the Sovereigns or Ministers of the Great Powers assembled at Aix-la-Chapelle, and the Conferences began. The first question to be decided was whether the Allied Army might safely be withdrawn from France; the second, in what form the concert of Europe should hereafter be maintained. On the first question there was no disagreement: the evacuation of France was resolved upon and promptly executed. The second question was a more difficult one. Richelieu, on behalf of King Louis XVIII., represented that France now stood on the same footing as any other European Power, and proposed that the Quadruple Alliance of 1815 should be converted into a genuine European federation by adding France to it as a fifth member. The plan had been communicated to the English Government, and would probably have received its assent but for the strong opposition raised by Canning within the Cabinet. Canning took a gloomy but a true view of the proposed concert of the Powers. He foresaw that it would really amount to a combination of governments against liberty. Therefore, while recognising the existing engagements of this country, he urged that England ought to join in no combination except that to which it had already pledged itself, namely, the combination made with the definite object of resisting French disturbance. To combine with three Powers to prevent Napoleon or the Jacobins from again becoming masters of France was a reasonable act of policy: to combine with all the Great Powers of Europe against nothing in particular was to place the country on the side of governments against peoples, and to involve England in any enterprise of repression which the Courts might think fit to undertake. Canning's warning opened the eyes of his colleagues to the view which was likely to be taken of such a general alliance by Parliament and by public opinion. Lord Castlereagh was forbidden to make this country a party to any abstract union of Governments. In memorable words the Prime Minister described the true grounds for the decision: "We must recollect in the whole of this business, and ought to make our Allies feel, that the general and European discussion of these questions will be in the British Parliament." * Fear of the rising voice of the nation, no longer forced by military necessities to sanction every measure of its rulers, compelled Lord Liverpool and Castlereagh to take account of scruples which were not their own. On the same grounds, while the Ministry agreed that Continental difficulties which might hereafter arise ought to be settled by a friendly discussion among the Great Powers, it declined to elevate this occasional deliberation into a system, and to assent to the periodical meeting of a Congress. Peace might or might not be promoted by the frequent gatherings of sovereigns and statesmen; but a council so formed, if permanent in its nature, would necessarily extinguish the indepen-

* Castlereagh, xii. 55, 62.

dence of every minor State, and hand over the government of all Europe to the Great Courts, if only they could agree with one another.

It was the refusal of England to enter into a general league that determined the form in which the results of the Conference of 1818 were embodied. In the first place the Quadruple Alliance against French revolution was renewed, and with such seriousness that the military centres were fixed, at which, in case of any outbreak, the troops of each of the Great Powers should assemble.* This Treaty, however, was kept secret, in order not to add to the difficulties of Richelieu. The published documents breathed another spirit.† Without announcing an actual alliance with King Louis XVIII., the Courts, including England, declared that through the restoration of legitimate and constitutional monarchy France had regained its place in the councils of Europe, and that it would hereafter co-operate in maintaining the general peace. For this end meetings of the sovereigns or their ministers might be necessary; such meetings would, however, be arranged by the ordinary modes of negotiation, nor would the affairs of any minor State be discussed by the Great Powers, except at the direct invitation of that State, whose representatives would then be admitted to the sittings. In these guarded words the intention of forming a permanent and organised Court of Control over Europe was disclaimed.

Declarations and Secret Treaty of Aix-la-Chapelle.

---

* Wellington, S. D., xii. 835.
† B. and F. State Papers, 1818—19, vi. 14.

A manifesto, addressed to the world at large, declared that the sovereigns of the five great States had no other object in their union than the maintenance of peace on the basis of existing treaties. They had formed no new political combinations: their rule was the observance of international law; their object the prosperity and moral welfare of their subjects.

The earnestness with which the statesmen of 1818, while accepting the conditions laid down by England, persevered in the project of a joint regulation of European affairs, may suggest the question whether the plan which they had at heart would not in truth have operated to the benefit of mankind. The answer is, that the value of any International Council depends firstly on the intelligence which it is likely to possess, and secondly on the degree in which it is really representative. Experience proved that the Congresses which followed 1818 possessed but a limited intelligence, and that they represented nothing at all but authority. The meeting at Aix-la-Chapelle was itself the turning-point in the constitutional history of Europe. Though no open declaration was made against constitutional forms, *Repressive tone of the Conference.* every sovereign and every minister who attended the Conference left it with the resolution to draw the reins of government tighter. A note of alarm had been sounded. Conspiracies in Belgium, an attempt on the life of Wellington, rumours of a plot to rescue Napoleon from St. Helena, combined with the outcry against the German Universities and the whispered tales from Moscow in filling the minds of statesmen with apprehensions. The change which had taken place in Alexander himself was of the most serious moment. Up to this time Metternich, the leader of European Conservatism, had felt that in the Czar there were sympathies with Liberalism and enlightenment which made the future of Europe doubtful.* To check the dissolution of existing power, to suppress all tendency to change, was the habitual object of Austria, and the Czar was the one person who had seemed likely to prevent the principles of Austria from becoming the law of Europe. Elsewhere Metternich had little to fear in the way of opposition. Hardenberg, broken in health and ill-supported by his King, had ceased to be a power. Yielding to the apprehensions of Frederick William, perhaps with the hope of dispelling them at some future time, he took his place among the alarmists of the day, and suffered the German policy of Prussia, to which so great a future lay open a few years before, to become the mere reflex of Austrian inaction and repression.† England, so long as it was represented on the Continent

<small>Metternich and Austrian principles henceforth dominant.</small>

---

* Gentz, D. I., i. 400. Gentz, the confidant and adviser of Metternich, was secretary to the Conference at Aix-la-Chapelle. His account of it in this despatch is of the greatest value, bringing out in a way in which no official documents do the conservative and repressive tone of the Conference. The prevalent fear had been that Alexander would break with his old Allies and make a separate league with France and Spain. See also Castlereagh, xii. 47.

† "I could write you a long letter about the honour which the Prussians pay to everything Austrian, our whole position, our measures, our language. Metternich has fairly enchanted them." Gentz, Nachlasse [Osten], i. 51.

by Castlereagh and Wellington, scarcely counted for anything on the side of liberty. The sudden change in Alexander removed the one check that stood in Austria's way; and from this time Metternich exercised an authority in Europe such as few statesmen have ever possessed. His influence, overborne by that of the Czar during 1814 and 1815, struck root at the Conference of Aix-la-Chapelle, maintained itself unimpaired during five eventful years, and sank only when the death of Lord Castlereagh allowed the real voice of England once more to be heard, and Canning, too late to forbid the work of repression in Italy and in Spain, inaugurated, after an interval of forced neutrality, that worthier concert which established the independence of Greece.

If it is the mark of a clever statesman to know where to press and where to give way, Metternich certainly proved himself one in 1818. Before the end of the Conference he delivered to Hardenberg and to the King of Prussia two papers containing a complete set of recommendations for the management of Prussian affairs. The contents of these documents were singular enough: it is still more singular that they form the history of what actually took place in Prussia during the succeeding years. Starting with the assumption that the party of revolution had found its lever in the promise of King Frederick William to create a Representative System, Metternich demonstrated in polite language to the very men who had made this promise, that any central Representation would inevitably overthrow the Prussian

Metternich's advice to Prussia, 1818.

State; pointed out that the King's dominions consisted of seven Provinces; and recommended Frederick William to fulfil his promise only by giving to each Province a Diet for the discussion of its own local concerns. Having thus warned the King against creating a National Parliament, like that which had thrown France into revolution in 1789, Metternich exhibited the specific dangers of the moment and the means of overcoming them. These dangers were Universities, Gymnastic establishments, and the Press. "The revolutionists," he said, "despairing of effecting their aim themselves, have formed the settled plan of educating the next generation for revolution. The Gymnastic establishment is a preparatory school for University disorders. The University seizes the youth as he leaves boyhood, and gives him a revolutionary training. This mischief is common to all Germany, and must be checked by joint action of the Governments. Gymnasia, on the contrary, were invented at Berlin, and spring from Berlin. For these, palliative measures are no longer sufficient. It has become a duty of State for the King of Prussia to destroy the evil. The whole institution in every shape must be closed and uprooted." With regard to the abuse of the Press, Metternich contented himself with saying that a difference ought to be made between substantial books and mere pamphlets or journals; and that the regulation of the Press throughout Germany at large could only be effected by an agreement between Austria and Prussia.*

* Metternich, iii. 171.

With a million men under arms, the sovereigns who had overthrown Napoleon trembled because thirty or forty journalists and professors pitched their rhetoric rather too high, and because wise heads did not grow upon schoolboys' shoulders. The Emperor Francis, whose imagination had failed to rise to the glories of the Holy Alliance, alone seems to have had some suspicion of the absurdity of the present alarms.* The Czar distinguished himself by his zeal against the lecturers who were turning the world upside down. As if Metternich had not frightened the Congress enough already, the Czar distributed at Aix-la-Chapelle a pamphlet published by one Stourdza, a Moldavian, which described Germany as on the brink of revolution, and enumerated half a score of mortal disorders which racked that unfortunate country. The chief of all was the vicious system of the Universities, which instead of duly developing the vessel of the Christian State from the cradle of Moses,† brought up young men to be despisers of law and instruments of a licentious press. The ingenious Moldavian, whose expressions in some places bear a singular resemblance to those of Alexander, while in others they are actually identical with reflections of Metternich's not then published, went on to enlighten the German Governments as to the best means of rescuing their subjects from their perilous

Stourdza's pamphlet.

* See his remarks in Metternich, iii. 269: an oasis of sense in this desert of commonplace.
† Stourdza, Denkschrift, &c., p. 31. The French original is not in the British Museum.

condition. Certain fiscal and administrative changes were briefly suggested, but the main reform urged was exactly that propounded by Metternich, the enforcement of a better discipline and of a more rigidly-prescribed course of study at the Universities, along with the supervision of all journals and periodical literature.

Stourdza's pamphlet, in which loose reasoning was accompanied by the coarsest invective, would have gained little attention if it had depended on its own merits or on the reputation of its author: it became a different matter when it was known to represent the views of the Czar. A vehement but natural outcry arose at the Universities against this interference of the foreigner with German domestic affairs. National independence, it seemed, had been won in the deadly struggle against France only in order that internal liberty, the promised fruit of this independence, should be sacrificed at the bidding of Russia. The Czar himself was out of reach: the vengeance of outraged patriotism fell upon an insignificant person who had the misfortune to be regarded as his principal agent. A dramatic author then famous, now forgotten, August Kotzebue, held the office of Russian agent in Central Germany, and conducted a newspaper whose object was to throw ridicule on the national movement of the day, and especially on those associations of students where German enthusiasm reached its climax. Many circumstances embittered popular feeling against this man, and caused him to be

The murder of Kotzebue, March 23, 1819.

regarded less as a legitimate enemy than as a traitor and an apostate. Kotzebue had himself been a student at Jena, and at one time had turned liberal sentiments to practical account in his plays. Literary jealousies and wounded vanity had subsequently alienated him from his country, and made him the willing and acrid hireling of a foreign Court. The reports which, as Russian agent, he sent to St. Petersburg were doubtless as offensive as the attacks on the Universities which he published in his journal; but it was an extravagant compliment to the man to imagine that he was the real author of the Czar's desertion from Liberalism to reaction. This, however, was the common belief, and it cost Kotzebue dear. A student from Erlangen, Carl Sand, who had accompanied the standard at the Wartburg festival, formed the silent resolve of sacrificing his own life in order to punish the enemy of his country. Sand was a man of pure and devout, though ill-balanced character. His earlier life marked him as one whose whole being was absorbed by what he considered a divine call. He thought of the Greeks who, even in their fallen estate, had so often died to free their country from Turkish oppression, and formed the deplorable conclusion that by murdering a decayed dramatist he could strike some great blow against the powers of evil.* He sought the

* The extracts from Sand's diaries, published in a little book in 1821 (Tagebücher, &c.) form a very interesting religious study. The last, written on Dec. 31, 1818, is as follows :—" I meet the last day of this year in an earnest festal spirit, knowing well that the Christmas which I have celebrated will be my last. If our strivings are to result in anything, if the cause of mankind is to succeed in our Fatherland, if all is not to be forgotten, all our enthusiasm spent in vain, the evil-doer, the traitor, the

unfortunate Kotzebue in the midst of his family, stabbed him to the heart, and then turned his weapon against himself. Recovering from his wounds, he was condemned to death, and perished, after a year's interval, on the scaffold, calling God to witness that he died for Germany to be free.

The effects of Sand's act were very great, and their real nature was at once recognised. Hardenberg, the moment that he heard of Kotzebue's death, exclaimed that a Prussian Constitution had now become impossible. Metternich, who had thought the Czar mad because he desired to found a peaceful alliance of sovereigns on religious principles, was not likely to make allowance for a kind of piety that sent young rebels over the country on missions of murder. The Austrian statesman was in Rome when the news of Kotzebue's assassination reached him. He saw that the time had come for united action throughout Germany, and, without making any public utterance, drew up a scheme of repressive measures, and sent out proposals for a gathering of the Ministers of all the principal German Courts. In the summer he travelled slowly northwards, met the King of Prussia at Teplitz, in Bohemia, and shortly afterwards opened the intended Conference of Ministers in the neighbouring town of

Action of Metternich.

corrupter of youth must die. Until I have executed this, I have no peace; and what can comfort me until I know that I have with upright will set my life at stake? O God, I pray only for the right clearness and courage of soul, that in that last supreme hour I may not be false to myself" (p. 174). The reference to the Greeks is in a letter in the English memoir, n. 40.

Carlsbad. A number of innocent persons had already, at his instigation, been arrested in Prussia and other States, under circumstances deeply discreditable to Government. Private papers were seized, and garbled extracts from them published in official prints as proof of guilt.* "By the help of God," Metternich wrote, "I hope to defeat the German Revolution, just as I vanquished the conqueror of the world. The revolutionists thought me far away, because I was five hundred leagues off. They deceived themselves; I have been in the midst of them, and now I am striking my blows."† Metternich's plan was to enforce throughout Germany, by means of legislation in the Federal Diet, the principle which he had already privately commended to the King of Prussia. There were two distinct objects of policy before him: the first, to prevent the formation in any German State of an assembly representing the whole community, like the English House of Commons or the French Chamber of Deputies; the second, to establish a general system of censorship over the Press and over the Universities, and to create a central authority, vested, as the representative of the Diet, with inquisitorial powers.

The first of these objects, the prevention of

* The papers of the poet Arndt were seized. Among them was a copy of certain short notes made by the King of Prussia, about 1808, on the uselessness of a *levée en masse*. One of these notes was as follows:— "As soon as a single clergyman is shot," (*i.e.*, by the French) "the thing would come to an end." These words were published in the Prussian official paper as an indication that Arndt, worse than Sand, advocated murdering clergymen! Welcker, Urkunden, p. 89.

† Metternich, iii. 217, 258.

general assemblies, had been rendered more difficult by recent acts of the Governments of Bavaria and Baden. A singular change had taken place in the relation between Prussia and the Minor States which had formerly constituted the Federation of the Rhine. *The South-Western States become constitutional as Prussia relapses.* When, at the Congress of Vienna, Prussian statesmen had endeavoured to limit the arbitrary rule of petty sovereigns by charging the Diet with the protection of constitutional right over all Germany, the Kings of Bavaria and Würtemberg had stoutly refused to part with sovereign power. To submit to a law of liberty, as it then seemed, was to lose their own separate existence, and to reduce themselves to dependence upon the Jacobins of Berlin. This apprehension governed the policy of the Minor Courts from 1813 to 1815. But since that time events had taken an unexpected turn. Prussia, which once threatened to excite popular movement over all Germany in its own interest, had now accepted Metternich's guidance, and made its representative in the Diet the mouthpiece of Austrian interest and policy. It was no longer from Berlin but from Vienna that the separate existence of the Minor States was threatened. The two great Courts were uniting against the independence of their weaker neighbours. The danger of any popular invasion of kingly rights in the name of German unity had passed away, and the safety of the lesser sovereigns seemed now to lie not in resisting the spirit of constitutional reform but in appealing to it. In proportion as Prussia abandoned itself to Metternich's direction, the Governments of the South-Western States familiarised themselves with the idea of a popular representation; and at the very time when the conservative programme was being drawn up for the Congress of Aix-la-Chapelle, the King of Bavaria published a Constitution. Baden followed after a short interval, and in each of these States, although the Legislature was divided into two Chambers, the representation established was not merely provincial, according to Metternich's plan, or wholly on the principle of separate Estates or Orders, as before the Revolution, but to some extent on the type of England and France, where the Lower Chamber, in theory, represented the public at large. This was enough to make Metternich condemn the new Constitutions as radically bad and revolutionary.* He was, however, conscious of the difficulty of making a direct attack upon them. This task he reserved for a later time. His policy at present was to obtain a declaration from the Diet which should prevent any other Government within the League from following in the same path; while, by means of Press-laws, supervision of the Universities, and a central commission of inquiry, he expected to make the position or rebellious professors and agitators so desperate that the forces of disorder, themselves not deeply rooted in German nature, would presently disappear.

Bavarian Constitution, May 26, 1818.

The Conference of Ministers at Carlsbad, which in the memory of the German people is justly associated

---

* Metternich, iii. 268.

with the suppression of their liberty for an entire generation, began and ended in the month of August, 1819. Though attended by the representatives of eight German Governments, it did little more than register the conclusions which Metternich had already formed.* The zeal with which the envoy of Prussia supported every repressive measure made it useless for the Ministers of the Minor Courts to offer an open opposition. Nothing more was required than that the Diet should formally sanction the propositions thus privately accepted by all the leading Ministers. On the 20th of September this sanction was given. The Diet, which had sat for three years without framing a single useful law, ratified all Metternich's oppressive enactments in as many hours. It was ordered that in every State within the Federation the Government should take measures for preventing the publication of any journal or pamphlet except after licence given, and each Government was declared responsible to the Federation at large for any objectionable writing published within its own territory. The sovereigns were required to appoint civil commissioners at the Universities, whose duty it should be to enforce public order, and to give a salutary direction to the teaching of the professors. They were also required to dismiss all professors who should overstep the bounds of their duty, and such dismissed persons were prohibited from being employed in any other State. It was enacted

Conference of Carlsbad, Aug., 1819.

------
* The minutes of the Conference are in Welcker, Urkunden, p. 104, *seq.* See also Weech, Correspondenzen.

T T

that within fifteen days of the passing of the decree an extraordinary Commission should assemble at Mainz to investigate the origin and extent of the secret revolutionary societies which threatened the safety of the Federation. The Commission was empowered to examine and, if necessary, to arrest any subject of any German State. All law-courts and other authorities were required to furnish it with information and with documents, and to undertake all inquiries which the Commission might order. The Commission, however, was not a law-court itself: its duty was to report to the Diet, which would then create such judicial machinery as might be necessary.*

These measures were of an exceptional, and purported to be of a temporary, character. There were, however, other articles which Metternich intended to raise to the rank of organic laws, and to incorporate with the Act of 1815, which formed the basis of the German Federation. The conferences of Ministers were accordingly resumed after a short interval, but at Vienna instead of at Carlsbad. They lasted for several months, a stronger opposition being now made by the Minor States than before. A second body of federal law was at length drawn up, and accepted by the Diet on the 8th of June, 1820.† The most important of its provisions was that which related to the Constitutions admissible

<small>Supplementary Act of Vienna, June, 1820.</small>

---

* Protokolle der Bundesversammlung, 8, 266. Nauwerck, Thätigkeit, &c., 2, 287.

† Ægidi, Der Schluss-Acte, ii. 361, 446.

within the German League. It was declared that in every State, with the exception of the four free cities, supreme power resided in the Sovereign and in him alone, and that no Constitution might do more than bind the Sovereign to co-operate with the Estates in certain definite acts of government.* In cases where a Government either appealed for help against rebellious subjects, or was notoriously unable to exert authority, the Diet charged itself with the duty of maintaining public order.

From this time whatever liberty existed in Germany was to be found in the Minor States, in Bavaria and Baden, and in Würtemberg, which received a Constitution a few days before the enrolment of the decrees of Carlsbad. In Prussia the reaction carried everything before it. Humboldt, the best and most liberal of the Ministers, resigned, protesting in vain against the ignominious part which the King had determined to play. He was followed by those of his colleagues whose principles were dearer to them than their places. Hardenberg remained in

The reaction in Prussia.

---

* Article 67. The intention being that no assembly in any German State might claim sovereign power as representing the people. If, for instance, the Bavarian Lower House had asserted that it represented the sovereignty of the people, and that the King was simply the first magistrate in the State, this would have been an offence against Federal law, and have entitled the Diet—*i.e.*, Metternich—to armed interference. The German State-papers of this time teem with the constitutional distinction between a Representative Assembly (*i.e.*, assembly representing popular sovereignty) and an Assembly of Estates (*i.e.*, of particular orders with limited, definite rights, such as the granting of a tax). In technical language, the question at issue was the true interpretation of the phrase *Landständische Verfassungen*, used in the 13th article of the original Act of Federation.

office, a dying man, isolated, neglected, thwarted; clinging to some last hope of redeeming his promises to the Prussian people, yet jealous of all who could have given him true aid; dishonouring by tenacity of place a career associated with so much of his country's glory, and ennobled in earlier days by so much fortitude in time of evil. There gathered around the King a body of men who could see in the great patriotic efforts and reforms of the last decade nothing but an encroachment of demagogues on the rights of power. They were willing that Prussia should receive its orders from Metternich and serve a foreign Court in the work of repression, rather than that it should take its place at the head of all Germany on the condition of becoming a free and constitutional State.* The stigma of disloyalty was attached to all who had kindled popular enthusiasm in 1808 and 1812. To have served the nation was to have sinned against the Government. Stein was protected by his great name from attack, but not from calumny. His friend Arndt, whose songs and addresses had so powerfully moved the heart of Germany during the War of Liberation, was subjected to repeated legal process, and, although unconvicted of any offence, was suspended from the exercise of his professorship for twenty years. Other persons, whose fault at the

---

* See, in Welcker, Urkunden, p. 356, the celebrated paper called "Memorandum of a Prussian Statesman, 1822," which at the same time recommends a systematic underhand rivalry with Austria, in preparation for an ultimate breach. Few State-papers exhibit more candid and cynical cunning.

most was to have worked for German unity, were brought before special tribunals, and after long trial either refused a public acquittal or sentenced to actual imprisonment. Free teaching, free discussion, ceased. The barrier of authority closed every avenue of political thought. Everywhere the agent of the State prescribed an orthodox opinion, and took note of those who raised a dissentient voice.

The pretext made at Carlsbad for this crusade against liberty, which was more energetically carried out in Prussia than elsewhere, was the existence of a conspiracy or agitation for the overthrow of Governments and of the present constitution of the German League. It was stated that proofs existed of the intention to establish by force a Republic one and indivisible, like that of France in 1793. *The Commission at Mainz.* But the very Commission which was instituted by the Carlsbad Ministers to investigate the origin and nature of this conspiracy disproved its existence. The Commission assembled at Mainz, examined several hundred persons and many thousand documents, and after two years' labour delivered a report to the Diet. The report went back to the time of Fichte's lectures and the formation of the Tugendbund in 1808, traced the progress of all the students' associations and other patriotic societies from that time to 1820; and, while exhibiting in the worst possible light the aims and conduct of the advocates of German unity, acknowledged that scarcely a single proof had been discovered of treasonable practice, and that the loyalty of the mass of the people was itself a sufficient guarantee against the impulses of the evil-minded.* Such was the impression of triviality and imposture produced at the Diet by this report, that the representatives of several States proposed that the Commission should forthwith be dissolved as useless and unnecessary. This, however, could not be tolerated by Metternich and his new disciples. The Commission was allowed to continue in existence, and with it the régime of silence and repression. The measures which had been accepted at Carlsbad as temporary and provisional became more and more a part of the habitual system of government. Prosecutions succeeded one another; letters were opened; spies attended the lectures of professors and the meetings of students; the newspapers were everywhere prohibited from discussing German affairs. In a country where there were so many printers and so many readers journalism could not altogether expire. It was still permissible to give the news and to offer an opinion about foreign lands: and for years to come the Germans, like beggars regaling themselves with the scents from rich men's kitchens,† followed every stage of the political struggles that were agitating France, England, and Spain, while they were not

---

* Ilse, Politische Verfolgungen, p. 31.

† The comparison is the Germans' own, not mine. "'How savoury a thing roast veal is!' said one Hamburg beggar to another. 'Where did you eat it?' said his friend, admiringly. 'I never ate it at all, but I smelt it as I passed a great man's house while the dog was being fed.'" (Ilse, p. 57.)

allowed to express a desire or to formulate a grievance of their own.

In the year 1822 Hardenberg died. All hope of a fulfilment of the promises made in Prussia in 1815 had already become extinct. Not many months after the Minister's death, King Frederick William established the Provincial Estates which had been recommended to him by Metternich, and announced that the creation of a central representative system would be postponed until such time as the King should think fit to introduce it. This meant that the project was finally abandoned; and Prussia in consequence remained without a Parliament until the Revolution of 1848 was at the door. The Provincial Estates, with which the King affected to temper absolute rule, met only once in three years. Their function was to express an opinion upon local matters when consulted by the Government: their enemies said that they were aristocratic and did harm, their partizans could not pretend that they did much good. In the bitterness of spirit with which, at a later time, the friends of liberty denounced the betrayal of the cause of freedom by the Prussian Court, a darker colour has perhaps been introduced into the history of this period than really belongs to it. The wrongs sustained by the Prussian nation have been compared to those inflicted by the despotism of Spain. But, however contemptible the timidity of King Frederick William, however odious the ingratitude shown to the truest friends of King

Prussian Provincial Estates, June, 1823.

Redeeming features of Prussian absolutism.

and people, the Government of 1819 is not correctly represented in such a parallel. To identify the thousand varieties of wrong under the common name of oppression, is to mistake words for things, and to miss the characteristic features which distinguish nations from one another. The greatest evils which a Government can inflict upon its subjects are probably religious persecution, wasteful taxation, and the denial of justice in the daily affairs of life. None of these were present in Prussia during the darkest days of reaction. The hand of oppression fell heavily on some of the best and some of the most enlightened men; it violated interests so precious as those of free criticism and free discussion of public affairs; but the great mass of the action of Government was never on the side of evil. The ordinary course of justice was still pure, the administration conscientious and thrifty. The system of popular education, which for the first time placed Prussia in advance of Saxony and other German States, dates from these years of warfare against liberty. A reactionary despotism built the schools and framed the laws whose reproduction in free England half a century later is justly regarded as the chief of all the liberal measures of our day. So strong, so lasting, was that vital tradition which made monarchy in Prussia an instrument for the execution of great public ends.

But the old harmony between rulers and subjects in Germany perished in the system of coercion which Metternich established in 1819. Patient as the Germans were, loyal as they had proved themselves to Frederick

William and to worse princes through good and evil, the galling disappointment of noble hopes, the silencing of the Press, the dissolution of societies,—calumnies, expulsions, prosecutions,—embittered many an honest mind against authority. *A new Liberalism grows up in Germany after 1820.* The Commission of Mainz did not find conspirators, but it made them. As years went by, and all the means of legitimately working for the improvement of German public life were one after another extinguished, men of ardent character thought of more violent methods. Secret societies, such as Metternich had imagined, came into actual being.* And among those who neither sank into apathy and despair nor enrolled themselves against existing power, a new body of ideas supplanted the old loyal belief in the regeneration of Germany by its princes. The Parliamentary struggles of France, the revolutionary movements in Italy and in Spain which began at this epoch, drew the imagination away from that pictured restoration of a free Teutonic past which had proved so barren of result, and set in its place the idea of a modern universal or European Liberalism. The hatred against France, especially among the younger men, disappeared. A distinction was made between the tyrant Napoleon and the people who were now giving to the rest of the Continent the example of a free and

Interest in France.

---

* The Commission at Mainz went on working till 1827. It seems to have begun to discover real revolutionary societies about 1824. There is a long list of persons remanded for trial in their several States, in Ilse, p. 595, with the verdicts and the sentences passed upon them, which vary from a few months' to nineteen years' imprisonment.

animated public life, and illuminating the age with a political literature so systematic and so ingenious that it seemed almost like a political philosophy. The debates in the French Assembly, the writings of French publicists, became the school of the Germans. Paris regained in foreign eyes something of the interest that it had possessed in 1789. Each victory or defeat of the French popular cause awoke the joy or the sorrow of German Liberals, to whom all was blank at home: and when at length the throne of the Bourbons fell, the signal for deliverance seemed to have sounded in many a city beyond the Rhine.

We have seen that in Central Europe the balance between liberty and reaction, wavering in 1815, definitely fell to the side of reaction at the Congress of Aix-la-Chapelle. It remains to trace the course of events which in France itself suspended the peaceful progress of the nation, and threw power for some years into the hands of a faction which belonged to the past. The measures carried by Decazes in 1817, which gave so much satisfaction to the French, were by no means viewed with the same approval either at London or at Vienna. The two principal of these were the Electoral Law, and a plan of military reorganisation which brought back great numbers of Napoleon's old officers and soldiers to the army. Richelieu, though responsible as the head of the Ministry, felt very grave fears as to the results of this legislation. He had already become anxious and distressed when the Congress of Aix-la-Chapelle met; and

France after 1818.

the events which took place in France during his absence, as well as the communications which passed between himself and the foreign Ministers, convinced him that a change of internal policy was necessary. The busy mind of Metternich had already been scheming against French Liberalism. Alarmed at the energy shown by Decazes, the Austrian statesman had formed the design of reconciling Artois and the Ultra-Royalists to the King's Government; and he now urged Richelieu, if his old opponents could be brought to reason, to place himself at the head of a coalition of all the conservative elements in the State.* While the Congress of Aix-la-Chapelle was sitting, the partial elections for the year 1818, the second under the new Electoral Law, took place. Among the deputies returned there were some who passed for determined enemies of the Bourbon restoration, especially Lafayette, whose name was so closely associated with the humiliations of the Court in 1789. Richelieu received the news with dismay, and on his return to Paris took steps which ended in the dismissal of Decazes, and the offer of a seat in the Cabinet to Villèle, the Ultra-Royalist leader. But the attempted combination failed. Richelieu accordingly withdrew from office; and a new Ministry was formed, of which Decazes, who had proved himself more powerful than his assailants, was the real though not the nominal chief.

Richelieu resigns, Dec., 1818. Decazes keeps power.

* Metternich, iii. 168; and see Wellington, S. D., xii. 878.

The victory of the young and popular statesman was seen with extreme displeasure by all the foreign Courts, nor was his success an enduring one. For a while the current of Liberal opinion in France and the favour of King Louis XVIII. enabled Decazes to hold his own against the combinations of his opponents and the ill-will of all the most powerful men in Europe. An attack made on the Electoral Law by the Upper House was defeated by the creation of sixty new Peers, among whom there were several who had been expelled in 1815. But the forces of Liberalism soon passed beyond the Minister's own control, and his steady dependence upon Louis XVIII. now raised against him as resolute an opposition among the enemies of the House of Bourbon as among the Ultra-Royalists. In the elections of 1819 the candidates of the Ministry were beaten by men of more pronounced opinions. Among the new members there was one whose victory caused great astonishment and alarm. The ex-bishop Grégoire, one of the authors of the destruction of the old French Church in 1790, and mover of the resolution which established the Republic in 1792, was brought forward from his retirement and elected Deputy by the town of Grenoble. To understand the panic caused by this election we must recall, not the events of the Revolution, but the legends of them which were current in 1819. The history of Grégoire by no means justifies the outcry which was raised against him; his real actions, however, formed the smallest

<small>Election of Grégoire, Sept., 1819.</small>

part of the things that were alleged or believed by his enemies. It was said he had applauded the execution of King Louis XVI., when he had in fact protested against it :* his courageous adherence to the character of a Christian priest throughout the worst days of the Convention, his labours in organising the Constitutional Church when the choice lay between that and national atheism, were nothing, or worse than nothing, in the eyes of men who felt themselves to be the despoiled heirs of that rich and aristocratic landed society, called the Feudal Church, which Grégoire had been so active in breaking up. Unluckily for himself, Grégoire, though humane in action, had not abstained from the rhodomontades against kings in general which were the fashion in 1793. Louis XVIII., forgetting that he had himself lately made the regicide Fouché a Minister, interpreted Grégoire's election by the people of Grenoble, to which the Ultra-Royalists had cunningly contributed, as a threat against the Bourbon family. He showed the displeasure usual with him when any slight was offered to his personal dignity, and drew nearer to his brother Artois and the Ultra-Royalists, whom he had hitherto shunned as his

* Grégoire, Mémoires, i.411. Had the Constitutional Church of France succeeded, Grégoire would have left a great name in religious history. Napoleon, by one of the most fatal acts of despotism, extinguished a society likely, from its democratic basis and its association with a great movement of reform, to become the most liberal and enlightened of all Churches, and left France to be long divided between Ultramontane dogma and a coarse kind of secularism. The life of Grégoire ought to be written in English. From the enormous number of improvements for which he laboured, his biography would give a characteristic picture of the finer side of the generation of 1789.

favourite Minister's worst enemies. Decazes, true to his character as the King's friend, now confessed that he had gone too far in the legislation of 1817, and that the Electoral Law, under which such a monster as Grégoire could gain a seat, required to be altered. A project of law was sketched, designed to restore the preponderance in the constituencies to the landed aristocracy. Grégoire's election was itself invalidated; and the Ministers who refused to follow Decazes in his new policy of compromise were dismissed from their posts.

A few months more passed, and an event occurred which might have driven a stronger Government than that of Louis XVIII. into excesses of reaction. The heirs to the Crown next in succession to the Count of Artois were his two sons, the Dukes of Angoulême and Berry.

<small>Murder of the Duke of Berry, Feb. 13, 1820.</small> Angoulême was childless: the Duke of Berry was the sole hope of the elder Bourbon line, which, if he should die without a son, would, as a reigning house, become extinct, the Crown of France not descending to a female.* The circumstance which made Berry's life so dear to Royalists made his destruction the all-absorbing purpose of an obscure fanatic, who abhorred the Bourbon family as the lasting symbol of the foreigner's victory over France. Louvel, a working man, had followed Napoleon to exile in Elba. After returning to his country he had dogged the footsteps of the Bourbon princes for years together, waiting for the chance of murder. On the

* The late Count of Chambord, or Henry V., son of the Duke of Berry, was born some months after his father's death.

night of the 13th of February, 1820, he seized the Duke of Berry as he was leaving the Opera House, and plunged a knife into his breast. The Duke lingered for some hours, and expired early the next morning in the presence of King Louis XVIII., the Princes, and all the Ministers. Terrible as the act was, it was the act of a single resolute mind: no human being had known of Louvel's intention. But it was impossible that political passion should await the quiet investigation of a law-court. No murder ever produced a stronger outburst of indignation among the governing classes, or was more skilfully turned to the advantage of party. The Liberals felt that their cause was lost. While fanatical Ultra-Royalists, abandoning themselves to a credulity worthy of the Reign of Terror, accused Decazes himself of com- *Reaction sets in.* plicity with the assassin, their leaders fixed upon the policy which was to be imposed on the King. It was in vain that Decazes brought forward his reactionary Electoral Law, and proposed to invest the officers of State with arbitrary powers of arrest and to re-establish the censorship of the Press. The Count of Artois insisted upon the dismissal of the Minister, as the only consolation which could be given to him for the murder of his son. The King yielded; and, as an Ultra-Royalist administration was not yet possible, Richelieu unwillingly returned to *Fall of Decazes. Richelieu Minister, Feb., 1820.* office, assured by Artois that his friends had no other desire than to support his own firm and temperate rule.

Returning to power under such circumstances, Richelieu became, in spite of himself, the Minister of reaction. The Press was fettered, the legal safeguards of personal liberty were suspended, the electoral system was transformed by a measure which gave a double vote to men of large property. So violent were the passions which this retrograde march of Government excited, that for a moment Paris seemed to be on the verge of revolution. Tumultuous scenes occurred in the streets; but the troops, on whom everything depended, obeyed the orders given to them, and the danger passed away. The first elections under the new system reduced the Liberal party to impotence, and brought back to the Chamber a number of men who had sat in the reactionary Parliament of 1816. Villèle and other Ultra-Royalists were invited to join Richelieu's Cabinet. For a while it seemed as if the passions of Church and aristocracy might submit to the curb of a practical statesmanship, friendly, if not devoted, to their own interests. But restraint was soon cast aside. The Count of Artois saw the road to power open, and broke his promise of supporting the Minister who had taken office at his request. Censured and thwarted in the Chamber of Deputies, Richelieu confessed that he had undertaken a hopeless task, and bade farewell to public life. King Louis, now nearing the grave, could struggle no longer against the brother who was waiting to ascend his throne. The next Ministry was nominated not by the King but by Artois. Around

Progress of the reaction in France.

Villèle, the real head of the Cabinet, there was placed a body of men who represented not the new France, or even that small portion of it which was called to exercise the active rights of citizenship, but the social principles of a past age, and that Catholic or Ultramontane revival which was now freshening the surface but not stirring the depths of the great mass of French religious indifference. A religious society known as the Congregation, which had struck its first roots under the storm of Republican persecution, and grown up during the Empire, a solitary yet unobserved rallying-place for Catholic opponents of Napoleon's despotism, now expanded into a great organism of government. The highest in blood and in office sought membership in it: its patronage raised ambitious men to the stations they desired, its hostility made itself felt against the small as well as against the great. The spirit which now gained the ascendancy in French government was clerical even more than it was aristocratic. It was monarchical too, but rather from dislike to the secularist tone of Liberalism and from trust in the orthodoxy of the Count of Artois than from any fixed belief in absolutist principles. There might be good reason to oppose King Louis XVIII.; but what priest, what noble, could doubt the divine right of a prince who was ready to compensate the impoverished emigrants out of the public funds, and to commit the whole system of public education to the hands of the clergy?

In the middle class of France, which from this time

began to feel itself in opposition to the Bourbon Government, there had been no moral change corresponding to that which made so great a difference between the governing authority of 1819 and that of 1822. Public opinion, though strongly affected, was not converted into something permanently unlike itself by the murder of the Duke of Berry. The courtiers, the devotees, the great ladies, who had laid a bold hand upon power, had not the nation on their side, although for a while the nation bore their sway submissively. But the fate of the Bourbon monarchy was in fact decided when Artois and his confidants became its representatives. France might have forgotten that the Bourbons owed their throne to foreign victories; it could not be governed in perpetuity by what was called the *Parti Prêtre*. Twenty years taken from the burden of age borne by Louis XVIII., twenty years of power given to Decazes, might have prolonged the rule of the restored family perhaps for some generations. If military pride found small satisfaction in the contrast between the Napoleonic age and that which immediately succeeded it, there were enough parents who valued the blood of their children, there were enough speakers and writers who valued the liberty of discussion, enough capitalists who valued quiet times, for the new order to be recognised as no unhopeful one. France has indeed seldom had a better government than it possessed between 1816 and 1820, nor could an equal period be readily named during which the French nation, as a whole, enjoyed greater happiness.

Political reaction had reached its full tide in Europe generally about five years after the end of the great war. The phenomena were by no means the same in all countries, nor were the accidents of personal influence without a large share in the determination of events: yet, underlying all differences, we may trace the operation of certain great causes which were not limited by the boundaries of individual States. The classes in which any fixed belief in constitutional government existed were nowhere very large; outside the circle of state officials there was scarcely any one who had had experience in the conduct of public affairs. In some countries, as in Russia and Prussia, the conception of progress towards self-government had belonged in the first instance to the holders of power: it had exercised the imagination of a Czar, or appealed to the understanding of a Prussian Minister, eager, in the extremity of ruin, to develop every element of worth and manliness existing within his nation. The cooling of a warm fancy, the disappearance of external dangers, the very agitation which arose when the idea of liberty passed from the rulers to their subjects, sufficed to check the course of reform. And by the side of the Kings and Ministers who for a moment had attached themselves to constitutional theories there stood the old privileged orders, or what remained of them, the true party of reaction, eager to fan the first misgivings and alarms of Sovereigns, and to arrest a development more prejudicial to their own power and importance than to the dignity and security

General causes of the victory of reaction in Europe.

of the Crown. Further, there existed throughout Europe the fatal and ineradicable tradition of the convulsions of the first Revolution, and of the horrors of 1793. No votary of absolutism, no halting and disquieted friend of freedom, could ever be at a loss for images of woe in presaging the results of popular sovereignty; and the action of one or two infatuated assassins owed its wide influence on Europe chiefly to the ancient name and memory of Jacobinism.

There was also in the very fact that Europe had been restored to peace by the united efforts of all the governments something adverse to the success of a constitutional or a Liberal party in any State. Constitutional systems had indeed been much praised at the Congress of Vienna; but the group of men who actually controlled Europe in 1815, and who during the five succeeding years continued in correspondence and in close personal intercourse with one another, had, with one exception, passed their lives in the atmosphere of absolute government, and learnt to regard the conduct of all great affairs as the business of a small number of very eminent individuals. Castlereagh, the one Minister of a constitutional State, belonged to a party which, to a degree almost unequalled in Europe, identified political duty with the principle of hostility to change. It is indeed in the correspondence of the English Minister himself, and in relation to subjects of purely domestic government in England, that the community of thought which now existed between all the leading statesmen of Europe finds its most singular exhibition. Both Metternich and Hardenberg took as much interest in the suppression of Lancashire Radicalism, and in the measures of coercion which the British Government thought it necessary to pass in the year 1819, as in the chastisement of rebellious pamphleteers upon the Rhine, and in the dissolution of the students' clubs at Jena. It was indeed no very great matter for the English people, who were now close upon an era of reform, that Castlereagh received the congratulations of Vienna and Berlin for suspending the Habeas Corpus Act and the right of public meeting,* or that Metternich believed that no one but himself knew the real import of the shouts with which the London mob greeted Sir Francis Burdett.† Neither the impending reform of the English Criminal Law nor the emancipation of Irish Catholics resulted from the enlightenment of foreign Courts, or could be hindered by their indifference. But on the Continent of Europe the progress towards constitutional freedom was indeed likely to be a slow and a chequered one when the Ministers of absolutism formed so close and intimate a band, when the nations contained within them such small bodies of men in any degree versed in public affairs, and when the institutions on which it was proposed to base the liberty of the future were so destitute of that strength which springs from connection with the past.

---

* Castlereagh, xii. 162, 259. "The monster Radicalism still lives," Castlereagh sorrowfully admits to Metternich.
† Metternich, iii. 369. "A man must be like me, born and brought up amid the storm of politics, to know what is the precise meaning of a shout of triumph like those which now burst from Burdett and Co. He may have read of it, but I have seen it with my eyes. I was living at the time of the Federation of 1789. I was fifteen, and already a man."

CHAPTER III.

Movements in the Mediterranean States beginning in 1820—Spain from 1814 to 1820—The South American Colonies—The Army at Cadiz: Action of Quiroga and Riego—Movement at Corunna—Ferdinand accepts the Constitution of 1812—Naples from 1815 to 1820—The Court-party, the Muratists, the Carbonari—The Spanish Constitution proclaimed at Naples—Constitutional movement in Portugal—Alexander's proposal with regard to Spain —The Conference and Declaration of Troppau—Protest of England—Conference of Laibach—The Austrians invade Naples and restore absolute Monarchy—Insurrection in Piedmont, which fails—Spain from 1820 to 1822—Death of Castlereagh—The Congress of Verona—Policy of England —The French invade Spain—Restoration of absolute Monarchy, and violence of the reaction—England prohibits the conquest of the Spanish Colonies by France, and subsequently recognises their independence— Affairs in Portugal—Canning sends troops to Lisbon—The Policy of Canning—Estimate of his place in the history of Europe.

WHEN the guardians of Europe, at the end of the first three years of peace, scanned from their council-chamber at Aix-la-Chapelle that goodly heritage which, under Providence, their own parental care was henceforth to guard against the assaults of malice and revolution, they had fixed their gaze chiefly on France, Germany, and the Netherlands, as the regions most threatened by the spirit of change. The forecast was not an accurate one. In each of these countries Government proved during the succeeding years to be much more than a match for its real or imaginary foes: it was in the Mediterranean States, which had excited comparatively little anxiety, that the first successful attack was made upon established power. Three movements arose successively in the three

The Mediterranean movements, beginning in 1820.

southern peninsulas, at the time when Metternich was enjoying the silence which he had imposed upon Germany, and the Ultra-Royalists of France were making good the advantage which the crime of an individual and the imprudence of a party had thrown into their hands. In Spain and in Italy a body of soldiers rose on behalf of constitutional government: in Greece a nation rose against the rule of the foreigner. In all three countries the issue of these movements was, after a longer or shorter interval, determined by the Northern Powers. All three movements were at first treated as identical in their character, and all alike condemned as the work of Jacobinism. But the course of events, and a change of persons in the government of one great State, brought about a truer view of the nature of the struggle in Greece. The ultimate action of Europe in the affairs of that country was different from its action in the affairs of Italy and Spain. It is now only remembered as an instance of political recklessness or stupidity that a conflict of race against race and of religion against religion should for a while have been confused by some of the leading Ministers of Europe with the attempt of a party to make the form of domestic government more liberal. The Hellenic rising had indeed no feature in common with the revolutions of Naples and Cadiz; and, although in order of time the opening of the Greek movement long preceded the close of the Spanish movement, the historian, who has neither the politician's motive for making a confusion, nor the protection of his excuse of ignorance, must in this case neglect the accidents of chronology, and treat the two as altogether apart.

King Ferdinand of Spain, after overthrowing the Constitution which he found in existence on his return to his country, had conducted himself as if his object had been to show to what lengths a legitimate monarch might abuse the fidelity of his subjects and defy the public opinion of Europe. The leaders of the Cortes, whom he had arrested in 1814, after being declared innocent by one tribunal after another, were sentenced to long terms of imprisonment by an arbitrary decree of the King, without even the pretence of judicial forms. Men who had been conspicuous in the struggle of the nation against Napoleon were neglected or disgraced; many of the highest posts were filled by politicians who had played a double part, or had even served under the invader. Priests and courtiers intrigued for influence over the King; even when a capable Minister was placed in power through the pressure of the ambassadors, and the King's name was set to edicts of administrative reform, these edicts were made a dead letter by the powerful band who lived upon the corruption of the public service. Nothing was sacred except the interest of the clergy; this, however, was enough to keep the rural population on the King's side. The peasant, who knew that his house would not now be burnt by the French, and who heard that true religion had at length triumphed over its enemies, understood, and cared to understand, nothing more. Rumours of kingly misgovernment and oppression scarcely reached

Spain between 1814 and 1820.

his ears. Ferdinand was still the child of Spain and of the Church; his return had been the return of peace; his rule was the victory of the Catholic faith.

But the acquiescence of the mass of the people was not shared by the officers of the army and the educated classes in the towns. The overthrow of the Constitution was from the first condemned by soldiers who had won distinction under the government of the Cortes; and a series of acts of military rebellion, though isolated and on the smallest scale, showed that the course on which Ferdinand had entered was not altogether free from danger. The attempts of General Mina in 1814, and of Porlier and Lacy in succeeding years, to raise the soldiery on behalf of the Constitution, failed, through the indifference of the soldiery themselves, and the power which the priesthood exercised in garrison-towns. Discontent made its way in the army by slow degrees; and the ultimate declaration of a military party against the existing Government was due at least as much to Ferdinand's absurd system of favouritism, and to the wretched condition into which the army had been thrown, as to an attachment to the memory or the principles of constitutional rule. Misgovernment made the treasury bankrupt; soldiers and sailors received no pay for years together; and the hatred with which the Spanish people had now come to regard military service is curiously shown by an order of the Government that all the beggars in Madrid and other great towns should be seized on a certain night (July 23, 1816), and

The nation satisfied: the officers discontented.

enrolled in the army.* But the very beggars were more than a match for Ferdinand's administration. They heard of the fate in store for them, and mysteriously disappeared, so frustrating a measure by which it had been calculated that Spain would gain sixty thousand warriors.

The military revolution which at length broke out in the year 1820 was closely connected with Struggle of Spain with its Colonies, 1810—1820. the struggle for independence now being made by the American colonies of Spain; and in its turn it affected the course of this struggle and its final result. The colonies had refused to accept the rule either of Joseph Bonaparte or of the Cortes of Cadiz when their legitimate sovereign was dispossessed by Napoleon. While acting for the most part in Ferdinand's name, they had engaged in a struggle with the National Government of Spain. They had tasted independence; and although on the restoration of Ferdinand they would probably have recognised the rights of the Spanish Crown if certain concessions had been made, they were not disposed to return to the condition of inferiority in which they had been held during the last century, or to submit to rulers who proved themselves as cruel and vindictive in moments of victory as they were incapable of understanding the needs of the time. The struggle accordingly continued. Regiment after regiment was sent from Spain, to perish of fever, of forced marches, or on the field. The Government of King Ferdinand, despairing of its own resources, looked

* Baumgarten, Geschichte Spaniens, ii. 175.

around for help among the European Powers. England would have lent its mediation, and possibly even armed assistance, if the Court of Madrid would have granted a reasonable amount of freedom to the colonies, and have opened their ports to British commerce. This, however, was not in accordance with the views of Ferdinand's advisers. Strange as it may appear, the Spanish Government demanded that the alliance of Sovereigns, which had been framed for the purpose of resisting the principle of rebellion and disorder in Europe, should intervene against its revolted subjects on the other side of the Atlantic, and it implied that England, if acting at all, should act as the instrument of the Alliance.* Encouragement was given to the design by the Courts of Paris and St. Petersburg. Whether a continent claimed its independence, or a German schoolboy wore a forbidden ribbon in his cap, the chiefs of the Holy Alliance now assumed the frown of offended Providence, and prepared to interpose their own superior power and wisdom to save a misguided world from the consequences of its own folly. Alexander had indeed for a time hoped that the means of subduing the colonies might be supplied by himself; and in his zeal to supplant England in the good graces of Ferdinand he sold the King a fleet of war on very moderate terms. To the scandal of Europe the ships, when they reached Cadiz, turned out to be thoroughly rotten and unseaworthy. As it was certain

* See the note of Fernan Nuñez, in Wellington, S. D., xii. 582. "Les efforts unanimes de ces mêmes Puissances ont détruit le systême dévastateur, d'où naquit la rébellion Américaine; mais il leur restait encore à le détruire dans l'Amérique Espagnole."

that the Czar's fleet and the Spanish soldiers, however holy their mission, would all go to the bottom together as soon as they encountered the waves of the Atlantic, the expedition was postponed, and the affairs of America were brought before the Conference of Aix-la-Chapelle. The Envoys of Russia and France submitted a paper, in which, anticipating the storm-warnings of more recent times, they described the dangers to which monarchical Europe would be exposed from the growth of a federation of republics in America; and they suggested that Wellington, as "the man of Europe," should go to Madrid, to preside over a negotiation between the Court of Spain and all the ambassadors with reference to the terms to be offered to the Transatlantic States.* England, however, in spite of Lord Castlereagh's dread of revolutionary contagion, adhered to the principles which it had already laid down; and as the counsellors of King Ferdinand declined to change their policy, Spain was left to subdue its colonies by itself.

It was in the army assembled at Cadiz for embarkation in the summer of 1819 that the conspiracy against Ferdinand's Government found its leaders. Secret societies had now spread themselves over the principal Spanish towns, and looked to the soldiery on the coast for the signal of revolt. Abisbal, commander at Cadiz, intending to make himself safe against all contingencies, encouraged for a while the plots of the discontented officers: then, foreseeing the failure of the movement, he arrested the

<small>Conspiracy in the Army of Cadiz.</small>

* Wellington, S. D. xii. 807.

principal men by a stratagem, and went off to Madrid, to reveal the conspiracy to the Court and to take credit for saving the King's crown (July, 1819).* If the army could have been immediately despatched to America, the danger would possibly have passed away. This, however, was prevented by an outbreak of yellow fever, which made it necessary to send the troops into cantonments for several months. The conspirators gained time to renew their plans. The common soldiers, who had hitherto been faithful to the Government, heard in their own squalor and inaction the fearful stories of the few sick and wounded who returned from beyond the seas, and learnt to regard the order of embarkation as a sentence of death. Several battalions were won over to the cause of constitutional liberty by their commanders. The leaders imprisoned a few months before were again in communication with their followers. After the treachery of Abisbal, it was agreed to carry out the revolt without the assistance of generals or grandees. The leaders chosen were two colonels, Quiroga and Riego, of whom the former was in nominal confinement in a monastery near Medina Sidonia, twenty miles east of Cadiz, while Riego was stationed at Cabezas, a few marches distant on the great road to Seville. The first day of the year 1820 was fixed for the insurrection. It was determined that Riego should descend upon the head-quarters which were at Arcos, and arrest the generals before they could hear anything of the movement, while Quiroga, moving

* Jullian, Précis Historique, p. 78.

from the east, gathered up the battalions stationed on the road, and threw himself into Cadiz, there to await his colleague's approach.

The first step in the enterprise proved successful. Riego, proclaiming the Constitution of 1812, surprised the head-quarters, seized the generals, and rallied several companies to his standard. Quiroga, how-Action of Quiroga and Riego, Jan., 1820.ever, though he gained possession of San Fernando, at the eastern end of the peninsula of Leon, on which Cadiz is situated, failed to make his entrance into Cadiz. The commandant, hearing of the capture of the head-quarters, had closed the city gates, and arrested the principal inhabitants whom he suspected of being concerned in the plot. The troops within the town showed no sign of mutiny. Riego, when he arrived at the peninsula of Leon, found that only five thousand men in all had joined the good cause, while Cadiz, with a considerable garrison and fortifications of great strength, stood hostile before him. He accordingly set off with a small force to visit and win over the other regiments which were lying in the neighbouring towns and villages. The commanders, however, while not venturing to attack the mutineers, drew off their troops to a distance, and prevented them from entering into any communication with Riego. The adventurous soldier, leaving Quiroga in the peninsula of Leon, then marched into the interior of Andalusia (January 27), endeavouring to raise the inhabitants of the towns. But the small numbers of his band, and the knowledge that Cadiz and the greater part of the army still held by the Government, prevented the inhabitants from joining the insurrection, even where they received Riego with kindness and supplied the wants of his soldiers. During week after week the little column traversed the country, now cut off from retreat, exhausted by forced marches in drenching rain, and harassed by far stronger forces sent in pursuit. The last town that Riego entered was Cordova. The enemy was close behind him. No halt was possible. He led his band, now numbering only two hundred men, into the mountains, and there bade them disperse (March 11).

With Quiroga lying inactive in the peninsula of Leon and Riego hunted from village to village, it seemed as if the insurrection which they had begun could only end in the ruin of its leaders. But the movement had in fact effected its object. While the courtiers around King Ferdinand, unwarned by the news from Cadiz, continued their intrigues against one another, the rumour of rebellion spread over the country. If no great success had been achieved by the rebels, it was also certain that no great blow had been struck by the Government. *Corunna proclaims the Constitution, Feb. 20.* The example of bold action had been set; the shock given at one end of the peninsula was felt at the other; and a fortnight before Riego's band dispersed, the garrison and the citizens of Corunna together declared for the Constitution (February 20). From Corunna the revolutionary movement spread to Ferrol, and to all the other coast-towns of Galicia. The news reached

Madrid, terrifying the Government, and exciting the spirit of insurrection in the capital itself. The King summoned a council of the leading men around him. The wisest of them advised him to publish a moderate Constitution, and, by convoking a Parliament immediately, to stay the movement, which would otherwise result in the restoration of the Assembly and the Constitution of 1812. They also urged the King to abolish the Inquisition forthwith. Ferdinand's brother, Don Carlos, the head of the clerical party, succeeded in preventing both measures. Though the generals in all quarters of Spain wrote that they could not answer for the troops, there were still hopes of keeping down the country by force of arms. Abisbal, who was at Madrid, was ordered to move with reinforcements towards the army in the south.

Abisbal's defection, March 4.

He set out, protesting to the King that he knew the way to deal with rebels. When he reached Ocaña he proclaimed the Constitution himself (March 4).

It was now clear that the cause of absolute monarchy was lost. The ferment in Madrid increased. On the night of the 6th of March all the great bodies of State assembled for council in the King's palace, and early on the 7th Ferdinand published a proclamation, stating that he had determined to summon the Cortes immediately. This declaration satisfied no one, for the Cortes designed by the King might be the mere revival of a mediæval form, and the history of 1814 showed how little value was to be attached to Ferdinand's promises. Crowds gathered

Ferdinand accepts the Constitution of 1812, March 9.

in the great squares of Madrid, crying for the Constitution of 1812. The statement of the Minister of War that the Guard was on the point of joining the people now overcame even the resistance of Don Carlos and the confessors; and after a day wasted in dispute, Ferdinand announced to his people that he was ready to take the oath to the Constitution which they desired. The next day was given up to public rejoicings; the book of the Constitution was carried in procession through the city with the honours paid to the Holy Sacrament, and all political prisoners were set at liberty. The prison of the Inquisition was sacked, the instruments of torture broken in pieces. On the 9th the leaders of the agitation took steps to make the King fulfil his promise. A mob invaded the court and threshold of the palace. At their demand the municipal council of 1814 was restored; its members were sent, in company with six deputies chosen by the populace, to receive the pledges of the King. Ferdinand, all smiles and bows, while he looked forward to the day when force or intrigue should make him again absolute master of Spain, and enable him to take vengeance upon the men who were humiliating him, took the oath of fidelity to the Constitution of 1812.* New Ministers were immediately called to office, and a provisional Junta was placed by their side as the representative of the public until the new Cortes should be duly elected.

Tidings of the Spanish revolution passed rapidly over Europe, disquieting the courts and everywhere reviving

* Historia de la vida de Fernando VII., ii. 158.

the hopes of the friends of popular right. Before four months had passed, the constitutional movement begun in Cadiz was taken up in Southern Italy. The kingdom of Naples was one of those States which had profited the most by French conquest. During the nine years that its crown was held by Joseph Bonaparte and Murat, the laws and institutions which accompanied Napoleon's supremacy had rudely broken up the ancient fixity of confusions which passed for government, and had aroused no insignificant forces of new social life. The feudal tenure of land, and with it something of the feudal structure of society, had passed away: the monasteries had been dissolved; the French civil code, and a criminal code based upon that of France, had taken the place of a thousand conflicting customs and jurisdictions; taxation had been made, if not light, yet equitable and simple; justice was regular, and the same for baron and peasant; brigandage had been extinguished; and, for the first time in many centuries, the presence of a rational and uniform administration was felt over all the south of Italy. Nor on the restoration of King Ferdinand had any reaction been permitted to take place like that which in a moment destroyed the work of reform in Spain and in Westphalia. England and Austria insisted that there should be neither vengeance nor counter-revolution. Queen Marie Caroline, the principal agent in the cruelties of 1799, was dead; Ferdinand himself was old and indolent, and willing to leave affairs in the hands of Ministers more intelligent

Condition of Naples, 1815–1820.

than himself. Hence the laws and the administrative system of Murat remained on the whole unchanged.* As in France, a Bourbon Sovereign placed himself at the head of a political order fashioned by Napoleon and the Revolution. Where changes in the law were made, or acts of State revoked, it was for the most part in consequence of an understanding with the Holy See. Thus, while no attempt was made to eject the purchasers of Church-lands, the lands not actually sold were given back to the Church; a considerable number of monasteries were restored; education was allowed to fall again into the hands of the clergy; the Jesuits were recalled, and the Church regained its jurisdiction in marriage-causes, as well as the right of suppressing writings at variance with the Catholic faith.

But the legal and recognised changes which followed Ferdinand's return by no means expressed the whole change in the operation of government. If there were not two con- flicting systems at work, there were two conflicting bodies of partisans in the State. Like the emigrants who returned with Louis XVIII., a multitude of Neapolitans, high and low, who had either accom- panied the King in his exile to Sicily or fought for him on the mainland in 1799 and 1806, now expected their reward. In their interest the efficiency of the public service was sacrificed and the course of justice perverted. Men who had committed notorious crimes escaped punishment if they had been numbered among

margin: Hostility between the Court party and the Muratists

* Carrascosa, Mémoires, p. 25; Colletta, ii. 155.

the King's friends; the generals and officials who had served under Murat, though not removed from their posts, were treated with discourtesy and suspicion. It was in the army most of all that the antagonism of the two parties was felt. A medal was struck for service in Sicily, and every year spent there in inaction was reckoned as two in computing seniority. Thus the younger officers of Murat found their way blocked by a troop of idlers, and at the same time their prospects suffered from the honest attempts made by Ministers to reduce the military expenditure. Discontent existed in every rank. The generals were familiar with the idea of political change, for during the last years of Murat's reign they had themselves thought of compelling him to grant a Constitution : the younger officers and the sergeants were in great part members of the secret society of the Carbonari, which in the course of the last few years had grown with the weakness of the Government, and had now become the principal power in the Neapolitan kingdom.

The origin of this society, which derived its name and its symbolism from the trade of the charcoal-burner, as Freemasonry from that of the builder, is uncertain. Whether its first aim was resistance to Bourbon tyranny after 1790, or the expulsion of the French and Austrians from Italy, in the year 1814 it was actively working for constitutional government in opposition to Murat, and receiving encouragement from Sicily, where Ferdinand was then playing the part of constitutional King.

The Carbonari.

The maintenance of absolute government by the restored Bourbon Court severed the bond which for a time existed between legitimate monarchy and conspiracy; and the lodges of the Carbonari, now extending themselves over the country with great rapidity, became so many centres of agitation against despotic rule. By the year 1819 it was reckoned that one person out of every twenty-five in the kingdom of Naples had joined the society. Its members were drawn from all classes, most numerously perhaps from the middle class in the towns; but even priests had been initiated, and there was no branch of the public service that had not Carbonari in its ranks. The Government, apprehending danger from the extension of the sect, tried to counteract it by founding a rival society of Calderari, or Braziers, in which every miscreant who before 1815 had murdered and robbed in the name of King Ferdinand and the Catholic faith received a welcome. But though the number of such persons was not small, the growth of this fraternity remained far behind that of its model; and the chief result of the competition was that intrigue and mystery gained a greater charm than ever for the Italians, and that all confidence in Government perished, under the sense that there was a hidden power in the land which was only awaiting the due moment to put forth its strength in revolutionary action.

After the proclamation of the Spanish Constitution, an outbreak in the kingdom of Naples had become inevitable. The Carbonari of Salerno, where the sect had its head-quarters, had intended to rise at the beginning of June; their action, however, was postponed for some months, and it was anticipated by the daring movement of a few sergeants belonging to a cavalry regiment stationed at Nola, and of a lieutenant, named Morelli, whom they had persuaded to place himself at their head. Leading out a squadron of a hundred and fifty men in the direction of Avellino on the morning of July 2nd, Morelli proclaimed the Constitution. One of the soldiers alone left the band; force or persuasion kept others to the standard, though they disapproved of the enterprise. The inhabitants of the populous places that lie between Nola and Avellino welcomed the squadron, or at least offered it no opposition: the officer commanding at Avellino came himself to meet Morelli, and promised him assistance. The band encamped that night in a village; on the next day they entered Avellino, where the troops and townspeople, headed by the bishop and officers, declared in their favour. From Avellino the news of the movement spread quickly over the surrounding country. The Carbonari were everywhere prepared for revolt; and before the Government had taken a single step in its own defence, the Constitution had been joyfully and peacefully accepted, not only by the people but by the militia and the regular troops, throughout the greater part of the district that lies to the east of Naples.

Morelli's movement, July 2, 1820.

The King was on board ship in the bay, when, in the afternoon of July 2nd, intelligence came of Morelli's revolt at Nola. Nothing was done by the Ministry on that day, although Morelli and his band might have been captured in a few hours if any resolute officer, with a few trustworthy troops, had been sent against them. On the next morning, when the garrison of Avellino had already joined the mutineers, and taken up a strong position commanding the road from Naples, General Carrascosa was sent, not to reduce the insurgents—for no troops were given to him—but to pardon, to bribe, and to coax them into submission.* Carrascosa failed to effect any good; other generals, who, during the following days, attempted to attack the mutineers, found that their troops would not follow them, and that the feeling of opposition to the Government, though it nowhere broke into lawlessness, was universal in the army as well as the nation. If the people generally understood little of politics, they had learnt enough to dislike arbitrary taxation and the power of arbitrary arrest. Not a single hand or voice was anywhere raised in defence of absolutism. Escaping from Naples, where he was watched by the Government, General Pepe, who was at once the chief man among the Carbonari and military commandant of the province in which Avellino lies, went to place himself at the head of the revolution. Naples itself had hitherto remained quiet, but on the night of July 6th a deputation from the Carbonari

Affairs at Naples, July 2—7.

---
* Carrascosa, p. 44.

informed the King that they could no longer preserve tranquillity in the city unless a Constitution was granted. The King, without waiting for morning, published an edict declaring that a Constitution should be drawn up within eight days; immediately afterwards he appointed a new Ministry, and, feigning illness, committed the exercise of royal authority to his son, the Duke of Calabria.

Ferdinand's action was taken by the people as a stratagem. He had employed the device of a temporary abdication some years before in cajoling the Sicilians; and the delay of eight days seemed unnecessary to ardent souls who knew that a Spanish Constitution was in existence and did not know of its defects in practice. There was also on the side of the Carbonari the telling argument that Ferdinand, as a possible successor to his nephew, the King of Spain, actually had signed the Spanish Constitution in order to preserve his own contingent rights to that crown. What Ferdinand had accepted as Infante of Spain he might well accept as King of Naples. The cry was therefore for the immediate proclamation of the Spanish Constitution of 1812. The court yielded, and the Duke of Calabria, as viceroy, published an edict making this Constitution the law of the kingdom of the Two Sicilies. But the tumult continued, for deceit was still feared, until the edict appeared again, signed by the King himself. Then all was rejoicing. Pepe, at the head of a large body of troops, militia and Carbonari, made a triumphal entry

Ferdinand takes the Oath to the Spanish Constitution, July 13.

into the city, and, in company with Morelli and other leaders of the military rebellion, was hypocritically thanked by the Viceroy for his services to the nation. On the 13th of July the King, a halo but venerable-looking man of seventy, took the oath to the Constitution before the altar in the royal chapel. The form of words had been written out for him; but Ferdinand was fond of theatrical acts of religion, and did not content himself with reading certain solemn phrases. Raising his eyes to the crucifix above the altar, he uttered aloud a prayer that if the oath was not sincerely taken the vengeance of God might fall upon his head. Then, after blessing and embracing his sons, the venerable monarch wrote to the Emperor of Austria, protesting that all that he did was done under constraint, and that his obligations were null and void.*

A month more passed, and in a third kingdom absolute government fell before the combined action of soldiers and people. The Court of Lisbon had

* Gentz, D. I., ii. 108, 122. It was rather too much even for the Austrians. "La conduite de ce malheureux souverain n'a été, dès le commencement des troubles, qu'un tissu de faiblesse et de duplicité," &c. "Voilà l'allié que le ciel a mis entre nos mains, et dont nous avons à rétablir les intérêts!" Ferdinand was guilty of such monstrous perjuries and cruelties that the reader ought to be warned not to think of him as a saturnine and Machiavellian Italian. He was a son of the Bourbon Charles III. of Spain. His character was that of a jovial, rather stupid farmer, whom a freak of fortune had made a king from infancy. A sort of grotesque comic element runs through his life, and through every picture drawn by persons in actual intercourse with him. The following, from one of Bentinck's despatches of 1814 (when Ferdinand had just heard that Austria had promised to keep Murat in Naples), is very characteristic: "I found his Majesty very much afflicted and very much roused. He expressed his determination never to renounce the rights which God had given him. ... He said he might be poor, but he would die honest, and

migrated to Brazil in 1807, when the troops of Napoleon first appeared upon the Tagus, and Portugal had since then been governed by a Regency, acting in the name of the absent Sovereign. The events of the Peninsular War had reduced Portugal almost to the condition of a dependency of Great Britain. Marshal Beresford, the English commander-in-chief of its army, kept his post when the war was over, and with him there remained a great number of English officers who had led the Portuguese regiments in Wellington's campaigns. The presence of these English soldiers was unwelcome, and commercial rivalry embittered the natural feeling of impatience towards an ally who remained as master rather than guest. Up to the year 1807 the entire trade with Brazil had been confined by law to Portuguese merchants; when, however, the Court had established itself beyond the Atlantic, it had opened the ports of Brazil to British ships, in return for the assistance given by our own country against Napoleon. Both England and Brazil profited by the new commerce, but the Portuguese traders, who had of old had the monopoly, were ruined. The change in the seat of government was in fact seen to be nothing less than a reversal of

<small>Affairs in Portugal, 1807—1820.</small>

---

his children should not have to reproach him for having given up their rights. He was the son of the honest Charles III. . . . he was his unworthy offspring, but he would never disgrace his family. . . . On my going away he took me by the hand, and said he hoped I should esteem him as he did me, and begged me to take a Pheasant pye to a gentleman who had been his constant shooting companion." Records, Sicily, vol. 97. Ferdinand was the last sovereign who habitually kept a professional fool, or jester, in attendance upon him.

RISING AT OPORTO.

the old relations between the European country and its colony. Hitherto Brazil had been governed in the interests of Portugal; but with a Sovereign fixed at Rio Janeiro, it was almost inevitable that Portugal should be governed in the interests of Brazil. Declining trade, the misery and impoverishment resulting from a long war, resentment against a Court which could not be induced to return to the kingdom, and a foreigner who could not be induced to quit it, filled the army and all classes in the nation with discontent. Conspiracies were discovered as early as 1817, and the conspirators punished with all the barbarous ferocity of the Middle Ages. Beresford, who had not sufficient tact to prevent the execution of a sentence ordering twelve persons to be strangled, beheaded, and then burnt in the streets of Lisbon, found, during the two succeeding years, that the state of the country was becoming worse and worse. In the spring of 1820, when the Spanish revolution had made some change in the neighbouring kingdom, either for good or evil, inevitable, Beresford set out for Rio Janeiro, intending to acquaint the King with the real condition of affairs, and to use his personal efforts in hastening the return of the Court to Lisbon. Before he could recross the Atlantic, the Government which he left behind him at Lisbon had fallen.

The grievances of the Portuguese army made it the natural centre of disaffection, but the military conspirators had their friends among all classes. On the 24th of August, 1820, the Revolution at Oporto, August, 1820.

signal of revolt was given at Oporto. Priests and magistrates, as well as the town-population, united with officers of the army in declaring against the Regency, and in establishing a provisional Junta, charged with the duty of carrying on the government in the name of the King until the Cortes should assemble and frame a Constitution. No resistance was offered by any of the civil or military authorities at Oporto. The Junta entered upon its functions, and began by dismissing all English officers, and making up the arrears of pay due to the soldiers. As soon as the news of the revolt reached Lisbon, the Regency itself volunteered to summon the Cortes, and attempted to conciliate the remainder of the army by imitating the measures of the Junta of Oporto.* The troops, however, declined to act against their comrades, and on the 15th of September the Regency was deposed, and a provisional Junta installed in the capital. Beresford, who now returned from Brazil, was forbidden to set foot on Portuguese soil. The two rival governing-committees of Lisbon and Oporto coalesced; and after an interval of confusion the elections to the Cortes were held, resulting in the return of a body of men whose loyalty to the Crown was not impaired by their hostility to the Regency. The King, when the first tidings of the constitutional movement reached Brazil, gave a qualified consent to the summoning of the Cortes which was announced by the Regency, and promised to return to Europe. Beresford, continuing his voyage

* British and Foreign State Papers, vii. 361, 998.

to England without landing at Lisbon, found that the Government of this country had no disposition to interfere with the domestic affairs of its ally.

It was the boast of the Spanish and Italian Liberals that the revolutions effected in 1820 were undisgraced by the scenes of outrage which had followed the capture of the Bastille and the overthrow of French absolutism thirty years before.* The gentler character of these southern movements proved, however, no extenuation in the eyes of the leading statesmen of Europe: on the contrary, the declaration of soldiers in favour of a Constitution seemed in some quarters more ominous of evil than any excess of popular violence. The alarm was first sounded at St. Petersburg. As soon as the Czar heard of Riego's proceedings at Cadiz, he began to meditate intervention; and when it was known that Ferdinand had been forced to accept the Constitution of 1812, he ordered his ambassadors to propose that all the Great Powers, acting through their Ministers at Paris, should address a remonstrance to the representative of Spain, requiring the Cortes to disavow the crime of the 8th of March, by which they had been called into being, and to offer a pledge of obedience to their King by enacting the most rigorous laws against sedition and revolt.† In that case, and in that alone, the Czar desired to add, would

marginal note: Alexander proposes joint action with regard to Spain, April, 1820.

* Except in Sicily, where, however, the course of events had not the same publicity as on the mainland.
† Verbatim from the Russian Note of April 18. B. and F. State Papers, vii. 943.

the Powers maintain their relations of confidence and amity with Spain.

This Russian proposal was viewed with some suspicion at Vienna; it was answered with a direct and energetic negative from London. Canning was still in the Ministry. The words with which in 1818 he had protested against a league between England and autocracy were still ringing in the ears of his colleagues. Lord Liverpool's Government knew itself to be unpopular in the country; every consideration of policy as well as of self-interest bade it resist the beginnings of an intervention which, if confined to words, was certain to be useless, and, if supported by action, was likely to end in that alliance between France and Russia which had been the nightmare of English statesmen ever since 1814, and in a second occupation of Spain by the very generals whom Wellington had spent so many years in dislodging. Castlereagh replied to the Czar's note in terms which made it clear that England would never give its sanction to a collective interference with Spain.* Richelieu, the nominal head of the French Government, felt too little confidence in his position to act without the concurrence of Great Britain; and the crusade of absolutism against Spanish liberty was in consequence postponed until the victory of the Ultra-Royalists at Paris was complete, and the overthrow of Richelieu had brought to the head of the French State a group of men who felt no scruple in entering upon an aggressive war.

England prevents joint diplomatic intervention.

* Parliamentary Debates, N. S., viii. 1136.

But the shelter of circumstances which for a while protected Spain from the foreigner, did not extend to Italy, when in its turn the Neapolitan revolution called a northern enemy into the field. *Naples and the Great Powers.* Though the kingdom of the Two Sicilies was in itself much less important than Spain, the established order of the Continent was more directly threatened by a change in its government. No European State was exposed to the same danger from a revolution in Madrid as Austria from a revolution in Naples. The Czar had invoked the action of the Courts against Spain, not because his own dominions were in peril, but because the principle of monarchical right was violated: with Austria the danger pressed nearer home. The establishment of constitutional liberty in Naples was *Austria.* almost certain to be followed by an insurrection in the Papal States and a national uprising in the Venetian provinces; and among all the bad results of Austria's false position in Italy, one of the worst was that in self-defence it was bound to resist every step made towards political liberty beyond its own frontier. The dismay with which Metternich heard of the collapse of absolute government at Naples* was understood and even shared by the English Ministry, who at this moment were deprived of their best guide by Canning's withdrawal. Austria, in peace

* Gentz, D. I., ii. 70. " M. le Prince Metternich s'est rendu chez l'Empereur pour le mettre au fait de ces tristes circonstances. Depuis que je le connais, je ne l'ai jamais vu aussi frappé d'aucun événement qu'il l'était hier avant son départ."

just as much as in war, had uniformly been held to be the natural ally of England against the two aggressive Courts of Paris and St. Petersburg. It seemed perfectly right and natural to Lord Castlereagh that Austria, when its own interests were endangered by the establishment of popular sovereignty at Naples, should intervene to restore King Ferdinand's power; the more so as the secret treaty of 1815, by which Metternich had bound this sovereign to maintain absolute monarchy, had been communicated to the ambassador of Great Britain, and had received his approval. But the right to intervene in Italy belonged, according to Lord Castlereagh, to Austria alone. The Sovereigns of Europe had no more claim, as a body, to interfere with Naples than they had to interfere with Spain. Therefore, while the English Government sanctioned and even desired the intervention of Austria, as a State acting in protection of its own interests against revolution in a neighbouring country, it refused to sanction any joint intervention of the European Powers, and declared itself opposed to the meeting of a Congress where any such intervention might be discussed.*

<small>England admits Austrian but not joint intervention.</small>

Had Metternich been free to follow his own impulses, he would have thrown an army into Southern Italy as soon as soldiers and stores could be collected, and have made an end of King Ferdinand's troubles forthwith. It was, however, impossible for him to disregard the wishes of the Czar, and to

* Castlereagh, xii. 311.

abandon all at once the system of corporate action, which was supposed to have done such great things for Europe.* A meeting of sovereigns and Ministers was accordingly arranged, and at the end of October the Emperor of Austria received the Czar and King Frederick William in the little town of Troppau, in Moravia. France had itself first recommended the summoning of a Congress to deal with Neapolitan affairs, and it was believed for a while that England would be isolated in its resistance to a joint intervention. But before the Congress assembled, the firm language of the English Ministry had drawn Richelieu over to its side;† and although one of the two French envoys made himself the agent of the Ultra-Royalist faction, it was not possible for him to unite his country with the three Eastern Courts. France, through the weakness of its Government and the dissension between its representatives, counted for nothing at the Congress. England sent its ambassador from Vienna, but with instructions

Conference at Troppau, Oct., 1820.

---

* Gentz, D. I., ii. 76. Metternich, iii. 395. "Our fire-engines were not full in July, otherwise we should have set to work immediately."

† Gentz, ii. 85. Gentz was secretary at the Congress of Troppau, as he had been at Vienna and Aix-la-Chapelle. His letters exhibit the Austrian and absolutist view of all European politics with striking clearness. He speaks of the change in Richelieu's action as disagreeable but not fatal. "Ces pruderies politiques sont sans doute fâcheuses. . . . . La Russie, l'Autriche, et la Prusse, heureusement libres encore dans leurs mouvements, et assez puissantes pour soutenir ce qu'elles arrêtent, pourraient adopter sans le concours de l'Angleterre et de la France un système tel que les besoins du moment le demandent." The description of the three despotisms as "happily free in their movements" is very characteristic of the time.

W W

to act as an observer and little more; and in consequence the meeting at Troppau resolved itself into a gathering of the three Eastern autocrats and their Ministers. As Prussia had ceased to have any independent foreign policy whatever, Metternich needed only to make certain of the support of the Czar in order to range on his side the entire force of eastern and central Europe in the restoration of Neapolitan despotism.

Then the plan of the Austrian statesman was not, however, to be realised without some effort. Alexander had watched with jealousy Metternich's recent assumption of a dictatorship over the minor German Courts; he had never admitted Austria's right to dominate in Italy; and even now some vestiges of his old attachment to liberal theories made him look for a better solution of the Neapolitan problem than in that restoration of despotism pure and simple which Austria desired. While condemning every attempt of a people to establish its own liberties, Alexander still believed that in some countries sovereigns would do well to make their subjects a grant of what he called sage and liberal institutions. It would have pleased him best if the Neapolitans could have been induced by peaceful means to abandon their Constitution, and to accept in return certain chartered rights as a gift from their King; and the concurrence of the two Western Powers might in this case possibly have been regained. This project of a compromise, by which Ferdinand would have been freed from his secret engagement with Austria, was exactly what Metternich

Contest between Metternich and Capodistrias.

desired to frustrate. He found himself matched, and not for the first time, against a statesman who was even more subtle than himself. This was Count Capodistrias, a Greek who from a private position had risen to be Foreign Minister of Russia, and was destined to become the first sovereign, in reality if not in title, of his native land. Capodistrias, the sympathetic partner of the Czar's earlier hopes, had not travelled so fast as his master along the reactionary road. He still represented what had been the Italian policy of Alexander some years before, and sought to prevent the re-establishment of absolute rule at Naples, at least by the armed intervention of Austria. Metternich's first object was to discredit the Minister in the eyes of his sovereign. It is said that he touched the Czar's keenest fears in a conversation relating to a mutiny that had just taken place among the troops at St. Petersburg, and so in one private interview cut the ground from under Capodistrias' feet; he also humoured the Czar by reviving that monarch's own favourite scheme for a mutual guarantee of all the Powers against revolution in any part of Europe. Alexander had proposed in 1818 that the Courts should declare resistance to authority in any country to be a violation of European peace, entitling the Allied Powers, if they should think fit, to suppress it by force of arms. This doctrine, which would have empowered the Czar to throw the armies of a coalition upon London if the Reform Bill had been carried by force, had hitherto failed to gain international acceptance owing to the opposition of Great Britain. It was now formally accepted by Austria and Prussia. Alexander saw the federative system of European monarchy, with its principle of collective intervention, recognised as an established fact by at least three of the great Powers;* and in return he permitted Metternich to lay down the lines which, in the case of Naples, this intervention should follow. It was determined to invite King Ferdinand to meet his brother-sovereigns at Laibach, in the Austrian province of Carniola, and through him to address a summons to the Neapolitan people, requiring them, in the name of the three Powers, and under threat of invasion, to abandon their Constitution. This determination was announced, as a settled matter, to the envoys of England and France; and a circular was issued from Troppau by the three Powers to all the Courts of Europe (Dec. 8), embodying the doctrine of federative intervention, and expressing a hope that England and France would approve its immediate application in the case of Naples.†

The principle of intervention laid down by three Courts.

Circular of Troppau, Dec. 8, 1820.

There was no ground whatever for this hope with

---

* This is the system conveniently but incorrectly named Holy Alliance, from its supposed origination in the unmeaning Treaty of Holy Alliance in 1815. The reader will have seen that it took five years of reaction to create a definitive agreement among the monarchs to intervene against popular changes in other States, and that the principles of any operative league planned by Alexander in 1815 would have been largely different from those which he actually accepted in 1820. The Alexander who designed the Holy Alliance was the Alexander who had forced Louis XVIII. to grant the Charta.

† Castlereagh, xii. 330.

regard to England. On the contrary, in proportion as the three Courts strengthened their union and insisted on their claim to joint jurisdiction over Europe, they drove England away from them. *Protest of England.* Lord Castlereagh had at first promised the moral support of this country to Austria in its enterprise against Naples; but when this enterprise ceased to be the affair of Austria alone, and became part of the police-system of the three despotisms, it was no longer possible for the English Government to view it with approval or even with silence. The promise of a moral support was withdrawn: England declared that it stood strictly neutral with regard to Naples, and protested against the doctrine contained in the Troppau circular, that a change of government in any State gave the Allied Powers the right to intervene.* France made no such protest; but it was still hoped at Paris that an Austrian invasion of Southern Italy, so irritating to French pride, might be averted. King Louis XVIII. endeavoured, but in

* Metternich, iii. 394. B. and F. State Papers, viii. 1160. Gentz, D. I., ii. 112. The best narrative of the Congress of Troppau is in Duvergier de Hauranne, vi. 93. The Life of Canning by his secretary, Stapleton, though it is a work of some authority on this period, is full of misstatements about Castlereagh. Stapleton says that Castlereagh took no notice of the Troppau circular of December 8 until it had been for more than a month in his possession, and suggests that he would never have protested at all but for the unexpected disclosure of the circular in a German newspaper. As a matter of fact, the first English protest against the Troppau doctrine, expressed in a memorandum, "très long, très positif, assez dur même, et assez tranchant dans' son langage," was handed in to the Congress on December 16 or 19, along with a very unwelcome note to Metternich. There is some gossip of another of

vain, to act the part of mediator, and to reconcile the Neapolitan House of Bourbon at once with its own subjects, and with the Northern Powers.

The summons went out from the Congress to King Ferdinand to appear at Laibach. It found him enjoying all the popularity of a constitutional King, surrounded by Ministers who had governed under Murat, exchanging compliments with a democratic Parliament, lavishing distinctions upon the men who had overthrown his authority, and swearing to everything that was set before him. As the Constitution prohibited the King from leaving the country without the consent of the Legislature, it was necessary for Ferdinand to communicate to Parliament the invitation which he had received from the Powers, and to take a vote of the Assembly on the subject of his journey. Ferdinand's Ministers possessed some political experience; they recognised that it would be impossible to maintain the existing Constitution against the hostility of three great States, and hoped that the Parliament would consent to Ferdinand's departure on condition that he pledged himself to uphold certain specified principles of free government. A message to the Assembly was accordingly made public, in which the King expressed his desire to mediate with the

Conference at Laibach, Jan. 1821.

Canning's secretaries in Greville's Memoirs, i. 105, to the effect that Castlereagh's private despatches to Troppau differed in tone from his official ones, which were only written "to throw dust in the eyes of Parliament." It is sufficient to read the Austrian documents of the time, teeming as they do with vexation and disappointment at England's action, to see that this is a fiction.

Powers on this basis. But the Ministers had not reckoned with the passions of the people. As soon as it became known that Ferdinand was about to set out, the leaders of the Carbonari mustered their bands. A host of violent men streamed into Naples from the surrounding country. The Parliament was intimidated, and Ferdinand was prohibited from leaving Naples until he had sworn to maintain the Constitution actually in force, that, namely, which Naples had borrowed from Spain. Ferdinand, whose only object was to escape from the country as quickly as possible, took the oath with his usual effusions of patriotism. He then set out for Leghorn, intending to cross from thence into Northern Italy. No sooner had he reached the Tuscan port than he addressed a letter to each of the five principal sovereigns of Europe, declaring that his last acts were just as much null and void as all his earlier ones. He made no attempt to justify, or to excuse, or even to explain his conduct; nor is there the least reason to suppose that he considered the perjuries of a prince to require a justification. "These sorry protests," wrote the secretary of the Congress of Troppau, "will happily remain secret. No Cabinet will be anxious to draw them from the sepulchre of its archives. Till then there is not much harm done."

Ferdinand reached Laibach, where the Czar rewarded him for the fatigues of his journey by a present of some Russian bears. His arrival *Ferdinand at Laibach.* was peculiarly agreeable to Metternich, whose intentions corresponded exactly with his own; and the fact that he had been compelled to swear to maintain the Spanish Constitution at Naples acted favourably for the Austrian Minister, inasmuch as it enabled him to say to all the world that negotiation was now out of the question.* Capodistrias, brought face to face with failure, twisted about, according to his rival's expression, like a devil in holy water, but all in vain. It was decided that Ferdinand should be restored as absolute monarch by an Austrian army, and that, whether the Neapolitans resisted or submitted, their country should be occupied by Austrian troops for some years to come. The only difficulty remaining was to vest King Ferdinand's conduct in some respectable disguise. Capodistrias, when nothing else was to be gained, offered to invent an entire correspondence, in which Ferdinand should proudly uphold the Constitution to which he had sworn, and protest against the determination of the Powers to force the sceptre of absolutism back into his hand.† This device, however, was thought too transparent. A letter was sent in the King's name to his son, the Duke of Calabria, stating that he had found the three Powers determined not to tolerate an order of things sprung from revolution; that submission

<small>Demands of the Allies on Naples.</small>

---

* Had Ferdinand's first proposals been accepted by the Neapolitan Parliament, France and England, it was thought, might have insisted on a compromise at Laibach. "Les Gouvernements de France et d'Angleterre auraient fortement insisté sur l'introduction d'un régime constitutionnel et représentatif, régime que la Cour de Vienne croit absolument incompatible avec la position des États de l'Italie, et avec la sûreté de ses propres États." Gentz, D. I., ii. 110.

† Gentz, Nachlasse (P. Osten), i. 67. Lest the reader should take a prejudice against Capodistrias for his cunning, I ought to mention here

alone would avert war; but that even in case of submission certain securities for order, meaning the occupation of the country by an Austrian army, would be exacted. The letter concluded with the usual promises of reform and good government. It reached Naples on the 9th of February, 1821. No answer was either expected or desired. On the 6th the order had been given to the Austrian army to cross the Po.

There was little reason to fear any serious resistance on the part of the Neapolitans. The administration of the State was thoroughly disorganised; the agitation of the secret societies had destroyed all spirit of obedience among the soldiers; a great part of the army was absent in Sicily, keeping guard over a people who, under wiser management, might have doubled the force which Naples now opposed to the invader. When the despotic government of Ferdinand was overthrown, the island of Sicily, or that part of it which was represented by Palermo, had claimed the separate political existence which it had possessed between 1806 and 1815, offering to remain united to Naples in the person of the sovereign, but demanding a National Parliament and a National Constitution of its own. The revolutionary Ministers of Naples had, however, no more sympathy with the wishes of the Sicilians than the Spanish Liberals of 1812 had

State of Naples and Sicily.

---

that he was a man of austere disinterestedness in private life, and one of the few statesmen of the time who did not try to make money by politics. His ambition, which was very great, rose above all the meaner objects which tempt most men. The contrast between his personal goodness and his unscrupulousness in diplomacy will become more clear later on.

with those of the American Colonists. They required the islanders to accept the same rights and duties as any other province of the Neapolitan kingdom, and, on their refusal, sent over a considerable force and laid siege to Palermo.* The contest soon ended in the submission of the Sicilians, but it was found necessary to keep twelve thousand troops on the island in order to prevent a new revolt. The whole regular army of Naples numbered little more than forty thousand; and although bodies of Carbonari and of the so-called Militia set out to join the colours of General Pepe and to fight for liberty, they remained for the most part a disorderly mob, without either arms or discipline. The invading army of Austria, fifty thousand strong, not only possessed an immense superiority in organisation and military spirit, but actually outnumbered the forces of the defence. At the first encounter, which took place at Rieti, in the Papal States, the Neapolitans were put to the rout. Their army melted away, as it had in Murat's campaign in 1815. Nothing was heard among officers and men but accusations of treachery; not a single strong point was defended; and on the 24th of March the Austrians made their entry into Naples. Ferdinand, halting at Florence, sent on before him the worst instruments of his former despotism. It was indeed impossible for these men to renew, under Austrian protection, the scenes of reckless bloodshed which had followed the restoration

The Austrians enter Naples, March 24, 1821.

Third Neapolitan restoration.

* Colletta, ii. 230.—Bianchi, Diplomazia, ii. 47.

of 1799; and a great number of compromised persons had already been provided with the means of escape. But the hand of vengeance was not easily stayed. Courts-martial and commissions of judges began in all parts of the kingdom to sentence to imprisonment and death. An attempted insurrection in Sicily and some desperate acts of rebellion in Southern Italy cost the principal actors their lives; and when an amnesty was at length proclaimed, an exception was made against those who were now called the deserters, and who were lately called the Sacred Band, of Nola, that is to say, the soldiers who had first risen for the Constitution. Morelli, who had received the Viceroy's treacherous thanks for his conduct, was executed, along with one of his companions; the rest were sent in chains to labour among felons. Hundreds of persons were left lying, condemned or uncondemned, in prison; others, in spite of the amnesty, were driven from their native land; and that great, long-lasting stream of fugitives now began to pour into England, which, in the early memories of many who are not yet old, has associated the name of Italian with the image of an exile and a sufferer.

There was a moment in the campaign of Austria against Naples when the invading army was threatened with the most serious danger. An insurrection broke out in Piedmont, and the troops of that country attempted to unite with the patriotic party of Lombardy in a movement which would have thrown all Northern Italy upon the rear of

Insurrection in Piedmont, March 10.

the Austrians. In the first excess of alarm, the Czar ordered a hundred thousand Russians to cross the Galician frontier, and to march in the direction of the Adriatic. It proved unnecessary, however, to continue this advance. The Piedmontese army was divided against itself; part proclaimed the Spanish Constitution, and, on the abdication of the King, called upon his cousin, the Regent, Charles Albert of Carignano, to march against the Austrians; part adhered to the rightful heir, the King's brother, Charles Felix, who was absent at Modena, and who, with an honesty in strong contrast to the frauds of the Neapolitan Court, refused to temporise with rebels, or to make any compromise with the Constitution. The scruples of the Prince of Carignano, after he had gone some way with the military party of action, paralysed the movement of Northern Italy. Unsupported by Piedmontese troops, the conspirators of Milan failed to raise any open insurrection. Austrian soldiers thronged westwards from the Venetian fortresses, and entered Piedmont itself; the collapse of the Neapolitan army destroyed the hopes of the bravest patriots ; and the only result of the Piedmontese movement was that the grasp of Austria closed more tightly on its subject provinces, while the martyrs of Italian freedom passed out of the sight of the world, out of the range of all human communication, buried for years to come in the silent, unvisited prison of the North.*

* Gualterio, Ultimi Rivolgimenti, iii. 46. Silvio Pellico, Le mie prigioni, ch. 57.

Thus the victory of absolutism was completed, and the law was laid down to Europe that a people seeking its liberties elsewhere than in the grace and spontaneous generosity of its legitimate sovereign became a fit object of attack for the armies of the three Great Powers. It will be seen in a later chapter how Metternich persuaded the Czar to include under the anathema issued by the Congress of Laibach (May, 1821),* the outbreak of the Greeks, which at this moment began, and how Lord Castlereagh supported the Austrian Minister in denying to these rebels against the Sultan all right or claim to the consideration of Europe. Spain was for the present left unmolested; but the military operations of 1821 prepared the way for a similar crusade against that country by occasioning the downfall of Richelieu's Ministry, and throwing the government of France entirely into the hands of the Ultra-Royalists. All parties in the French Chamber, whether they condemned or approved the suppression of Neapolitan liberty, censured a policy which had kept France in inaction, and made Austria supreme in Italy. The Ultra-Royalists profited by the general discontent to overthrow the Minister whom they had promised to support (Dec., 1821); and from this time a war with Spain, conducted either by France alone or in combination with the three Eastern Powers, became the dearest hope of the rank and file of the dominant faction. Villèle, their nominal chief, remained what he had been before,

margin: The French Ultra-Royalists urging attack on Spain.

* B. and F. State Papers, viii. 1203.

a statesman among fanatics, and desired to maintain the attitude of observation as long as this should be possible. A body of troops had been stationed on the southern frontier in 1820 to prevent all intercourse with the Spanish districts afflicted with the yellow fever. This epidemic had passed away, but the number of the troops was now raised to a hundred thousand. It was, however, the hope of Villèle that hostilities might be averted unless the Spaniards should themselves provoke a combat, or, by resorting to extreme measures against King Ferdinand, should compel Louis XVIII. to intervene on behalf of his kinsman. The more violent section of the French Cabinet, represented by Montmorency, the Foreign Minister, called for an immediate march on Madrid, or proposed to delay operations only until France should secure the support of the other Continental Powers.

The condition of Spain in the year 1822 gave ample encouragement to those who longed to employ the arms of France in the royalist cause.

Spain from 1820 to 1822.

The hopes of peaceful reform, which for the first few months after the revolution had been shared even by foreign politicians at Madrid, had long vanished. In the moment of popular victory Ferdinand had brought the leaders of the Cortes from their prisons and placed them in office. These men showed a dignified forgetfulness of the injuries which they had suffered. Misfortune had calmed their impetuosity, and taught them more of the real condition of the Spanish people. They entered upon their task with seriousness and good faith, and would have proved the best friends of constitutional monarchy if Ferdinand had had the least intention of co-operating with them loyally. But they found themselves encountered from the first by a double enemy. The clergy, who had overthrown the Constitution six years before, intrigued or openly declared against it as soon as it was revived; the more violent of the Liberals, with Riego at their head, abandoned themselves to extravagances like those of the club-orators of Paris in 1791, and did their best to make any peaceable administration impossible. After combating these anarchists, or Exaltados, with some success, the Ministry was forced to call in their aid, when, at the instigation of the Papal Nuncio, the King placed his veto upon a law dissolving most of the monasteries* (Oct., 1820). Ferdinand now openly combined with the enemies of the Constitution, and attempted to transfer the command of the army to one of his own agents. The plot failed; the Ministry sent the alarm over the whole country, and Ferdinand stood convicted before his people as a conspirator against the Constitution which he had sworn to defend. The agitation of the clubs, which the Ministry had hitherto suppressed, broke out anew. A storm of accusations assailed Ferdinand himself. He was compelled at the end of the year 1820 to banish from Madrid most of the persons who had been his confidants; and although his dethronement was not yet proposed, he had already

Ferdinand plots with the Serviles against the Constitution.

* Baumgarten, ii. 825.

become, far more than Louis XVI. of France under similar conditions, the recognised enemy of the revolution, and the suspected patron of every treason against the nation.

The attack of the despotic Courts on Naples in the spring of 1821 heightened the fury of parties in Spain, encouraging the Serviles, or Absolutists, in their plots, and forcing the Ministry to yield to the cry for more violent measures against the enemies of the Constitution. In the south of Spain the Exaltados gained possession of the principal military and civil commands, and openly refused obedience to the central administration when it attempted to interfere with their action. Seville, Carthagena, and Cadiz acted as if they were independent Republics, and even spoke of separation from Spain. Defied by its own subordinates in the provinces, and unable to look to the King for any sincere support, the moderate governing party lost all hold upon the nation. In the Cortes elected in 1822 the Exaltados formed the majority, and Riego was appointed President. Ferdinand now began to concert measures of action with the French Ultra-Royalists. The Serviles, led by priests, and supported by French money, broke into open rebellion in the north. When the session of the Cortes ended, the King attempted to overthrow his enemies by military force. Three battalions of the Royal Guard, which had been withdrawn from Madrid, received secret orders to march upon the capital (July 6, 1822), where Ferdinand was expected to place himself at their head. They were, however,

The Ministry between the Exaltados and Serviles, 1821.

met and defeated in the streets by other regiments, and Ferdinand, vainly attempting to dissociate himself from the action of his partisans, found his crown, if not his life, in peril. He wrote to Louis XVIII. that he was a prisoner. Attempted coup d'état, July 6, 1822. Though the French King gave nothing more than good counsel, the Ultra-Royalists in the French Cabinet and in the army now strained every nerve to accelerate a war between the two countries. The Spanish Absolutists seized the town of Seo d'Urgel, and there set up a provisional government. Civil war spread over the northern provinces. Royalists revolt in the north. The Ministry, which was now formed of Riego's friends, demanded and obtained from the Cortes dictatorial powers like those which the French Committee of Public Safety had wielded in 1793, but with far other result. Spain found no Danton, no Carnot, at this crisis, when the very highest powers of intellect and will would have been necessary to arouse and to arm a people far less disposed to fight for liberty than the French were in 1793. One man alone, General Mina, checked and overthrew the rebel leaders of the north with an activity superior to their own. The Government, boastful and violent in its measures, effected scarcely anything in the organisation of a national force, or in preparing the means of resistance against those foreign armies with whose attack the country was now plainly threatened.

When the Congress of Laibach broke up in the spring of 1821, its members determined to renew their meeting in the following year, in order to decide whether the Austrian army might then be withdrawn from Naples, and to discuss other questions affecting their common interests. The progress of the Greek insurrection and a growing strife between Russia and Turkey, had since then thrown all Italian difficulties into the shade. The Eastern question stood in the front rank of European politics; next in importance came the affairs of Spain. It was certain that these, far more than the occupation of Naples, would supply the real business of the Congress of 1822. England had a far greater interest in both questions than in the Italian negotiations of the two previous years. It was felt that the system of abstention which England had then followed could be pursued no longer, and that the country must be represented not by some casual and wandering diplomatist, but by its leading Minister, Lord Castlereagh. The intentions of the other Powers in regard to Spain were matter of doubt; it was the fixed policy of Great Britain to leave the Spanish revolution in Europe to run its own course, and to persuade the other Powers to do the same. But the difficulties connected with Spain did not stop at the Spanish frontier. The South American colonies had now in great part secured their independence. They had developed a trade with Great Britain which made it impossible for this country to ignore their flag and the decisions of their law courts. The British navigation-laws had already been modified by Parliament in favour of their shipping; and although it was no business of the English Government to grant a formal title to communities which had made themselves free, the practical recognition of the American States by the appointment of diplomatic agents could in several cases not be justly delayed. Therefore, without interfering with any colonies which were still fighting or still negotiating with Spain, the British Minister proposed to inform the Allied cabinets of the intention of this country to accredit agents to some of the South American Republics, and to recommend to them the adoption of a similar policy.

Such was the tenour of the instructions which, a few weeks before his expected departure for the Continent, Castlereagh drew up for his own guidance, and submitted to the Cabinet and the King.* Had he lived to fulfil the mission with which he was charged, the recognition of the South American Republics, which adds so bright a ray to the fame of Canning, would probably have been the work of the man who, more than any other, is associated in popular belief with the traditions of a hated and outworn system of oppression. Two more years of life, two more years of change in the relations of England to the Continent, would have given Castlereagh a different figure in the history both of Greece and of America. No English statesman in modern times has been so severely judged. Circumstances, down to the close of his career, withheld from Castlereagh the opportunities which fell to his successor; ties from which others were free made it hard for him to accelerate the breach with

margin: Death of Castlereagh, Aug. 12, 1822.

* Wellington Despatches, N. S., i. 284.

the Allies of 1814. Antagonists showed Castlereagh no mercy, no justice. The man whom Byron disgraced himself by ridiculing after his death possessed in a rich measure the qualities which, in private life, attract esteem and love. His public life, if tainted in earlier days by the low political morality of the time, rose high above that of every Continental statesman of similar rank, with the single exception of Stein. The best testimony to his integrity is the irritation which it caused to Talleyrand.* If the consciousness of labour unflaggingly pursued in the public cause, and animated on the whole by a pure and earnest purpose, could have calmed the distress of a breaking mind, the decline of Castlereagh's days might have been one of peace. His countrymen would have recognised that, if blind to the rights of nations, Castlereagh had set to foreign rulers the example of truth and good faith. But the burden of his life was too heavy to bear. Mists of despondency obscured the outlines of the real world, and struck chill into his heart. Death, self-invoked, brought relief to the over-wrought brain, and laid Castlereagh, with all his cares, in everlasting sleep.

The vacant post was filled by Canning, by far the most gifted of the band of statesmen who had begun their public life in the school of Pitt. Wellington undertook to represent England at the Congress of 1822, which was now about to open at Vienna. His departure was, however, delayed for several weeks, and the preliminary meeting,

Canning Foreign Secretary. Wellington deputed to the Congress, Sept., 1822.

* Talleyrand et Louis XVIII., p. 233.

at which it had been intended to transact all business not relating to Italy, was almost over before his arrival. Wellington accordingly travelled on to Verona, where Italian affairs were to be dealt with; and the Italian Conference, which the British Government had not intended to recognise, thus became the real Congress of 1822. Anxious as Lord Castlereagh had been on the question of foreign interference with Spain, he hardly understood the imminence of the danger. In passing through Paris, Wellington learnt for the first time that a French or European invasion of Spain would be the foremost object of discussion among the Powers; and on reaching Verona he made the unwelcome discovery that the Czar was bent upon sending a Russian army to take part, as the mandatary of Europe, in overthrowing the Spanish Constitution. Alexander's desire was to obtain a joint declaration from the Congress like that which had been issued against Naples by the three Courts at Troppau, but one even more formidable, since France might be expected in the present case to give its concurrence, which had been withheld before. France indeed occupied, according to the absolutist theory of the day, the same position in regard to a Jacobin Spain as Austria in regard to a Jacobin Naples, and might perhaps claim to play the leading military part in the crusade of repression. But the work was likely to be a much more difficult one than that of 1821. The French troops, said the Czar, were not trustworthy; and there was a party in France

Congress of Verona, Oct., 1822.

which might take advantage of the war to proclaim the second Napoleon or the Republic. King Louis XVIII. could not therefore be allowed to grapple with Spain alone. It was necessary that the principal force employed by the alliance should be one whose loyalty and military qualities were above suspicion: the generals who had marched from Moscow to Paris were not likely to fail beyond the Pyrenees: and a campaign of the Russian army in Western Europe promised to relieve the Czar of some of the discontent of his soldiers, who had been turned back after entering Galicia in the previous year, and who had not been allowed to assist their fellow-believers in Greece in their struggle against the Sultan.*

Wellington had ascertained, while in Paris, that King Louis XVIII. and Villèle were determined under no circumstances to give Russian troops a passage through France. His knowledge of this fact enabled him to speak with some confidence to Alexander. It was the earnest desire of the English Government to avert war, and its first object was therefore to prevent the Congress, as a body, from sending an ultimatum to Spain. If all the Powers united in a declaration like that of Troppau, war was inevitable; if France were left to settle its own disputes with its neighbour, English mediation might possibly preserve peace. The statement of Wellington, that England would rather sever itself from the great alliance than consent to a joint declaration against Spain, had no

<small>No joint declaration made by the Congress against Spain.</small>

* Wellington, i. 343.

doubt its effect in preventing such a declaration being proposed; but a still weightier reason against it was the direct contradiction between the intentions of the French Government and those of the Czar. If the Czar was determined to be the soldier of Europe, while on the other hand King Louis absolutely denied him a passage through France, it was impossible that the Congress should threaten Spain with a collective attack. No great expenditure of diplomacy was therefore necessary to prevent the summary framing of a decree against Spain like that which had been framed against Naples two years before. In the first despatches which he sent back to England Wellington expressed his belief that the deliberations of the Powers would end in a decision to leave the Spaniards to themselves.

But the danger was only averted in appearance. The impulse to war was too strong among the French Ultra-Royalists for the Congress to keep silence on Spanish affairs. Villèle indeed still hoped for peace, and, unlike other members of his Cabinet, he desired that, if war should arise, France should maintain entire freedom of action, and enter upon the struggle as an independent Power, not as the instrument of the European concert. This did not prevent him, however, from desiring to ascertain what assistance would be forthcoming, if France should be hard pressed by its enemy. Instructions were given to the French envoys at Verona to sound the Allies on this question.* It was out of the inquiry

margin: Course of the negotiation against Spain.

* Duvergier de Hauranne, vii, 140.

so suggested that a negotiation sprang which virtually combined all Europe against Spain. The envoy Montmorency, acting in the spirit of the war party, demanded of all the Powers whether, in the event of France withdrawing its ambassador from Madrid, they would do the same, and whether, in case of war, France would receive their moral and material support. Wellington in his reply protested against the framing of hypothetical cases; the other envoys answered Montmorency's questions in the affirmative. The next step was taken by Metternich, who urged that certain definite acts of the Spanish people or Government ought to be specified as rendering war obligatory on France and its allies, and also that, with a view of strengthening the Royalist party in Spain, notes ought to be presented by all the ambassadors at Madrid, demanding a change in the Constitution. This proposal was in its turn submitted to Wellington and rejected by him. It was accepted by the other plenipotentiaries, and the acts of the Spanish people were specified on which war should necessarily follow. These were, the commission of any act of violence against a member of the royal family, the deposition of the King, or an attempt to change the dynasty. A secret clause was added to the second part of the agreement, to the effect that if the Spanish Government made no satisfactory answer to the notes requiring a change in the Constitution, all the ambassadors should be immediately withdrawn. A draft of the notes to be presented was sketched; and Montmorency, who thought that he had probably gone too far in his stipulations, returned to Paris to submit the drafts to the King before handing them over to the ambassadors at Paris for transmission to Madrid.

It was with great dissatisfaction that Villèle saw how his colleague had committed France to the direction of the three Eastern Powers. There was no likelihood that the Spanish Government would make the least concession of the kind required, and in that case France stood pledged, if the action of Montmorency was ratified, to withdraw its ambassador from Madrid at once. Villèle accordingly addressed himself to the ambassadors at Paris, asking that the despatch of the notes might be postponed. No notice was taken of his request: the notes were despatched forthwith. Roused by this slight, Villèle appealed to the King not to submit to the dictation of foreign Courts. Louis XVIII. declared in his favour against all the rest of the Cabinet, and Montmorency had to retire from office. But the decision of the King meant that he disapproved of the negotiations of Verona as shackling the movements of France, not that he had freed himself from the influence of the war-party. Chateaubriand, the most reckless agitator for hostilities, was appointed Foreign Minister. The mediation of Great Britain was rejected;* and in his speech at the opening of the Chambers of 1823, King

Villèle and Montmorency.

Speech of Louis XVIII., Jan. 27, 1823.

---

* Canning denied that it was offered, but the despatches in Wellington prove it. These papers, supplemented by the narrative of Duvergier

Louis himself virtually published the declaration of war.

The ambassadors of the three Eastern Courts had already presented their notes at Madrid demanding a change in the Constitution; and, after receiving a high-spirited answer from the Ministers, they had quitted the country. Canning, while using every diplomatic effort to prevent an unjust war, had made it clear to the Spaniards that England could not render them armed assistance. The reasons against such an intervention were indeed overwhelming. Russia, Austria, and Prussia would have taken the field rather than have permitted the Spanish Constitution to triumph; and although, if leagued with Spain in a really national defence like that of 1808, Great Britain might perhaps have protected the peninsula against all the Powers of Europe combined, it was far otherwise when the cause at stake was one to which a majority of the Spanish nation had shown itself to be indifferent, and against which the northern provinces had actually taken up arms. The Government and the Cortes were therefore left to defend themselves as best they could against their enemies. They displayed their weakness by enacting laws of extreme severity against deserters, and

England in 1823.

---

de Hauranne, drawn from the French documents which he specifies, are the authority for the history of the Congress. Canning's celebrated speech of April, 1823, is an effective *ex parte* composition rather than a historical summary. The reader who goes to the originals will be struck by the immense superiority of Wellington's statements over those of all the Continental statesmen at Verona, in point, in force, and in good sense, as well as in truthfulness. The Duke nowhere appears to greater advantage.

by retiring, along with the recalcitrant King, from Madrid to Seville. On the 7th of April the French troops, led by the Duke of Angoulême, crossed the frontier. The priests and a great part of the peasantry welcomed them as deliverers: the forces opposed to them fell back without striking a blow. As the invader advanced towards the capital, gangs of royalists, often led by monks, spread such terror and devastation over the northern provinces that the presence of foreign troops became the only safeguard for the peaceable inhabitants.* Madrid itself was threatened by the corps of a freebooter named Bessières. The commandant sent his surrender to the French while they were still at some distance, begging them to advance as quickly as possible in order to save the city from pillage. The message had scarcely been sent when Bessières and his bandits appeared in the suburbs. The governor drove them back, and kept the royalist mob within the city at bay for four days more. On the 23rd of May the advance-guard of the French army entered the capital. French invasion of Spain, April, 1823.

It had been the desire of King Louis XVIII. and Angoulême to save Spain from the violence of royalist and priestly fanaticism. On reaching Madrid, Angoulême intended to appoint a provisional government himself; he was, however, compelled by orders from Paris to leave the Angoulême, the Regency, and the ambassadors.

* Report of Angoulême, Duvergier d'Hauranne, vii. "Là où sont nos troupes, nous maintenons la paix avec beaucoup de peine; mais là où nous ne sommes pas, on massacre, on brûle, on pille, on vole. Les corps Espagnols, se disant royalistes, ne cherchent qu'à voler et à piller."

election in the hands of the Council of Castille, and a Regency came into power whose first acts showed in what spirit the victory of the French was to be used. Edicts were issued declaring all the acts of the Cortes affecting the monastic orders to be null and void, dismissing all officials appointed since March 7, 1820, and subjecting to examination those who, then being in office, had not resigned their posts.* The arrival of the ambassadors of the three Eastern Powers encouraged the Regency in their antagonism to the French commander. It was believed that the Cabinet of Paris was unwilling to restore King Ferdinand as an absolute monarch, and intended to obtain from him the grant of institutions resembling those of the French Charta. Any such limitation of absolute power was, however, an object of horror to the three despotic Courts. Their ambassadors formed themselves into a council with the express object of resisting the supposed policy of Angoulême. The Regency grew bolder, and gave the signal for general retribution upon the Liberals by publishing an order depriving all persons who had served in the voluntary militia since March, 1820, of their offices, pensions, and titles. The work inaugurated in the capital was carried much further in the provinces.

* Decretos del Rey Fernando, vii. 35, 50, 75. This process, which was afterwards extended even to common soldiers, was called Purificacion. Committees were appointed to which all persons coming under the law had to send in detailed evidence of correct conduct in and since 1820, signed by some well-known royalists. But the committees also accepted any letters of denunciation that might be sent to them, and were bound by law to keep them secret, so that in practice the Purificacion became a vast system of anonymous persecution.

The friends of the Constitution, and even soldiers who were protected by their capitulation with the French, were thrown into prison by the new local authorities. The violence of the reaction reached such a height that Angoulême, now on the march to Cadiz, was compelled to publish an ordinance forbidding arrests to be made without the consent of a French commanding officer, and ordering his generals to release the persons who had been arbitrarily imprisoned. The council of ambassadors, blind in their jealousy of France to the danger of an uncontrolled restoration, drew up a protest against his ordinance, and desired that the officers of the Regency should be left to work their will.

After spending some weeks in idle debates at Seville, the Cortes had been compelled by the appearance of the French on the Sierra Morena to retire to Cadiz. *The Cortes at Cadiz.* As King Ferdinand refused to accompany them, he was declared temporarily insane, and forced to make the journey (June 12). Angoulême, following the French vanguard after a considerable interval, appeared before Cadiz in August, and sent a note to King Ferdinand, recommending him to publish an amnesty, and to promise the restoration of the mediæval Cortes. It was hoped that the terms suggested in this note might be accepted by the Government in Cadiz as a basis of peace, and so render an attack upon the city unnecessary. The Ministry, however, returned a defiant answer in the King's name. The siege of Cadiz accordingly began in earnest. On the 30th of August the fort of the Trocadero was stormed; three weeks later the city was bombarded. In reply to all proposals for negotiation Angoulême stated that he could only treat when King Ferdinand was within his own lines. There was not the least hope of prolonging the defence of Cadiz with success, for the combat was dying out even in those few districts of Spain where the constitutional troops had fought with energy. Ferdinand himself pretended that he bore no grudge against his Ministers, and that the Liberals had nothing to fear from his release. On the 30th of September he signed, as if with great satisfaction, an absolute and universal amnesty.*

Ferdinand liberated, Oct. 1.

On the following day he was conveyed with his family across the bay to Angoulême's head-quarters.

The war was over: the real results of the French invasion now came into sight. Ferdinand had not been twelve hours in the French camp when, surrounded by monks and royalist desperadoes, he published a proclamation invalidating every act of the constitutional Government of the last three years, on the ground that his sanction had been given under constraint. The same proclamation ratified the acts of the Regency of Madrid. As the Regency of Madrid had declared all persons concerned in the removal of the King to Cadiz to be liable to the penalties of high treason, Ferdinand had in fact ratified a sentence of death against several of the men from whom he had just parted in friendship.† Many of

Violence of the Restoration.

---

* Historia de la vida de Fernando VII., 1842, iii. 152.
† Decretos del Rey Fernando, vii. 45.

THE SIEGE OF CADIZ.
KING FERDINAND BEING CONVEYED ACROSS THE BAY TO ANGOULÊME'S
HEAD-QUARTERS.

(p. 222.)

these victims of the King's perfidy were sent into safety by the French. But Angoulême was powerless to influence Ferdinand's policy and conduct. Don Saez, the King's confessor, was made First Secretary of State. On the 4th of October an edict was issued banishing for ever from Madrid, and from the country fifty miles round it, every person who during the last three years had sat in the Cortes, or who had been a Minister, counsellor of State, judge, commander, official in any public office, magistrate, or officer in the so-called voluntary militia. It was ordered that throughout Spain a solemn service should be celebrated in expiation of the insults offered to the Holy Sacrament; that missions should be sent over the land to combat the pernicious and heretical doctrines associated with the late outbreak, and that the bishops should relegate to monasteries of the strictest observance the priests who had acted as the agents of an impious faction.* Thus the war of revenge was openly declared against the defeated party. It was in vain that Angoulême indignantly reproached the King, and that the ambassadors of the three Eastern

* Decretos, vii. 154. The preamble to this law is perhaps the most astonishing of all Ferdinand's devout utterances. "My soul is confounded with the horrible spectacle of the sacrilegious crimes which impiety has dared to commit against the Supreme Maker of the universe. The ministers of Christ have been persecuted and sacrificed; the venerable successor of St. Peter has been outraged; the temples of the Lord have been profaned and destroyed; the Holy Gospel depreciated; in fine, the inestimable legacy which Jesus Christ gave in his last supper to secure our eternal felicity, the Sacred Host, has been trodden under foot. My soul shudders, and will not be able to return to tranquillity until, in union with my children, my faithful subjects, I offer to God holocausts of piety," &c. But for some specimens of Ferdinand's command of the vernacular, of a very different character, see Wellington, N. S., ii. 87.

Courts pressed him to draw up at least some kind of amnesty. Ferdinand travelled slowly towards Madrid, saying that he could take no such step until he reached the capital. On the 7th of November, Riego was hanged. Thousands of persons were thrown into prison, or compelled to fly from the country. Except where order was preserved by the French, life and property were at the mercy of royalist mobs and the priests who led them; and although the influence of the Russian statesman Pozzo di Borgo at length brought a respectable Ministry into office, this only roused the fury of the clerical party, and led to a cry for the deposition of the King, and for the elevation of his more fanatical brother, Don Carlos, to the throne. Military commissions were instituted at the beginning of 1824 for the trial of accused persons, and a pretended amnesty, published six months later, included in its fifteen classes of exception the participators in almost every act of the revolution. Ordinance followed upon ordinance, multiplying the acts punishable with death, and exterminating the literature which was believed to be the source of all religious and social heterodoxy. Every movement of life was watched by the police; every expression of political opinion was made high treason. Young men were shot for being freemasons; women were sent to prison for ten years for possessing a portrait of Riego. The relation of the restored Government to its subjects was in fact that which belonged to a state of civil war. Insurrections arose among the fanatics who were now taking the name of the Carlist or Apostolic party, as well as among a despairing remnant of the Constitutionalists. After a feeble outbreak of the latter at Tarifa, a hundred and twelve persons were put to death by the military commissions within eighteen days.* It was not until the summer of 1825 that the jurisdiction of these tribunals and the Reign of Terror ended.

France had won a cheap and inglorious victory: the three Eastern Courts had seen their principle of absolutism triumph at the cost of everything that makes government morally better than anarchy. One consolation remained for those who felt that there was little hope for freedom on the Continent of Europe. The crusade against Spanish liberty had put an end for ever to the possibility of a joint conquest of Spanish America in the interest of despotism. *[margin: England prohibits the conquest of Spanish colonies by France or its allies.]* The attitude of England was no longer what it had been in 1818. When the Czar had proposed at the Congress of Aix-la-Chapelle that the allied monarchs should suppress the republican principle beyond the seas, Castlereagh had only stated that England could bear no part in such an enterprise; he had not said that

---

* Revolution d'Espagne, examen critique (Paris, 1836), p. 151; from the lists in the Gaceta de Madrid. The Gaceta for these years is wanting from the copy in the British Museum; and in the large collection in that library of historical and periodical literature relating to Spain I can find no first-hand authorities for the judicial murders of these years. Nothing relating to the subject was permitted to be printed in Spain for many years afterwards. The work cited in this note, though bearing a French title, and published at Paris in 1836, was in fact a Spanish book written in 1824. The critical inquiry which has substantiated many of the worst traditions of the French Reign of Terror from local records still remains to be undertaken for this period of Spanish history.

England would effectually prevent others from attempting it. This was the resolution by which Canning, isolated and baffled by the conspiracy of Verona, proved that England could still do something to protect its own interest and the interests of mankind against a league of autocrats. There is indeed little doubt that the independence of the Spanish colonies would have been recognised by Great Britain soon after the war of 1823, whoever might have been our Minister for Foreign Affairs; but this recognition was a different matter in the hands of Canning from what it would have been in the hands of his predecessor. The contrast between the two men was one of spirit rather than of avowed rules of action. Where Castlereagh offered apologies to the Continental sovereigns, Canning uttered defiance.* The treaties of 1815, which connected England so closely with the foreign courts, were no work of his; though he sought not to repudiate them, he delighted to show that in spite of them England had still its own policy, its own sympathies, its own traditions. In face of the council of kings and its assumption of universal

---

* See e.g., Stapleton, Canning and his Times, p. 378. Wellington often suggested the use of less peremptory language. Despatches, i. 134, 188. Metternich wrote as follows on hearing at Vienna of Castlereagh's death: "Castlereagh was the only man in his country who had gained any experience in foreign affairs. He had learned to understand me. He was devoted to me in heart and spirit, not only from personal inclination, but from conviction. I awaited him here as my second self." iii. 391. Metternich, however, was apt to exaggerate his influence over the English Minister. It was a great surprise to him that Castlereagh, after gaining decisive majorities in the House of Commons on domestic questions in 1820, in no wise changed the foreign policy expressed in the protest against the Declaration of Troppau.

jurisdiction, he publicly described himself as an enthusiast for the independence of nations. If others saw little evidence that France intended to recompense itself for its services to Ferdinand by appropriating some of his rebellious colonies, Canning was quick to lay hold of every suspicious circumstance. At the beginning of the war of 1823 he gave a formal warning to the ambassador of Louis XVIII. that France would not be permitted to bring any of these provinces under its dominion, whether by conquest or cession.* When the war was over, he rejected the invitation of Ferdinand's Government to take part in a conference at Paris, where the affairs of South America were to be laid before the Allied Powers.† What these Powers might or might not think on the subject of America was now a matter of indifference, for the policy of England was fixed, and it was useless to debate upon a conclusion that could not be altered. British consular agents were appointed in most of the colonies before the close of the year 1823; and after some interval the independence of Buenos Ayres, Colombia, and Mexico was formally recognised by the conclusion of commercial treaties. "I called the New World into existence," cried Canning, when reproached with permitting the French occupation of Spain, "in order to redress the balance of the Old." The boast, famous in our Parliamentary history, has left an erroneous impression

<small>England recognises the independence of the colonies. 1824-5.</small>

---

* Stapleton, Political Life of Canning, ii. 18.
† Wellington, i. 188.

of the part really played by Canning at this crisis. He did not call the New World into existence; he did not even assist it in winning independence, as France had assisted the United States fifty years before; but when this independence had been won, he threw over it the ægis of Great Britain, declaring that no other European Power should reimpose the yoke which Spain had not been able to maintain.

Affairs in Portugal. The overthrow of the Spanish Constitution by foreign arms led to a series of events in Portugal which forced England to a more direct intervention in the Peninsula than had yet been necessary, and heightened the conflict that had sprung up between its policy and that of Continental absolutism. The same parties and the same passions, political and religious, existed in Portugal as in Spain, and the enemies of the Constitution found the same support at foreign Courts. The King of Portugal, John VI., was a weak but not ill-meaning man; his wife, who was a sister of Ferdinand of Spain, and his son Don Miguel were the chiefs of the conspiracy against the Cortes. In June, 1823, a military revolt, arranged by Miguel, brought the existing form of government to an end: the King promised, however, when dissolving the Cortes, that a Constitution should be bestowed by himself upon Portugal; and he seems to have intended to keep his word. The ambassadors of France and Austria were, however, busy in throwing hindrances in the way, and Don Miguel prepared to use violence to prevent his father from making any concession to the

Liberals. King John, in fear for his life, applied to England for troops; Canning declined to land soldiers at Lisbon, but sent a squadron, with orders to give the King protection. The winter of 1823 was passed in intrigues; in May, 1824, Miguel arrested the Ministers and surrounded the King's palace with troops. After several days of confusion King John made his escape to the British ships, and Miguel, who was alternately cowardly and audacious, then made his submission, and was ordered to leave the country. King John died in the spring of 1826 without having granted a Constitution. Pedro, his eldest son, had already been made Emperor of Brazil; and, as it was impossible that Portugal and Brazil could again be united, it was arranged that Pedro's daughter, when of sufficient age, should marry her uncle Miguel, and so save Portugal from the danger of a contested succession. Before renouncing the crown of Portugal, Pedro granted a Constitution to that country. A Regency had already been appointed by King John, in which neither the Queen-dowager nor Miguel was included.

<small>Constitution granted by Pedro. May, 1826.</small>

Miguel had gone to Vienna. Although a sort of Caliban in character and understanding, this Prince met with the welcome due to a kinsman of the Imperial house, and to a representative of the good cause of absolutism. He was received by Metternich with great interest, and his fortunes were taken under the protection of the Austrian Court. In due time, it was hoped, this savage and ignorant churl would do yeoman's service to

Austrian principles in the Peninsula. But the Regency and the new Constitution of Portugal had not to wait for the tardy operation of Metternich's covert hostility.

Desertion of Portuguese soldiery, 1826. The soldiery who had risen at Miguel's bidding in 1823 now proclaimed him King, and deserted to Spanish soil. Within the Spanish frontier they were received by Ferdinand's representatives with open arms. The demands made by the Portuguese ambassador at Madrid for their dispersion and for the surrender of their weapons were evaded. The cause of these armed bands on the frontier became the cause of the Clerical and Ultra-Royalist party over all Europe. Money was sent to them from France and Austria. They were joined by troops of Spanish Carlists or Apostolicals; they were fed, clothed, and organised, if not by the Spanish Government itself, at least by those over whose action the Spanish Government exercised control.* Thus raised to considerable military strength, they made incursions into Portugal, and at last attempted a regular invasion.

Spain permits the desertors to attack Portugal. The Regency of Lisbon, justly treating these outrages as the act of the Spanish Government, and appealing to the treaties which bound Great Britain to defend Portugal against foreign attack, demanded the assistance of this country. More was involved in the action taken by Canning than a possible contest with Spain; the seriousness of the danger lay in the fact that Spain was still occupied by French armies, and that a war with Spain might, and probably

* Parl. Hist., 12th Dec., 1826.

would, involve a war with France, if not with other Continental Powers. But the English Ministry waited only for the confirmation of the alleged facts by their own ambassador. The treaty-rights of Portugal were undoubted; the temper of the English Parliament and nation, strained to the utmost by the events of the last three years, was such that a war against Ferdinand and against the destroyers of Spanish liberty would have caused more rejoicing than alarm. Nine days after the formal demand of the Portuguese arrived, four days after their complaint was substantiated by the report of our ambassador, Canning announced to the House of Commons that British troops were actually on the way to Lisbon. In words that alarmed many of his own party, and roused the bitter indignation of every Continental Court, Canning warned those whose acts threatened to force England into war, that the war, if war arose, would be a war of opinion, and that England, however earnestly she might endeavour to avoid it, could not avoid seeing ranked under her banner all the restless and discontented of any nation with which she might come into conflict. As for the Portuguese Constitution which formed the real object of the Spanish attack, it had not, Canning said, been given at the instance of Great Britain, but he prayed that Heaven might prosper it. It was impossible to doubt that a Minister who spoke thus, and who, even under expressions of regret, hinted at any alliance with the revolutionary elements in France and Spain, was formidably in earnest. The words and the action of Canning produced

Canning sends troops to Lisbon, Dec., 1826.

the effect which he desired. The Government of Ferdinand discovered the means of checking the activity of the Apostolicals: the presence of the British troops at Lisbon enabled the Portuguese Regency to throw all its forces upon the invaders and to drive them from the country. They were disbanded when they re-crossed the Spanish frontier; the French Court loudly condemned their immoral enterprise; and the Constitution of Portugal seemed, at least for the moment, to have triumphed over its open and its secret enemies.

The tone of the English Government had indeed changed since the time when Metternich could express a public hope that the three Eastern Powers would have the approval of this country in their attack upon the Constitution of Naples. In 1820 such a profession might perhaps have passed for a mistake; in 1826 it would have been a palpable absurdity. Both in England and on the Continent it was felt that the difference between the earlier and the later spirit of our policy was summed up in the contrast between Canning and Castlereagh. It has become an article of historical faith that Castlereagh's melancholy death brought one period of our foreign policy to a close and inaugurated another: it has been said that Canning liberated England from its Continental connexions; it has even been claimed for him that he performed for Europe no less a task than the dissolution of the Holy Alliance.* The figure of Canning is indeed one that will for ever fill a great space

The policy of Canning.

* Stapleton, Life of Canning, i. 134. Martineau, p. 144.

in European history; and the more that is known of the opposition which he encountered both from his sovereign and from his great rival Wellington, the greater must be our admiration for his clear, strong mind, and for the conquering force of his character. But the legend which represents English policy as taking an absolutely new departure in 1822 does not correspond to the truth of history. Canning was a member of the Cabinet from 1816 to 1820; it is a poor compliment to him to suppose that he either exercised no influence upon his colleagues or acquiesced in a policy of which he disapproved; and the history of the Congress of Aix-la-Chapelle proves that his counsels had even at that time gained the ascendant. The admission made by Castlereagh in 1820, after Canning had left the Cabinet, that Austria, as a neighbouring and endangered State, had a right to suppress the revolutionary constitution of Naples, would probably not have gained Canning's assent; in all other points, the action of our Government at Troppau and Laibach might have been his own. Canning loved to speak of his system as one of neutrality, and of non-interference in that struggle between the principles of despotism and of democracy which seemed to be spreading over Europe. He avowed his sympathy for Spain as the object of an unjust and unprovoked war, but he most solemnly warned the Spaniards not to expect English assistance. He prayed that the Constitution of Portugal might prosper, but he expressly disclaimed all connection with its origin, and defended Portugal not because it was a Constitutional State, but because England was bound by treaties to defend it against foreign invasion. The arguments against intervention on behalf of Spain which Canning addressed to the English sympathisers with that country might have been uttered by Castlereagh; the denial of the right of foreign Powers to attack the Spanish Constitution, with which Castlereagh headed his own instructions for Verona, might have been written by Canning.

The statements that Canning withdrew England from the Continental system, and that he dissolved the Holy Alliance, cannot be accepted without large correction. *Canning and the European concert.* The general relations existing between the Great Powers were based, not on the ridiculous and obsolete treaty of Holy Alliance, but on the Acts which were signed at the Conference of Aix-la-Chapelle. The first of these was the secret Quadruple Treaty which bound England and the three Eastern Powers to attack France in case a revolution in that country should endanger the peace of Europe; the second was the general declaration of all the five Powers that they would act in amity and take counsel with one another. From the first of these alliances Canning certainly did not withdraw England. He would perhaps have done so in 1823 if the Quadruple Treaty had bound England to maintain the House of Bourbon on the French throne; but it had been expressly stated that the deposition of the Bourbons would not necessarily and in itself be considered by England as endangering the peace of Europe. This treaty remained in full force up to Canning's death; and if a revolutionary army had marched from Paris upon Antwerp, he would certainly have claimed the assistance of the three Eastern Powers. With respect to the general concert of Europe, established or confirmed by the declaration of Aix-la-Chapelle, this had always been one of varying extent and solidity. Both France and England had held themselves aloof at Troppau. The federative action was strongest and most mischievous not before but after the death of Castlereagh, and in the period that followed the Congress of Verona; for though the war against Spain was conducted by France alone, the three Eastern Powers had virtually made themselves responsible for the success of the enterprise, and it was the influence of their ambassadors at Paris and Madrid which prevented any restrictions from being imposed upon Ferdinand's restored sovereignty.

Canning is invested with a spurious glory when it is said that his action in Spain and in Portugal broke up the league of the Continental Courts. Canning indeed shaped the policy of our own country with equal independence and wisdom, but the political centre of Europe was at this time not London but Vienna. The keystone of the European fabric was the union of Austria and Russia, and this union was endangered, not by anything that could take place in the Spanish Peninsula, but by the conflicting interests of these two great States in regard to the Ottoman Empire. From the moment when the Treaty of Paris was signed, every Austrian politician fixed his gaze upon the roads leading to the Lower Danube, and anxiously noted the signs of coming war, or of continued peace, between Russia and the Porte.* It was the triumph of Metternich to have diverted the Czar's thoughts during the succeeding years from his grievances against Turkey, and to have baffled the Russian diplomatists and generals who, like Capodistrias, sought to spur on their master to enterprises of Eastern conquest. At the Congress of Verona the shifting and incoherent manœuvres of Austrian statecraft can indeed only be understood on the supposition that Metternich was thinking all the time less of Spain than of Turkey, and struggling at whatever cost to maintain that personal influence over Alexander which had hitherto prevented the outbreak of war in the East. But the antagonism so long suppressed broke out at last. The progress of the Greek insurrection brought Austria and Russia not indeed into war, but into the most embittered hostility with one another. It was on this rock that the ungainly craft which men called the Holy Alliance at length struck and went to pieces. Canning played his part well in the question of the East, but he did not create this question. There were forces at work which, without his intervention, would probably have made an end of the despotic amities of 1815. It is not necessary to the title of a great statesman that he should have called into being the elements which make a new political order possible; it is sufficient praise that he should have known how to turn them to account.

* Gentz, Nachlasse (Osten), ii. 103.

CHAPTER IV.

Condition of Greece: its Races and Institutions—The Greek Church—Communal System—The Ægean Islands—The Phanariots—Greek Intellectual Revival: Koraes—Beginning of Greek National Movement; Contact of Greece with the French Revolution and Napoleon—The Hetæria Philike—Hypsilanti's Attempt in the Danubian Provinces: its Failure—Revolt of the Morea: Massacres: Execution of Gregorius, and Terrorism at Constantinople—Attitude of Russia, Austria, and England—Extension of the Revolt: Affairs at Hydra—The Greek Leaders—Fall of Tripolitza—The Massacre of Chios—Failure of the Turks in the Campaign of 1822—Dissensions of the Greeks—Mahmud calls upon Mohomet Ali for Aid—Ibrahim conquers Crete and invades the Morea—Siege of Mesolonghi—Philhellenism in Europe—Russian Proposal for Intervention—Conspiracies in Russia: Death of Alexander: Accession of Nicholas—Military Insurrection at St. Petersburg—Anglo-Russian Protocol—Treaty between England, Russia, and France—Death of Canning—Navarino War between Russia and Turkey—Campaigns of 1828 and 1829—Treaty of Adrianople—Capodistrias President of Greece—Leopold accepts and then declines the Greek Crown—Murder of Capodistrias—Otho, King of Greece.

OF the Christian races which at the beginning of the third decade of this century peopled the European provinces of the Ottoman Empire, the Greek was that which had been least visibly affected by the political and military events of the Napoleonic age. Servia, after a long struggle, had in the year 1817 gained local autonomy under its own princes, although Turkish troops still garrisoned its fortresses, and the sovereignty of the Sultan was acknowledged by the payment of tribute. The Romanic districts, Wallachia and Moldavia, which, in the famous interview of Tilsit, Napoleon had bidden the Czar to make his own, were restored by Russia to the Porte in

Greece in the Napoleonic age.

the Treaty of Bucharest in 1812, but under conditions which virtually established a Russian protectorate. Greece, with the exception of the Ionian Islands, had neither been the scene of any military operations, nor formed the subject of any treaty. Yet the age of the French Revolution and of the Napoleonic wars had silently wrought in the Greek nation the last of a great series of changes which fitted it to take its place among the free peoples of Europe. The signs were there from which those who could read the future might have gathered that the political resurrection of Greece was near at hand. There were some who, with equal insight and patriotism, sought during this period to lay the intellectual foundation for that national independence which they foresaw that their children would win with the sword.

The forward movement of the Greek nation may be said, in general terms, to have become visible during the first half of the eighteenth century. Serfage had then disappeared; the peasant was either a freeholder, or a farmer paying a rent in kind for his land. In the gradual and unobserved emancipation of the labouring class the first condition of national revival had already been fulfilled. The peasantry had been formed which, when the conflict with the Turk broke out, bore the brunt of the long struggle. In comparison with the Prussian serf, the Greek cultivator at the beginning of the eighteenth century was an independent man: in comparison with the English labourer, he was well fed

Greece in the eighteenth century.

and well housed. The evils to which the Greek population was exposed, wherever Greeks and Turks lived together, were those which brutalised or degraded the Christian races in every Ottoman province. There was no redress for injury inflicted by a Mohammedan official or neighbour. If a wealthy Turk murdered a Greek in the fields, burnt down his house, and outraged his family, there was no court where the offender could be brought to justice. The term by which the Turk described his Christian neighbour was "our rayah," that is, "our subject." A Mohammedan landowner might terrorise the entire population around him, carry off the women, flog and imprison the men, and yet feel that he had committed no offence against the law; for no law existed but the Koran, and no Turkish court of justice but that of the Kadi, where the complaint of the Christian passed for nothing.

This was the monstrous relation that existed between the dominant and the subject nationalities, not in Greece only, but in every part of the Ottoman Empire where Mohammedans and Christians inhabited the same districts. The second great and general evil was the extortion practised by the tax-gatherers, and this fell upon the poorer Mohammedans equally with the Christians, except in regard to the poll-tax, or haratsch, the badge of servitude, which was levied on Christians alone. All land payed tithe to the State; and until the tax-gatherer had paid his visit it was not permitted to the peasant to cut the ripe crop. This rule enabled the tax-gatherer, whether a Mohammedan or Christian, to inflict ruin upon those who did not bribe himself or his masters; for by merely postponing his visit he could destroy the value of the harvest. Round this central institution of tyranny and waste, there gathered, except in the districts protected by municipal privileges, every form of corruption natural to a society where the State heard no appeals, and made no inquiry into the processes employed by those to whom it sold the taxes. What was possible in the way of extortion was best seen in the phenomenon of well-built villages being left tenantless, and the population of rich districts dying out in a time of peace, without pestilence, without insurrection, without any greater wrong on the part of the Sultan's government than that normal indifference which permitted the existence of a community to depend upon the moderation or the caprice of the individual possessors of force.

Such was the framework, or, as it may be said, the common-law of the mixed Turkish and Christian society of the Ottoman Empire. On this background we have now to trace the social and political features which stood out in Greek life, which preserved the race from losing its separate nationality, and which made the ultimate recovery of its independence possible. In the first outburst of sympathy and delight with which

<small>Origin of modern Greece Byzantine, not classic.</small> every generous heart in western Europe hailed the standard of Hellenic freedom upraised in 1821, the twenty centuries which separated the Greece of literature from the Greece of to-day were strangely forgotten. The imagination went

straight back to Socrates and Leonidas, and pictured in the islander or the hillsman who rose against Mahmud II. the counterpart of those glorious beings who gave to Europe the ideals of intellectual energy, of plastic beauty, and of poetic truth. The illusion was a happy one, if it excited on behalf of a brave people an interest which Servia or Montenegro might have failed to gain; but it led to a re-action when disappointments came; it gave inordinate importance to the question of the physical descent of the Greeks; and it produced a false impression of the causes which had led up to the war of independence, and of the qualities, the habits, the bonds of union, which exercised the greatest power over the nation. These were, to a great extent, unlike anything existing in the ancient world; they had originated in Byzantine, not in classic Greece;. and where the scenes of old Hellenic history appeared to be repeating themselves, it was due more to the continuing influence of the same seas and the same mountains than to the survival of any political fragments of the past. The Greek population had received a strong Slavonic infusion many centuries before. More recently, Albanian settlers had expelled the inhabitants from certain districts both in the mainland and in the Morea. Attica, Bœotia, Corinth, and Argolis were at the outbreak of the war of independence peopled in the main by a race of Albanian descent, who still used, along with some Greek, the Albanian language.*

_{Slavonic and Albanian elements.}

* About the year 1830 the theory was started by Fallmerayer, a Tyrolese writer, that the modern Greeks were the descendants of Slavonic

The sense of a separate nationality was, however, weak among these settlers, who, unlike some small Albanian communities in the west of the Morea, were Christians, not Mohammedans. Neighbourhood, commerce, identity of religion and similarity of local institutions were turning these Albanians into Greeks; and no community of pure Hellenic descent played a greater part in the national war, or exhibited more of the maritime energy and daring which we associate peculiarly with the Hellenic name, than the islanders of Hydra and Spetza, who had crossed from the Albanian parts of the Morea and taken possession of these desert rocks not a hundred years before. The same phenomenon of an assimilation of Greeks and Albanians was seen in southern Epirus, the border-ground between the two races. The Suliotes, Albanian mountaineers, whose military exploits form one of the most extraordinary chapters in history, showed signs of Greek influences before the Greek war of independence began, and in this war they made no distinction between the Greek cause and their own. Even the rule of the ferocious Ali Pasha at Janina had been favourable to the extension of Greek civilisation in Epirus. Under this Mohammedan tyrant Janina contained more schools than

invaders, with scarcely a drop of Greek blood in their veins. Fallmerayer was believed by some good scholars to have proved that the old Greek race had utterly perished. More recent inquiries have discredited both Fallmerayer and his authorities, and tend to establish the conclusion that, except in certain limited districts, the Greeks left were always numerous enough to absorb the foreign incomers. (Hopf, Griechenland; in Ersch and Gruber's Encyklopädie, vol. 85, p. 100.) The Albanian population of Greece in 1820 is reckoned at about one-sixth.

Athens. The Greek population of the district increased; and in the sense of a common religious antagonism to the Mohammedan, the Greek and the Albanian Christians in Epirus forgot their difference of race.

The central element in modern Greek life was the religious profession of the Orthodox Eastern Church. Where, as in parts of Crete, the Greek adopted Mohammedanism, all the other elements of his nationality together did not prevent him from amalgamating with the Turk. The sound and popular forces of the Church belonged to the lower clergy, who, unlike the priests of the Roman Church, were married and shared the life of the people. If ignorant and bigoted, they were nevertheless the real guardians of national spirit; and if their creed was a superstition rather than a religion, it at least kept the Greeks in a wholesome antagonism to the superstition of their masters. The higher clergy stood in many respects in a different position. The Patriarch of Constantinople was a great officer of the Porte. His dignities and his civil jurisdiction had been restored and even enlarged by the Mohammedan conquerors of the Greek Empire, with the express object of employing the Church as a means of securing obedience to themselves: and it was quite in keeping with the history of this great office that, when the Greek national insurrection at last broke out, the Patriarch Gregorius IV. should have consented, though unwillingly, to launch the curse of the Church against it. The Patriarch gained his office by purchase, or through intrigues at the Divan; he paid an enormous annual backsheesh for it; and he was liable to be murdered or deposed as soon as his Mussulman patrons lost favour with the Sultan, or a higher bid was made for his office by a rival ecclesiastic. To satisfy the claims of the Palace the Patriarch was compelled to be an extortioner himself. The bishoprics in their turn were sold in his ante-chambers, and the Bishops made up the purchase-money by fleecing their clergy. But in spite of a deserved reputation for venality, the Bishops in Greece exercised very great influence, both as ecclesiastics and as civil magistrates. Whether their jurisdiction in lawsuits between Christians arose from the custom of referring disputes to their arbitration or was expressly granted to them by the Sultan, they virtually displaced in all Greek communities the court of the Kadi, and afforded the merchant or the farmer a tribunal where his own law was administered in his own language. Even a Mohammedan in dispute with a Christian would sometimes consent to bring the matter before the Bishops' Court rather than enforce his right to obtain the dilatory and capricious decision of an Ottoman judge.

The Bishops, civil magistrates.

The condition of the Greeks living in the country that now forms the Hellenic Kingdom and in the Ægæan Islands exhibited strong local contrasts. It was, however, common to all that, while the Turk held the powers of State in his hand, the details of local administration in each district were left to the inhabitants, the Turk caring nothing about these matters so long as the due amount of taxes was paid and the due supply of sailors provided. The apportionment of taxes among households and villages seems to have been the germ of self-government from which several types of municipal organisation, some of them of great importance in the history of the Greek nation, developed. In the Paschalik of the Morea the taxes were usually farmed by the Voivodes, or Beys, the Turkish governors of the twenty-three provinces into which the Morea was divided. But in each village or township the inhabitants elected officers called Proestoi, who, besides collecting the taxes and managing the affairs of their own communities, met in a district-assembly, and there determined what share of the district-taxation each community should bear. One Greek officer, called Primate, and one Mohammedan, called Ayan, were elected to represent the district, and to take part in the council of the Pasha of the Morea, who resided at Tripolitza.* The Primates exercised considerable power. Created originally by the Porte to expedite the collection of the revenue, they became a Greek aristocracy. They were indeed an aristocracy of no very noble kind. Agents of a tyrannical master, they shared the vices of the tyrant and of the slave. Often farmers of the taxes themselves, obsequious and intriguing in the palace of the Pasha at Tripolitza, grasping and despotic in their native districts, they were described as a species of Christian Turk. But whatever their vices, they saved

Communal organisation.

The Morea.

---

* Maurer, Das Griechische Volk, i. 64.

the Greeks from being left without leaders. They formed a class accustomed to act in common, conversant with details of administration, and especially with the machinery for collecting and distributing supplies. It was this financial experience of the Primates of the Morea which gave to the rebellion of the Greeks what little unity of organisation it exhibited in its earliest stage.

On the north of the Gulf of Corinth the features of the communal system were less distinct than in the Morea. There was, however, in the mountain-country of Ætolia and Pindus a rough military organisation which had done great service to Greece in keeping alive the national spirit and habits of personal independence. The Turks had found a local militia established in this wild region at the time of their conquest, and had not interfered with it for some centuries. The Armatoli, or native soldiery, recruited from peasants, shepherds, and muleteers, kept Mohammedan influences at a distance, until, in the eighteenth century, the Sultans made it a fixed rule of policy to diminish their numbers and to reduce the power of their captains. Before 1820 the Armatoli had become comparatively few and weak; but as they declined, bands of Klephts, or brigands, grew in importance; and the mountaineer who was no longer allowed to practice arms as a guardian of order, enlisted himself among the robbers. Like the freebooters of our own northern border, these brigands became the heroes of song. Though they

Northern Greece. The Armatoli and Klephts.

plundered the Greek as well as the Mohammedan, the national spirit approved their exploits. It was, no doubt, something, that the physical energy of the marauder and the habit of encountering danger should not be wholly on the side of the Turk and the Albanian. But the influence of the Klephts in sustaining Greek nationality has been overrated. They had but recently become numerous, and the earlier organisation of the northern Armatoli was that to which the sound and vigorous character of the Greek peasantry in these regions, the finest part of the Greek race on the mainland, was really due.*

In the islands of the Ægæan the condition of the Greeks was on the whole happy and prosperous. Some of these islands had no Turkish population; in others the caprice of a Sultana, the goodwill of the Capitan Pasha who governed the Archipelago, or the judicious offer of a sum of money when money was wanted by the Porte, had so lightened the burden of Ottoman sovereignty, that the Greek island-community possessed more liberty than was to be found in any part of Europe, except

The Ægæan Islands.

* The Greek songs illustrate the conversion of the Armatole into the Klepht in the age preceding the Greek revolution. Thus, in the fine ballad called, "The Tomb of Demos," which Goethe has translated, the dying man says—

καὶ φέρτε τὸν πνευματικὸν νὰ μ' ἐξομολογήσῃ
νὰ τὸν εἰπῶ τὰ κρίματα ὅσα 'χω καμωμένα
τριάντα χρόνι' ἁρματωλὸς,. κ' εἴκοσι ἔχω κλέφτης.

"Bring the priest that he may shrive me; that I may tell him the sins that I have committed, thirty years an Armatole and twenty years a Klepht."—Fauriel, Chants Populaires, i. 56.

Switzerland. The taxes payable to the central government, including the haratsch or poll-tax levied on all Christians, had often been commuted for a fixed sum, which was raised without the interposition of the Turkish tax-gatherer. In Hydra, Spetza, and Psara, the so-called nautical islands, the supremacy of the Turk was felt only in the obligation to furnish sailors to the Ottoman navy, and in the payment of a tribute of about £100 per annum. The government of these three islands was entirely in the hands of the inhabitants. In Chios, though a considerable Mussulman population existed by the side of the Greek, there was every sign of peace and prosperity. Each island bore its own peculiar social character, and had its municipal institutions of more or less value. The Hydriote was quarrelsome, turbulent, quick to use the knife, but outspoken, honest in dealing, and an excellent sailor. The picture of Chian life, as drawn even by those who have judged the Greeks most severely, is one of singular beauty and interest; the picture of a self-governing society in which the family trained the citizen in its own bosom, and in which, while commerce enriched all, the industry of the poor within their homes and in their gardens was refined by the practice of an art. The skill which gave its value to the embroidery and to the dyes of Chios was exercised by those who also worked the hand-loom and cultivated the mastic and the rose. The taste and the labour of man requited nature's gifts of sky, soil, and sea;

Chios.

and in the pursuit of occupations which stimulated, not deadened, the faculties of the worker, idleness and intemperance were alike unknown.* How bright a scene of industry, when compared with the grime and squalor of the English factory-town, where the human and the inanimate machine grind out their yearly mountains of iron-ware and calico, in order that the employer may vie with his neighbours in soulless ostentation, and the workman consume his millions upon millions in drink.

The territory where the Greeks formed the great majority of the population included beyond the boundaries of the present Hellenic Kingdom the islands adjacent to the coast of Asia Minor, Crete, and the Chalcidic peninsula in Macedonia. But the activity of the race was not confined within these limits. If the Greek was a subject in his own country, he was master in the lands of some of his neighbours. A Greek might exercise power over other Christian subjects of the Porte either as an ecclesiastic, or as the delegate of the Sultan in certain fixed branches of the administration. The authority of the Patriarch of Constantinople was recognised over the whole of the European provinces of Turkey, except Servia. The Bishops in all these provinces were Greeks; the services of the Church were conducted in the Greek tongue; the revenues of the greater part of the Church-lands, and the fees of all the ecclesiastical courts, went into

<small>The Greeks have ecclesiastical power in other Turkish provinces.</small>

* Finlay, Greece under Ottoman Domination, p. 284.

Greek pockets. In things religious, and in that wide range of civil affairs which in communities belonging to the Eastern Church appertains to the higher religious office, the Greeks had in fact regained the ascendancy which they had possessed under the Byzantine Empire. The dream of the Churchman was not the creation of an independent kingdom of Greece, but the restoration of the Eastern Empire under Greek supremacy. When it was seen that the Slav and the Rouman came to the Greek for law, for commercial training, for religious teaching, and looked to the Patriarch of Constantinople as the ultimate judge of all disputes, it was natural that the belief should arise that, when the Turk passed away, the Greek would step into his place. But the influence of the Greeks, great as it appeared to be, did not in reality reach below the surface, except in Epirus. The bishops were felt to be foreigners and extortioners. There was no real process of assimilation at work, either in Bulgaria or in the Danubian Provinces. The slow and plodding Bulgarian peasant, too stupid for the Greek to think of him as a rival, preserved his own unchanging tastes and nationality, sang to his children the songs which he had learnt from his parents, and forgot the Greek which he had heard in the Church when he re-entered his home.*
In Roumania, the only feeling towards the Greek intruder was one of intense hatred.

Four great offices of the Ottoman Empire were

* Kanitz, Donau-Bulgarien, i. 123.

always held by Greeks. These were the offices of Dragoman,* or Secretary, of the Porte, Dragoman of the Fleet, and the governorships, called Hospodariates, of Wallachia and Moldavia. The varied business of the Patriarchate of Constantinople, the administration of its revenues, the conduct of its law-courts, had drawn a multitude of pushing and well-educated Greeks to the quarter of Constantinople called the Phanar, in which the palace of the Patriarch is situated. Merchants and professional men inhabited the same district. These Greeks of the capital, the so-called Phanariots, gradually made their way into the Ottoman administration as Turkish energy declined, and the conquering race found that it could no longer dispense with the weapons of calculation and diplomacy. The Treaty of Carlowitz, made in 1699, after the unsuccessful war in which the Turks laid siege to Vienna, was negotiated on behalf of the Porte by Alexander Maurokordatos, a Chian by birth, who had become physician to the Sultan and was virtually the Foreign Minister of Turkey. His sons, Nicholas and Constantine, were made Hospodars of Wallachia and Moldavia early in the eighteenth century; and from this time forward, until the outbreak of the Greek insurrection, the governorships of the Roumanian provinces were entrusted to Phanariot families.

sidenote: The Phanariot officials of the Porte.

sidenote: Greek Hospodars.

---

* Literally, *Interpreter*; the old theory of the Turks being that in their dealings with foreign nations they had only to receive petitions, which required to be translated into Turkish.

The result was that a troop of Greek adventurers passed to the north of the Danube, and seized upon every office of profit in these unfortunate lands. There were indeed individuals among the Hospodars, especially among the Maurokordati, who rendered good service to their Roumanian subjects; but on the whole the Phanariot rule was grasping, dishonest, and cruel.* Its importance in relation to Greece was not that it Hellenised the Danubian countries, for that it signally failed to do; but that it raised the standard of Greek education, and enlarged the range of Greek thought, by opening a political and administrative career to ambitious men. The connection of the Phanariots with education was indeed an exceedingly close one. Alexander Maurokordatos was the ardent and generous founder of schools for the instruction of his countrymen in Constantinople as well as in other cities, and for the improvement of the existing language of Greece. His example was freely followed throughout the eighteenth century. It is, indeed, one of the best features in the Greek character that the owner of wealth has so often been, and still so often is, the promoter of the culture of his race. As in Germany in the last century, and in Hungary and Bohemia at a more recent date, the national revival of Greece was preceded by a striking revival of interest in the national language.

The knowledge of ancient Greek was never wholly lost among the priesthood, but it had become useless.

* Zallones, Πραγματεια περι των Φαναριωτων, p. 71. *Kognalitchan, La Walachie,* i. 371.

Nothing was read but the ecclesiastic commonplace of a pedantic age; and in the schools kept by the clergy before the eighteenth century the ancient language was taught only as a means of imparting divinity. The educational movement promoted by men like Maurokordatos had a double end; it revived the knowledge of the great age of Greece through its literature, and it taught the Greek to regard the speech which he actually used not as a mere barbarous patois which each district had made for itself, but as a language different indeed from that of the ancient world, yet governed by its own laws, and capable of performing the same functions as any other modern tongue. It was now that the Greek learnt to call himself Hellen, the name of his forefathers, instead of Romaios, a Roman. As the new schools grew up and the old ones were renovated or transformed, education ceased to be merely literary. In the second half of the eighteenth century science returned in an humble form to the land that had given it birth; and the range of instruction was widened by men who had studied law, physics, and moral philosophy at foreign universities. Something of the liberal spirit of the inquirers of Western Europe arose among the best Greek teachers. Though no attack was made upon the doctrines of the Church, and no direct attack was made upon the authority of the Sultan, the duty of religious toleration was proclaimed in a land where bigotry had hitherto reigned supreme, and the political freedom of ancient Greece was held up as a glorious ideal to a less happy age. Some of the higher clergy and of the Phanariot instruments of Turkish rule took fright at the independent spirit of the new learning, and for a while it seemed as if the intellectual as well as the political progress of Greece might be endangered by ecclesiastical ill-will. But the attachment of the Greek people to the Church was so strong and so universal that, although satire might be directed against the Bishops, a breach with the Church formed no part of the design of any patriot. The antagonism between episcopal and national feeling, strongest about the end of the eighteenth century, declined during succeeding years, and had almost disappeared before the outbreak of the war of liberation.

The greatest scholar of modern Greece was also one of its greatest patriots. Koraes, known as the legislator of the Greek language, was born in 1748, of Chian parents settled at Smyrna. The love of learning, combined with an extreme independence of character, made residence insupportable to him in a land where the Turk was always within sight, and where few opportunities existed for gaining wide knowledge. His parents permitted him to spend some years at Amsterdam, where a branch of their business was established. Recalled to Smyrna at the age of thirty, Koraes almost abandoned human society. The hand of a beautiful heiress could not tempt him from the austere and solitary life of the scholar; and quitting his home, he passed through

<small>Koraes, 1748—1833.</small>

the medical school of Montpellier, and settled at Paris. He was here when the French Revolution began. The inspiration of that time gave to his vast learning and inborn energy a directly patriotic aim. For forty years Koraes pursued the work of serving Greece by the means open to the scholar. The political writings in which he addressed the Greeks themselves or appealed to foreigners in favour of Greece, admirable as they are, do not form the basis of his fame. The peculiar task of Koraes was to give to the reviving Greek nation the national literature and the form of expression which every civilised people reckons among its most cherished bonds of unity. Master, down to the minutest details, of the entire range of Greek writings, and of the history of the Greek language from classical times down to our own century, Koraes was able to select the Hellenic authors, Christian as well as Pagan, whose works were best suited for his countrymen in their actual condition, and to illustrate them as no one could who had not himself been born and bred among Greeks. This was one side of Koraes' literary task. The other was to direct the language of the future Hellenic kingdom into its true course. Classical writing was still understood by the educated in Greece, but the spoken language of the people was something widely different. Turkish and Albanian influences had barbarised the vocabulary; centuries of ignorance had given play to every natural irregularity of local dialect. When the restoration of Greek independence came within

The language of modern Greece.

view, there were some who proposed to revive artificially each form used in the ancient language, and thus, without any real blending, to add the old to the new: others, seeing this to be impossible, desired that the common idiom, corrupt as it was, should be accepted as a literary language. Koraes chose the middle and the rational path. Taking the best written Greek of the day as his material, he recommended that the forms of classical Greek, where they were not wholly obsolete, should be fixed in the grammar of the language. While ridiculing the attempt to restore modes of expression which, even in the written language, had wholly passed out of use, he proposed to expunge all words that were in fact not Greek at all, but foreign, and to replace them by terms formed according to the natural laws of the language. The Greek, therefore, which Koraes desired to see his countrymen recognise as their language, and which he himself used in his writings, was the written Greek of the most cultivated persons of his time, purged of its foreign elements, and methodised by a constant reference to a classical model, which, however, it was not to imitate pedantically. The correctness of this theory has been proved by its complete success. The patois which, if it had been recognised as the language of the Greek kingdom, would now have made Herodotus and Plato foreign authors in Athens, is indeed still preserved in familiar conversation, but it is little used in writing and not taught in schools. A language year by year more closely approximating in its forms to that of classical

Greece unites the Greeks both with their past and among themselves, and serves as the instrument of a widening Hellenic civilization in the Eastern Mediterranean. The political object of Koraes has been completely attained: no people in Europe is now prouder of its native tongue, or turns it to better account in education, than his countrymen. In literature, the renovated language has still its work before it. The lyric poetry that has been written in Greece since the time of Koraes is not wanting, if a foreigner may express an opinion, in tenderness and grace. The writer who shall ennoble Greek prose with the energy and directness of the ancient style has yet to arise.*

The intellectual advance of the Greeks in the eighteenth century was closely connected with the development of their commerce, and this in its turn was connected with events in the greater cycle of European history. A period of comparative peace and order in the Levantine waters, following the final expulsion of

<small>Development of Greek commerce. 1750—1820.</small>

---

* A French translation of the Autobiography of Koraes, along with his portrait, will be found in the Lettres Inédites de Coray, Paris, 1877. The vehicle of expression usually chosen by Koraes for addressing his countrymen was the Preface (written in modern Greek) to the edition of an ancient author. The second half of the Preface to the Politics of Aristotle, 1822, is a good specimen of his political spirit and manner. It was separately edited by the Swiss scholar, Orelli, with a translation, for the benefit of the German Philhellenes. Among the principal linguistic prefaces are those to Heliodorus, 1804, and the Prodromos, or introduction, to the series of editions called Bibliotheca Græca, begun in 1805, and published at the expense of the brothers Zosimas of Odessa. Most of the editions published by Koraes bear on their title-page a statement of the patriotic purpose of the work, and indicate the persons who

the Venetians from the Morea in 1718, gave play to the natural aptitude of the Greek islanders for coasting-trade. Their ships, still small and unfit to venture on long voyages, plied between the harbours in the Ægæan and in the Black Sea, and brought profit to their owners in spite of the imposition of burdens from which not only many of the Mussulman subjects of the Sultan, but foreign nations protected by commercial treaties, were free. It was at this epoch, after Venice had lost its commercial supremacy in the Eastern Mediterranean, that Russia began to exercise a direct influence upon the fortunes of Greece. The Empress Catherine had formed the design of conquering Constantinople, and intended, under the title of Protectress of the Christian Church, to use the Greeks as her allies. In the war which broke out between Russia and Turkey in 1768, a Russian expeditionary force landed in the Morea, and the

bore the expense. The edition of the Ethics, published immediately after the massacre of Chios, bears the affecting words: "At the expense of those who have so cruelly suffered in Chios." The costly form of these editions, some of which contain fine engravings, seems somewhat inappropriate for works intended for national instruction. Koraes, however, was not in a hurry. He thought, at least towards the close of his life, that the Greeks ought to have gone through thirty years more of commercial and intellectual development before they drew the sword. They would in that case, he believed, have crushed Turkey by themselves, and have prevented the Greek kingdom from becoming the sport of European diplomacy. Much miscellaneous information on Greek affairs before 1820 (rather from the Phanariot point of view) will be found, combined with literary history, in the Cours de Littérature Grecque of Rhizos Néroulos, 1827. The more recent treatise of R. Rhaukabes on the same subject (also in French, Paris, 1877) exhibits what appears to be characteristic of the modern Greeks, the inability to distinguish between mere passable performances and really great work.

Greeks were persuaded to take up arms. The Moreotes themselves paid dearly for the trust which they had placed in the orthodox Empress. They were virtually abandoned to the vengeance of their oppressors; but to Greece at large the conditions on which peace was made proved of immense benefit. The Treaty of Kainardji, signed in 1774, gave Russia the express right to make representations at Constantinople on behalf of the Christian inhabitants of the Danubian provinces; it also bound the Sultan to observe certain conditions in his treatment of the Greek islanders. Out of these clauses, Russian diplomacy constructed a general right of interference on behalf of any Christian subjects of the Porte. The Treaty also opened the Black Sea to Russian ships of commerce, and conferred upon Russia the commercial privileges of the most favoured nation.* The result of this compact was a very remarkable one. The Russian Government permitted hundreds of Greek shipowners to hoist its own flag, and so changed the footing of Greek merchantmen in every port of the Ottoman Empire. The burdens which had placed the Greek trader at a disadvantage, when compared with the Mohammedan, vanished. A host of Russian consular agents, often Greeks themselves, was scattered over the Levant. Eager for opportunities of attaching the Greeks to their Russian patrons, quick to make their newly-won power felt by the Turks, these men extracted a definite meaning from the clauses of the

Treaty of Kainardji, 1774.

* Zinkeisen, Geschichte des Osmanischen Reiches, v. 959.

Treaty of Kainardji, by which the Porte had bound itself to observe the rights of its Christian subjects. The sense of security in the course of their business, no less than the emancipation from commercial fetters, gave an immense impulse to Greek traders. Their ships were enlarged; voyages, hitherto limited to the Levant, were extended to England and even to America; and a considerable armament of cannon was placed on board each ship for defence against the attack of Algerian pirates.

Before the end of the eighteenth century another war between Turkey and Russia, resulting in the cession of the district of Oczakoff on the northern shore of the Black Sea, made the Greeks both carriers and vendors of the corn-export of Southern Russia. The city of Odessa was founded on the ceded territory.

Foundation of Odessa, 1792.

The merchants who raised it to its sudden prosperity were not Russians but Greeks; and in the course of a single generation many a Greek trading-house, which had hitherto deemed the sum of £3,000 to be a large capital, rose to an opulence little behind that of the great London firms. Profiting by the neutrality of Turkey or its alliance with England during a great part of the revolutionary war, the Greeks succeeded to much of the Mediterranean trade that was lost by France and its dependencies. The increasing intelligence of the people was shown in the fact that foreigners were no longer employed by Greek merchants as their travelling agents in distant countries; there were countrymen enough of their own who could negotiate with an Englishman or a Dane in his own language. The richest Greeks were no doubt those of Odessa and Salonica, not of Hellas proper; but even the little islands of Hydra and Spetza, the refuge of the Moreotes whom Catherine had forsaken in 1770, now became communities of no small wealth and spirit. Psara, which was purely Greek, formed with these Albanian colonies the nucleus of an Ægæan naval Power. The Ottoman Government, cowed by its recent defeats, and perhaps glad to see the means of increasing its resources, made no attempt to check the growth of the Hellenic armed marine. Under the very eyes of the Sultan, the Hydriote and Psarian captains, men as venturesome as the sea-kings of ancient Greece, accumulated the artillery which was hereafter to hold its own against many an Ottoman man-of-war, and to sweep the Turkish merchantmen from the Ægæan. Eighteen years before the Greek insurrection broke out, Koraes, calling the attention of Western Europe to the progress made by his country, wrote the following significant words:—" If the Ottoman Government could have foreseen that the Greeks would create a merchant-navy, composed of several hundred vessels, most of them regularly armed, it would have crushed the movement at its commencement. It is impossible to calculate the effects which may result from the creation of this marine, or the influence which it may exert both upon the destiny of the oppressed nation and upon that of its oppressors." *

* Koraes, Mémoire sur l'état actuel de la civilization de la Grèce: republished in the Lettres Inédites, p. 464. This memoir, read by

Like its classic sisterland in the Mediterranean, Greece was stirred by the far-sounding voices of the French Revolution. The Declaration of the Rights of Man, the revival of a supposed antique Republicanism, the victories of Hoche and Bonaparte, successively kindled the enthusiasm of a race already restless under the Turkish yoke. France drew to itself some of the hopes that had hitherto been fixed entirely upon Russia. Images and ideas of classic freedom invaded the domain where the Church had hitherto been all in all; the very sailors began to call their boats by the names of Spartan and Athenian heroes, as well as by those of saints and martyrs. In 1797 Venice fell, and Bonaparte seized its Greek possessions, the Ionian Islands. There was something of the forms of liberation in the establishment of French rule; the inhabitants of Zante were at least permitted to make a bonfire of the stately wigs worn by their Venetian masters. Great changes seemed to be near at hand. It was not yet understood that France fought for empire, not for justice; and the man who, above all others, represented the early spirit of the revolution among the Greeks, the poet Rhegas, looked to Bonaparte to give the signal for the rising of the whole of the Christian populations subject to Mohammedan rule. Rhegas, if he was not a wise politician, was a thoroughly brave man, and he was able to serve his country as a martyr. While engaged in Austria in

Marginal note: Influence of the French Revolution on Greece.

Koraes to a learned society in Paris, in January, 1803, is one of the most luminous and interesting historical sketches ever penned.

conspiracies against the Sultan's Government, and probably in intrigues with Bernadotte, French ambassador at Vienna, he was arrested by the agents of Thugut, and handed over to the Turks. He was put to death at Belgrade, with five of his companions, in May, 1798. The songs of Rhegas soon passed through every household in Greece. They were a precious treasure to his countrymen, and they have immortalised his name as a patriot. But the work which he had begun languished for a time after his death. The series of events which followed Bonaparte's invasion of Egypt extinguished the hope of the liberation of Greece by the French Republic. Among the higher Greek clergy the alliance with the godless followers of Voltaire was seen with no favourable eye. The Porte was even able to find a Christian Patriarch to set his name to a pastoral, warning the faithful against the sin of rebellion, and reminding them that, while Satan was creating the Lutherans and Calvinists, the infinite mercy of God had raised up the Ottoman Power in order that the Orthodox Church might be preserved pure from the heresies of the West.*

Death of Rhegas, 1798.

From the year 1798 down to the Peace of Paris, Greece was more affected by the vicissitudes of the

---

*. Διδασκαλία Πατρική, by, or professing to be by, Anthimos, Patriarch of Jerusalem, and printed "at the expense of the Holy Sepulchre," p. 13. This curious work, in which the Patriarch at last breaks out into doggrel, has found its way to the British Museum. It was answered by Koraes. For the effect of Rhegas' songs on the people, see Fauriel, ii. 18. Mr. Finlay seems to be mistaken in calling Anthimos' book an answer to the tract of Eugenios Bulgaris on religious toleration. That was written about thirty years before.

Ionian Islands and by the growth of dominion of Ali Pasha in Albania than by the earlier revolutionary ideas. France was deprived of its spoils by the combined Turkish and Russian fleets in the coalition of 1799, and the Ionian Islands were made into a Republic under the protection of the Czar and the Sultan. It was in the native administration of Corfu that the career of Capodistrias began. At the peace of Tilsit the Czar gave these islands back to Napoleon, and Capodistrias, whose ability had gained general attention, accepted an invitation to enter the Russian service. The islands were then successively beleaguered and conquered by the English, with the exception of Corfu; and after the fall of Napoleon they became a British dependency. Thus the three greatest Powers of Europe were during the first years of this century in constant rivalry on the east of the Adriatic, and a host of Greeks, some fugitives, some adventurers, found employment among their armed forces. The most famous chieftain in the war of liberation, Theodore Kolokotrones, a Klepht of the Morea, was for some years major of a Greek regiment in the pay of England. In the meantime, Ali Pasha, on the neighbouring mainland, neither rested himself nor allowed any of his neighbours to rest. The Suliotes, vanquished after years of heroic defence, migrated in a body to the Ionian Islands in 1804. Every Klepht and Armatole of the Epirote border had fought at some time either for Ali or against him; for in the extension of his violent and crafty rule Ali was a friend to-day and an enemy to-morrow alike to Greek, Turk, and Albanian. When his power was at its height, Ali's court at Janina was as much Greek as it was Mohammedan: soldiers, merchants, professors, all, as it was said, with a longer or a shorter rope round their necks, played their part in the society of the Epirote capital.* Among the officers of Ali's army there were some who were soon to be the military rivals of Kolokotrones in the Greek insurrection: Ali's physician, Dr. Kolettes, was gaining an experience and an influence among these men which afterwards placed him at the head of the Government. For good or for evil, it was felt that the establishment of a virtually independent kingdom of Albania must deeply affect the fate of Greece; and when at length Ali openly defied the Sultan, and Turkish armies closed round his castle at Janina, the conflict between the Porte and its most powerful vassal gave the Greeks the signal to strike for their own independence.

The secret society, which under the name of Hetæria Philike, or association of friends, inaugurated the rebellion of Greece, was founded in 1814, after it had become clear that the Congress of Vienna would take no steps on behalf of the Christian subjects of the Porte. The founders of this society were traders of Odessa, and its earliest members seem to have been drawn more from the Greeks in Russia and in the Danubian provinces than from those of Greece

The Hetæria Philike.

* Leake, Travels in Northern Greece, ch. v., 36, 37.

Proper. The object of the conspiracy was the expulsion of the Turk from Europe, and the re-establishment of a Greek Eastern Empire. It was pretended by the council of directors that the Emperor Alexander had secretly joined them; and the ingenious fiction was circulated that a society for the preservation of Greek antiquities, for which Capodistrias had gained the patronage of the Czar and other eminent men at the Congress of Vienna, was in fact this political association in disguise. The real chiefs of the conspiracy always spoke of themselves as acting under the instructions of a nameless superior power. They were as little troubled by scruple in thus deceiving their followers as they were in planning a general massacre of the Turks, and in murdering their own agents when they wished to have them out of the way. The ultimate design of the Hetæria was an unsound one, and its operations were based upon an imposture; but in exciting the Greeks against Turkish rule, and in inspiring confidence in its own resources and authority, it was completely successful. In the course of six years every Greek of note, both in Greece itself and in the adjacent countries, had joined the association. The Turkish Government had received warnings of the danger which threatened it, but disregarded them until revolt was on the point of breaking out. The very improvement in the condition of the Christians, the absence of any crying oppression or outrage in Greece during late years, probably lulled the anxieties of Sultan Mahmud, who, terrible as he afterwards proved himself, had not hitherto been without sympathy for the Rayah. But the history of France, no less than the history of Greece, shows that it is not the excess, but the sense, of wrong that produces revolution. A people may be so crushed by oppression as to suffer all conceivable misery with patience. It is when the pulse has again begun to beat strong, when the eye is fixed no longer on the ground, and the knowledge of good and evil again burns in the heart, that the right and the duty of resistance is felt.

Early in 1820 the ferment in Greece had become so general that the chiefs of the Hetæria were compelled to seek at St. Petersburg for the Russian leader who had as yet existed only in their imagination. There was no dispute as to the person to whom the task of restoring the Eastern Empire rightfully belonged. Capodistrias, at once a Greek and Foreign Minister of Russia, stood in the front rank of European statesmen; he was known to love the Greek cause; he was believed to possess the strong personal affection of the Emperor Alexander. The deputies of the Hetæria besought him to place himself at its head. Capodistrias, however, knew better than any other man the force of those influences which would dissuade the Czar from assisting Greece. He had himself published a pamphlet in the preceding year recommending his countrymen to take no rash step; and, apart from all personal considerations, he probably believed that he could serve Greece better as Minister of Russia than by connecting himself with any dangerous enterprise. He rejected the offers of the

Capodistrias and Hypsilanti.

Hetærists, who then turned to a soldier of some distinction in the Russian army, Prince Alexander Hypsilanti, a Greek exile, whose grandfather, after governing Wallachia as Hospodar, had been put to death by the Turks for complicity with the designs of Rhegas. It is said that Capodistrias encouraged Hypsilanti to attempt the task which he had himself declined, and that he allowed him to believe that if Greece once rose in arms the assistance of Russia could not long be withheld.* Hypsilanti, sacrificing his hopes of the recovery of a great private fortune, through the intercession of the Czar at Constantinople, placed himself at the head of the Hetæria, and entered upon a career, for which, with the exception of personal courage proved in the campaigns against Napoleon, he seems to have possessed no single qualification.

In October, 1820, the leading Hetærists met in council at Ismail to decide whether the insurrection against the Turk should begin in Greece itself or in the Danubian provinces. Most of the Greek officers in the service of Sutsos, the Hospodar of Moldavia, were ready to join the revolt. With the exception of a few companies serving as police, there were no Turkish soldiers north of the Danube, the Sultan having bound himself by the Treaty of Bucharest to send no troops into the Principalities without the Czar's consent. It does not appear

The Hetærist plan.

---

* Mendelssohn Bartholdy, Geschichte Griechenlands, i. 145, from the papers of Hypsilanti's brother. Otherwise in Prokesch-Osten, Abfall der Griechen, i. 13.

that the Hetærists had yet formed any calculation as to the probable action of the Roumanian people: they had certainly no reason to believe that this race bore good-will to the Greeks, or that it would make any effort to place a Greek upon the Sultan's throne. The conspirators at Ismail were so far on the right track that they decided that the outbreak should begin, not on the Danube, but in Peloponnesus. Hypsilanti, however, full of the belief that Russia would support him, reversed this conclusion, and determined to raise his standard in Moldavia.* And now for the first time some account was taken of the Roumanian population. It was known that the mass of the people groaned under the feudal oppression of the Boyards, or landowners, and that the Boyards themselves detested the government of the Greek Hospodars. A plan found favour among Hypsilanti's advisers that the Wallachian peasantry should first be called to arms by a native leader for the redress of their own grievances, and that the Greeks should then step in and take control of the insurrectionary movement. Theodor Wladimiresco, a Roumanian who had served in the Russian army, was ready to raise the standard of revolt among his countrymen. It did not occur to the Hetærists that Wladimiresco might have a purpose of his own, or that the Roumanian population might prefer to see the Greek adventure fail. No sovereign by divine right had a firmer belief in his prerogative within his own dominions than Hypsilanti in his power

* Gordon, Greek Revolution, i. 96.

to command or outwit Roumanians, Slavs, and all other Christian subjects of the Sultan.

The feint of a native rising was planned and executed. In February, 1821, while Hypsilanti waited on the Russian frontier, Wladimiresco proclaimed the abolition of feudal services, and marched with a horde of peasants upon Bucharest. On the 6th of March the Hetærists began their own insurrection by a deed of blood that disgraced the Christian cause. Karavius, a conspirator commanding the Greek troops of the Hospodar at Galatz, let loose his soldiers and murdered every Turk who could be hunted down. Hypsilanti crossed the Pruth next day, and appeared at Jassy with a few hundred followers. A proclamation was published in which the Prince called upon all Christian subjects of the Porte to rise, and declared that a great European Power, meaning Russia, supported him in his enterprise. Sutsos, the Hospodar, at once handed over all the apparatus of government, and supplied the insurgents with a large sum of money. Two thousand armed men, some of them regular troops, gathered round Hypsilanti at Jassy. The roads to the Danube lay open before him; the resources of Moldavia were at his disposal; and had he at once thrown a force into Galatz and Ibraila, he might perhaps have made it difficult for Turkish troops to gain a footing on the north of the Danube.

Hypsilanti in Roumania, March, 1821.

But the incapacity of the leader became evident from the moment when he began his enterprise. He loitered for a week at Jassy, holding court and conferring titles, and then, setting out for Bucharest, wasted three weeks more upon the road. In the meantime the news of the insurrection, and of the fraudulent use that had been made of his own name, reached the Czar, who was now engaged at the Congress of Laibach. Alexander was at this moment abandoning himself heart and soul to Metternich's reactionary influence, and ordering his generals to make ready a hundred thousand men to put down the revolution in Piedmont. He received with dismay a letter from Hypsilanti invoking his aid in a rising which was first described in the phrases of the Holy Alliance as the result of a divine inspiration, and then exhibited as a masterwork of secret societies and widespread conspiracy. A stern answer was sent back. Hypsilanti was dismissed from the Russian service; he was ordered to lay down his arms, and a manifesto was published by the Russian Consul at Jassy declaring that the Czar repudiated and condemned the enterprise with which his name had been connected. The Patriarch of Constantinople, helpless in the presence of Sultan Mahmud, now issued a ban of excommunication against the leader and all his followers. Some weeks later the Congress of Laibach officially branded the Greek revolt as a work of the same anarchical spirit which had produced the revolutions of Italy and Spain.*

<small>The Czar disavows the movement.</small>

The disavowal of the Hetærist enterprise by the Czar was fatal to its success. Hypsilanti, indeed, put on a

* B. and F. State Papers, viii. 1208.

bold countenance and pretended that the public utterances of the Russian Court were a mere blind, and in contradiction to the private instructions given him by the Czar; but no one believed him. The Roumanians, when they knew that aid was not coming from Russia, held aloof, or treated the insurgents as enemies.

The enterprise fails.

Turkish troops crossed the Danube, and Hypsilanti fell back from Bucharest towards the Austrian frontier. Wladimiresco followed him, not however to assist him in his struggle, but to cut off his retreat and to betray him to the enemy. It was in vain that the bravest of Hypsilanti's followers, Georgakis, a Greek from Olympus, sought the Wallachian at his own headquarters, exposed his treason to the Hetærist officers who surrounded him, and carried him, a doomed man, to the Greek camp. Wladimiresco's death was soon avenged. The Turks advanced. Hypsilanti was defeated in a series of encounters, and fled ignobly from his followers, to seek a refuge, and to find a prison, in Austria. Bands of his soldiers, forsaken by their leader, sold their lives dearly in a hopeless struggle. At Skuleni, on the Pruth, a troop of four hundred men refused to cross to Russian soil until they had given battle to the enemy. Standing at bay, they met the onslaught of ten times their number of pursuers. Georgakis, who had sworn that he would never fall alive into the enemy's hands, kept his word. Surrounded by Turkish troops in the tower of a monastery, he threw open the doors for those of his comrades who could to escape, and then setting fire to a chest of powder, perished in the explosion, together with his assailants.

The Hetærist invasion of the Principalities had ended in total failure, and with it there passed away for ever the dream of re-establishing the Eastern Empire under Greek ascendency. But while this enterprise, planned in vain reliance upon foreign aid and in blind assumption of leadership over an alien race, collapsed through the indifference of a people to whom the Greeks were known only as oppressors, that genuine uprising of the Greek nation, which, in spite of the nullity of its leaders, in spite of the crimes, the disunion, the perversity of a race awaking from centuries of servitude, was to add one more to the free peoples of Europe, broke out in the real home of the Hellenes, in the Morea and the islands of the Ægæan. Soon after Hypsilanti's appearance in Moldavia the Turkish governor of the Morea, anticipating a general rebellion of the Greeks, had summoned the Primates of his province to Tripolitza, with the view of seizing them as hostages. The Primates of the northern district set out, but halted on their way, debating whether they should raise the standard of insurrection or wait for events. While they lingered irresolutely at Kalavryta the decision passed out of their hands, and the people rose throughout the Morea. The revolt of the Moreot Greeks against their oppressors was from the first, and with set purpose, a war of extermination. "The Turk," they sang in their warsongs, "shall live no longer, neither in Morea nor in the

Revolt of the Morea, April 2, 1821.

whole earth." This terrible resolution was, during the first weeks of the revolt, carried into literal effect. The Turks who did not fly from their country-houses to the towns where there were garrisons or citadels to defend them, were attacked and murdered with their entire families, men, women and children. This was the first act of the revolution; and within a few weeks after the 2nd of April, on which the first outbreaks occurred, the open country was swept clear of its Ottoman population, which had numbered about 25,000, and the residue of the lately dominant race was collected within the walls of Patras, Tripolitza, and other towns, which the Greeks forthwith began to beleaguer.*

The news of the revolt of the Morea and of the massacre of Mohammedans reached Constantinople, striking terror into the politicians of the Turkish capital, and rousing the Sultan Mahmud to a vengeance tiger-like in its ferocity, but deliberate and calculated like every bloody deed of this resolute and able sovereign. Reprisals had already been made upon the Greeks at Constantinople for the acts of Hypsilanti, and a number of innocent persons had been put to death by the executioner, but no general attack upon the Christians had been suggested, nor had the work of punishment passed out of the hands of the government itself. Now, however, the fury of the Mohammedan populace was let loose upon the infidel. The Sultan called upon his subjects to arm themselves

Terrorism at Constantinople.

---

* Finlay, i. 187; Gordon, i. 203; K. Mendelssohn, Geschichte Griechenlands, i. 191; Prokesch-Osten, Abfall der Griechen, i. 20.

THE HANGING OF THE GREEK PATRIARCH AT CONSTANTINOPLE.

(p. 275.)

in defence of their faith. Executions were redoubled; soldiers and mobs devastated Greek settlements on the Bosphorus; and on the most sacred day of the Greek Church a blow was struck which sent a thrill over Eastern Europe. The Patriarch of Constantinople had celebrated the service which ushers in the dawn of Easter Sunday, when he was summoned by the Dragoman of the Porte to appear before a Synod hastily assembled. *Execution of the Patriarch, April 22.* There an order of the Sultan was read declaring Gregorius IV. a traitor, and degrading him from his office. The Synod was commanded to elect his successor. It did so. While the new Archbishop was receiving his investiture, Gregorius was led out, and was hanged, still wearing his sacred robes, at the gate of his palace. His body remained during Easter Sunday and the two following days at the place of execution. It was then given to the Jews to be insulted, dragged through the streets, and cast into the sea. The Archbishops of Adrianople, Salonica, and Tirnovo suffered death on the same Easter Sunday. The body of Gregorius, floating in the waves, was picked up by a Greek ship and carried to Odessa. Brought, as it was believed, by a miracle to Christian soil, the relics of the Patriarch received at the hands of the Russian government the funeral honours of a martyr. Gregorius had no doubt had dealings with the Hetærists; but he was put to death untried; and whatever may have been the real extent of his offence, he was executed not for this but in order to strike terror into the Sultan's Christian subjects.

During the succeeding months, in Asia Minor as well as in Macedonia and at Constantinople itself, there were wholesale massacres of the Christians, and the churches of the Greeks were pillaged or destroyed by their enemies, both Jews and Turks. Smyrna, Adrianople, and Salonica, in so far as these towns were Greek, were put to the sack; thousands of the inhabitants were slain by the armed mobs who held command, or were sold into slavery. It was only the fear of a war with Russia which at length forced Sultan Mahmud to stop these deeds of outrage and to restore some of the conditions of civilised life in the part of his dominions which was not in revolt. The Russian army and nation would have avenged the execution of the Patriarch by immediate war if popular instincts had governed its ruler. Strogonoff, the ambassador at Constantinople, at once proposed to the envoys of the other Powers to unite in calling up war-ships for the protection of the Christians. Joint action was, however, declined by Lord Strangford, the representative of England, and the Porte was encouraged by the attitude of this politician to treat the threats of Strogonoff with indifference. There was an interval during which the destiny of a great part of Eastern Europe depended upon the fluctuations of a single infirm will. The Czar had thoroughly identified himself while at Laibach with the principles and the policy of European conservatism, and had assented to the declaration in which Metternich placed the Greek rebellion, together with the Spanish and

Italian insurrections, under the ban of Europe. Returning to St. Petersburg, Alexander, in spite of the veil that intercepts from every sovereign the real thoughts and utterances of his people, found himself within the range of widely different influences. Russian passions were not roused by what might pass in Italy or Spain. The Russian priest, the soldier, the peasant understood nothing of theories of federal intervention, and of the connection between Neapolitan despotism and the treaties of 1815: but his blood boiled when he heard that the chief priest of his Church had been murdered by the Sultan, and that a handful of his brethren were fighting for their faith unhelped. Alexander felt to some extent the throb of national spirit. There had been a time in his life when a single hour of strong emotion or of overpowering persuasion had made him renounce every obligation and unite with Napoleon against his own allies; and there were those who in 1821 believed that the Czar would as suddenly break loose from his engagements with Metternich and throw himself, with a fanatical army and nation, into a crusade against the Turk. Sultan Mahmud had himself given to the Russian party of action a ground for denouncing him in the name of Russian honour and interests independently of all that related to Greece. In order to prevent the escape of suspected persons, the Porte had ordered Russian vessels to be searched at Constantinople, and it had forced all corn-ships coming from the Euxine to discharge their cargoes at the Bosphorus, under the apprehension that the corn-supplies of the capital would be cut off by Greek vessels in command of the Ægæan. Further, Russia had by treaty the right to insist that the Danubian Principalities should be governed by their civil authorities, the Hospodars, and not by Turkish Pashas. The insurrection in Wallachia had been put down, but the rule of Hospodars had not been restored; Turkish generals, at the head of their forces, still administered their provinces under military law. On all these points Russia had at least the semblance of grievances of its own. The outrages which shocked all Europe were not the only wrong which Russian pride called upon the Czar to redress. The influence of Capodistrias revived at St. Petersburg. A despatch was sent to Constantinople declaring that the Porte had begun a war for life or death with the Christian religion, and that its continued existence among the Powers of Europe must depend upon its undertaking to restore the churches which had been destroyed, to guarantee the inviolability of Christian worship in the future, and to discriminate in its punishments between the innocent and the guilty. Presenting this ultimatum from his master, Strogonoff, in accordance with his instructions, demanded a written answer within eight days. No such answer came. On the 27th of July the ambassador quitted Constantinople. War seemed to be on the point of breaking out.

<small>Russian ambassador leaves Constantinople, July 27.</small>

The capital where these events were watched with the greatest apprehension was Vienna. The fortunes of the Ottoman Empire have always been most intimately connected with those of Austria; and although the long struggle of the House of Hapsburg with Napoleon and its wars in recent times with Prussia and with Italy have made the western aspect of Austrian policy more prominent and more familiar than its eastern one, the eastern interests of the monarchy have always been at least as important in the eyes of its actual rulers. Before the year 1720 Austria, not Russia, was the great enemy of Turkey and the aggressive Power of the east of Europe. After 1780 the Emperor Joseph had united with Catherine of Russia in a plan for dividing the Sultan's dominions in Europe, and actually waged a war for this purpose. In 1795 the alliance, with the same object, had been prospectively revived by Thugut; in 1809, after the Treaty of Tilsit, Metternich had determined in the last resort to combine with Napoleon and Alexander in dismembering Turkey, if all diplomatic means should fail to prevent a joint attack on the Porte by France and Russia. But this resolution had been adopted by Metternich only as a matter of necessity, and in view of a combination which threatened to reduce Austria to the position of a vassal State. Metternich's own definite and consistent policy after 1814 was the maintenance of the Ottoman Empire. His statesmanship was, as a rule, governed by fear; and his fear of Alexander was second only to his old fear of Napoleon. Times were changed since Joseph and Thugut could hope to enter upon a game of aggression with Russia upon equal terms. The Austrian army had been beaten in every battle that it had fought

Eastern policy of Austria.

during nearly twenty years. Province after province had been severed from it, without, except in the Tyrol, raising a hand in its support; and when in 1821 the Minister compared Austria's actual Empire and position in Europe, won and maintained in great part by his own diplomacy, with the ruin to which a series of wars had brought it ten years before, he might well thank Heaven that international Congresses were still so much in favour with the Courts, and tremble at the clash of arms which from the remote Morea threatened to call Napoleon's northern conquerors once more into the field.*

England was not, like Austria, exposed to actual danger by the advance of Russia towards the Ægæan; but the growth of Russian power had been viewed with alarm by English politicians since 1788, when Pitt had formed a triple alliance with Prussia and Holland for the purpose of defending the Porte against the attacks of Catherine and Joseph. The interest of Great Britain in the maintenance of the Ottoman Empire had not been laid down as a principle before that date, nor was it then acknowledged by the Whig party. It was asserted by Pitt from considerations relating to the European balance of power, not, as in our own times, with a direct reference to England's position in India. The course of events from 1792 to 1807 made England and Russia for a while natural allies; but this friendship was turned into hostility by the Treaty of Tilsit; and although after a

Eastern policy of England.

---

* Metternich, iii. 622, 717; Prokesch-Osten, i. 281, 303. B. and F. State Papers, viii. 1247.

few years Alexander was again fighting for the same cause as Great Britain, and the public opinion of this country enthusiastically hailed the issue of the Moscow campaign, English statesmen never forgot the interview upon the Niemen, and never, in the brightest moments of victory, regarded Alexander without some secret misgivings. During the campaign of 1814 in France, Castlereagh's willingness to negotiate with Bonaparte was due in great part to the fear that Alexander's high-wrought resolutions would collapse before Napoleon could be thoroughly crushed, and that reaction would carry him into a worse peace than that which he then disdained.* The negotiations at the Congress of Vienna brought Great Britain and Russia, as it has been seen, into an antagonism which threatened to end in the resort to arms; and the tension which then and for some time afterwards existed between the two governments led English Ministers to speak, certainly in exaggerated and misleading language, of the mutual hostility of the English and the Russian nations. From 1815 to 1821 the Czar had been jealously watched. It had been rumoured over and over again that he was preparing to invade the Ottoman Empire; and when the rebellion of the Greeks broke out, the one thought of Castlereagh and his colleagues was that Russia must be prevented from throwing itself into the fray, and that the interests of Great Britain required that the authority of the Sultan should as soon as possible be restored throughout his dominions.

* Records, Continent. iii.

Both at London therefore and at Vienna the rebellion of Greece was viewed by governments only as an unfortunate disturbance which was likely to excite war between Russia and its neighbours, and to imperil the peace of Europe at large. It may seem strange that the spectacle of a nation rising to assert its independence should not even have aroused the question whether its claims deserved to be considered. But to do justice, at least to the English Ministers of 1821, it must be remembered how terrible, how overpowering, were the memories left by the twenty years of European war that had closed in 1815, and at how vast a cost to mankind the regeneration of Greece would have been effected, if, as then seemed probable, it had ranged the Great Powers again in arms against one another, and re-kindled the spirit of military aggression which for a whole generation had made Europe the prey of rival coalitions. It is impossible to read the letter in which Castlereagh pleaded with the Czar to sacrifice his own glory and popularity to the preservation of European peace, without perceiving in what profound earnestness the English statesman sought to avert the renewal of an epoch of conflict, and how much the apprehension of coming calamity predominated in his own mind over the mere jealousy of an extension of Russian power.* If Castlereagh had no thought for Greece itself, it was because the larger interests of Europe wholly absorbed him, and because he lacked the imagination and the insight to conceive of a better

Marginal note: Fears of a new period of warfare.

---

* Castlereagh, viii. 16; Metternich, iii. 504.

adjustment of European affairs under the widening recognition of national rights. The Minister of Austria, to whom at this crisis Castlereagh looked as his natural ally, had no doubt the same dread of a renewed convulsion of Europe, but in his case it was mingled with considerations of a much narrower kind. It is not correct to say that Metternich was indifferent to the Greek cause; he actually hated it, because it gave a stimulus to the liberal movement of Germany. In his empty and pedantic philosophy of human action, Metternich linked together every form of national aspiration and unrest as something presumptuous and wanton. He understood nothing of the debt that mankind owes to the spirit of freedom. He was just as ready to dogmatise upon the wickedness of the English Reform Bill as he was to trace the hand of Capodistrias in every tumult in Servia or the Morea: and even if there had been no fear of Russian aggression in the background, he would instinctively have condemned the Greek revolt when he saw that the light-headed professors in the German Universities were beginning to agitate in its favour, and that the recalcitrant Minor Courts regarded it with some degree of sympathy.

Metternich and the Greeks.

The policy of Metternich in the Eastern Question had for its object the maintenance of the existing order of things; and as it was certain that some satisfaction or other must be given to Russian pride, Metternich's counsel was that the grievances of the Czar which were specifically Russian should be clearly distinguished from questions relating to the independence of Greece; and that on the former the Porte should be recommended to agree with its adversary quickly, the good offices of Europe being employed within given limits on the Czar's behalf; so that, the Russian causes of complaint being removed, Alexander might without loss of honour leave the Greeks to be subdued, and resume the diplomatic relations with Constantinople which had been so perilously severed by Strogonoff's departure. It remained for the Czar to decide whether, as head of Russia and protector of the Christians of the East, he would solve the Eastern Question by his own sword, or whether, constant to the principle and ideal of international action to which he had devoted himself since 1815, he would commit his cause to the joint mediation of Europe, and accept such solution of the problem as his allies might attain. In the latter case it was clear that no blow would be struck on behalf of Greece. For a year or more the balance wavered; at length the note of triumph sounded in the Austrian Cabinet. Capodistrias, the representative of the Greek cause at St. Petersburg, rightly measured the force of the opposing impulses in the Czar's mind. He saw that Alexander, interested as he was in Italy and Spain, would never break with that federation of the Courts which he had himself created, nor shake off the influences of legitimism which had dominated him since the Congress of Aix-la-Chapelle. Submitting when contention had become hopeless, and anticipating his inevitable fall by a voluntary retirement from public affairs, Capodistrias, still high in credit and reputation, quitted St. Petersburg under the form of leave of absence, and withdrew to Geneva, there to await events, and to enjoy the distinction of a patriot whom love for Greece had constrained to abandon one of the most splendid positions in Europe. Grave, melancholy, and austere, as one who suffered with his country, Capodistrias remained in private life till the vanquished cause had become the victorious one, and the liberated Greek nation called him to place himself at its head. *Capodistrias retires, Aug. 1822.*

An international diplomatic campaign of vast activity and duration began in the year 1821, but the contest of arms was left, as Metternich desired, to the Greeks and the Turks alone. The first act of the war was the insurrection of the Morea: the second was the extension of this insurrection over parts of Continental Greece and the Archipelago, and its summary extinction by the Turk in certain districts, which in consequence remained for the future outside the area of hostilities, and so were not ultimately included in the Hellenic Kingdom. Central Greece, that is, the country lying immediately north of the Corinthian Gulf, broke into revolt a few weeks later than the Morea. The rising against the Mohammedans was distinguished by the same merciless spirit: the men were generally massacred; the women, if not killed, were for the most part sold into slavery; and when, after *Extension of the Greek revolt.* *Central Greece.*

an interval of three years, Lord Byron came to Missolonghi, he found that a miserable band of twenty-three captive women formed the sole remnant of the Turkish population of that town. Thessaly, with some exceptions, remained passive, and its inaction was of the utmost service to the Turkish cause; for Ali Pasha in Epirus was now being besieged by the Sultan's armies, and if Thessaly had risen in the rear of these troops, they could scarcely have escaped destruction. Khurshid, the Ottoman commander conducting the siege of Janina, held firmly to his task, in spite of the danger which threatened his communications, and in spite of the circumstance that his whole household had fallen into the hands of the Moreot insurgents. His tenacity saved the border-provinces for the Ottoman Empire.

Fall of Ali Pasha, Feb., 1822.

No combination was effected between Ali and the Greeks, and at the beginning of 1822 the Albanian chieftain lost both his stronghold and his life. In the remoter district of Chalcidice, on the Macedonian coast, where the promontory of Athos and the two parallel peninsulas run out into the Ægæan, and a Greek population, clearly severed from the Slavic inhabitants of the mainland, maintained its own communal and religious organisation, the national revolt broke out under Hetærist leaders. The monks of Mount Athos, like their neighbours, took up arms. But there was little sympathy between the privileged chiefs of these abbeys and the desperate men who had come to head the revolt. The struggle was soon abandoned;

Chalcidice.

and, partly by force of arms, partly by negotiation, the authority of the Sultan was restored without much difficulty throughout this region.

The settlements of the Ægæan which first raised the flag of Greek independence were the so-called Nautical Islands, Hydra, Spetza, and Psara, where the absence of a Turkish population and the enjoyment of a century of self-government had allowed the bold qualities of an energetic maritime race to grow to their full vigour. Hydra and Spetza were close to the Greek coast, Psara was on the farther side of the archipelago, almost within view of Asia Minor; so that in joining the insurrection its inhabitants showed great heroism, for they were exposed to the first attack of any Turkish force that could maintain itself for a few hours at sea, and the whole adjacent mainland was the recruiting-ground of the Sultan. At Hydra the revolt against the Ottoman was connected with the internal struggles of the little community, and these in their turn were connected with the great economical changes of Europe which, at the opposite end of the continent, and in a widely-different society, led to the enactment of the English Corn Laws, and to the strife of classes which resulted from them. During Napoleon's wars the carrying-trade of most nations had become extinct; little corn reached England, and few besides Greek ships navigated the Euxine and Mediterranean. When peace opened the markets and the ports of all nations, just as the renewed importation of foreign corn threatened

The Ægæan Islands.

to lower the profits of English farmers and the rents of English landlords, so the reviving freedom of navigation made an end of the monopoly of the Hydriote and Psarian merchantmen. The shipowners formed an oligarchy in Hydra; the captains and crews of their ships, though they shared the profits of each voyage, were excluded from any share in the government of the island. Failure of trade, want and inactivity, hence led to a political opposition. The shipowners, wealthy and privileged men, had no inclination to break with the Turk; the captains and sailors, who had now nothing to lose, declared for Greek independence. There was a struggle in which for a while nothing but the commonest impulses of need and rapacity came into play; but the greater cause proved its power: Hydra threw in its lot with Greece; and although private greed and ill-faith, as well as great cruelty, too often disgraced both the Hydriote crews and those of the other islands, the nucleus of a naval force was now formed which made the achievement of Greek independence possible. The three islands which led the way were soon followed by the wealthier and more populous Samos and by the greater part of the Archipelago. Crete, inhabited by a mixed Greek and Turkish population, also took up arms, and was for years to come the scene of a bloody and destructive warfare.

Within the Morea the first shock of the revolt had made the Greeks masters of everything outside the fortified towns. The reduction of these places was at once undertaken by the insurgents. Tripolitza, lately the seat of the Turkish Government, was the centre of operations, and in the neighbourhood of this town the first provisional government of the Greeks, called the Senate of Kaltesti, was established. Demetrius Hypsilanti, a brother of the Hetærist leader, whose failure in Roumania was not yet known, landed in the Morea and claimed supreme power. He was tumultuously welcomed by the peasant-soldiers, though the Primates, who had hitherto held undisputed sway, bore him no good will. Two other men became prominent at this time as leaders in the Greek war of liberation. These were Maurokordatos, a descendant of the Hospodars of Wallachia—a politician superior to all his rivals in knowledge and breadth of view, but wanting in the faculty of action required by the times—and Kolokotrones, a type of the rough fighting Klepht; a mere savage in attainments, scarcely able to read or write, cunning, grossly avaricious and faithless, incapable of appreciating either military or moral discipline, but a born soldier in his own irregular way, and a hero among peasants as ignorant as himself. There was yet another, who, if his character had been equal to his station, would have been placed at the head of the government of the Morea. This was Petrobei, chief of the family of Mauromichalis, ruler of the rugged district of Maina, in the south-west of Peloponnesus, where the Turk had never established more than nominal sovereignty. A jovial, princely person, exercising among his clansmen a mild Homeric sway, Petrobei, surrounded by his nine vigorous sons, was the most picturesque figure in Greece. But he had no genius for great things. A sovereignty, which in other hands might have expanded to national dominion, remained with Petrobei a mere ornament and curiosity; and the power of the deeply-rooted clan-spirit of the Maina only made itself felt when, at a later period, the organisation of a united Hellenic State demanded its sacrifice.

Anarchy, egotism, and ill-faith disgraced the Greek insurrection from its beginning to its close. There were, indeed, some men of unblemished honour among the leaders, and the peasantry in the ranks fought with the most determined courage year after year; but the action of most of those who figured as representatives of the people brought discredit upon the national cause. Their first successes were accompanied by gross treachery and cruelty. Had the Greek leaders been Bourbon kings, nurtured in all the sanctities of divine right, instead of tax-gatherers and cattle-lifters, truants from the wild school of Turkish violence and deceit, they could not have perjured themselves with lighter hearts. On the surrender of Navarino, in August, 1821, after a formal capitulation providing for the safety of its Turkish inhabitants, men, women, and children were indiscriminately massacred. The capture of Tripolitza, which took place two months later, was changed from a peaceful triumph into a scene of frightful slaughter by the avarice of individual chiefs, who, while negotiations were pending, made their way into the town, and

Fall of Tripolitza, Oct. 5, 1821.

bargained with rich inhabitants to give them protection in return for their money and jewels. The soldiery, who had undergone the labours of the siege for six months, saw that their reward was being pilfered from them. Defying all orders, and in the absence of Demetrius Hypsilanti, the commander-in-chief, they rushed upon the fortifications of Tripolitza, and carried them by storm. A general massacre of the inhabitants followed. For three days the work of carnage was continued in the streets and houses, until few out of a population of many thousands remained living. According to the testimony of Kolokotrones himself, the roads were so choked with the dead, that as he rode from the gateway to the citadel his horse's hoofs never touched the ground.*

In the opening scenes of the Greek insurrection the barbarity of Christians and of Ottomans was perhaps on a level. The Greek revenged himself with the ferocity of the slave who breaks his fetters; the Turk resorted to wholesale massacre and extermination as the normal means of government in troubled times. And as experience has shown that the savagery of the European yields in one generation to the influences of civilised rule, while the Turk remains as inhuman to-day as he was under Mahmud II., so the history of 1822 proved that the most devilish passions of the Greek were in the end but a poor match for disciplined Turkish prowess in the work of butchery. It was no easy matter for the Sultan to

The Massacre of Chios, April—June, 1822.

* Kolokotrones, Διήγησις Συμβάντων, p. 82; Tricoupes, Ἱστορία ii., 61, 62.

requite himself for the sack of Tripolitza upon Kolokotrones and his victorious soldiers; but there was a peaceful and inoffensive population elsewhere, which offered all the conditions for free, unstinted, and unimperilled vengeance which the Turk desires. A body of Samian troops had landed in Chios, and endeavoured, but with little success, to excite the inhabitants to revolt, the absence of the Greek fleet rendering them an almost certain prey to the Sultan's troops on the mainland. The Samian leader nevertheless refused to abandon the enterprise, and laid siege to the citadel, in which there was a Turkish garrison. Before this fortress could be reduced, a relieving army of seven thousand Turks, with hosts of fanatical volunteers, landed on the island. The Samians fled; the miserable population of Chios was given up to massacre. For week after week the soldiery and the roving hordes of Ottomans slew, pillaged, and sold into slavery at their pleasure. In parts of the island where the inhabitants took refuge in the monasteries, they were slaughtered by thousands together; others, tempted back to their homes by the promulgation of an amnesty, perished family by family. The lot of those who were spared was almost more pitiable than of those who died. The slave-markets of Egypt and Tunis were glutted with Chian captives. The gentleness, the culture, the moral worth of the Chian community made its fate the more tragical. No district in Europe had exhibited a civilisation more free from the vices of its type: on no community had there fallen in modern times so terrible a catastrophe. The estimates of the destruction of life at Chios are loosely framed; among the lowest is that which sets the number of the slain and the enslaved at thirty thousand. The island, lately thronging with life and activity, became a thinly-populated place. After a long period of depression and the slow return of some fraction of its former prosperity, convulsions of nature have in our own day again made Chios a ruin. A new life may arise when the Turk is no longer master of its shores, but the old history of Chios is closed for ever.

The impression made upon public opinion in Europe by the massacre of 1822 was a deep and lasting one, although it caused no immediate change in the action of Governments. The general feeling of sympathy for the Greeks and hatred for the Turks, which ultimately forced the Governments to take up a different policy, was intensified by a brilliant deed of daring by which a Greek captain avenged the Chians upon their devastator, and by the unexpected success gained by the insurgents on the mainland against powerful armies of the Sultan. The Greek executive, which was now headed by Maurokordatos, had been guilty of gross neglect in not sending over the fleet in time to prevent the Turks from landing in Chios. When once this landing had been effected, the ships which afterwards arrived were powerless to prevent the massacre, and nothing could be attempted except against the Turkish fleet itself. The instrument of destruction employed by the Greeks was the fire-ship, which had been used with success against the Turk in

Exploit of Kanaris, June 18th, 1822.

these same waters in the war of 1770. The sacred month of the Ramazan was closing, and on the night of June 18, Kara Ali, the Turkish commander, celebrated the festival of Bairam with above a thousand men on board his flag-ship. The vessel was illuminated with coloured lanterns. In the midst of the festivities, Constantine Kanaris, a Psarian captain, brought his fire-ship unobserved right up to the Turkish man-of-war, and drove his bowsprit firmly into one of her portholes; then, after setting fire to the combustibles, he stepped quietly into a row-boat, and made away. A breeze was blowing, and in a moment the Turkish crew were enveloped in a mass of flames. The powder on board exploded; the boats were sunk; and the vessel, with its doomed crew, burned to the water-edge, its companions sheering off to save themselves from the shower of blazing fragments that fell all around. Kara Ali was killed by a broken mast; a few of his men saved their lives by swimming or were picked up by rescuers; the rest perished. Such was the consternation caused by the deed of Kanaris, that the Ottoman fleet forthwith quitted the Ægæan waters, and took refuge under the guns of the Dardanelles. Kanaris, unknown before, became from this exploit a famous man in Europe. It was to no stroke of fortune or mere audacity that he owed his success, but to the finest combination of nerve and nautical skill. His feat, which others were constantly attempting, but with little success, to imitate, was repeated by him in the same year. He was the most brilliant of Greek seamen, a simple and modest hero; and after his splendid achievements in the war of liberation, he served his country well in a political career. Down to his death in a hale old age, he was with justice the idol and pride of the Greek nation.

The fall of the Albanian rebel, Ali Pasha, in the spring of 1822 made it possible for Sultan Mahmud, who had hitherto been crippled by the resistance of Janina, to throw his whole land-force against the Hellenic revolt; and the Greeks of the mainland, who had as yet had to deal only with scattered detachments or isolated garrisons, now found themselves exposed to the attack of two powerful armies. Kurshid, the conqueror of Ali Pasha, took up his headquarters at Larissa in Thessaly, and from this base the two invading armies marched southwards on diverging lines. The first, under Omer Brionis, was ordered to make its way through Southern Epirus to the western entrance of the Corinthian Gulf, and there to cross into the Morea; the second, under Dramali, to reduce Central Greece, and enter the Morea by the isthmus of Corinth; the conquest of Tripolitza and the relief of the Turkish coast-fortresses which were still uncaptured being the ultimate end to be accomplished by the two armies in combination with one another and with the Ottoman fleet. Not less than fifty thousand men were under the orders of the Turkish commanders, the division of Dramali being by far the larger of the two. Against this formidable enemy the Greeks possessed poor means of defence, nor

Double invasion of Greece, 1822.

were their prospects improved when Maurokordatos, the President, determined to take a military command, and to place himself at the head of the troops in Western Greece. There were indeed urgent reasons for striking with all possible force in this quarter. The Suliotes, after seventeen years of exile in Corfu, had returned to their mountains, and were now making common cause with Greece. They were both the military outwork of the insurrection, and the political link between the Hellenes and the Christian communities of Albania, whose action might become of decisive importance in the struggle against the Turks. Maurokordatos rightly judged the relief of Suli to be the first and most pressing duty of the Government. Under a capable leader this effort would not have been beyond the power of the Greeks; directed by a politician who knew nothing of military affairs, it was perilous in the highest degree. Maurokordatos, taking the command out of abler hands, pushed his troops forward to the neighbourhood of Arta, mismanaged everything, and after committing a most important post to Botzares, an Albanian chieftain of doubtful fidelity, left two small regiments exposed to the attack of the Turks in mass. One of these regiments, called the corps of Philhellenes, was composed of foreign officers who had volunteered to serve in the Greek cause as common soldiers. Its discipline was far superior to anything that existed among the Greeks themselves; and at its head were men who had fought in Napoleon's campaigns. But this corps, which might have

Destruction of the Philhellenes near Arta, July 16.

become the nucleus of a regular army, was sacrificed to the incapacity of the general and the treachery of his confederate. Betrayed and abandoned by the Albanian, the Philhellenes met the attack of the Turks gallantly, and almost all perished. Maurokordatos and the remnant of the Greek troops now retired to Missolonghi. The Suliotes, left to their own resources, were once more compelled to quit their mountain home, and to take refuge in Corfu. Their resistance, however, delayed the Turks for some months, and it was not until the beginning of November that the army of Omer Brionis, after conquering the intermediate territory, appeared in front of Missolonghi. Here the presence of Maurokordatos produced a better effect than in the field. He declared that he would never leave the town as long as a man remained to fight the Turks. Defences were erected, and the besiegers kept at bay for two months. On the 6th of January, 1823, Brionis ordered an assault. It was beaten back with heavy loss; and the Ottoman commander, hopeless of maintaining his position throughout the winter, abandoned his artillery, and retired into the interior of the country.*

Unsuccessful siege of Missolonghi, Nov., 1822.

In the meantime Dramali had advanced from Thessaly with twenty-four thousand infantry and six thousand cavalry, the most formidable armament that had been seen in Greece since the final struggle between the Turks and Venetians in 1715. At the terror of his approach

* Gordon, i. 383; Finlay, i. 330; Mendelssohn, i. 269.

all hopes of resistance vanished. He marched through Bœotia and Attica, devastating the country, and reached the isthmus of Corinth in July, 1822. The mountain-passes were abandoned by the Greeks; the Government, whose seat was at Argos, dispersed; and Dramali moved on to Nauplia, where the Turkish garrison was on the point of surrendering to the Greeks. The entrance to the Morea had been won; the very shadow of a Greek government had disappeared, and the definite suppression of the revolt seemed now to be close at hand. But two fatal errors of the enemy saved the Greek cause. Dramali neglected to garrison the passes through which he had advanced; and the commander of the Ottoman fleet, which ought to have met the land-force at Nauplia, disobeyed his instructions and sailed on to Patras. Two Greeks, at this crisis of their country's history, proved themselves equal to the call of events. Demetrius Hypsilanti, now President of the Legislature, refused to fly with his colleagues, and threw himself, with a few hundred men, into the Acropolis of Argos. Kolokotrones, hastening to Tripolitza, called out every man capable of bearing arms, and hurried back to Argos, where the Turks were still held at bay by the defenders of the citadel. Dramali could no longer think of marching into the interior of the Morea. The gallantry of Demetrius had given time for the assemblage of a considerable force, and the Ottoman general now discovered the ruinous effect of his neglect to garrison the passes in his rear. These were seized by Kolokotrones.

The summer-drought threatened the Turkish army with famine; the fleet which would have rendered them independent of land-supplies was a hundred miles away; and Dramali, who had lately seen all Greece at his feet, now found himself compelled to force his way back through the enemy to the isthmus of Corinth. The measures taken by Kolokotrones to intercept his retreat were skilfully planned, and had they been adequately executed not a man of the Ottoman army would have escaped. It was only through the disorder and the cupidity of the Greeks themselves that a portion of Dramali's force succeeded in cutting its way back to Corinth. Baggage was plundered while the retreating enemy ought to have been annihilated, and divisions which ought to have co-operated in the main attack sought trifling successes of their own. But the losses and the demoralisation of the Turkish army were as ruinous to it as total destruction. Dramali himself fell ill and died; and the remnant of his troops which had escaped from the enemy's hands perished in the neighbourhood of Corinth from sickness and want.

<small>His retreat and destruction, Aug., 1822.</small>

The decisive events of 1822 opened the eyes of European Governments to the real character of the Greek national rising, and to the probability of its ultimate success. The forces of Turkey were exhausted for the moment, and during the succeeding year no military operations could be undertaken by the Sultan on anything like the same scale. It would perhaps have been better for the Greeks

<small>Greek Civil Wars, 1824.</small>

themselves if the struggle had been more continuously sustained. Nothing but foreign pressure could give unity to the efforts of a race distracted by so many local rivalries, and so many personal ambitions and animosities. Scarcely was the extremity of danger passed when civil war began among the Greeks themselves. Kolokotrones set himself up in opposition to the Legislature, and seized on some of the strong places in the Morea. This first outbreak of the so-called military party against the civil authorities was, however, of no great importance. The Primates of the Morea took part with the representatives of the islands and of Central Greece against the disturber of the peace, and an accommodation was soon arranged. Konduriottes, a rich ship-owner of Hydra, was made President, with Kolettes, a politician of great influence in Central Greece, as his Minister. But in place of the earlier antagonism between soldier and civilian, a new and more dangerous antagonism, that of district against district, now threatened the existence of Greece. The tendency of the new government to sacrifice everything to the interest of the islands at once became evident. Konduriottes was a thoroughly incompetent man, and made himself ridiculous by appointing his friends, the Hydriote sea-captains, to the highest military and civil posts. Rebellion again broke out, and Kolokotrones was joined by his old antagonists, the Primates of the Morea. A serious struggle ensued, and the government, which was really conducted by Kolettes, displayed an energy that surprised both its friends and its foes. The

Morea was invaded by a powerful force from Hydra. No mercy was shown to the districts which supported the rebels. Kolokotrones was thoroughly defeated, and compelled to give himself up to the Government. He was carried to Hydra and thrown into prison, where he remained until new peril again rendered his services indispensable to Greece.

After the destruction of Dramali's army and the failure of the Ottoman navy to effect any result whatever, the Sultan appears to have conceived a doubt whether the subjugation of Greece might not in fact be a task beyond his own unaided power. Even if the mainland were conquered, it was certain that the Turkish fleet could never reduce the islands, nor prevent the passage of supplies and reinforcements from these to the ports of the Morea. Strenuous as Mahmud had hitherto shown himself in crushing his vassals who, like Ali Pasha, attempted to establish an authority independent of the central government, he now found himself compelled to apply to the most dangerous of them all for assistance. Mehemet Ali, Pasha of Egypt, had risen to power in the disturbed time that followed the expulsion of Napoleon's forces from Egypt. His fleet was more powerful than that of Turkey. He had organised an army composed of Arabs, negroes, and fellahs, and had introduced into it, by means of French officers, the military system and discipline of Europe. The same reform had been attempted in Turkey seventeen years before by Mahmud's predecessor, Selim III., but it had been

Mahmud calls for the help of Egypt.

successfully resisted by the soldiery of Constantinople, and Selim had paid for his innovations with his life. Mahmud, silent and tenacious, had long been planning the destruction of the Janissaries, the mutinous and degraded representatives of a once irresistible force, who would now neither fight themselves nor permit their rulers to organise any more effective body of troops in their stead. It is possible that the Sultan may have believed that a victory won over the enemies of Islam by the remodelled forces of Egypt would facilitate the execution of his own plans of military reform; it is also possible that he may not have been unwilling to see his vassal's resources dissipated by a distant and hazardous enterprise. Not without some profound conviction of the urgency of the present need, not without some sinister calculation as to the means of dealing with an eventual rival in the future, was the offer of aggrandisement—if we may judge from the whole tenor of Sultan Mahmud's career and policy—made to the Pasha of Egypt by his jealous and far-seeing master. The Pasha was invited to assume the supreme command of the Ottoman forces by land and sea, and was promised the island of Crete in return for his co-operation against the Hellenic revolt. Messages to this effect reached Alexandria at the beginning of 1824. Mehemet, whose ambition had no limits, welcomed the proposals of his sovereign with ardour, and, while declining the command for himself, accepted it on behalf of Ibrahim, his adopted son.

The most vigorous preparations for war were now made at Alexandria. The army was raised to 90,000 men, and new ships were added to the navy from English dockyards. A scheme was framed for the combined operation of the Egyptian and the Turkish forces which appeared to render the ultimate conquest of Greece certain. It was agreed that the island of Crete, which is not sixty miles distant from the southern extremity of the Morea, should be occupied by Ibrahim, and employed as his place of arms; that simultaneous or joint attacks should then be made upon the principal islands of the Ægæan; and that after the capture of these strongholds and the destruction of the maritime resources of the Greeks, Ibrahim's troops should pass over the narrow sea between Crete and the Morea, and complete their work by the reduction of the mainland, thus left destitute of all chance of succour from without. Crete, like Sicily, is a natural stepping-stone between Europe and Africa; and when once the assistance of Egypt was invoked by the Sultan, it was obvious that Crete became the position which above all others it was necessary for the Greeks to watch and to defend. But the wretched Government of Konduriottes was occupied with its domestic struggles. The appeal of the Cretans for protection remained unanswered, and in the spring of 1824 a strong Egyptian force landed on this island, captured its fortresses, and suppressed the resistance of the inhabitants with the most frightful cruelty. The base of operations had been won, and the combined attacks of the Egyptian and Turkish fleets upon the smaller islands followed. Casos,

Turkish-Egyptian plans.

Egyptians conquer Crete, April, 1824.

about thirty miles east of Crete, was surprised by the Egyptians, and its population exterminated. Psara was selected for the attack of the Turkish fleet. Since the beginning of the insurrection the Psariotes had been the scourge and terror of the Ottoman coasts. The services that they had rendered in the Greek navy had been priceless; and if there was one spot of Greek soil which ought to have been protected as long as a single boat's crew remained afloat, it was the little rock of Psara. Yet, in spite of repeated warnings, the Greek Government allowed the Turkish fleet to pass the Dardanelles unobserved, and some clumsy feints were enough to blind it to the real object of an expedition whose aim was known to all Europe. There were ample means for succouring the islanders, as subsequent events proved; but when the Turkish admiral, Khosrew, with 10,000 men on board, appeared before Psara, the Greek fleet was far away. The Psariotes themselves were over-confident. They trusted to their batteries on land, and believed their rocks to be impregnable. They were soon undeceived. While a corps of Albanians scaled the cliffs behind the town, the Turks gained a footing in front, and overwhelmed their gallant enemy by weight of numbers. No mercy was asked or given. Eight thousand of the Psarians were slain or carried away as slaves. Not more that one-third of the population succeeded in escaping to the neighbouring islands.*

Destruction of Psara, July, 1824.

---

* Gordon, ii. 138. The news of this catastrophe reached Metternich at Ischl on July 30th. "Prince Metternich was taking an excursion, in which,

The first part of the Turko-Egyptian plan had thus been successfully accomplished, and if Khosrew had attacked Samos immediately after his first victory, this island would probably have fallen before help could arrive. But, like other Turkish commanders, Khosrew loved intervals of repose, and he now sailed off to Mytilene to celebrate the festival of Bairam. In the meantime the catastrophe of Psara had aroused the Hydriote Government to a sense of its danger. A strong fleet was sent across the Ægæan, and adequate measures were taken to defend Samos both by land and sea. The Turkish fleet was attacked with some success, and though Ibrahim with the Egyptian contingent now reached the coast of Asia Minor, the Greeks proved themselves superior to their adversaries combined. The operations of the Mussulman commanders led to no result; they were harassed and terrified by the Greek fireships; and when at length all hope of a joint conquest of Samos had been abandoned, and Ibrahim set sail for Crete to carry out his own final enterprise alone, he was met on the high seas by the Greeks, and driven back to the coast of Asia Minor. During the autumn of 1824 the disasters of the preceding months were to some extent retrieved, and the situation of the Egyptian fleet would have become

Greek successes off the coast of Asia Minor, September, 1824.

unfortunately, I could not accompany him. I at once sent Francis after him with this important letter, which he received at a spot where the name of the Capitan Pasha had probably never been heard before. The prince soon came back to me; and (*pianissimo*, in order that the friends of Greece might not hear it) we congratulate one another on the event, which may very well prove *le commencement de la fin* for the Greek insurrection." (Gentz.)

one of some peril if the Greeks had maintained their guard throughout the winter. But they underrated the energy of Ibrahim, and surrendered themselves to the belief that he would not repeat the attempt to reach Crete until the following spring. Careless, or deluded by false information, they returned to Hydra, and left the seas unwatched. Ibrahim saw his opportunity, and, setting sail for Crete at the beginning of December, he reached it without falling in with the enemy.

Ibrahim reaches Crete. December, 1824.

The snowy heights of Taygetus are visible on a clear winter's day from the Cretan coast; yet, with their enemy actually in view of them, the Greeks neglected to guard the passage to the Morea. On the 22nd of February, 1825, Ibrahim crossed the sea unopposed and landed five thousand men at Modon. He was even able to return to Crete and bring over a second contingent of superior strength before any steps were taken to hinder his movements. The fate of the mainland was now settled. Ibrahim marched from Modon upon Navarino, defeated the Greek forces on the way, and captured the garrison placed in the Island of Sphakteria—the scene of the first famous surrender of the Spartans—before the Greek fleet could arrive to relieve it. The forts of Navarino then capitulated, and Ibrahim pushed on his victorious march towards the centre of the Morea. It was in vain that the old chief Kolokotrones was brought from his prison at Hydra to take supreme command. The conqueror of Dramali was unable to resist the

Ibrahim in the Morea, Feb., 1825.

onslaught of Ibrahim's regiments, recruited from the fierce races of the Soudan, and fighting with the same arms and under the same discipline as the best troops in Europe. Kolokotrones was driven back through Tripolitza, and retired as the Russians had retired from Moscow, leaving a deserted capital behind him. Ibrahim gave his troops no rest; he hurried onwards against Nauplia, and on the 24th of June reached the summit of the mountain-pass that looks down upon the Argolic Gulf. "Ah, little island," he cried, as he saw the rock of Hydra stretched below him, "how long wilt thou escape me?" At Nauplia itself the Egyptian commander rode up to the very gates and scanned the defences, which he hoped to carry at the first assault. Here, however, a check awaited him. In the midst of general flight and panic, Demetrius Hypsilanti was again the undaunted soldier. He threw himself with some few hundreds of men into the mills of Lerna, and there beat back Ibrahim's vanguard when it attempted to carry this post by storm. The Egyptian recognised that with men like these in front of him Nauplia could be reduced only by a regular siege. He retired for a while upon Tripolitza, and thence sent out his harrying columns, slaughtering and devastating in every direction. It seemed to be his design not merely to exhaust the resources of his enemy but to render the Morea a desert, and to exterminate its population. In the very birthplace of European civilisation, it was said, this savage, who had already been nominated Pasha of the Morea, intended to extinguish the European race and name, and to found for himself upon the ashes of Greece a new barbaric state composed of African negroes and fellaheen. That such design had actually been formed was denied by the Turkish government in answer to official inquiries, and its existence was not capable of proof. But the brutality of one age is the stupidity of the next, and Ibrahim's violence recoiled upon himself. Nothing in the whole struggle between the Sultan and the Greeks gave so irresistible an argument to the Philhellenes throughout Europe, or so directly overcame the scruples of Governments in regard to an armed intervention in favour of Greece, as Ibrahim's alleged policy of extermination and re-settlement. The days were past when Europe could permit its weakest member to be torn from it and added to the Mohammedan world.

One episode of the deepest tragic interest yet remained in the Turko-Hellenic conflict before the Powers of Europe stepped in and struck with weapons stronger than those which had fallen from dying hands. The town of Missolonghi was now beleaguered by the Turks, who had invaded Western Greece while Ibrahim was overrunning the Morea. Missolonghi had already once been besieged without success; and, as in the case of Saragossa, the first deliverance appears to have inspired the townspeople with the resolution, maintained even more heroically at Missolonghi than at the Spanish city, to die rather than capitulate. From the time when Reschid, the Turkish commander, opened the second attack by

Siege of Missolonghi, April, 1825—April, 1826.

land and sea in the spring of 1825, the garrison and the inhabitants met every movement of the enemy with the most obstinate resistance. It was in vain that Reschid broke through the defences with his artillery, and threw mass after mass upon the breaches which he made. For month after month the assaults of the Turks were uniformly repelled, until at length the arrival of a Hydriote squadron forced the Turkish fleet to retire from its position, and made the situation of Reschid himself one of considerable danger. And now, as winter approached, and the guerilla bands in the rear of the besiegers grew more and more active, the Egyptian army with its leader was called from the Morea to carry out the task in which the Turks had failed. The Hydriote sea-captains had departed, believing their presence to be no longer needed; and although they subsequently returned for a short time, their services were grudgingly rendered and ineffective. Ibrahim, settling down to his work at the beginning of 1826, conducted his operations with the utmost vigour, boasting that he would accomplish in fourteen days what the Turks could not effect in nine months. But his veteran soldiers were thoroughly defeated when they met the Greeks hand to hand; and the Egyptian, furious with his enemy, his allies, and his own officers, confessed that Missolonghi could only be taken by blockade. He now ordered a fleet of flat-bottomed boats to be constructed and launched upon the lagoons that lie between Missolonghi and the open sea. Missolonghi was thus completely surrounded; and when the Greek admirals appeared for the last time and endeavoured to force an entrance through the shallows, they found the besieger in full command of waters inaccessible to themselves, and after one unsuccessful effort abandoned Missolonghi to its fate. In the third week of April, 1826, exactly a year after the commencement of the siege, the supply of food was exhausted. The resolution, long made, that the entire population, men, women, and children, should fall by the enemy's sword rather than surrender, was now actually carried out. On the night of the 22nd of April all the Missolonghiots, with the exception of those whom age, exhaustion, or illness made unable to leave their homes, were drawn up in bands at the city gates, the women armed and dressed as men, the children carrying pistols. Preceded by a body of soldiers, they crossed the moat under Turkish fire. The attack of the vanguard carried everything before it, and a way was cut through the Turkish lines. But at this moment some cry of confusion was mistaken by those who were still on the bridges for an order to retreat. A portion of the non-combatants returned into the town, and with them the rearguard of the military escort. The leading divisions, however, continued their march forward, and would have escaped with the loss of some of the women and children, had not treachery already made the Turkish commander acquainted with the routes which they intended to follow. They had cleared the Turkish camp, and were expecting to meet the bands of Greek armatoli, who had promised to fall upon the enemy's rear,

THE SORTIE FROM MISSOLONGHI.

(p. 310.)

when, instead of friends, they encountered troop after troop of Ottoman cavalry and of Albanians placed in ambush along the road between Missolonghi and the mountains. Here, exhausted and surprised, they were cut down without mercy, and out of a body numbering several thousand not more than fifteen hundred men, with a few women and children, ultimately reached places of safety. Missolonghi itself was entered by the Turks during the sortie. The soldiers who had fallen back during the confusion on the bridges, proved that they had not acted from cowardice. They fought unflinchingly to the last, and three bands, establishing themselves in the three powder magazines of the town, set fire to them when surrounded by the Turks, and perished in the explosion. Some thousands of women and children were captured around and within the town, or wandering on the mountains; but the Turks had few other prisoners. The men were dead or free.

From Missolonghi the tide of Ottoman conquest rolled eastward, and the Acropolis of Athens was in its turn the object of a long and arduous siege. The Government, which now held scarcely any territory on the mainland except Nauplia, where it was itself threatened by Ibrahim, made the most vigorous efforts to prevent the Acropolis from falling into Reschid's hands. All, however, was in vain. The English officers, Church and Cochrane, who were now placed at the head of the military and naval forces of Greece, failed ignominiously in the attacks which they made on Reschid's besieging army; and the

Fall of the Acropolis of Athens, June 5, 1827.

garrison capitulated on June 5, 1827. But the time was past when the liberation of Greece could be prevented by any Ottoman victory. The heroic defence of the Missolonghiots had achieved its end. Greece had fought long enough to enlist the Powers of Europe on its side; and in the same month that Missolonghi fell the policy of non-intervention was definitely abandoned by those Governments which were best able to carry their intentions into effect. If the struggle had ended during the first three years of the insurrection, no hand would have been raised to prevent the restoration of the Sultan's rule. Russia then lay as if spellbound beneath the diplomacy of the Holy Alliance; and although in the second year of the war the death of Castlereagh and the accession of Canning to power had given Greece a powerful friend instead of a powerful foe within the British Ministry, it was long before England stirred from its neutrality. Canning indeed made no secret of his sympathies for Greece, and of his desire to give the weaker belligerent such help as a neutral might afford; but when he took up office the time had not come when intervention would have been useful or possible. Changes in the policy of other great Powers and in the situation of the belligerents themselves were, he considered, necessary before the influence of England could be successfully employed in establishing peace in the East.

A vigorous movement of public opinion in favour of Greece made itself felt throughout Western Europe as the struggle continued; and the vivid and romantic interest excited over the whole civilised world by the death of Lord Byron in 1823, among the people whom he had come to free, probably served the Greek cause better than all that Byron could have achieved had his life been prolonged. In France and England, where public opinion had great influence on the action of the Government, as well as in Germany, where it had none whatever, societies were formed for assisting the Greeks with arms, stores, and money. The first proposal, however, for a joint intervention in favour of Greece came from St. Petersburg. The undisguised good-will of Canning towards the insurgents led the Czar's Government to anticipate that England itself might soon assume that championship of the Greek cause which Russia, at the bidding of Metternich and of Canning's predecessor, had up to that time declined. If the Greeks were to be befriended, it was intolerable that others should play the part of the patron. Accordingly, on the 12th of January, 1824, a note was submitted in the Czar's name to all the Courts of Europe, containing a plan for a settlement of the Greek question, which it was proposed that the great Powers of Europe should enforce upon Turkey either by means of an armed demonstration or by the threat of breaking off all diplomatic relations. According to this scheme, Greece, apart from the islands, was to be divided into three Principalities, each tributary to the Sultan and garrisoned by Turkish troops, but in other respects autonomous, like the Principalities of Moldavia and Wallachia. The islands were to retain their municipal

First Russian project of joint intervention, 12 Jan., 1824.

organisation as before. In one respect this scheme was superior to all that have succeeded it, for it included in the territory of the Greeks both Crete and Epirus; in all other respects it was framed in the interest of Russia alone. Its object was simply to create a second group of provinces, like those on the Danube, which should afford Russia a constant opportunity for interfering with the Ottoman Empire, and which at the same time should prevent the Greeks from establishing an independent and self-supporting State. The design cannot be called insidious, for its object was so palpable that not a single politician in Europe was deceived by it; and a very simple ruse of Metternich's was enough to draw from the Russian Government an explicit declaration against the independence of Greece, which was described by the Czar as a mere chimera. But of all the parties concerned, the Greeks themselves were loudest in denunciation of the Russian plan. Their Government sent a protest against it to London, and was assured by Canning in reply that the support of this country should never be given to any scheme for disposing of the Greeks without their own consent. Elsewhere the Czar's note was received with expressions of politeness due to a Court which it might be dangerous to contradict; and a series of conferences was opened at St. Petersburg for the purpose of discussing propositions which no one intended to carry into execution. Though Canning ordered the British ambassador at St. Petersburg to dissociate himself from these proceedings, the conferences dragged on, with long adjournments, from the spring of 1824 to the summer of the following year.*

In the meantime a strong spirit of discontent was rising in the Russian army and nation. The religious feeling no less than the pride of the people was deeply wounded by Alexander's refusal to aid the Greeks in their struggle, and by the pitiful results of his attempted diplomatic concert. Alone among the European nations the Russians understood the ecclesiastical character of the Greek insurrection, and owed nothing of their sympathy with it to the spell of classical literature and art. *Discontent and conspiracies in Russia.* It is characteristic of the strength of the religious element in the political views of the Russian people, that the floods of the Neva which overwhelmed St. Petersburg in the winter of 1825 should have been regarded as a sign of divine anger at the Czar's inaction in the struggle between the Crescent and the Cross. But other causes of discontent were not wanting in Russia. Though Alexander had forgotten his promises to introduce constitutional rule, there were many, especially in the army, who had not done so. Officers who served in the invasion of France in 1815, and in the three years' occupation which followed it, returned from Western Europe with ideas of social progress and of constitutional rights which they could never have gathered in their own country. And when the bright hopes which had been excited by the recognition of these same ideas by the Czar passed away, and

* Prokesch-Osten, i. 258, iv. 68. B. and F. State Papers, xii. 902. Stapleton, Canning, p. 496; Metternich, iv. 127. Wellington, N.S. ii. 372-396.

Russia settled down into the routine of despotism and corruption, the old unquestioning loyalty of the army was no longer proof against the workings of the revolutionary spirit. In a land where legal means of opposition to government and of the initiation of reform were wholly wanting, discontent was forced into its most dangerous form, that of military conspiracy. The army was honeycombed with secret societies. Both in the north and in the south of Russia men of influence worked among the younger officers, and gained a strong body of adherents to their design of establishing a constitution by force. The southern army contained the most resolute and daring conspirators. These men had definitely abandoned the hope of effecting any public reform as long as Alexander lived, and they determined to sacrifice the sovereign, as his father and others before him had been sacrificed, to the political necessities of the time. If the evidence subsequently given by those implicated in the conspiracy is worthy of credit, a definite plan had been formed for the assassination of the Czar in the presence of his troops at one of the great reviews intended to be held in the south of Russia in the autumn of 1825. On the death of the monarch a provisional government was at once to be established, and a constitution proclaimed.

Alexander, aware of the rising indignation of his people, and irritated beyond endurance by the failure of his diplomatic efforts, had dissolved the St. Petersburg Conferences in August, 1825, and declared that Russia would henceforth act according to its own discretion. He quitted St. Petersburg and travelled to the Black

Sea, accompanied by some of the leaders of the war-party. Here, plunged in a profound melancholy, conscious that all his early hopes had only served to surround him with conspirators, and that his sacrifice of Russia's military interests to international peace had only rendered his country impotent before all Europe, he still hesitated to make the final determination between peace and war. A certain mystery hung over his movements, his acts, and his intentions. Suddenly, while all Europe waited for the signal that should end the interval of suspense, the news was sent out from a lonely port on the Black Sea that the Czar was dead. Alexander, still under fifty years of age, had welcomed the illness which carried him from a world of cares, and closed a career in which anguish and disappointment had succeeded to such intoxicating glory and such unbounded hope. Young as he still was for one who had reigned twenty-four years, Alexander was of all men the most life-weary. Power, pleasure, excitement, had lavished on him hours of such existence as none but Napoleon among all his contemporaries had enjoyed. They had left him nothing but the solace of religious resignation, and the belief that a Power higher than his own might yet fulfil the purposes in which he himself had failed. Ever in the midst of great acts and great events, he had missed greatness himself. Where he had been best was exactly where men inferior to himself considered him to have been worst—in his hopes; and these hopes he had himself abandoned and renounced. Strength, insight, unity

Death of the Czar, Dec. 1, 1825.

of purpose, the qualities which enable men to mould events, appeared in him but momentarily or in semblance. For want of them the large and fair horizon of his earlier years was first obscured and then wholly blotted out from his view, till in the end nothing but his pietism and his generosity distinguished him from the politicians of repression whose instrument he had become.

The sudden death of Alexander threw the Russian Court into the greatest confusion, for it was not known who was to succeed him. The heir to the throne was his brother Constantine, an ignorant and brutal savage, who had just sufficient sense not to desire to be Czar of Russia, though he considered himself good enough to tyrannise over the Poles. Constantine had renounced his right to the crown some years before, but the renunciation had not been made public, nor had the Grand Duke Nicholas, Constantine's younger brother, been made aware that the succession was irrevocably fixed upon himself. Accordingly, when the news of Alexander's death reached St. Petersburg, and the document embodying Constantine's abdication was brought from the archives by the officials to whose keeping it had been entrusted, Nicholas refused to acknowledge it as binding, and caused the troops to take the oath of allegiance to Constantine, who was then at Warsaw. Constantine, on the other hand, proclaimed his brother emperor. An interregnum of three weeks followed, during which messages passed between Warsaw and St. Petersburg, Nicholas positively

Military insurrection at St. Petersburg, Dec. 26, 1825.

refusing to accept the crown unless by his elder brother's direct command. This at length arrived, and on the 26th of December Nicholas assumed the rank of sovereign. But the interval of uncertainty had been turned to good account by the conspirators at St. Petersburg. The oath already taken by the soldiers to Constantine enabled the officers who were concerned in the plot to denounce Nicholas as a usurper, and to disguise their real designs under the cloak of loyalty to the legitimate Czar. Ignorant of the very meaning of a constitution, the common soldiers mutinied because they were told to do so; and it is said that they shouted the word Constitution, believing it to be the name of Constantine's wife. When summoned to take the oath to Nicholas, the Moscow Regiment refused it, and marched off to the place in front of the Senate House, where it formed square, and repulsed an attack made upon it by the Cavalry of the Guard. Companies from other regiments now joined the mutineers, and symptoms of insurrection began to show themselves among the civil population. Nicholas himself did not display the energy of character which distinguished him through all his later life; on the contrary, his attitude was for some time rather that of resignation than of self-confidence. Whether some doubt as to the justice of his cause haunted him, or a trial like that to which he was now exposed was necessary to bring to its full strength the iron quality of his nature, it is certain that the conduct of the new Czar during these critical hours gave to those around him little indication of the indomitable will which was henceforth to govern Russia. Though the great mass of the army remained obedient, it was but slowly brought up to the scene of revolt. Officers of high rank were sent to harangue the insurgents, and one of these, General Miloradovitsch, a veteran of the Napoleonic campaigns, was mortally wounded while endeavouring to make himself heard. It was not until evening that the artillery was ordered into action, and the command given by the Czar to fire grape-shot among the insurgents. The effect was decisive. The mutineers fled before a fire which they were unable to return, and within a few minutes the insurrection was over. It had possessed no chief of any military capacity; its leaders were missing at the moment when a forward march or an attack on the palace of the Czar might have given them the victory; and among the soldiers at large there was not the least desire to take part in any movement against the established system of Russia. The only effect left by the conspiracy within Russia itself was seen in the rigorous and uncompromising severity with which Nicholas henceforward enforced the principle of autocratic rule. The illusions of the previous reign were at an end. A man with the education and the ideas of a drill-sergeant and the religious assurance of a Covenanter was on the throne; rebellion had done its worst against him; and woe to those who in future should deviate a hair's breadth from their duty of implicit obedience to the sovereign's all-sufficing power.*

---

* Korff, Accession of Nicholas, p. 253; Herzen, Russische Verschwörung, p. 106; Mendelssohn, i. 806. Schnitzler, Histoire Intime, i. 195.

It has been stated, and with some probability of truth, that the military insurrection of 1825 disposed the new Czar to a more vigorous policy abroad. The conspirators, when on their trial, declared it to have been their intention to throw the army at once into an attack upon the Turks; and in so doing they would certainly have had the feeling of the nation on their side. Nicholas himself had little or no sympathy for the Greeks. They were a democratic people, and the freedom which they sought to gain was nothing but anarchy. "Do not speak of the Greeks," he said to the representative of a foreign power; "I call them the rebels."
Nevertheless, little as Nicholas wished to serve the Greek democracy, both inclination and policy urged him to make an end of his predecessor's faint-hearted system of negotiation, and to bring the struggle in the East to a summary close. Canning had already, in conversation with the Russian ambassador at London, discussed a possible change of policy on the part of the two rival Courts. He now saw that time had come for establishing new relations between Great Britain and Russia, and for attempting that co-operation in the East which he had held to be impracticable during Alexander's reign. The Duke of Wellington was sent to St. Petersburg, nominally to offer the usual congratulations to the new sovereign, in reality to dissuade him from going to war, and to propose either the separate intervention of England or a joint intervention by England and Russia on behalf of Greece. The mission was successful. It was in vain that Metternich

Anglo-Russian Protocol, April 4, 1826.

endeavoured to entangle the new Czar in the diplomatic web that had so long held his predecessor. The spell of the Holy Alliance was broken. Nicholas looked on the past influence of Austria on the Eastern Question only with resentment; he would hear of no more conferences of ambassadors; and on the 4th of April, 1826, a Protocol was signed at St. Petersburg, by which Great Britain and Russia fixed the conditions under which the mediation of the former Power was to be tendered to the Porte. Greece was to remain tributary to the Sultan; it was, however, to be governed by its own elected authorities, and to be completely independent in its commercial relations. The policy known in our own day as that of bag-and-baggage expulsion was to be carried out in a far more extended sense than that in which it has been advocated by more recent champions of the subject races of the East; the Protocol of 1826 stipulating for the removal not only of Turkish officials but of the entire surviving Turkish population of Greece. All property belonging to the Turks, whether on the continent or in the islands, was to be purchased by the Greeks.*

Thus was the first step taken in the negotiations which ended in the establishment of Hellenic independence. The Protocol, which had been secretly signed, was submitted after some interval to the other Courts of Europe. At Vienna it was received with the utmost disgust. Metternich had at first declared the union

---

* B. and F. State Papers, xiv. 630; Metternich, iv. 161, 212, 320, 372; Wellington, N. S., ii. 85, 148, 244; Gentz, D. L, iii. 315.

of England and Russia to be an impossibility. When this union was actually established, no language was sufficiently strong to express his mortification and his spite. At one moment he declared that Canning was a revolutionist who had entrapped the young and inexperienced Czar into an alliance with European radicalism; at another, that England had made itself the cat's-paw of Russian ambition. Not till now, he protested, could Europe understand what it had lost in Castlereagh. Nor did Metternich confine himself to lamentations. While his representatives at Paris and Berlin spared no effort to excite the suspicion of those Courts against the Anglo-Russian project of intervention, the Austrian ambassador at London worked upon King George's personal hostility to Canning, and conspired against the Minister with that important section of the English aristocracy which was still influenced by the traditional regard for Austria. Berlin, however, was the only field where Metternich's diplomacy still held its own. King Frederick William had not yet had time to acquire the habit of submission to the young Czar Nicholas, and was therefore saved the pain of deciding which of two masters he should obey. In spite of his own sympathy for the Greeks, he declined to connect Prussia with the proposed joint-intervention, and remained passive, justifying this course by the absence of any material interests of Prussia in the East. Being neither a neighbour of the Ottoman Empire nor a maritime Power, Prussia had in fact no direct means of making its influence felt.

France, on whose action much more depended, was now governed wholly in the interests of the Legitimist party. Louis XVIII. had died in 1824, and the Count of Artois had succeeded to the throne, under the title of Charles X. The principles of the Legitimists would logically have made them defenders of the hereditary rights of the Sultan against his rebellious subjects; but the Sultan, unlike Ferdinand of Spain, was not a Bourbon nor even a Christian; and in a case where the legitimate prince was an infidel and the rebels were Christians, the conscience of the most pious Legitimist might well recoil from the perilous task of deciding between the divine rights of the Crown and the divine rights of the Church, and choose, in so painful an emergency, the simpler course of gratifying the national love of action. There existed, both among Liberals and among Ultramontanes, a real sympathy for Greece, and this interest was almost the only one in which all French political sections felt that they had something in common. Liberals rejoiced in the prospect of making a new free State in Europe; Catholics, like Charles X. himself, remembered Saint Louis and the Crusades; diplomatists understood the extreme importance of the impending breach between Austria and Russia, and of the opportunity of allying France with the latter Power. Thus the natural and disinterested impulse of the greater part of the public coincided exactly with the dictates of a far-seeing policy; and the Government, in spite of its Legitimist principles and of some assurances given to Metternich in

Treaty between England, Russia, and France, July, 1827.

Admirals commanding the Mediterranean squadrons of the three Powers.*

Scarcely was the Treaty of London signed when Canning died. He had definitely broken from the policy of his predecessors, that policy which, for the sake of guarding against Russia's advance, had condemned the Christian races of the East to eternal subjection to the Turk, and bound up Great Britain with the Austrian system of resistance to the very principle and name of national independence. Canning was no blind friend to Russia. As keenly as any of his adversaries he appreciated the importance of England's interests in the East; of all English statesmen of that time he would have been the last to submit to any diminution of England's just influence or power. But, unlike his predecessors, he saw that there were great forces at work which, whether with England's concurrence or in spite of it, would accomplish that revolution in the East for which the time was now come; and he was statesman enough not to acquiesce in the belief that the welfare of England was in permanent and necessary antagonism to the moral interests of mankind and the better spirit of the age. Therefore, instead of attempting to maintain the integrity of the Ottoman Empire, or holding aloof and resorting to threats and armaments while Russia accomplished the liberation of Greece by itself, he united with Russia in this work, and relied on concerted action as the best preventive against the undue extension of Russia's influence in the East. In

Death of Canning, August, 1827.

Policy of Canning.

---

* B. and F. State Papers, xiv. 632; xvii. 20; Wellington, N. S., iv. 57.

committing England to armed intervention, Canning no doubt hoped that the settlement of the Greek question arranged by the Powers would be peacefully accepted by the Sultan, and that a separate war between Russia and the Porte, on this or any other issue, would be averted. Neither of these hopes was realised. The joint-intervention had to be enforced by arms, and no sooner had the Allies struck their common blow than a war between Turkey and Russia followed. How far the course of events might have been modified had Canning's life not been cut short it is impossible to say; but whether his statesmanship might or might not have averted war on the Danube, the balance of results proved his policy to have been the right one. Greece was established as an independent State, to supply in the future a valuable element of resistance to Slavic preponderance in the Levant; and the encounter between Russia and Turkey, so long dreaded, produced none of those disastrous effects which had been anticipated from it. On the relative value of Canning's statesmanship as compared with that of his predecessors, the mind of England and of Europe has long been made up. He stands among those who have given to this country its claim to the respect of mankind. His monument, as well as his justification, is the existence of national freedom in the East; and when half a century later a British Government reverted to the principle of non-intervention, as it had been understood by Castlereagh, and declined to enter into any effective co-operation with Russia for the emancipation of Bulgaria, even then, when the precedent of Canning's action in 1827 stood in direct and glaring contradiction to the policy of the hour, no effective attempt was made by the leaders of the party to which Canning had belonged to impugn his authority, or to explain away his example. It might indeed be alleged that Canning had not explicitly resolved on the application of force; but those who could maintain that Canning would, like Wellington, have used the language of apology and regret when Turkish obstinacy had made it impossible to effect the object of his intervention by any other means, had indeed read the history of Canning's career in vain.*

The death of Canning, which brought his rival, the Duke of Wellington, after a short interval to the head of affairs, caused at the moment no avowed change in the execution of his plans. In accordance with the provisions of the Treaty of London the mediation of the allied Powers was at once tendered to the belligerents, and an armistice demanded. The armistice

* Parl. Deb., May 11, 1877. Nothing can be more misleading than to say that Canning never contemplated the possibility of armed action because a clause in the Treaty of 1827 made the formal stipulation that the contracting Powers would not "take part in the hostilities between the contending parties." How, except by armed force, could the Allies "prevent, in so far as might be in their power, all collision between the contending parties," which, in the very same clause, they undertook to do? And what was the meaning of the stipulation that they should "transmit instructions to their Admirals conformable to these provisions"? Wellington himself, *before* the battle of Navarino, condemned the Treaty of London on the very ground that it "specified means of compulsion which were neither more nor less than measures of war;" and he protested against the statement that the treaty arose directly out of the Protocol of St. Petersburg, which was his own work. Wellington, N.S., iv. 137, 221.

was accepted by the Greeks; it was contemptuously refused by the Turks. In consequence of this refusal the state of war continued, as it would have been absurd to ask the Greeks to sit still and be massacred because the enemy declined to lay down his arms. The Turk being the party resisting the mediation agreed upon, it became necessary to deprive him of the power of continuing hostilities. Heavy reinforcements had just arrived from Egypt, and an expedition was on the point of sailing from Navarino, the gathering place of Ibrahim's forces, against Hydra, the capture of which would have definitely made an end of the Greek insurrection. Admiral Codrington, the commander of the British fleet, and the French Admiral De Rigny, were now off the coast of Greece. They addressed themselves to Ibrahim, and required from him a promise that he would make no movement until further orders should arrive from Constantinople. Ibrahim made this promise verbally on the 25th of September. A few days later, however, Ibrahim learnt that while he himself was compelled to be inactive, the Greeks, continuing hostilities as they were entitled to do, had won a brilliant naval victory under Captain Hastings within the Gulf of Corinth. Unable to control his anger, he sailed out from the harbour of Navarino, and made for Patras. Codrington, who had stationed his fleet at Zante, heard of the movement, and at once threw himself across the track of the Egyptian, whom he compelled to turn back by an energetic threat to sink his fleet. Had the French and

Intervention of the Admirals, Sept., 1827.

Russian contingents been at hand, Codrington would have taken advantage of Ibrahim's sortie to cut him from all Greek harbours, and to force him to return direct to Alexandria, thus peaceably accomplishing the object of the intervention. This, however, to the misfortune of Ibrahim's seamen, the English admiral could not do alone. Ibrahim re-entered Navarino, and there found the orders of the Sultan for which it had been agreed that he should wait. These orders were dictated by true Turkish infatuation. They bade Ibrahim continue the subjugation of the Morea with the utmost vigour, and promised him the assistance of Reschid Pasha, his rival in the siege of Missolonghi. Ibrahim, perfectly reckless of the consequences, now sent out his devastating columns again. No life, and nothing that could support life, was spared. Not only were the crops ravaged, but the fruit trees, which are the permanent support of the country, were cut down at the roots. Clouds of fire and smoke from burning villages showed the English officers who approached the coast in what spirit the Turk met their proposals for a pacification. "It is supposed that if Ibrahim remained in Greece," wrote Captain Hamilton, "more than a third of its inhabitants would die of absolute starvation."

It became necessary to act quickly, the more so as the season was far advanced, and a winter blockade of Ibrahim's fleet was impossible. A message was sent to the Egyptian head-quarters, requiring that hostilities should cease, that the Morea should be evacuated, and the Turko-Egyptian

Battle of Navarino, Oct. 20th, 1827.

fleet return to Constantinople and Alexandria. In answer to this message there came back a statement that Ibrahim had left Navarino for the interior of the country, and that it was not known where to find him. Nothing now remained for the admirals but to make their presence felt. On the 18th of October it was resolved that the English, French, and Russian fleets, which were now united, should enter the harbour of Navarino in battle order. The movement was called a demonstration, and in so far as the admirals had not actually determined upon making an attack, it was not directly a hostile measure; but every gun was ready to open fire, and it was well understood that any act of resistance on the part of the opposite fleet would result in hostilities. Codrington, as senior officer, took command of the allied squadron, and the instructions which he gave to his colleagues for the event of a general engagement concluded with Nelson's words, that no captain could do very wrong who placed his ship alongside that of an enemy.

Thus, ready to strike hard, the English admiral sailed into the harbour of Navarino at noon on October 20, followed by the French and the Russians. The allied fleet advanced to within pistol-shot of the Ottoman ships and there anchored. A little to the windward of the position assigned to the English corvette *Dartmouth* there lay a Turkish fire-ship. A request was made that this dangerous vessel might be removed to a safer distance; it was refused, and a boat's crew was then sent to cut its cable. The boat was received with musketry fire. This was answered by the *Dartmouth* and by a French ship, and the battle soon became general. Codrington, still desirous to avoid bloodshed, sent his pilot to Moharem Bey, who commanded in Ibrahim's absence, proposing to withhold fire on both sides. Moharem replied with cannon-shot, killing the pilot and striking Codrington's own vessel. This exhausted the patience of the English admiral, who forthwith made his adversary a mere wreck. The entire fleets on both sides were now engaged. The Turks had a superiority of eight hundred guns and fought with courage. For four hours the battle raged at close quarters in the land-locked harbour, while twenty thousand of Ibrahim's soldiers watched from the surrounding hills the struggle in which they could take no part. But the result of the combat was never for a moment doubtful. The confusion and bad discipline of the Turkish fleet made it an easy prey. Vessel after vessel was sunk or blown to pieces, and before evening fell the work of the allies was done. When Ibrahim returned from his journey on the following day he found the harbour of Navarino strewed with wrecks and dead bodies. Four thousand of his seamen had fallen; the fleet which was to have accomplished the reduction of Hydra was utterly ruined.*

Over all Greece it was at once felt that the nation was saved. The intervention of the Powers had been sudden and decisive beyond the most sanguine hopes;

* Bourchier's Codrington, ii. 62. Admiralty Despatches, Nov. 10, 1827. Parl. Deb., Feb. 14, 1828.

and though this intervention might be intended to establish something less than the complete independence of Greece, the violence of the first collision bade fair to carry the work far beyond the bounds originally assigned to it. The atti- *Inaction of England after Navarino.*
tude of the Porte after the news of the battle of Navarino reached Constantinople was exactly that which its worst enemies might have desired. So far from abating anything in its resistance to the mediation of the three Powers, it declared the attack made upon its navy to be a crime and an outrage, and claimed satisfaction for it from the ambassadors of the Allied Powers. Arguments proved useless, and the united demand for an armistice with the Greeks having been finally and contemptuously refused, the ambassadors, in accordance with their instructions, quitted the Turkish capital (Dec. 8). Had Canning been still living, it is probable that the first blow of Navarino would have been immediately followed by the measures necessary to make the Sultan submit to the Treaty of London, and that the forces of Great Britain would have been applied with sufficient vigour to render any isolated action on the part of Russia both unnecessary and impossible. But at this critical moment a paralysis fell over the English Government. Canning's policy was so much his own, he had dragged his colleagues so forcibly with him in spite of themselves, that when his place was left empty no one had the courage either to fulfil or to reverse his intentions, and the men who succeeded him acted as if they were trespassers in the fortress

which Canning had taken by storm. The very ground on which Wellington, no less than Canning, had justified the agreement made with Russia in 1826 was the necessity of preventing Russia from acting alone; and when Russian and Turkish ships had actually fought at Navarino, and war was all but formally declared, it became more imperative than ever that Great Britain should keep the most vigorous hold upon its rival, and by steady, consistent pressure let it be known to both Turks and Russians that the terms of the Treaty of London and no others must be enforced. To retire from action immediately after dealing the Sultan one dire, irrevocable blow, without following up this stroke or attaining the end agreed upon—to leave Russia to take up the armed compulsion where England had dropped it, and to win from its crippled adversary the gains of a private and isolated war—was surely the weakest of all possible policies that could have been adopted. Yet this was the policy followed by English Ministers during that interval of transition and incoherence that passed between Canning's death and the introduction of the Reform Bill.

By the Russian Government nothing was more ardently desired than a contest with Turkey, in which England and France, after they had destroyed the Turkish fleet, should be mere on-lookers, debarred by the folly of the Porte itself from prohibiting or controlling hostilities between it and its neighbour. There might indeed be some want of a pretext for war, since all the points of contention between Russia and Turkey other than those relating to Greece had been finally settled in Russia's favour by a Treaty signed at Akerman in October, 1826. But the spirit of infatuation had seized the Sultan, or a secret hope that the Western Powers would in the last resort throw over the Court of St. Petersburg, led him to hurry on hostilities by a direct challenge to Russia. A proclamation which reads like the work of some frantic dervish, though said to have been composed by Mahmud himself, called the Mussulman world to arms. Russia was denounced as the instigator of the Greek rebellion, and the arch-enemy of Islam. The Treaty of Akerman was declared to have been extorted by compulsion and to have been signed only for the purpose of gaining time. "Russia has imparted its own madness to the other Powers and persuaded them to make an alliance to free the Rayah from his Ottoman master. But the Turk does not count his enemies. The law forbids the people of Islam to permit any injury to be done to their religion; and if all the unbelievers together unite against them, they will enter on the war as a sacred duty, and trust in God for protection." This proclamation was followed by a levy of troops and the expulsion of most of the Christian residents in Constantinople. Russia needed no other pretext. The fanatical outburst of the Sultan was treated by the Court of St. Petersburg as if it had been the deliberate expression of some civilised Power, and was answered on the 26th of April, 1828, by a declaration of war. In order to soften the effect of this step and to reap the full benefit of its subsisting relations with France and England, Russia gave a provisional undertaking to confine its operations as a belligerent to the mainland and the Black Sea, and within the Mediterranean to act still as one of the allied neutrals under the terms of the Treaty of London.

The moment seized by Russia for the declaration of war was one singularly favourable to itself and unfortunate for its adversary. Not only had the Turkish fleet been destroyed by the neutrals, but the old Turkish force of the Janissaries had been destroyed by its own master, and the new-modelled regiments which were to replace it had not yet been organised. The Sultan had determined in 1826 to postpone his long-planned military reform no longer, and to stake everything on one bold stroke against the Janissaries. Troops enough were brought up from the other side of the Bosphorus to make Mahmud certain of victory. The Janissaries were summoned to contribute a proportion of their number to the regiments about to be formed on the European pattern; and when they proudly refused and raised the standard of open rebellion they were cut to pieces and exterminated by Mahmud's Anatolian soldiers in the midst of Constantinople.* The principal difficulty in the way of a reform of the Turkish army was thus removed and the work of reorganisation was earnestly taken in hand; but before there was time to complete it the enemy entered the field. Mahmud had to meet

Military condition of Turkey.

* Rosen, Geschichte der Türkei, i. 57.

the attack of Russia with an army greatly diminished in number, and confused by the admixture of European and Turkish discipline. The resources of the empire were exhausted by the long struggle with Greece, and, above all, the destruction of the Janissaries had left behind it an exasperation which made the Sultan believe that rebellion might at any moment break out in his own capital. Nevertheless, in spite of its inherent weakness and of all the disadvantages under which it entered into war, Turkey succeeded in prolonging its resistance through two campaigns, and might, with better counsels, have tried the fortune of a third.

The actual military resources of Russia were in 1828 much below what they were believed to be by all Europe. The destruction of Napoleon's army in 1812 and the subsequent exploits of Alexander in the campaigns which ended in the capture of Paris had left behind them an impression of Russian energy and power which was far from corresponding with the reality, and which, though disturbed by the events of 1828, had by no means vanished at the time of the Crimean War. The courage and patience of the Russian soldier were certainly not over-rated; but the progress supposed to have been made in Russian military organisation since the campaign of 1799, when it was regarded in England and Austria as little above that of savages, was for the most part imaginary. The proofs of a radically bad system —scanty numbers, failing supplies, immense sickness—

Military condition of Russia.

were never more conspicuous than in 1828. Though Russia had been preparing for war for at least seven years, scarcely seventy thousand soldiers could be collected on the Pruth. The general was Wittgenstein, one of the heroes of 1812, but now a veteran past effective work. Nicholas came to the camp to make things worse by headstrong interference. The best Russian officer, Paskiewitsch, was put in command of the forces about to operate in Asia Minor, and there, thrown on his own resources and free to create a system of his own, he achieved results in strong contrast to the failure of the Russian arms on the Danube.

In entering on the campaign of 1828, it was necessary for the Czar to avoid giving any unnecessary causes of anxiety to Austria, which had already made unsuccessful attempts to form a coalition against him. The line of operations was therefore removed as far as possible from the Austrian frontier; and after the Rou-

Campaign of 1828.

manian principalities had been peacefully occupied, the Danube was crossed at a short distance above the point where its mouths divide (June 7). The Turks had no intention of meeting the enemy in a pitched battle; they confined themselves to the defence of fortresses, the form of warfare to which, since the decline of the military art in Turkey, the patience and abstémiousness of the race best fit them. Ibraila and Silistria on the Danube, Varna and Shumla in the neighbourhood of the Balkans, were their principal strongholds, and of these Ibraila was at once besieged by a considerable force, while Silistria was watched by a weak contingent, and the vanguard of the army pushed on through the Dobrudscha towards the Black Sea, where, with the capture of the minor coast-towns, it expected to enter into communication with the fleet. The first few weeks of the campaign were marked by considerable successes. Ibraila capitulated on the 18th of June, and the military posts in the Dobrudscha fell one after another into the hands of the invaders, who met with no effective resistance in this district. But their serious work was only now beginning. The Russian army, in spite of its weakness, was divided into three parts, occupied severally in front of Silistria, Shumla, and Varna. At Shumla the mass of the Turkish army, under Omer Brionis, was concentrated. The force brought against it by the invader was inadequate to its task, and the attempts which were made to lure the Turkish army from its entrenched camp into the open field proved unsuccessful. The difficulties of the siege proved so great that Wittgenstein after a while proposed to abandon offensive operations at this point, and to leave a mere corps of observation before the enemy until Varna should have fallen. This, however, was forbidden by the Czar. As the Russians wasted away before Shumla with sickness and fatigue, the Turks gained strength, and on the 24th of September Omer broke out from his entrenchments and moved eastwards to the relief of Varna. Nicholas again over-ruled his generals, and ordered his cousin, Prince Eugene of Würtemberg, to attack the advancing Ottomans with the troops then actually at his disposal. Eugene did so, and suffered a severe defeat. A vigorous movement of the Turks would probably have made an end of the campaign, but Omer held back at the critical moment, and on the 10th of October Varna surrendered. This, however, was the only conquest made by the Russians. The season was too far advanced for them either to cross the Balkans or to push forward operations against the uncaptured fortresses. Shumla and Silistria remained in the hands of their defenders, and the Russians, after suffering enormous losses in proportion to the smallness of their numbers, withdrew to Varna and the Danube, to resume the campaign in the spring of the following year.*

The spirits of the Turks and of their European friends were raised by the unexpected failure of the Czar's arms. Metternich resumed his efforts to form a coalition, and tempted French Ministers with the prospect of recovering the Rhenish provinces, but in vain. The Sultan began negotiations, but broke them off when he found that the events of the campaign had made no difference in the enemy's tone. The prestige of Russia was in fact at stake, and Nicholas would probably have faced a war with Austria and Turkey combined rather than have made peace without restoring the much-diminished reputation of his troops. The winter was therefore spent in bringing up distant reserves. Wittgenstein was removed from his command; the Czar withdrew from military operations in which he had done nothing but mischief; and Diebitsch, a Prussian by

* Moltke, Russisch-Turkische Feldzug, p. 226. Rosen, i. 67.

birth and training, was placed at the head of the army, untrammelled by the sovereign presence or counsels which had hampered his predecessor.

Campaign of 1829.

The intention of the new commander was to cross the Balkans as soon as Silistria should have fallen, without waiting for the capture of Shumla. In pursuance of this design the fleet was despatched early in the spring of 1829 to seize a port beyond the mountain-range. Diebitsch then placed a corps in front of Silistria, and made his preparations for the southward march; but before any progress had been made in the siege the Turks themselves took the field. Reschid Pasha, now Grand Vizier, moved eastwards from Shumla at the beginning of May against the weak Russian contingent that still lay in winter quarters between that place and Varna. The superiority of his force promised him an easy victory; but after winning some unimportant successes, and advancing to a considerable distance from his stronghold, he allowed himself to be held at bay until Diebitsch, with the army of the Danube, was ready to fall upon his rear. The errors of the Turks had given to the Russian commander, who hastened across Bulgaria on hearing of his colleague's peril, the choice of destroying their army, or of seizing Shumla by a *coup-de-main*. Diebitsch determined upon attacking his enemy in the open field, and on the 10th of June Reschid's army, attempting to regain the roads to Shumla, was put to total rout at Kulewtscha. A fortnight later Silistria surrendered, and Diebitsch, reinforced by the troops that had besieged that fortress, was now able to commence his march across the Balkans.

Rumour magnified into hundreds of thousands the scanty columns which for the first time carried the Russian flag over the Balkan range. Resistance everywhere collapsed. The mountains were crossed without difficulty, and on the 19th of August the invaders appeared before Adrianople, which immediately surrendered. Putting on the boldest countenance in order to conceal his real weakness, Diebitsch now struck out right and left, and sent detachments both to the Euxine and the Ægæan coast. The fleet co-operated with him, and the ports of the Black Sea, almost as far south as the Bosphorus, fell into the invaders' hands. The centre of the army began to march upon Constantinople. If the Sultan had known the real numbers of the force which threatened his capital, a force not exceeding twenty thousand men, he would probably have recognised that his assailant's position was a more dangerous one than his own. Diebitsch had advanced into the heart of the enemy's country with a mere handful of men. Sickness was daily thinning his ranks; his troops were dispersed over a wide area from sea to sea; and the warlike tribes of Albania threatened to fall upon his communications from the west. For a moment the Sultan spoke of fighting upon the walls of Constantinople; but the fear of rebellion within his own capital, the discovery of conspiracies, and the disasters sustained by his arms in Asia, where Kars and Erzeroum had fallen into the

Crossing of the Balkans, July, 1829.

enemy's hands, soon led him to make overtures of peace and to accept the moderate terms which the Russian Government, aware of its own difficulties, was willing to grant. It would have been folly for the Czar to stimulate the growing suspicion of England and to court the attack of Austria by prolonging hostilities; and although King Charles X. and the French Cabinet, reverting to the ideas of Tilsit, proposed a partition of the Ottoman Empire, and a general re-arrangement of the map of Europe which would have given Belgium and the Palatinate to France, the plan was originated too late to produce any effect.* Russia had everything to lose and nothing to gain by a European war. It had reduced Turkey to submission, and might fairly hope to maintain its ascendency at Constantinople during coming years without making any of those great territorial changes which would have given its rivals a pretext for intervening on the Sultan's behalf. Under the guise of a generous forbearance the Czar extricated himself from a dangerous position with credit and advantage. As much had been won as could be maintained without hazard; and on the 14th of September peace was concluded in Adrianople.

The Treaty of Adrianople gave Russia a slight increase of territory in Asia, incorporating with the Czar's dominions the ports of Anapa and Poti on the eastern coast of the Black Sea; but its most important

* Viel-Castel, xx. 16. Russia was to have had the Danubian Provinces; Austria was to have had Bosnia and Servia; Prussia was to have had Saxony and Holland; the King of Holland was to have reigned at Constantinople.

provisions were those which confirmed and extended the Protectorate exercised by the Czar over the Danubian Principalities, and guaranteed the commercial rights of Russian subjects throughout the Ottoman Empire both by land and sea. In order more effectively to exclude the Sultan's influence from Wallachia and Moldavia, the office of Hospodar, hitherto tenable for seven years, was now made an appointment for life, and the Sultan specifically engaged to permit no interference on the part of his neighbouring Pashas with the affairs of these provinces. No fortified point was to be retained by the Turks on the left bank of the Danube; no Mussulman was to be permitted to reside within the Principalities; and those possessing landed estates there were to sell them within eighteen months. The Porte pledged itself never again to detain Russian ships of commerce coming from the Black Sea, and acknowledged that such an act would amount to an infraction of treaties justifying Russia in having recourse to reprisals. The Straits of Constantinople and the Dardanelles were declared free and open to the merchant ships of all Powers at peace with the Porte, upon the same conditions which were stipulated for vessels under the Russian flag. The same freedom of trade and navigation was recognised within the Black Sea. All treaties and conventions hitherto concluded between Turkey and Russia were recognised as in force, except in so far as modified by the present agreement. The Porte further gave its adhesion to the Treaty of London relating to Greece, and to an Act entered into

Treaty of Adrianople, Sept. 14, 1829.

by the Allied Powers in March, 1829, for regulating the Greek frontier. An indemnity in money was declared to be owing to Russia; and as the amount of this remained to be fixed by mutual agreement, the means were still left open to the Russian Government for exercising a gentle pressure at Constantinople, or for rewarding the compliance of the conquered.*

The war between Turkey and Russia, while it left the European frontier between the belligerents unchanged, exercised a two-fold influence upon the settlement of Greece. On the one hand, by exciting the fears and suspicions of Great Britain, it caused the Government of our own country, under the Duke of Wellington, to insist on the limitation of the Greek State to the narrowest possible area †; on the other hand, by reducing Turkey itself almost to the condition of a Russian dependency, it led to the abandonment of the desire to maintain the Sultan's supremacy in any form over the emancipated provinces, and resulted in the establishment of an absolutely independent Hellenic kingdom. An important change had taken place within Greece itself just at the time when the allied Powers determined upon intervention. The parts of the local leaders were played out, and in April, 1827, Capodistrias, ex-Minister of Russia, was elected President for seven years. Capodistrias accepted the call. He was then, as he had been throughout the insurrection, at a distance from Greece;

Capodistrias elected President of Greece, April, 1827.

---

* Hertslet, Map of Europe by Treaty, ii. 813. Rosen, i. 108.
† Wellington, N. S., iv. 297.

and before making his way thither, he visited the principal Courts of Europe, with the view of ascertaining what moral or financial support he should be likely to receive from them. His interview with the Czar Nicholas led to a clear statement by that sovereign of the conditions which he expected Capodistrias, in return for Russia's continued friendship, to fulfil. Greece was to be rescued from revolution : in other words, personal was to be substituted for popular government. The State was to remain tributary to the Sultan: that is, in both Greece and Turkey the door was to be kept open for Russia's interference. Whether Capodistrias had any intention of fulfilling the latter condition is doubtful. His love for Greece and his own personal ambition prevented his regard for Russia, strong though this might be, from making him the mere instrument of the Court of St. Petersburg; and while outwardly acquiescing in the Czar's decision that Greece should remain a tributary State, he probably resolved from the first to aim at establishing its complete independence. With regard to the Czar's demand that the system of local self-government should be superseded within Greece itself by one of autocratic rule, Capodistrias was in harmony with his patron. He had been the Minister of a centralised despotism himself. His experience was wholly that of the official of an absolute sovereign; and although Capodistrias had represented the more liberal tendencies of the Russian Court when it was a question of arguing against Metternich about the complete or the partial restoration of despotic rule in Italy, he had no real acquaintance and no real sympathy with the action of free institutions, and moved in the same circle of ideas as the autocratic reformers of the eighteenth century, of whom Joseph II. was the type.*

The Turks were still masters of the Morea when Capodistrias reached Greece. The battle of Navarino had not caused Ibrahim to relax his hold upon the fortresses, and it was deemed necessary by the Allies to send a French army-corps to dislodge him from his position. This expeditionary force, under General Maison, landed in Greece in the summer of 1828, and Ibrahim, not wishing to fight to the bitter end, contented himself with burning Tripolitza to the ground and sowing it with salt, and then withdrew. The war between Turkey and Russia had now begun. Capodistrias assisted the Russian fleet in blockading the Dardanelles, and thereby gained for himself the marked ill-will of the British Government. At a conference held in London by the representatives of France, England, and Russia, in November, 1828, it was resolved that the operations of the Allies should be limited to the Morea and the islands. Capodistrias, in consequence of this decision, took the most vigorous measures for continuing the war against Turkey. What the allies refused to guarantee must be won by force of arms; and during the winter of 1829, while Russia pressed upon Turkey from the Danube, Capodistrias succeeded in reconquering Missolonghi and the whole tract of country

The Protocols of Nov., 1828, and March, 1829.

* Mendelssohn, Graf Capodistrias, p. 64.

immediately to the north of the Gulf of Corinth. The Porte, in prolonging its resistance after the November conference, played, as usual, into its enemy's hands. The negotiations at London were resumed in a spirit somewhat more favourable to Greece, and a Protocol was signed on the 22nd of March, 1829, extending the northern frontier of Greece up to a line drawn from the Gulf of Arta to the Gulf of Volo. Greece, according to this Protocol, was still to remain under the Sultan's suzerainty: its ruler was to be a hereditary prince belonging to one of the reigning European families, but not to any of the three allied Courts.*

The mediation of Great Britain was now offered to the Porte upon the terms thus laid down, and for the fourteenth time its mediation was rejected. But the end was near at hand. Diebitsch crossed the Balkans, and it was in vain that the Sultan then proposed the terms which he had scouted in November. The Treaty of Adrianople enforced the decisions of the March Protocol. Greece escaped from a limitation of its frontier, which would have left both Athens and Missolonghi Turkish territory. The principle of the admission of the provinces north of the Gulf of Corinth within the Hellenic State was established, and nothing remained for the friends of the Porte but to cut down to the narrowest possible area the district which had been loosely indicated in the London Protocol. While Russia, satisfied with its own successes against the Ottoman Empire and anxious to

Leopold accepts the Greek Crown, Feb., 1830.

---

* B. and F. State Papers, xvii. p. 132. Prokesch-Osten, v. 136.

play the part of patron of the conquered, ceased to interest itself in Greece, the Government of Great Britain contested every inch of territory proposed to be ceded to the new State, and finally induced the Powers to agree upon a boundary-line which did not even in letter fulfil the conditions of the treaty. Northern Acarnania and part of Ætolia were severed from Greece, and the frontier was drawn from the mouth of the river Achelous to a spot near Thermopylæ. On the other hand, as Russian influence now appeared to be firmly established and likely to remain paramount at Constantinople, the Western Powers had no motive to maintain the Sultan's supremacy over Greece. This was accordingly by common consent abandoned; and the Hellenic Kingdom, confined within miserably narrow limits on the mainland, and including neither Crete nor Samos among its islands, was ultimately offered in full sovereignty to Prince Leopold of Saxe-Coburg, the widower of Charlotte, daughter of George IV. After some negotiations, in which Leopold vainly asked for a better frontier, he accepted the Greek crown on the 11th of February, 1830.

In the meantime, Capodistrias was struggling hard to govern and to organise according to his own conceptions a land in which every element of anarchy, ruin, and confusion appeared to be arrayed against the restoration of civilised life. The country was devastated, depopulated, and in some places utterly barbarised. Out of a population of little more than a million, it was reckoned that three hundred

Government of Capodistrias.

thousand had perished during the conflict with the Turk. The whole fabric of political and social order had to be erected anew; and, difficult as this task would have been for the wisest ruler, it was rendered much more difficult by the conflict between Capodistrias' own ideal and the character of the people among whom he had to work. Communal or local self-government lay at the very root of Greek nationality. In many different forms this intense provincialism had maintained itself unimpaired up to the end of the war, in spite of national assemblies and national armaments. The Hydriote ship-owners, the Primates of the Morea, the guerilla leaders of the north, had each a type of life and a body of institutions as distinct as the dialects which they spoke or the saints whom they cherished in their local sanctuaries. If antagonistic in some respects to national unity, this vigorous local life had nevertheless been a source of national energy while Greece had still its independence to win; and now that national independence was won, it might well have been made the basis of a popular and effective system of self-government. But to Capodistrias, as to greater men of that age, the unity of the State meant the uniformity of all its parts; and, shutting his eyes to all the obstacles in his path, he set himself to create an administrative system as rigorously centralised as that which France had received from Napoleon. Conscious of his own intellectual superiority over his countrymen, conscious of his own integrity and of the sacrifice of all his personal wealth in his country's service, he put no measure on his expressions of scorn for the freebooters and peculators whom he believed to make up the Greek official world, and he both acted and spoke as if, in the literal sense of the words, all who ever came before him were thieves and robbers. The peasants of the mainland, who had suffered scarcely less from Klephts and Primates than from Turks, welcomed Capodistrias' levelling despotism, and to the end his name was popular among them; but among the classes which had supplied the leaders in the long struggle for independence, and especially among the ship-owners of the Archipelago, who felt the contempt expressed by Capodistrias for their seven years' efforts to be grossly unjust, a spirit of opposition arose which soon made it evident that Capodistrias would need better instruments than those which he had around him to carry out his task of remodelling Greece.

It was in the midst of this growing antagonism that the news reached Capodistrias that Leopold of Saxe-Coburg had been appointed King of Greece. The resolution made by the Powers in March, 1829, that the sovereign of Greece should belong to some reigning house, had perhaps not wholly destroyed the hopes of Capodistrias that he might become Prince or Hospodar of Greece himself. There were difficulties in the way of filling the throne, and these difficulties, after the appointment of Leopold, Capodistrias certainly did not seek to lessen. His subtlety, his command of the indirect methods of effecting a purpose, were so great and so habitual to him that there was little chance of his taking any overt step for preventing Leopold's accession to the crown; there

Leopold renounces the crown, May, 1830.

appears, however, to be evidence that he repressed the indications of assent which the Greeks attempted to offer to Leopold; and a series of letters written by him to that prince was probably intended, though in the most guarded language, to give Leopold the impression that the task which awaited him was a hopeless one. Leopold himself, at the very time when he accepted the crown, was wavering in his purpose. He saw with perfect clearness that the territory granted to the Greek State was too small to secure either its peace or its independence. The severance of Acarnania and Northern Ætolia meant the abandonment of the most energetic part of the Greek inland population, and a probable state of incessant warfare upon the northern frontier; the relinquishment of Crete meant that Greece, bankrupt as it was, must maintain a navy to protect the south coast of the Morea from Turkish attack. These considerations had been urged upon the Powers by Leopold before he accepted the crown, and he had been induced for the moment to withdraw them. But he had never fully acquiesced in the arrangements imposed upon him: he remained irresolute for some months; and at last, whether led to this decision by the letters of Capodistrias or by some other influences, he declared the conditions under which he was called upon to rule Greece to be intolerable, and renounced the crown (May, 1830).*

Capodistrias thus found himself delivered from his

* Stockmar, i. 80.; Mendelssohn; Capodistrias, p. 272. B. and F. State Papers, xvii. 453.

rival, and again face to face with the task to which duty or ambition called him. The candidature of Leopold had embittered the relations between Capodistrias and all who confronted him in Greece, for it gave him the means of measuring their hostility to himself by the fervour of their addresses to this unknown foreigner. A dark shadow fell over his government. As difficulties thickened and resistance grew everywhere more determined, the President showed himself harsher and less scrupulous in the choice of his means. The men about him were untrustworthy; to crush them, he filled the offices of government with relatives and creatures of his own who were at once tyrannous and incapable. Thwarted and checked, he met opposition by imprisonment and measures of violence, suspended the law-courts, and introduced the espionage and the police-system of St. Petersburg. At length armed rebellion broke out, and while Miaoulis, the Hydriote admiral, blew up the best ships of the Greek navy to prevent them falling into the President's hands, the wild district of Maina, which had never admitted the Turkish tax-gatherer, refused to pay taxes to the Hellenic State. The revolt was summarily quelled by Capodistrias, and several members of the family of Mauromichalis, including the chief Petrobei, formerly feudal ruler of Maina, were arrested. Some personal insult, imaginary or real, was moreover offered by Capodistrias to this fallen foe, after the aged mother of Petrobei, who had lost sixty-four kinsmen in the war against the Turks, had begged for his release.

Government and death of Capodistrias

The vendetta of the Maina was aroused. A son and a nephew of Petrobei laid wait for the President, and as he entered the Church of St. Spiridion at Nauplia on the 9th of October, 1831, a pistol-shot and blow from a yataghan laid him dead on the ground. He had been warned that his life was sought, but had refused to make any change in his habits, or to allow himself to be attended by a guard.

The death of Capodistrias excited sympathies and regrets which to a great extent silenced criticism upon his government, and which have made his name one of those most honoured by the Greek nation. His fall threw the country into anarchy. An attempt was made by his brother Augustine to retain autocratic power, but the result was universal dissension and the interference of the foreigner. At length the Powers united in finding a second sovereign for Greece, and brought the weary scene of disorder to a close. Prince Otho of Bavaria was sent to reign at Athens, and with him there came a group of Bavarian officials, to whom the Courts of Europe persuaded themselves that the future of Greece might be safely entrusted. A frontier somewhat better than that which had been offered to Leopold was granted to the new sovereign, but neither Crete, Thessaly, nor Epirus was included within his kingdom. Thus hemmed in within intolerably narrow limits, while burdened with the expenses of an independent state, alike unable to meet the calls upon its national exchequer and to exclude the intrigues of foreign Courts, Greece offered during the next generation little that justified the hopes that

Otho King of Greece, Feb. 1, 1833.

had been raised as to its future. But the belief of mankind in the invigorating power of national independence is not wholly vain, nor, even under the most hostile conditions, will the efforts of a liberated people fail to attract the hope and the envy of those branches of its race which still remain in subjection. Poor and inglorious as the Greek kingdom was, it excited the restless longings not only of Greeks under Turkish bondage but of the prosperous Ionian Islands under English rule; and in 1864 the first step in the expansion of the Hellenic kingdom was accomplished by the transfer of these islands from Great Britain to Greece. Our own day has seen Greece further strengthened and enriched by the annexation of Thessaly. The commercial and educational development of the kingdom is now as vigorous as that of any State in Europe: in agriculture and in manufacturing industry it still lingers far behind. Following the example of Cavour and the Sardinian statesmen who judged no cost too great in preparing for Italian union, the rulers of Greece burden the national finances with the support of an army and navy excessive in comparison both with the resources and with the present requirements of the State. To the ideal of a great political future the material progress of the land has been largely sacrificed. Whether, in the re-adjustment of frontiers which must follow upon the gradual extrusion of the Turk from Eastern Europe, Greece will gain from its expenditure advantages proportionate to the undoubted evils which it has involved, the future alone can decide.

CHAPTER V.

France before 1830—Reign of Charles X.—Ministry of Martignac—Ministry of Polignac—The Duke of Orleans—War in Algiers—The July Ordinances—Revolution of July—Louis Philippe King—Nature and Effects of the July Revolution—Affairs in Belgium—The Belgian Revolution—The Great Powers—Intervention, and Establishment of the Kingdom of Belgium—Affairs of Poland—Insurrection at Warsaw—War between Russia and Poland—Overthrow of the Poles: End of the Polish Constitution—Affairs of Italy—Insurrection in the Papal States—France and Austria—Austrian Intervention—Ancona occupied by the French—Affairs of Germany—Prussia; the Zollverein—Brunswick, Hanover, Saxony—The Palatinate—Reaction in Germany—Exiles in Switzerland; Incursion into Savoy—Dispersion of the Exiles—France under Louis Philippe: Successive Risings—Period of Parliamentary Activity—England after 1830: The Reform Bill.

WHEN the Congress of Vienna re-arranged the map of Europe after Napoleon's fall, Lord Castlereagh expressed the opinion that no prudent statesman would forecast a duration of more than seven years for any settlement that might then be made. At the end of a period twice as long, the Treaties of 1815 were still the public law of Europe. The grave had peacefully closed over Napoleon; the revolutionary forces of France had given no sign of returning life. As the Bourbon monarchy struck root, and the elements of opposition grew daily weaker in France, the perils that lately filled all minds appeared to grow obsolete, and the very Power against which the anti-revolutionary treaties of 1815 had been in the main directed took its place, as of natural right, by the side of Austria and Russia in the struggle against revolution. The attack of Louis XVIII. upon the Spanish Constitutionalists marked the complete reconciliation of France with the Continental dynasties which had combined against it in 1815; and from this time the Treaties of Chaumont and Aix-la-Chapelle, though their provisions might be still unchallenged, ceased to represent the actual relations existing between the Powers. There was no longer a moral union of the Courts against a supposed French revolutionary State; on the contrary, when Eastern affairs reached their crisis, Russia detached itself from its Hapsburg ally, and definitely allied itself with France. If after the Peace of Adrianople any one Power stood isolated, it was Austria; and if Europe was threatened by renewed aggression, it was not under revolutionary leaders or with revolutionary watchwords, but as the result of an alliance between Charles X. and the Czar of Russia. After the Bourbon Cabinet had resolved to seek an extension of French territory at whatever sacrifice of the balance of power in the East, Europe could hardly expect that the Court of St. Petersburg would long reject the advantages offered to it. The frontiers of 1815 seemed likely to be obliterated by an enterprise which would bring Russia to the Danube and France to the Rhine. From this danger the settlement of 1815 was saved by the course of events that took place within France itself. The Revolution of 1830, insignificant in its immediate effects upon the French people, largely influenced the governments and the nations of Europe; and while within certain narrow limits it gave a stimulus to constitutional liberty, its more general result was to revive the union of the three Eastern Courts which had broken down in 1820, and to reunite the principal members of the Holy Alliance by the sense of a common interest against the Liberalism of the West.

In the person of Charles X. reaction and clericalism had ascended the French throne. The minister, Villèle, who had won power in 1820 as the repre-

Government of Charles X., 1824 –1827

sentative of the ultra-Royalists, had indeed learnt wisdom while in office, and down to the death of Louis XVIII. in 1824 he had kept in check the more violent section of his party. But he now retained his post only at the price of compliance with the Court, and gave the authority of his name to measures which his own judgment condemned. It was characteristic of Charles X. and of the reactionaries around him that out of trifling matters they provoked more exasperation than a prudent Government would have aroused by changes of infinitely greater importance. Thus in a sacrilege-law which was introduced in 1825 they disgusted all reasonable men by attempting to revive the barbarous mediæval punishment of amputation of the hand; and in a measure conferring some fractional rights upon the eldest son in cases of intestacy they alarmed the whole nation by a preamble declaring the French principle of the equal division of inheritances to be incompatible with monarchy. Coming from a Government which had thus already forfeited public confidence, a law granting the emigrants a compensation of £40,000,000 for their estates which had been confiscated during the Revolution excited the strongest opposition, although, apart from questions of equity, it benefited the nation by for ever setting at rest all doubt as to the title of the purchasers of the confiscated lands. The financial operations by which, in order to provide the vast sum allotted to the emigrants, the national debt was converted from a five per cent. to a three per cent. stock, alienated all stockholders and especially the powerful bankers of Paris. But more than any single legislative act, the alliance of the Government with the priestly order, and the encouragement given by it to monastic corporations, whose existence in France was contrary to law, offended the nation. The Jesuits were indicted before the law-courts by Montlosier, himself a Royalist and a member of the old noblesse. A vehement controversy sprang up between the ecclesiastics and their opponents, in which the Court was not spared. The Government, which had lately repealed the law of censorship, now restored it by edict. The climax of its unpopularity was reached; its hold upon the Chamber was gone, and the very measure by which Villèle, when at the height of his power, had endeavoured to give permanence to his administration, proved its ruin. He had abolished the system of partial renovation, by which one-fifth of the Chamber or Deputies was annually returned, and substituted for it the English system of septennial Parliaments with general elections. In 1827 King Charles, believing his Ministers to be stronger in the country than in the

Chamber, exercised his prerogative of dissolution. The result was the total defeat of the Government, and the return of an assembly in which the Liberal opposition outnumbered the partisans of the Court by three to one. Villèle's Ministry now resigned. King Charles, unwilling to choose his successor from the Parliamentary majority, thought for a moment of violent resistance, but subsequently adopted other counsels, and, without sincerely intending to bow to the national will, called to office the Vicomte de Martignac, a member of the right centre, and the representative of a policy of conciliation and moderate reform (January 2, 1828).

It was not the fault of this Minister that the last chance of union between the French nation and the elder Bourbon line was thrown away.

Ministry of Martignac, 1828—29.

Martignac brought forward a measure of decentralisation conferring upon the local authorities powers which, though limited, were larger than they had possessed at any time since the foundation of the Consulate; and he appealed to the Liberal sections of the Chamber to assist him in winning an instalment of self-government which France might well have accepted with satisfaction. But the spirit of opposition within the Assembly was too strong for a coalition of moderate men, and the Liberals made the success of Martignac's plan impossible by insisting on concessions which the Minister was unable to grant. The reactionists were ready to combine with their opponents. King Charles himself was in secret antagonism to his Minister, and watched with malicious joy his failure to control the majority in the Chamber. Instead of throwing all his influence on to the side of Martignac, and rallying all doubtful forces by the pronounced support of the Crown, he welcomed Martignac's defeat as a proof of the uselessness of all concessions, and dismissed the Minister from office, declaring that the course of events had fulfilled his own belief in the impossibility of governing in accord with a Parliament. The names of the Ministers who were now called to power excited anxiety and alarm not only in France but throughout the political circles of Europe. They were the names of men known as the most violent and embittered partisans of reaction; men whose presence in the councils of the King could mean nothing but a direct attack upon the existing Parliamentary system of France. At the head was Jules Polignac, then French ambassador at London, a man half-crazed with religious delusions, who had suffered a long imprisonment for his share in Cadoudal's attempt to kill Napoleon, and on his return to France in 1814 had refused to swear to the Charta because it granted religious freedom to non-Catholics. Among the subordinate members of the Ministry were General Bourmont, who had deserted to the English at Waterloo, and La Bourdonnaye, the champion of the reactionary Terrorists in 1816.*

Polignac Ministér, Aug. 9, 1829.

The Ministry having been appointed immediately after the close of the session of 1829, an interval of several months passed before they were brought face to

* Viel-Castel, xix. 574. Duvergier de Hauranne, x. 85.

face with the Chambers. During this interval the prospect of a conflict with the Crown became familiar to the public mind, though no general impression existed that an actual change of dynasty was close at hand.

Prospects in 1830. The Orleanists.

The Bonapartists were without a leader, Napoleon's son, their natural head, being in the power of the Austrian Court; the Republicans were neither numerous nor well organised, and the fatal memories of 1793 still weighed upon the nation; the great body of those who contemplated resistance to King Charles X. looked only to a Parliamentary struggle, or, in the last resort, to the refusal of payment of taxes in case of a breach of the Constitution. There was, however, a small and dexterous group of politicians which, at a distance from all the old parties, schemed for the dethronement of the reigning branch of the House of Bourbon, and for the elevation of Louis Philippe, Duke of Orleans, to the throne. The chief of this intrigue was Talleyrand. Slighted and thwarted by the Court, the old diplomatist watched for the signs of a falling Government, and when the familiar omens met his view he turned to the quarter from which its successor was most likely to arise. Louis Philippe stood high in credit with all circles of Parliamentary Liberals. His history had been a strange and eventful one. He was the son of that Orleans who, after calling himself Égalité, and voting for the death of his cousin, Louis XVI., had himself perished during the Reign of Terror. Young Louis Philippe had been a member of the Jacobin Club, and had fought for the Republic at Jemappes. Then, exiled and reduced to penury, he had earned his bread by teaching mathematics in Switzerland, and had been a wanderer in the new as well as in the old world. After a while his fortunes brightened. A marriage with the daughter of Ferdinand of Sicily restored him to those relations with the reigning houses of Europe which had been forfeited by his father, and inspired him with the hope of gaining a crown. During Napoleon's invasion of Spain he had caballed with politicians in that country who were inclined to accept a substitute for their absent sovereign; at another time he had entertained hopes of being made king of the Ionian Islands. After the peace of Paris, when the allied sovereigns and their ministers visited England, Louis Philippe was sent over by his father-in-law to intrigue among them against Murat, and in pursuance of this object he made himself acquainted not only with every foreign statesman then in London but with every leading English politician. He afterwards settled in France, and was reinstated in the vast possessions of the House of Orleans, which, though confiscated, had not for the most part been sold during the Revolution. His position at Paris under Louis XVIII. and Charles X. was a peculiar one. Without taking any direct part in politics or entering into any avowed opposition to the Court, he made his home, the Palais Royale, a gathering-place for all that was most distinguished in the new political and literary society of the capital; and while the Tuileries affected the pomp and the ceremoniousness of the old *régime*, the Duke of Orleans moved with the familiarity of a citizen among citizens. 'He was a clever, ready, sensible man, equal, as it seemed, to any practical task likely to come in his way, but in reality void of any deep insight, of any far-reaching aspiration, of any profound conviction. His affectation of a straightforward middle-class geniality covered a decided tendency towards intrigue and a strong love of personal power. Later events indeed gave rise to the belief that, while professing the utmost loyalty towards Charles X., Louis Philippe had been scheming to oust him from his throne; but the evidence really points the other way, and indicates that, whatever secret hopes may have suggested themselves to the Duke, his strongest sentiment during the Revolution of 1830 was the fear of being driven into exile himself, and of losing his possessions. He was not indeed of a chivalrous nature; but when the Crown came in his way, he was guilty of no worse offence than some shabby evasions of promises.

Early in March, 1830, the French Chambers assembled after their recess. The speech of King Charles at the opening of the session was resolute and even threatening. It was answered by an address from the Lower House, requesting him to dismiss his Ministers. The deputation which presented this address was received by the King in a style that left no doubt as to his intentions, and on the following day the Chambers were prorogued for six months. It was known that they would not be

Meeting and Prorogation of the Chambers, March, 1830.

permitted to meet again, and preparations for a renewed general election were at once made with the utmost vigour by both parties throughout France. The Court unsparingly applied all the means of pressure familiar to French governments; it moreover expected to influence public opinion by some striking success in arms or in diplomacy abroad. The negotiations with Russia for the acquisition of Belgium were still before the Cabinet, and a quarrel with the Dey of Algiers gave Polignac the opportunity of beginning a war of conquest in Africa. General Bourmont left the War Office, to wipe out the infamy still attaching to his name by a campaign against the Arabs; and the Government trusted that, even in the event of defeat at the elections, the nation at large would at the most critical moment be rallied to its side by an announcement of the capture of Algiers.

While the dissolution of Parliament was impending, Polignac laid before the King a memorial expressing his own views on the courses open to Government in case of the elections proving adverse. The Charta contained a clause which, in loose and ill-chosen language, declared it to be the function of the King "to make the regulations and ordinances necessary for the execution of the laws and for the security of the State." These words, which no doubt referred to the exercise of the King's normal and constitutional powers, were interpreted by Polignac as authorising the King to suspend the Constitution itself, if the Representative Assembly should be at variance with the King's

Polignac's project.

Ministers. Polignac in fact entertained the same view of the relation between executive and deliberative bodies as those Jacobin directors who made the *coup-d'état* of Fructidor, 1797; and the measures which he ultimately adopted were, though in a softened form, those adopted by Barras and Laréveillère after the Royalist elections in the sixth year of the Republic. To suspend the Constitution was not, he suggested, to violate the Charta, for the Charta empowered the sovereign to issue the ordinances necessary for the security of the State; and who but the sovereign and his advisers could be the judges of this necessity? This was simple enough; there was nevertheless among Polignac's colleagues some doubt both as to the wisdom and as to the legality of his plans. King Charles who, with all his bigotry, was anxious not to violate the letter of the Charta, brooded long over the clause which defined the sovereign's powers. At length he persuaded himself that his Minister's interpretation was the correct one, accepted the resignation of the dissentients within the Cabinet, and gave his sanction to the course which Polignac recommended.*

The result of the general election, which took place in June, surpassed all the hopes of the Opposition and all the fears of the Court. The entire body of Deputies which had voted the obnoxious address to the Crown in March was returned, and the partisans of Government lost in addition fifty seats. The Cabinet, which had not up to this time resolved

Elections of 1830.

* Procès des Ex-Ministres, i. 189.

upon the details of its action, now deliberated upon several projects submitted to it, and, after rejecting all plans that might have led to a compromise, determined to declare the elections null and void, to silence the press, and to supersede the existing electoral system by one that should secure the mastery of the Government both at the polling-booths and in the Chamber itself. All this was to be done by Royal Edict, and before the meeting of the new Parliament. The date fixed for the opening of the Chambers had been placed as late as possible in order to give time to General Bourmont to win the victory in Africa from which the Court expected to reap so rich a harvest of prestige. On the 9th of July news arrived that Algiers had fallen. The announcement, which was everywhere made with the utmost pomp, fell flat on the country. The conflict between the Court and the nation absorbed all minds, and the rapturous congratulations of Bishops and Prefects scarcely misled even the blind *côterie* of the Tuileries. Public opinion was no doubt with the Opposition; King Charles, however, had no belief that the populace of Paris, which alone was to be dreaded as a fighting body, would take up arms on behalf of the middle-class voters and journalists against whom his Ordinances were to be directed. The populace neither read nor voted: why should it concern itself with constitutional law? Or why, in a matter that related only to the King and the Bourgeoisie, should it not take part with the King against this new and bastard aristocracy which lived on others' labour? Politicians who could not fight were troublesome only when they were permitted to speak and to write. There was force enough at the King's command to close the gates of the Chamber of Deputies, and to break up the printing-presses of the journals; and if King Louis XVI. had at last fallen by the hands of men of violence, it was only because he had made concessions at first to orators and politicians. Therefore, without dreaming that an armed struggle would be the immediate result of their action, King Charles and Polignac determined to prevent the meeting of the Chamber, and to publish, a week before the date fixed for its opening, the Edicts which were to silence the brawl of faction and to vindicate monarchical government in France.

Accordingly, on the 26th of July, a series of Ordinances appeared in the *Moniteur*, signed by the King and countersigned by the Ministers. The first Ordinance forbade the publication of any journal without royal permission; the second dissolved the Chamber of Deputies; the third raised the property-qualification of voters, established a system of double-election, altered the duration of Parliaments, and re-enacted the obsolete clause of the Charta, confining the initiative in all legislation to the Government. Other Ordinances convoked a Chamber to be elected under the new rules, and called to the Council of State a number of the most notorious ultra-Royalists and fanatics in France. Taken together, the Ordinances left scarcely anything standing

The Ordinances. July 26, 1830.

of the Constitutional and Parliamentary system of the day. The blow fell first on the press, and the first step in resistance was taken by the journalists of Paris, who, under the leadership of the young Thiers, editor of the *National*, published a protest declaring that they would treat the Ordinances as illegal, and calling upon the Chambers and nation to join in this resistance. For a while the journalists seemed likely to stand alone. Paris at large remained quiet, and a body of the recently elected Deputies, to whom the journalists appealed as representatives of the nation, proved themselves incapable of any action or decision whatsoever. It was not from these timid politicians, but from a body of obscure Republicans, that the impulse proceeded which overthrew the Bourbon throne. Unrepresented in Parliament and unrepresented in the press, there were a few active men who had handed down the traditions of 1792, and who, in sympathy with the Carbonari and other conspirators abroad, had during recent years founded secret societies in Paris, and enlisted in the Republican cause a certain number of workmen, of students, and of youths of the middle classes. While the journalists discussed legal means of resistance and the Deputies awaited events, the Republican leaders met and determined upon armed revolt. They were assisted, probably without direct concert, by the printing firms and other employers of labour, who, in view of the general suspension of the newspapers, closed their establishments on the morning of July 27, and turned their workmen into the streets.

3 H

Thus on the day after the appearance of the Edicts the aspect of Paris changed. Crowds gathered, and revolutionary cries were raised. Marmont, who was suddenly ordered to take command of the troops, placed them around the Tuileries, and captured two barricades which were erected in the neighbourhood; but the populace was not yet armed, and no serious conflict took place. In the evening Lafayette reached Paris, and the revolution had now a real, though not an avowed, leader. A body of his adherents met during the night at the office of the *National*, and, in spite of Thiers' resistance, decided upon a general insurrection. Thiers himself, who desired nothing but a legal and Parliamentary attack upon Charles X., quitted Paris to await events. The men who had outvoted him placed themselves in communication with all the district committees of Paris, and began the actual work of revolt by distributing arms. On the morning of Wednesday, July 28th, the first armed bands attacked and captured the arsenals and several private depôts of weapons and ammunition. Barricades were erected everywhere. The insurgents swelled from hundreds to thousands, and, converging on the old rallying-point of the Commune of Paris, they seized the Hôtel de Ville, and hoisted the tricolor flag on its roof. Marmont wrote to the King, declaring the position to be most serious, and advising concession; he then put his troops in motion, and succeeded, after a severe conflict, in capturing several points of vantage, and in expelling the rebels from the Hôtel de Ville.

In the meantime the Deputies, who were again assembled at the house of one of their number in pursuance of an agreement made on the previous day, gained sufficient courage to adopt a protest declaring that in spite of the Ordinances they were still the legal representatives of the nation. They moreover sent a deputation to Marmont, begging him to put a stop to the fighting, and offering their assistance in restoring order if the King would withdraw his Edicts. Marmont replied that he could do nothing without the King's command, but he despatched a second letter to St. Cloud, urging compliance. The only answer which he received was a command to concentrate his troops and to act in masses. The result of this was that the positions which had been won by hard fighting were abandoned before evening, and that the troops, famished and exhausted, were marched back through the streets of Paris to the Tuileries. On the march some fraternised with the people, others were surrounded and disarmed. All eastern Paris now fell into the hands of the insurgents; the middle-class, as in 1789 and 1792, remained inactive, and allowed the contest to be decided by the populace and the soldiery. Messages from the capital constantly reached St. Cloud, but the King so little understood his danger and so confidently reckoned on the victory of the troops in the Tuileries that he played whist as usual during the evening; and when the Duc de Mortemart, French Ambassador at St. Petersburg, arrived at nightfall, and pressed for an audience, the King refused to receive him until the next morning.

When morning came, the march of the insurgents against the Tuileries began. Position after position fell into their hands. The regiments stationed in the Place Vendôme abandoned their commander, and marched off to place themselves at the disposal of the Deputies. Marmont ordered the Swiss Guard, which had hitherto defended the Louvre, to replace them; and in doing so he left the Louvre for a moment without any garrison. The insurgents saw the building empty, and rushed into it. From the windows they commanded the Court of the Tuileries, where the troops in reserve were posted; and soon after mid-day all was over. A few isolated battalions fought and perished, but the mass of the soldiery with their commander fell back upon the Place de la Concorde, and then evacuated Paris.*

July 29.

The Duke of Orleans was all this time in hiding. He had been warned that the Court intended to arrest him, and, whether from fear of the Court or of the populace, he had secreted himself at a hunting-lodge in his woods, allowing none but his wife and his sister to know where he was concealed. His partisans, of whom the rich and popular banker, Laffitte, was the most influential among the Deputies, were watching for an opportunity to bring forward his name; but their chances of success seemed slight. The Deputies at large wished only for the withdrawal of the Ordinances,

---

* Lafayette, vi. 383. Marmont, viii. 238. Dupin, Revolution de Juillet, p. 7. Odilon Barrot, i. 105. Sarrans, Lafayette i. 217. Berard, Revolution de 1830, p. 60. Hillebrand, Die Juli-Revolution, p. 87.

and were wholly averse from a change of dynasty. It was only through the obstinacy of King Charles himself, and as the result of a series of accidents, that the Crown passed from the elder Bourbon line. King Charles would not hear of withdrawing the Ordinances until the Tuileries had actually fallen; he then gave way and charged the Duc de Mortemart to form a new Ministry, drawn from the ranks of the Opposition. But instead of formally repealing the Edicts by a public Decree, he sent two messengers to Paris to communicate his change of purpose to the Deputies by word of mouth. The messengers betook themselves to the Hôtel de Ville, where a municipal committee under Lafayette had been installed; and, when they could produce no written authority for their statements, they were referred by this committee to the general body of Deputies, which was now sitting at Laffitte's house. The Deputies also demanded a written guarantee. Laffitte and Thiers spoke in favour of the Duke of Orleans, but the Assembly at large was still willing to negotiate with Charles X., and only required the presence of the Duc de Mortemart himself, and a copy of the Decree repealing the Ordinances.

It was now near midnight. The messengers returned to St. Cloud, and were not permitted to deliver their intelligence until the King awoke next morning. Charles then signed the necessary document, and Mortemart set out for Paris; but the night's delay had given the Orleanists time to act, and before the King was up Thiers had placarded the streets of

July 30.

Paris with a proclamation extolling Orleans as the prince devoted to the cause of the Revolution, as the soldier of Jemappes, and the only constitutional King now possible. Some hours after this manifesto had appeared the Deputies again assembled at Laffitte's house, and waited for the appearance of Mortemart. But they waited in vain. Mortemart's carriage was stopped on the road from St. Cloud, and he was compelled to make his way on foot by a long circuit and across a score of barricades. When he approached Laffitte's house, half dead with heat and fatigue, he found that the Deputies had adjourned to the Palais Bourbon, and, instead of following them, he ended his journey at the Luxemburg, where the Peers were assembled. His absence was turned to good account by the Orleanists. At the morning session the proposition was openly made to call Louis Philippe to power; and when the Deputies reassembled in the afternoon and the Minister still failed to present himself, it was resolved to send a body of Peers and Deputies to Louis Philippe to invite him to come to Paris and to assume the office of Lieutenant-General of the kingdom. No opposition was offered to this proposal in the House of Peers, and a deputation accordingly set out to search for Louis Philippe at his country house at Neuilly. The prince was not to be found; but his sister, who received the deputation, undertook that he should duly appear in Paris. She then communicated with her brother in his hiding-place, and induced him, in spite of the resistance of his wife, to set out for the capital. He arrived at the Palais Royale late on the night of the 30th. Early the next morning he received a deputation from the Assembly, and accepted the powers which they offered him. A proclamation was then published, announcing to the Parisians that in order to save the country from anarchy and civil war the Duke of Orleans had assumed the office of Lieutenant-General of the kingdom.

But there existed another authority in Paris beside the Assembly of Representatives, and one that was not altogether disposed to permit Louis Philippe and his satellites to reap the fruits of the people's victory. *The Hôtel de Ville.* Lafayette and the Municipal Committee, which occupied the Hôtel de Ville, had transformed themselves into a provisional government, and sat surrounded by the armed mob which had captured the Tuileries two days before. No single person who had fought in the streets had risked his life for the sake of making Louis Philippe king; in so far as the Parisians had fought for any definite political idea, they had fought for the Republic. It was necessary to reconcile both the populace and the provisional government to the assumption of power by the new Regent; and with this object Louis Philippe himself proceeded to the Hôtel de Ville, accompanied by an escort of Deputies and Peers. It was a hazardous moment when he entered the crowd on the Place de Grève; but Louis Philippe's readiness of speech stood him in good stead, and he made his way unhurt through the throng into the building, where Lafayette received him. Compliments and promises were showered upon this veteran of 1789, who presently appeared on a balcony and embraced Louis Philippe, while the Prince grasped the tricolor flag, the flag which had not waved in Paris since 1815. The spectacle was successful. The multitude shouted applause; and the few determined men who still doubted the sincerity of a Bourbon and demanded the proclamation of the Republic were put off with the promise of an ultimate appeal to the French people.

In the meantime Charles X. had withdrawn to Rambouillet, accompanied by the members of his family and by a considerable body of troops. Here the news reached him that Orleans had accepted from the Chambers the office of Lieutenant-General. It was a severe blow to the old king, who, while others doubted of Louis Philippe's loyalty, had still maintained his trust in this prince's fidelity. For a moment he thought of retiring beyond the Loire and risking a civil war; but the troops now began to disperse, and Charles, recognising that his cause was hopeless, abdicated together with the dauphin in favour of his grandson the young Chambord, then called Duc de Bordeaux. He wrote to Louis Philippe, appointing him, as if on his own initiative, Lieutenant-General of the kingdom, and required him to proclaim Henry V. king, and to undertake the government during the new sovereign's minority. It is doubtful whether Louis Philippe had at this time formed any distinct resolve, and whether his answer to Charles X. was inspired by mere good nature or by conscious falsehood; for while replying officially that he would lay the king's letter before the Chambers, he privately wrote to Charles X. that he would retain his new office only until he could safely place the Duc de Bordeaux upon the throne. Having thus soothed the old man's pride, Louis Philippe requested him to hasten his departure from the neighbourhood of Paris; and when Charles ignored the message, he sent out some bands of the National Guard to terrify him into flight. This device succeeded, and the royal family, still preserving the melancholy ceremonial of a court, moved slowly through France towards the western coast. At Cherbourg they took ship and crossed to England, where they were received as private persons. Among the British nation at large the exiled Bourbons excited but little sympathy. They were, however, permitted to take up their abode in the palace of Holyrood, and here Charles X. resided for two years. But neither the climate nor the society of the Scottish capital offered any attraction to the old and failing chief of a fallen dynasty. He sought a more congenial shelter in Austria, and died at Goritz in November, 1836.

The first public notice of the abdication of King Charles was given by Louis Philippe in the Chamber of Deputies, which was convoked by him, as Lieutenant-General of the Kingdom, on the 3rd of August. In addressing the Deputies, Louis Philippe stated that he had received a letter containing the abdication both of the King and of the Dauphin, *Louis Philippe made King, Aug. 7.* but he uttered no single word regarding the Duc de Bordeaux, in whose favour both his grandfather and his uncle had renounced their rights. Had Louis Philippe mentioned that the abdications were in fact conditional, and had he declared himself protector of the Duc de Bordeaux during his minority, there is little doubt that the legitimate heir would have been peaceably accepted both by the Chamber and by Paris. Louis Philippe himself had up to this time done nothing that was inconsistent with the assumption of a mere Regency; the Chamber had not desired a change of dynasty; and, with the exception of Lafayette, the men who had actually made the Revolution bore as little goodwill to an Orleanist as to a Bourbon monarchy. But from the time when Louis Philippe passed over in silence the claims of the grandson of Charles X., his own accession to the throne became inevitable. It was left to an obscure Deputy to propose that the crown should be offered to Louis Philippe, accompanied by certain conditions couched in the form of modifications of the Charta. The proposal was carried in the Chamber on the 7th of August, and the whole body of representatives marched to the Palais Royale to acquaint the prince with its resolution. Louis Philippe, after some conventional expressions of regret, declared that he could not resist the call of his country. When the Lower Chamber had thus disposed of the crown, the House of Peers, which had proved itself a nullity throughout the crisis, adopted the same resolution, and tendered its congratulations in a similar fashion. Two days later Louis Philippe took the oath to the Charta as modified by the Assembly, and was proclaimed King of the French.

Thus ended a revolution, which, though greeted with enthusiasm at the time, has lost much of its splendour and importance in the later judgment of mankind. In comparison with the Revolution of 1789, the movement which overthrew the Bourbons in 1830 was a mere flutter on the surface. It was unconnected with any great change in men's ideas, and it left no great social or legislative changes behind it. Occasioned by a breach of the constitution on the part of the Executive Government, it resulted mainly in the transfer of administrative power from one set of politicians to another: the alterations which it introduced into the constitution itself were of no great importance. France neither had an absolute Government before 1830, nor had it a popular Government afterwards. Instead of a representative of divine right, attended by guards of nobles and counselled by Jesuit confessors, there was now a citizen-king, who walked about the streets of Paris with an umbrella under his arm and sent his sons to the public schools, but who had at heart as keen a devotion to dynastic interests as either of his predecessors, and a much greater capacity for personal rule. The bonds which kept the entire local administration of France in dependence upon the central authority were not loosened; officialism remained as strong as ever; the franchise was still limited to a mere fraction of the nation. On the other hand, within the administration itself the change wrought by the July Revolution was real and lasting. It extinguished the political power of the clerical interest. Not only were the Bishops removed from the House of Peers, but throughout all departments of Government the influence of the clergy, which had been so strong under Charles X., vanished away. The State took a distinctly secular colour. The system of public education was regulated with such police-like exclusiveness that priests who insisted upon opening schools of their own for Catholic teaching were enabled to figure as champions of civil liberty and of freedom of opinion against despotic power. The noblesse lost whatever political influence it had regained during the Restoration. The few surviving Regicides who had been banished in 1815 were recalled to France, among them the terrorist Barrère, who was once more returned to the Assembly. But the real winners in the Revolution of 1830 were not the men of extremes, but the middle-class of France. This was the class which Louis Philippe truly represented; and the force which for eighteen years kept Louis Philippe on the throne was the middle-class force of the National Guard of Paris. Against this sober, prosaic, unimaginative power there struggled the hot and restless spirit which had been let loose by the overthrow of the Bourbon dynasty, and which, fired at once with the political ideal of a Republic, with dreams of the regeneration of Europe by French armies, and with the growing antagonism between the labouring class and the owners of property, threatened for awhile to overthrow the newly-constituted monarchy in France, and to plunge Europe into war. The return of the tricolor flag, the long-silenced strains of the Republic and the Empire, the sense of victory with which men on the popular side witnessed the expulsion of the dynasty which had been forced upon France after Waterloo, revived that half-romantic military ardour which had undertaken the liberation of Europe in 1792. France appeared once more in the eyes of enthusiasts as the deliverer of nations. The realities of the past epoch of French military aggression, its robberies, its corruption, the execrations of its victims, were forgotten; and when one people after another took up the shout of liberty that was raised in Paris, and insurrections broke out in every quarter of Europe, it was with difficulty that Louis Philippe and the few men of caution about him could prevent the French nation from rushing into war.

The State first affected by the events of July was the kingdom of the Netherlands. The creation of this kingdom, in which the Belgian provinces formerly subject to Austria were united with Holland to serve as an effective barrier against French aggression on the north, had been one of Pitt's most cherished schemes, and it had been carried into effect ten years after his death by the Congress of Vienna. National and religious incongruities had been little considered by the statesmen of that day, and at the very moment of union the Catholic bishops of Belgium had protested against a constitution which gave equal toleration to all religions under the rule of a Protestant King. The Belgians had been uninterruptedly united with France for the twenty years preceding 1814; the

Affairs in Belgium.

French language was not only the language of their literature, but the spoken language of the upper classes; and though the Flemish portion of the population was nearly related to the Dutch, this element had not then asserted itself with the distinctness and energy which it has since developed. The antagonism between the northern and the southern Netherlands, though not insuperable, was sufficiently great to make a harmonious union between the two countries a work of difficulty, and the Government of The Hague had not taken the right course to conciliate its opponents. The Belgians, though more numerous, were represented by fewer members in the National Assembly than the Dutch. Offices were filled by strangers from Holland; finance was governed by a regard for Dutch interests; and the Dutch language was made the official language for the whole kingdom. But the chief grievances were undoubtedly connected with the claims of the clerical party in Belgium to a monopoly of spiritual power and the exclusive control of education. The one really irreconcilable enemy of the Protestant House of Orange was the Church; and the governing impulse in the conflicts which preceded the dissolution of the kingdom of the Netherlands in 1830 sprang from the same clerical interest which had thrown Belgium into revolt against the Emperor Joseph forty years before. There was again seen the same strange phenomenon of a combination between the Church and a popular or even revolutionary party. For the sake of an alliance against a constitution distasteful to both, the clergy of Belgium accepted the democratic principles of the political Opposition, and the Opposition consented for a while to desist from their attacks upon the Papacy. The contract was faithfully observed on both sides until the object for which it was made was attained.*

For some months before the Revolution of July, 1830, the antagonism between the Belgians and their Government had been so violent that no great shock from outside was necessary to produce an outbreak. The convulsions of Paris were at once felt at Brussels, and on the 25th of August the performance of a revolutionary opera in that city gave the signal for the commencement of insurrection. From the capital the rebellion spread from town to town throughout the southern Netherlands. The King summoned the Estates General, and agreed to the establishment of an administration for Belgium separate from that of Holland: but the storm was not allayed; and the appearance of a body of Dutch troops at Brussels was sufficient to dispel the expectation of a peaceful settlement. Barricades were erected; a conflict took place in the streets; and the troops, unable to carry the city by assault, retired to the outskirts and kept up a desultory attack for several days. They then withdrew, and a provisional government, which was immediately established, declared the independence of Belgium. For a moment there appeared some possibility that the Crown Prince of Holland, who had from the first assumed the part of mediator, might be

marginal note: Belgian Revolution, August, 1830.

---

* Juste, Révolution Belge, i. 85. Congrès National, i. 184.

accepted as sovereign of the newly-formed State; but the growing violence of the insurrection, the activity of French emissaries and volunteers, and the bombardment of Antwerp by the Dutch soldiers who garrisoned its citadel, made an end of all such hopes. Belgium had won its independence, and its connection with the House of Orange could be re-established only by force of arms.

The accomplishment of this revolution in one of the smallest Continental States threatened to involve all Europe in war. Though not actually effected under the auspices of a French army, it was undoubtedly to some extent effected in alliance with the French revolutionary party. It broke up a kingdom established by the European Treaties of 1814; and it was so closely connected with the overthrow of the Bourbon monarchy as to be scarcely distinguishable from those cases in which the European Powers had pledged themselves to call their armies into the field. Louis Philippe, however, had been recognised by most of the European Courts as the only possible alternative to a French Republic; and a general disposition existed to second any sincere effort that should be made by him to prevent the French nation from rushing into war. This was especially the case with England; and it was to England that Louis Philippe turned for co-operation in the settlement of the Belgian question. Louis Philippe himself had every possible reason for desiring to keep the peace. If war broke out, France would be opposed to all the Continental Powers together. Success was in the last degree improbable;

France and the Belgian Revolution.

it could only be hoped for by a revival of the revolutionary methods and propaganda of 1793; and failure, even for a moment, would certainly cost him his throne, and possibly his life. His interest no less than his temperament made him the strenuous, though concealed, opponent of the war-party in the Assembly; and he found in the old diplomatist who had served alike under the Bourbons, the Republic, and the Empire, an ally thoroughly capable of pursuing his own wise though unpopular policy of friendship and co-operation with England. Talleyrand, while others were crying for a revenge for Waterloo, saw that the first necessity for France was to rescue it from its isolation; and as at the Congress of Vienna he had detached Austria and England from the two northern Courts, so now, before attempting to gain any extension of territory, he sought to make France safe against the hostility of the Continent by allying it with at least one great Power. Russia had become an enemy instead of a friend. The expulsion of the Bourbons had given mortal offence to the Czar Nicholas, and neither Austria nor Prussia was likely to enter into close relations with a Government founded upon revolution. England alone seemed a possible ally, and it was to England that the French statesman of peace turned in the Belgian crisis. Talleyrand, now nearly eighty years old, came as ambassador to London, where he had served in 1792. He addressed himself to Wellington and to the new King, William IV., assuring them that, under the Government of Louis Philippe, France would not seek to use the Belgian revolution for its own aggrandisement; and, with his old aptness in the invention of general principles to suit a particular case, he laid down the principle of non-intervention as one that ought for the future to govern the policy of Europe. His efforts were successful. So complete an understanding was established between France and England on the Belgian question, that all fear of an armed intervention of the Eastern Courts on behalf of the King of Holland, which would have rendered a war with France inevitable, passed away. The regulation of Belgian affairs was submitted to a Conference at London. Hostilities were stopped, and the independence of the new kingdom was recognised in principle by the Conference before the end of the year. A Protocol defining the frontiers of Belgium and Holland, and apportioning to each State its share in the national debt, was signed by the representatives of the Powers in January, 1831.*

[marginal note: France and England]

Thus far, a crisis which threatened the peace of Europe had been surmounted with unexpected ease. But the first stage of the difficulty alone was passed; it still remained for the Powers to provide a king for Belgium, and to gain the consent of the Dutch and Belgian Governments to the territorial arrangements drawn up for them. The Belgians themselves, with whom a connection with France was popular, were disposed to elect as their sovereign the

[marginal note: Leopold elected King, June 4.]

---

* Wellington, N.S. vii. 309. B. and F. State Papers, xviii. 761. Metternich, v. 44. Hillebrand, Geschichte Frankreichs, i. 171. Stockmar, i. 148. Bulwer's Palmerston, ii. 5. Hertslet, Map of Europe, iii. 81.

Duc de Nemours, second son of Louis Philippe; and although Louis Philippe officially refused his sanction to this scheme, which in the eyes of all Europe would have turned Belgium into a French dependency, he privately encouraged its prosecution after a Bonapartist candidate, the son of Eugène Beauharnais, had appeared in the field. The result was that the Duc de Nemours was elected king on the 3rd of February, 1831. Upon this appointment the Conference of the Powers at London had already pronounced its veto, and the British Government let it be understood that it would resist any such extension of French influence by force. Louis Philippe now finally refused the crown for his son, and, the Bonapartist candidate being withdrawn, the two rival Powers agreed in recommending Prince Leopold of Saxe-Coburg, on the understanding that, if elected King of Belgium, he should marry a daughter of Louis Philippe. The Belgians fell in with the advice given them, and elected Leopold on the 4th of June. He accepted the crown, subject to the condition that the London Conference should modify in favour of Belgium some of the provisions relating to the frontiers and to the finances of the new State which had been laid down by the Conference, and which the Belgian Government had hitherto refused to accept.

The difficulty of arranging the Belgian frontier arose principally from the position of the Grand Duchy of Luxemburg. This territory, though subject to Austria before the French Revolution, had always been treated as distinct from the body of the Austrian

Netherlands. When, at the peace of 1814, it was given to the King of Holland in substitution for the ancient possessions of his family at Nassau, its old character as a member of the German federal union was restored to it, so that the King of Holland in respect of this portion of his dominions became a German prince, and the fortress of Luxemburg, the strongest in Europe after Gibraltar, was liable to occupation by German troops. The population of the Duchy had, however, joined the Belgians in their revolt, and, with the exception of the fortress itself, the territory had passed into possession of the Belgian Government. In spite of this actual overthrow of Dutch rule, the Conference of London had attached such preponderating importance to the military and international relations of Luxemburg that it had excluded the whole of the Duchy from the new Belgian State, and declared it still to form part of the dominions of the King of Holland. The first demand of Leopold was for the reversal or modification of this decision, and the Powers so far gave way as to substitute for the declaration of January a series of articles, in which the question of Luxemburg was reserved for future settlement. The King of Holland had assented to the January declaration; on hearing of its abandonment, he took up arms, and threw fifty thousand men into Belgium. Leopold appealed to France for assistance, and a French army immediately crossed the frontier. The Dutch now withdrew, and the French in their

Settlement of the Belgian frontier

turn were recalled, after Leopold had signed a treaty undertaking to raze the fortifications of five towns on his southern border. The Conference again took up its work, and produced a third scheme, in which the territory of Luxemburg was divided between Holland and Belgium. This was accepted by Belgium, and rejected by Holland. The consequence was that a treaty was made between Leopold and the Powers; and at the beginning of 1832 the kingdom of Belgium, as defined by the third award of the Conference, was recognised by all the Courts, Lord Palmerston on behalf of England resolutely refusing to France even the slightest addition of territory, on the ground that, if annexations once began, all security for the continuance of peace would be at an end. On this wise and firm policy the concert of Europe in the establishment of the Belgian kingdom was successfully maintained; and it only remained for the Western Powers to overcome the resistance of the King of Holland, who still held the citadel of Antwerp and declined to listen either to reason or authority. A French army corps was charged with the task of besieging the citadel; an English fleet blockaded the river Scheldt. After a severe bombardment the citadel surrendered. Hostilities ceased, and negotiations for a definitive settlement recommenced. As, however, the Belgians were in actual occupation of all Luxemburg with the exception of the fortress, they had no motive to accelerate a settlement which would deprive them of part of their existing possessions; on the other hand, the King of Holland held back through mere obstinacy. Thus the provisional state of affairs was prolonged for year after year, and it was not until April, 1839, that the final Treaty of Peace between Belgium and Holland was executed.

The consent of the Eastern Powers to the overthrow of the kingdom of the United Netherlands, and to the establishment of a State based upon a revolutionary movement, would probably have been harder to gain if in the autumn of 1830 Russia had been free to act with all its strength. But at this moment an outbreak took place in Poland, which required the concentration of all the Czar's forces within his own border. The conflict was rather a war of one armed nation against another than the insurrection of a people against its government. Poland—that is to say, the territory which had formerly constituted the Grand Duchy of Warsaw—had, by the treaties of 1814, been established as a separate kingdom, subject to the Czar of Russia, but not forming part of the Russian Empire. It possessed an administration and an army of its own, and the meetings of its Diet gave to it a species of parliamentary government to which there was nothing analogous within Russia proper. During the reign of Alexander the constitutional system of Poland had, on the whole, been respected; and although the real supremacy of an absolute monarch at St. Petersburg had caused the Diet to act as a body in opposition to the Russian Government, the personal connection existing between Alexander and the Poles had prevented any overt rebellion during his own

Affairs of Poland.

life-time. But with the accession of Nicholas all such individual sympathy passed away, and the hard realities of the actual relation between Poland and the Court of Russia came into full view. In the conspiracies of 1825 a great number of Poles were implicated. Eight of these persons, after a preliminary inquiry, were placed on trial before the Senate at Warsaw, which, in spite of strong evidence of their guilt, acquitted them. Pending the decision, Nicholas declined to convoke the Diet: he also stationed Russian troops in Poland, and violated the constitution by placing Russians in all branches of the administration. Even without these grievances the hostility of the mass of the Polish noblesse to Russia would probably have led sooner or later to insurrection. The peasantry, ignorant and degraded, were but instruments in the hands of their territorial masters. In so far as Poland had rights of self-government, these rights belonged almost exclusively to the nobles, or landed proprietors, a class so numerous that they have usually been mistaken in Western Europe for the Polish nation itself. The so-called emancipation of the serfs, effected by Napoleon after wresting the Grand Duchy of Warsaw from Prussia in 1807, had done little for the mass of the population; for, while abolishing the legal condition of servitude, Napoleon had given the peasant no vestige of proprietorship in his holding, and had consequently left him as much at the mercy of his landlord as he was before. The name of freedom appears in fact to have worked actual injury to the peasant; for in the enjoyment of a pretended power of free contract he was left without that protection of the officers of State which, under the Prussian régime from 1795 to 1807, had shielded him from the tyranny of his lord. It has been the fatal, the irremediable bane of Poland that its noblesse, until too late, saw no country, no right, no law, outside itself. The very measures of interference on the part of the Czar which this caste resented as unconstitutional were in part directed against the abuse of its own privileges; and although in 1830 a section of the nobles had learnt the secret of their country's fall, and were prepared to give the serf the real emancipation of proprietorship, no universal impulse worked in this direction, nor could the wrong of ages be undone in the tumult of war and revolution.

A sharp distinction existed between the narrow circle of the highest aristocracy of Poland and the mass of the poor and warlike noblesse. The former, represented by men like Czartoryski, the friend of Alexander I. and ex-Minister of Russia, understood the hopelessness of any immediate struggle with the superior power, and advocated the politic development of such national institutions as were given to Poland by the constitution of 1815, institutions which were certainly sufficient to preserve Poland from absorption by Russia, and to keep alive the idea of the ultimate establishment of its independence. It was among the lesser nobility, among the subordinate officers of the army and the population of Warsaw itself, who jointly formed the so-called democratic party, that the

Insurrection at Warsaw, Nov. 20.

LAFAYETTE AND LOUIS PHILIPPE.

(p. 276.)

spirit of revolt was strongest. Plans for an outbreak had been made during the Turkish war of 1828; but unhappily this opportunity, which might have been used with fatal effect against Russia, was neglected, and it was left for the French Revolution of 1830 to kindle an untimely and ineffective flame. The memory of Napoleon's campaigns and the wild voices of French democracy filled the patriots at Warsaw with vain hopes of a military union with western Liberalism, and overpowered the counsels of men who understood the state of Europe better. Revolt broke out on the 29th of November, 1830. The Polish regiments in Warsaw joined the insurrection, and the Russian troops, under the Grand Duke Constantine, withdrew from the capital, where their leader had narrowly escaped with his life.*

The Government of Poland had up to this time been in the hands of a Council nominated by the Czar as King of Poland, and controlled by instructions from a secretary at St. Petersburg. The chief of the Council was Lubecki, a Pole devoted to the Emperor Nicholas. On the victory of the insurrection at Warsaw, the Council was dissolved and a provisional Government installed. Though the revolt was the work of the so-called democratic party, the influence of the old governing families of the highest aristocracy was still so great that power was by common consent placed in their hands. Czartoryski became

<small>Attempted negotiation with the Czar.</small>

---

* Smitt, Geschichte des Polnischen Aufstandes, i. 112. Spazier, Geschichte des Aufstandes, L 177. Lelewel, Histoire de Pologne, i. 300.

president, and the policy adopted by himself and his colleagues was that of friendly negotiation with Russia. The insurrection of November was treated not as the beginning of a national revolt, but as a mere disturbance occasioned by unconstitutional acts of the Government. So little did the committee understand the character of the Emperor Nicholas, as to imagine that after the expulsion of his soldiers and the overthrow of his Ministers at Warsaw he would peaceably make the concessions required of him, and undertake for the future faithfully to observe the Polish constitution. Lubecki and a second official were sent to St. Petersburg to present these demands, and further (though this was not seriously intended) to ask that the constitution should be introduced into all the Russian provinces which had once formed part of the Polish State. The reception given to the envoys at the frontier was of an ominous character. They were required to describe themselves as officers about to present a report to the Czar, inasmuch as no representatives of rebels in arms could be received into Russia. Lubecki appears now to have shaken the dust of Poland off his feet; his colleague pursued his mission, and was admitted to the Czar's presence. Nicholas, while expressing himself in language of injured tenderness, and disclaiming all desire to punish the innocent with the guilty, let it be understood that Poland had but two alternatives, unconditional submission or annihilation. The messenger who in the meanwhile carried back to Warsaw the first despatches of the envoy, reported that the roads were already filled with Russian regiments moving on their prey.

Six weeks of precious time were lost through the illusion of the Polish Government that an accommodation with the Emperor Nicholas was possible. Had the insurrection at Warsaw been instantly followed by a general levy and the invasion of Lithuania, the resources of this large province might possibly have been thrown into the scale against Russia. Though the mass of the Lithuanian population, in spite of several centuries of union with Poland, had never been assimilated to the dominant race, and remained in language and creed more nearly allied to the Russians than the Poles, the nobles formed an integral part of the Polish nation, and possessed sufficient power over their serfs to drive them into the field to fight for they knew not what. The Russian garrisons in Lithuania were not strong, and might easily have been overpowered by a sudden attack. When once the population of Warsaw had risen in arms against Nicholas, the only possibility of success lay in the extension of the revolt over the whole of the semi-Polish provinces, and in a general call to arms. But beside other considerations which disinclined the higher aristocracy at Warsaw to extreme measures, they were influenced by a belief that the Powers of Europe might intervene on behalf of the constitution of the Polish kingdom as established by the treaty of Vienna; while, if the struggle passed beyond the borders of that kingdom, it would become a revolutionary movement to

Diebitsch invades Poland, Feb., 1831.

which no Court could lend its support. It was not until the envoy returned from St. Petersburg bearing the answer of the Emperor Nicholas that the democratic party carried all before it, and all hopes of a peaceful compromise vanished away. The Diet then passed a resolution declaring that the House of Romanoff had forfeited the Polish crown, and preparations began for a struggle for life or death with Russia. But the first moments when Russia stood unguarded and unready had been lost beyond recall. Troops had thronged westwards into Lithuania; the garrisons in the fortresses had been raised to their full strength; and in February, 1831, Diebitsch took up the offensive, and crossed the Polish frontier with a hundred and twenty thousand men.

The Polish army, though far inferior in numbers to the enemy which it had to meet, was no contemptible force. Among its officers there were many who had served in Napoleon's campaigns; it possessed, however, no general habituated to independent command; and the spirit of insubordination and self-will, which had wrought so much ruin in Poland, was still ready to break out when defeat had impaired the authority of the nominal chiefs. In the first encounters the advancing Russian army was gallantly met; and, although the Poles were forced to fall back upon Warsaw, the losses sustained by Diebitsch were so serious that he had to stay his operations and to wait for reinforcements. In March the Poles took up the offensive and surprised several isolated divisions of

Campaign in Poland, 1831.

the enemy; their general, however, failed to push his advantages with the necessary energy and swiftness; the junction of the Russians was at length effected, and on the 26th of May the Poles were defeated after obstinate resistance in a pitched battle at Ostrolenka. Cholera now broke out in the Russian camp. Both Diebitsch and the Grand Duke Constantine were carried off in the midst of the campaign, and some months more were added to the struggle of Poland, hopeless as this had now become. Incursions were made into Lithuania and Podolia, but without result. Paskiewitch, the conqueror of Kars, was called up to take the post left vacant by the death of his rival. New masses of Russian troops came in place of those who had perished in battle and in the hospitals; and while the Governments of Western Europe lifted no hand on behalf of Polish independence, Prussia, alarmed lest the revolt should spread into its own Polish provinces, assisted the operations of the Russian general by supplying stores and munition of war. Blow after blow fell upon the Polish cause. Warsaw itself became the prey of disorder, intrigue, and treachery; and at length the Russian army made its entrance into the capital, and the last soldiers of Poland laid down their arms, or crossed into Prussian or Austrian territory. The revolt had been rashly and unwisely begun : its results were fatal and lamentable. The constitution of Poland was abolished; it ceased to be a separate kingdom, and became a province of the Russian Empire. Its defenders were exiles over

<small>Capture of Warsaw, Sept. 8, 1831.</small>

the face of Europe or forgotten in Siberia. All that might have been won by the gradual development of its constitutional liberties without breach with the Czar's sovereignty was sacrificed.. The future of Poland, like that of Russia itself, now depended on the enlightenment and courage of the Imperial Government, and on that alone. The very existence of a Polish nationality and language seemed for a while to be threatened by the measures of repression that followed the victory of 1831: and if it be true that Russian autocracy has at length done for the Polish peasants what their native masters during centuries of ascendency refused to do, this emancipation would probably not have come the later for the preservation of some relics of political independence, nor would it have had the less value if unaccompanied by the proscription of so great a part of that class which had once been held to constitute the Polish nation.*

During the conflict on the banks of the Vistula, the attitude of the Austrian Government had been one of watchful neutrality. Its own Polish territory was not seriously menaced with disturbance, for in a great part of Galicia, the population, being of Ruthenian stock and belonging to the Greek Church, had nothing in common with the Polish and Catholic noblesse of their province, and looked back upon the days of Polish dominion as a time of suffering and wrong. Austria's danger in any period of European convulsion lay as yet rather on the

* Leroy-Beaulieu, Milutino, p. 199; L'Empire des Tsars, i. 380. Lelewel, Considérations, p. 317.

side of Italy than on the East, and the vigour of its policy in that quarter contrasted with the equanimity with which it watched the struggle of its Slavic neighbours. Since the suppression of the Neapolitan constitutional movement in 1821, the Carbonari and other secret societies of Italy had lost nothing of their activity. Their headquarters had been removed from Southern Italy to the Papal States, and the numerous Italian exiles in France and elsewhere kept up a busy communication at once with French revolutionary leaders like Lafayette and with the enemies of the established governments in Italy itself. The death of Pope Pius VIII., on November 30, 1830, and the consequent paralysis of authority within the Ecclesiastical States, came at an opportune moment; assurances of support arrived from Paris; and the Italian leaders resolved upon a general insurrection throughout the minor Principalities on the 5th of February, 1831. Anticipating the signal, Menotti, chief of a band of patriots at Modena, who appears to have been lured on by the Grand Duke himself, assembled his partisans on February 3. He was overpowered and imprisoned; but the outbreak of the insurrection in Bologna, and its rapid extension over the northern part of the Papal States, soon caused the Grand Duke to fly to Austrian territory, carrying his prisoner Menotti with him, whom he subsequently put to death. The new Pope, Gregory XVI., had scarcely been elected when the report reached him that Bologna had declared the temporal power of the Papacy

Insurrection in the Papal States, Feb., 1831.

to be at an end. Uncertain of the character of the revolt, he despatched Cardinal Benvenuti northwards, to employ conciliation or force as occasion might require. The Legate fell into the hands of the insurgents; the revolt spread southwards; and Gregory, now hopeless of subduing it by the forces at his own command, called upon Austria for assistance.*

Attitude of France.
The principle which, since the Revolution of July, the government of France had repeatedly laid down as the future basis of European politics was that of non-intervention. It had disclaimed any purpose of interfering with the affairs of its neighbours, and had required in return that no foreign intervention should take place in districts which, like Belgium and Savoy, adjoined its own frontier. But there existed no real unity of purpose in the councils of Louis Philippe. The Ministry had one voice for the representatives of foreign powers, another for the Chamber of Deputies, and another for Lafayette and the bands of exiles and conspirators who were under his protection. The head of the government at the beginning of 1831 was Laffitte, a weak politician, dominated by revolutionary sympathies and phrases, but incapable of any sustained or resolute action, and equally incapable of resisting Louis Philippe after the King had concluded his performance of popular leader, and assumed his real character as the wary and self-seeking chief of a reigning house. Whether the actual course of French policy would be governed by

* Bianchi, Ducati Estensi, i. 54. La Farina, v. 241. Farini, i. 34.

the passions of the streets or by the timorousness of Louis Philippe was from day to day a matter of conjecture. The official answer given to the inquiries of the Austrian ambassador as to the intentions of France in case of an Austrian intervention in Italy was, that such intervention might be tolerated in Parma and Modena, which belonged to sovereigns immediately connected with the Hapsburgs, but that if it was extended to the Papal States war with France would be probable, and if extended to Piedmont, certain. On this reply Metternich, who saw Austria's own dominion in Italy once more menaced by the success of an insurrectionary movement, had to form his decision. He could count on the support of Russia in case of war; he knew well the fears of Louis Philippe, and knew that he could work on these fears both by pointing to the presence of the young Louis Bonaparte and his brother with the Italian insurgents as evidence of the Bonapartist character of the movement, and by hinting that in the last resort he might himself let loose upon France Napoleon's son, the Duke of Reichstadt, now growing to manhood at Vienna, before whom Louis Philippe's throne would have collapsed as speedily as that of Louis XVIII. in 1814. Where weakness existed, Metternich was quick to divine it and to take advantage of it. He rightly gauged Louis Philippe. Taking at their true value the threats of the French Government, he declared that it was better for Austria to fall, if necessary, by war than by revolution; and, resolving at all hazards to suppress the Roman insurrection, he gave orders to the Austrian troops to enter the Papal States.

The military resistance which the insurgents could offer to the advance of the Pope's Austrian deliverers was insignificant, and order was soon restored. But all Europe expected the outbreak of war between Austria and France. The French ambassador at Constantinople had gone so far as to offer the Sultan an offensive and defensive alliance, and to urge him to make preparations for an attack upon both Austria and Russia on their southern frontiers. A despatch from the ambassador reached Paris describing the warlike overtures he had made to the Porte. Louis Philippe saw that if this despatch reached the hands of Laffitte and the war-party in the Council of Ministers the preservation of peace would be almost impossible. In concert with Sebastiani, the Foreign Minister, he concealed the despatch from Laffitte. The Premier discovered the trick that had been played upon him, and tendered his resignation. It was gladly accepted by Louis Philippe. Laffitte quitted office, begging pardon of God and man for the part that he had taken in raising Louis Philippe to the throne. His successor was Casimir Perier, a man of very different mould; resolute, clear-headed, and immovably true to his word; a constitutional statesman of the strictest type, intolerant of any species of disorder, and a despiser of popular movements, but equally proof against royal intrigues, and as keen to maintain the constitutional system of France

Austrians suppress Roman revolt, March, 1831.

Casimir Perier, March, 1831.

against the Court on one side and the populace on the other as he was to earn for France the respect of foreign powers by the abandonment of a policy of adventure, and the steady adherence to the principles of international obligation which he had laid down. Under his firm hand the intrigues of the French Government with foreign revolutionists ceased; it was felt throughout Europe that peace was still possible, and that if war was undertaken by France it would be undertaken only under conditions which would make any moral union of all the great Powers against France impossible. The Austrian expedition into the Papal States had already begun, and the revolutionary Government had been suppressed; the most therefore that Casimir Perier could demand was that the evacuation of the occupied territory should take place as soon as possible, and that Austria should add its voice to that of the other Powers in urging the Papal Government to reform its abuses. Both demands were granted. For the first time Austria appeared as the advocate of something like a constitutional system. A Conference held at Rome agreed upon a scheme of reforms to be recommended to the Pope; the prospects of peace grew daily fairer; and in July, 1831, the last Austrian soldiers quitted the Ecclesiastical States.*

It now remained to be seen whether Pope Gregory and his cardinals had the intelligence and good-will

---

* Bianchi, Diplomazia, iii. 48. Metternich, iv. 121. Hillebrand, Geschichte Frankreichs, i. 206. Haussonville, i. 32. B. and F. State Papers, xix. 1429. Guizot, Mémoires, ii. 290.

necessary for carrying out the reforms on the promise of which France had abstained from active intervention. If any such hopes existed they were doomed to speedy disappointment. The apparatus of priestly maladministration was restored in all its ancient deformity. An amnesty which had been promised by the Legate Benvenuti was disregarded, and the Pope set himself to strengthen his authority by enlisting new bands of ruffians and adventurers under the standard of St. Peter. Again insurrection broke out, and again at the Pope's request the Austrians crossed the frontier (January, 1832). Though their appearance was fatal to the cause of liberty, they were actually welcomed as protectors in towns which had been exposed to the tender mercies of the Papal condottieri. There was no disorder, no severity, where the Austrian commandants held sway; but their mere presence in central Italy was a threat to European peace; and Casimir Perier was not the man to permit Austria to dominate in Italy at its will. Without waiting for negotiations, he dispatched a French force to Ancona, and seized this town before the Austrians could approach it. The rival Powers were now face to face in Italy; but Perier had no intention of forcing on war if his opponent was still willing to keep the peace. Austria accepted the situation, and made no attempt to expel the French from the position they had seized. Casimir Perier, now on his death-bed, defended the step that he had taken against the remonstrances of ambassadors and against the protests of the Pope, and declared the presence of the French at Ancona to be no incentive to rebellion, but the mere assertion of the rights of a Power which had as good a claim to be in central Italy as Austria itself. Had his life been prolonged, he would probably have insisted upon the execution of the reforms which the Powers had urged upon the Papal government, and have made the occupation of Ancona an effectual means for reaching this end. But with his death the wrongs of the Italians themselves and the question of a reformed government in the Papal States gradually passed out of sight. France and Austria jealously watched one another on the debatable land; the occupation became a mere incident of the balance of power, and was prolonged for year after year, until, in 1838, the Austrians having finally withdrawn all their troops, the French peacefully handed over the citadel of Ancona to the Holy See.

The arena in which we have next to follow the effects of the July Revolution, in action and counteraction, is Germany. It has been seen that in the southern German States an element of representative government, if weak, yet not wholly ineffective, had come into being soon after 1815, and had survived the reactionary measures initiated by the conference of Ministers at Carlsbad. In Prussia the promises of King Frederick William to his people had never been fulfilled. Years had passed since exaggerated rumours of conspiracy had served as an excuse for withholding the Constitution. Hardenberg

Prussia in 1830.

had long been dead; the foreign policy of the country had taken a freer tone; the rigours of the police-system had departed; but the nation remained as completely excluded from any share in the government as it had been before Napoleon's fall. It had in fact become clear that during the lifetime of King Frederick William things must be allowed to remain in their existing condition; and the affection of the people for their sovereign, who had been so long and so closely united with Prussia in its sufferings and in its glories, caused a general willingness to postpone the demand for constitutional reform until the succeeding reign. The substantial merits of the administration might moreover have reconciled a less submissive people than the Prussians to the absolute government under which they lived. Under a wise and enlightened financial policy the country was becoming visibly richer. Obstacles to commercial development were removed, communications opened; and finally, by a series of treaties with the neighbouring German States, the foundations were laid for that Customs-Union which, under the name of the Zollverein, ultimately embraced almost the whole of non-Austrian Germany. As one Principality after another attached itself to the Prussian system, the products of the various regions of Germany, hitherto blocked by the frontier dues of each petty State, moved freely through the land, while the costs attending the taxation of foreign imports, now concentrated upon the external line of frontier, were enormously diminished. Patient, sagacious, and even liberal in its negotiations with

The Zollverein 1828—1836.

its weaker neighbours, Prussia silently connected with itself through the ties of financial union States which had hitherto looked to Austria as their natural head. The semblance of political union was carefully avoided, but the germs of political union were nevertheless present in the growing community of material interests. The reputation of the Prussian Government, no less than the welfare of the Prussian people, was advanced by each successive step in the extension of the Zollverein; and although the earlier stages alone had been passed in the years before 1830, enough had already been done to affect public opinion; and the general sense of material progress combined with other influences to close Prussia to the revolutionary tendencies of that year.

There were, however, other States in northern Germany which had all the defects of Prussian autocracy without any of its redeeming qualities. In Brunswick and in Hesse Cassel despotism existed in its most contemptible form; the violence of a half-crazy youth in the one case, and the caprices of an obstinate dotard in the other, rendering authority a mere nuisance to those who were subject to it. Here accordingly revolution broke out. The threatened princes had made themselves too generally obnoxious or ridiculous for any hand to be raised in their defence. Their disappearance excited no more than the inevitable lament from Metternich; and in both States systems of representative government were introduced by their successors. In Hanover and in Saxony agitation also began in favour of Parliamentary rule. The

Insurrections in Brunswick and Cassel.

disturbance that arose was not of a serious character, and it was met by the Courts in a conciliatory spirit. Constitutions were granted, the liberty of the Press extended, and trial by jury established. On the whole, the movement of 1830, as it affected northern Germany, was rationally directed and salutary in its results. Changes of real value were accomplished with a sparing employment of revolutionary means, and, in the more important cases, through the friendly co-operation of the sovereigns with their subjects. It was not the fault of those who had asked for the same degree of liberty in northern Germany which the south already possessed, that Germany at large again experienced the miseries of reaction and repression which had afflicted it ten years before.

Constitutions in Hanover and Saxony, 1830–1833.

Like Belgium and the Rhenish Provinces, the Bavarian Palatinate had for twenty years been incorporated with France. Its inhabitants had grown accustomed to the French law and French institutions, and had caught something of the political animation which returned to France after Napoleon's fall. Accordingly when the government of Munich, alarmed by the July Revolution, showed an inclination towards repressive measures, the Palatinate, severed from the rest of the Bavarian monarchy and in immediate contact with France, became the focus of a revolutionary agitation. The Press had already attained some activity and some influence in this province; and although the leaders of the party of progress were still to a great extent Professors, they had so far advanced

Movement in the Palatinate.

upon the patriots of 1818 as to understand that the liberation of the German people was not to be effected by the lecturers and the scholars of the Universities. The design had been formed of enlisting all classes of the public on the side of reform, both by the dissemination of political literature and by the establishment of societies not limited, as in 1818, to academic circles, but embracing traders as well as soldiers and professional men. Even the peasant was to be reached and instructed in his interests as a citizen. It was thought that much might be effected by associating together all the Oppositions in the numerous German Parliaments; but a more striking feature of the revolutionary movement which began in the Palatinate, and one strongly distinguishing it from the earlier agitation of Jena and Erfurt, was its cosmopolitan character. France in its triumph and Poland in its death-struggle excited equal interest and sympathy. In each the cause of European liberty appeared to be at stake. The Polish banner was saluted in the Palatinate by the side of that of united Germany; and from that time forward in almost every revolutionary movement of Europe, down to the insurrection of the Commune of Paris in 1871, Polish exiles have been active both in the organisation of revolt and in the field.

Until the fall of Warsaw, in September, 1831, the German governments, uncertain of the course which events might take in Europe, had shown a certain willingness to meet the complaints of their subjects, and had in especial relaxed the supervision

Reaction in Germany.

exercised over the press. The fall of Warsaw, which quieted so many alarms, and made the Emperor Nicholas once more a power outside his own dominions, inaugurated a period of reaction in Germany. The Diet began the campaign against democracy by suppressing various liberal newspapers, and amongst them the principal journal of the Palatinate. It was against this movement of repression that the agitation in the Palatinate and elsewhere was now directed. A festival, or demonstration, was held at the Castle of Hambach, near Zweibrücken, at which a body of enthusiasts called upon the German people to unite against their oppressors, and some even urged an immediate appeal to arms (May 27, 1832). Similar meetings, though on a smaller scale, were held in other parts of Germany. Wild words abounded, and the connection of the German revolutionists with that body of opponents of all established governments which had its council-chamber at Paris and its head in Lafayette was openly avowed. Weak and insignificant as the German demagogues were, their extravagance gave to Metternich and to the Diet sufficient pretext for revising the reactionary measures of 1819. Once more the subordination of all representative bodies to the sovereign's authority was laid down by the Diet as a binding principle for every German state. The refusal of taxes by any legislature was declared to be an act of rebellion which would be met by the armed intervention of the central Powers. All political meetings and associations were forbidden; the Press was silenced; the introduction of German books printed abroad was prohibited, and the Universities were again placed under the watch of the police (July, 1832).*

If among the minor sovereigns of Germany there were some who, as in Baden, sincerely desired the development of free institutions, the authority exercised by Metternich and his adherents in reaction bore down all the resistance that these courts could offer, and the hand of despotism fell everywhere heavily upon the party of political progress. The majority of German Liberals, not yet prepared for recourse to revolutionary measures, submitted to the pressure of the times, and disclaimed all sympathy with illegal acts; a minority, recognising that nothing was now to be gained by constitutional means, entered into conspiracies, and determined to liberate Germany by force. One insignificant group, relying upon the armed co-operation of Polish bands in France, and deceived by promises of support from some Würtemberg soldiers, actually rose in insurrection at Frankfort. A guard-house was seized, and a few soldiers captured; but the citizens of Frankfort stood aloof, and order was soon restored (April, 1833). It was not to be expected that the reactionary courts should fail to draw full advantage from this ill-timed outbreak of their enemies. Prussian troops marched into Frankfort, and Metternich had no difficulty in carrying through the Diet a decree establishing a commission to superintend and to report upon the proceedings

Attempt at Frankfort, April, 1833.

---

* Ilse, Untersuchungen, p. 262. Metternich, v. 347. Biedermann, Dreissig Jahre, i. 6.

instituted against political offenders throughout Germany. For several years these investigations continued, and the campaign against the opponents of government was carried on with various degrees of rigour in the different states. About two thousand persons altogether were brought to trial: in Prussia thirty-nine sentences of death were pronounced, but not executed. In the struggle against revolution the forces of monarchy had definitely won the victory. Germany again experienced, as it had in 1819, that the federal institutions which were to have given it unity existed only for the purposes of repression. The breach between the nation and its rulers, in spite of the apparent failure of the democratic party, remained far deeper and wider than it had been before; and although Metternich, victor once more over the growing restlessness of the age, slumbered on for another decade in fancied security, the last of his triumphs had now been won, and the next uprising proved how blind was that boasted statesmanship which deemed the sources of danger exhausted when once its symptoms had been driven beneath the surface.

In half the states of Europe there were now bodies of exasperated, uncompromising men, who devoted their lives to plotting against governments, and who formed, in their community of interest and purpose, a sort of obverse of the Holy Alliance, a federation of kings' enemies, a league of principle and creed, in which liberty and human right stood towards established rule as light to darkness. As the grasp of

Conspirators and exiles.

authority closed everywhere more tightly upon its baffled foes, more and more of these men passed into exile. Among them was the Genoese Mazzini, who, after suffering imprisonment in 1831, withdrew to Marseilles, and there, in combination with various secret societies, planned an incursion into the Italian province of Savoy. It was at first intended that this enterprise should be executed simultaneously with the German rising at Frankfort. Delays, however, arose, and it was not until the beginning of the following year that the little army, which numbered more Poles than Italians, was ready for its task. The incursion was made from Geneva in February, 1834, and ended disastrously.* Mazzini returned to Switzerland, where hundreds of exiles, secure under the shelter of the Republic, devised schemes of attack upon the despots of Europe, and even rioted in honour of freedom in the streets of the Swiss cities which protected them. The effect of the revolutionary movement of the time in consolidating the alliance of the three Eastern Powers, so rudely broken by the Greek War of Liberation, now came clearly into view. The sovereigns of Russia and Austria had met at Münchengrätz in Bohemia in the previous autumn, and, in concert with Prussia, had resolved upon common principles of action if their intervention should be required against disturbers of order. Notes were now addressed from every quarter to the Swiss Government, requiring the expulsion of all persons

* Mazzini, Scritti, iii. 310. Simoni, Conspirations Mazziniennes, p. 53. Metternich, v. 526. B. and F. State Papers, xxiv. 979.

concerned in enterprises against the peace of neighbouring States. Some resistance to this demand was made by individual cantons; but the extravagance of many of the refugees themselves alienated popular sympathy, and the greater part of them were forced to quit Switzerland and to seek shelter in England or in America. With the dispersion of the central band of exiles the open alliance which had existed between the revolutionists of Europe gradually passed away. The brotherhood of the kings had proved a stern reality, the brotherhood of the peoples a delusive vision. Mazzini indeed, who up to this time had scarcely emerged from the rabble of revolutionary leaders, was yet to prove how deeply the genius, the elevation, the fervour of one man struggling against the powers of the world may influence the history of his age; but the fire that purified the fine gold charred and consumed the baser elements; and of those who had hoped the most after 1830, many now sank into despair, or gave up their lives to mere restless agitation and intrigue.

Dispersion of the Swiss exiles, 1834.

It was in France that the revolutionary movement was longest maintained. During the first year of Louis Philippe's rule the opposition to his government was inspired not so much by Republicanism as by a wild and inconsiderate sympathy with the peoples who were fighting for liberty elsewhere, and by a headstrong impulse to take up arms on their behalf. The famous decree of the Convention in 1792, which promised the assistance of France to every nation in revolt against its rulers, was in fact the true expression of what was felt by a great part of the French nation in 1831; and in the eyes of these enthusiasts it was the unpardonable offence of Louis Philippe against the honour of France that he allowed Poland and Italy to succumb without drawing his sword against their conquerors. That France would have had to fight the three Eastern Powers combined, if it had allied itself with those in revolt against any one of the three, passed for nothing among the clamorous minority in the Chamber and among the orators of Paris. The pacific policy of Casimir Perier was misunderstood: it passed for mere poltroonery, when in fact it was the only policy that could save France from a recurrence of the calamities of 1815. There were other causes for the growing unpopularity of the King and of his Ministers, but the first was their policy of peace. As the attacks of his opponents became more and more bitter, the government of Casimir Perier took more and more of a repressive character. Disappointment at the small results produced in France itself by the Revolution of July worked powerfully in men's minds. The forces that had been set in motion against Charles X. were not to be laid at rest at the bidding of those who had profited by them, and a Republican party gradually took definite shape and organisation. Tumult succeeded tumult. In the summer of 1832 the funeral of General Lamarque, a popular soldier, gave the signal for insurrection at Paris. There was severe fighting in the streets; the National Guard, however, proved

Difficulties of Louis Philippe.

Insurrections, 1832–1834.

true to the king, and shared with the army in the honours of its victory. Repressive measures and an unbroken series of prosecutions against seditious writers followed this first armed attack upon the established government. The bitterness of the Opposition, the discontent of the working classes, far surpassed anything that had been known under Charles X. The whole country was agitated by revolutionary societies and revolutionary propaganda. Disputes between masters and workmen, which, in consequence of the growth of French manufacturing industry, now became both frequent and important, began to take a political colour. Polish and Italian exiles connected their own designs with attacks to be made upon the French Government from within; and at length, in April, 1834, after the passing of a law against trades-unions, the working classes of Lyons, who were on strike against their employers, were induced to rise in revolt. After several days' fighting the insurrection was suppressed. Simultaneous outbreaks took place at St. Etienne, Grenoble, and many other places in the south and centre of France; and on a report of the success of the insurgents reaching Paris, the Republic was proclaimed and barricades were erected. Again civil war raged in the streets, and again the forces of Government gained the victory. A year more passed, during which the investigations into the late revolt and the trial of a host of prisoners served rather to agitate than to reassure the public mind; and in the summer of 1835 an attempt was made upon the life of the King so terrible and destructive in its effects as to amount to a public calamity. An infernal machine composed of a hundred gun-barrels was fired by a Corsican named Fieschi, as the King with a large suite was riding through the streets of Paris on the anniversary of the Revolution of July. Fourteen persons were killed on the spot, among whom was Mortier, one of the oldest of the marshals of France; many others were fatally or severely injured. The King, however, with his three sons, escaped unhurt, and the repressive laws that followed this outrage marked the close of open revolutionary agitation in France. Whether in conse- Repressive Laws, Sept., 1835. quence of the stringency of the new laws, or of the exhaustion of a party discredited in public estimation by the crimes of a few of its members and the recklessness of many more, the constitutional monarchy of Louis Philippe now seemed to have finally vanquished its opponents. Repeated attempts were made on the life of the King, but they possessed for the most part little political significance. Order was welcome to the nation at large; and though in the growth of a socialistic theory and creed of life which dates from this epoch there lay a danger to Governments greater than any purely political, Socialism was as yet the affair of thinkers rather than of active workers either in the industrial or in the Parliamentary world. The Government had beaten its enemies outside the Chamber. Within the Chamber, the parties of extremes ceased to exercise any real influence. Groups were formed, and rival leaders played against one another for office; but they were separated by no far-reaching differences of aim, and by no real antagonism of constitutional principle. During the succeeding years of Louis Philippe's reign there was little visible on the surface but the normal rivalry of parties under a constitutional monarchy. The middle-class retained its monopoly of power: authority, centralised as before, maintained its old prestige in France, and softened opposition by judicious gifts of office and emolument. Revolutionary passion seemed to have died away: and the triumphs or reverses of party-leaders in the Chamber of Deputies succeeded to the harassing and doubtful conflict between Government and insurrection.

The near coincidence in time between the French Revolution of 1830 and the passing of the English Reform Bill is apt to suggest to those who look for the operation of wide general causes in history that the English Reform movement should be viewed as a part of the great current of political change which then traversed the continent of Europe. But on a closer examination this view is scarcely borne out by facts, and the coincidence of the two epochs of change appears to be little more than accidental. The general unity that runs through the history of the more advanced continental states is indeed stronger than appears to a superficial reader of history; but this correspondence of tendency does not always embrace England; on the contrary, the conditions peculiar to England usually preponderate over those common to England and other countries,

The English Reform movement.

exhibiting at times more of contrast than of similarity, as in the case of the Napoleonic epoch, when the causes which drew together the western half of the continent operated powerfully to exclude our own country from the current influences of the time, and made the England of 1815, in opinion, in religion, and in taste much more insular than the England of 1780. The revolution which overthrew Charles X. did no doubt encourage and stimulate the party of Reform in Great Britain; but, unlike the Belgian, the German, and the Italian movements, the English Reform movement would unquestionably have run the same course and achieved the same results even if the revolt against the ordinances of Charles X. had been successfully repressed, and the Bourbon monarchy had maintained itself in increased strength and reputation. A Reform of Parliament had been acknowledged to be necessary forty years before. Pitt had actually proposed it in 1785, and but for the outbreak of the French Revolution would probably have carried it into effect before the close of the last century. The development of English manufacturing industry which took place between 1790 and 1830, accompanied by the rapid growth of towns and the enrichment of the urban middle class, rendered the design of Pitt, which would have transferred the representation of the decayed boroughs to the counties alone, obsolete, and made the claims of the new centres of population too strong to be resisted. In theory the representative system of the country was completely transformed; but never was a measure which seemed to open the way to such boundless possibilities of change so thoroughly safe and so thoroughly conservative. In spite of the increased influence won by the wealthy part of the commercial classes, the House of Commons continued to be drawn mainly from the territorial aristocracy. Cabinet after Cabinet was formed with scarcely a single member included in it who was not himself a man of title, or closely connected with the nobility: the social influence of rank was not diminished; and although such measures as the Reform of Municipal Corporations attested the increased energy of the Legislature, no party in the House of Commons was weaker than that which supported the democratic demands for the Ballot and for Triennial Parliaments, nor was the repeal of the Corn Laws seriously considered until famine had made it inevitable. That the widespread misery which existed in England after 1832, as the result of the excessive increase of our population and the failure alike of law and of philanthropy to keep pace with the exigencies of a vast industrial growth, should have been so quietly borne, proves how great was the success of the Reform Bill as a measure of conciliation between Government and people. But the crowning justification of the changes made in 1832, and the complete and final answer to those who had opposed them as revolutionary, was not afforded until 1848, when, in the midst of European convulsion, the monarchy and the constitution of England remained unshaken. Bold as the legislation of Lord Grey appeared to men who had been brought up amidst the reactionary influences dominant in England since 1793, the Reform

Bill belongs not to the class of great creative measures which have inaugurated new periods in the life of nations, but to the class of those which, while least affecting the general order of society, have most contributed to political stability and to the avoidance of revolutionary change.

CHAPTER VI.

France and England after 1830—Affairs of Portugal—Don Miguel—Don Pedro invades Portugal—Ferdinand of Spain—The Pragmatic Sanction—Death of Ferdinand: Regency of Christina—The Constitution—Quadruple Alliance —Miguel and Carlos expelled from Portugal—Carlos enters Spain— The Basque Provinces—Carlist War; Zumalacarregui—The Spanish Government seeks French assistance, which is refused—Constitution of 1837—End of the War—Regency of Espartero—Isabella Queen—Affairs of the Ottoman Empire—Ibrahim invades Syria; his victories—Rivalry of France and Russia at Constantinople—Peace of Kutaya and Treaty of Unkiar Skelessi—Effect of this Treaty—France and Mehemet Ali—Commerce of the Levant—Second War between Mehemet and the Porte—Ottoman disasters—The Policy of the Great Powers—Quadruple Treaty without France—Ibrahim expelled from Syria—Final Settlement—Turkey after 1840 —Attempted reforms of Reschid Pasha.

ALLIANCES of opinion usually cover the pursuit on one or both sides of some definite interest; and to this rule the alliance which appeared to be springing up between France and England after the changes of 1830 was no exception. In the popular view, the bond of union between the two States was a common attachment to principles of liberty; and on the part of the Whig statesmen who now governed England this sympathy with free constitutional systems abroad was certainly a powerful force: but other motives than mere community of sentiment combined to draw the two Governments together, and in the case of France these immediate interests greatly outweighed any abstract preference for

France and England after 1830.

a constitutional ally. Louis Philippe had an avowed and obstinate enemy in the Czar of Russia, who had been his predecessor's friend: the Court of Vienna tolerated usurpers only where worse mischief would follow from attacking them; Prussia had no motive for abandoning the connexions which it had maintained since 1815. As the union between the three Eastern Courts grew closer in consequence of the outbreak of revolution beyond the borders of France, a good understanding with Great Britain became more and more obviously the right policy for Louis Philippe; on the other hand, the friendship of France seemed likely to secure England from falling back into that isolated position which it had occupied when the Holy Alliance laid down the law to Europe, and averted the danger to which the Ottoman Empire, as well as the peace of the world, had been exposed by the combination of French with Russian schemes of aggrandizement. If Canning, left without an ally in Europe, had called the new world into existence to redress the balance of the old, his Whig successors might well look with some satisfaction on that shifting of the weights which had brought over one of the Great Powers to the side of England, and anticipate, in the concert of the two great Western States, the establishment of a permanent force in European politics which should hold in check the reactionary influences of Vienna and St. Petersburg. To some extent these views were realised. A general relation of friendliness was recognised as subsisting between the Governments of Paris and London, and in certain

European complications their intervention was arranged in common. But even here the element of mistrust was seldom absent; and while English Ministers jealously watched each action of their neighbour, the French Government rarely allowed the ties of an inormal alliance to interfere with the prosecution of its own views. Although down to the close of Louis Philippe's reign the good understanding between England and France was still nominally in existence, all real confidence had then long vanished; and on more than one occasion the preservation of peace between the two nations had been seriously endangered.

It was in the establishment of the kingdom of Belgium that the combined action of France and England produced its first and most successful result. A second demand was made upon the Governments of the two constitutional Powers by the conflicts which agitated the Spanish Peninsula, and which were stimulated in the general interests of absolutism by both the Austrian and the Russian Court. The intervention of Canning in 1826 on behalf of the constitutional Regency of Portugal against the foreign supporters of Don Miguel, the head of the clerical and reactionary party, had not permanently restored peace to that country. Miguel indeed accepted the constitution, and, after betrothing himself to the infant sovereign, Donna Maria, who was still with her father, Pedro, in Brazil, entered upon the Regency which his elder brother had promised to him. But his actions soon disproved the professions of loyalty to the

Affairs of Portugal, 1826—1830.

constitution which he had made; and after dissolving the Cortes, and re-assembling the mediæval Estates, he caused himself to be proclaimed King (June, 1828). A reign of terror followed. The constitutionalists were completely crushed. Miguel's own brutal violence gave an example to all the fanatics and ruffians who surrounded him; and after an unsuccessful appeal to arms, those of the adherents of Donna Maria and the constitution who escaped from imprisonment or execution took refuge in England or in the Azore islands, where Miguel had not been able to establish his authority. Though Miguel was not officially recognised as Sovereign by most of the foreign Courts, his victory was everywhere seen with satisfaction by the partisans of absolutism; and in Great Britain, where the Duke of Wellington was now in power, the precedent of Canning's intervention was condemned, and a strict neutrality maintained. Not only was all assistance refused to Donna Maria, but her adherents who had taken refuge in England were prevented from making this country the basis of any operations against the usurper.

Such was the situation of Portuguese affairs when the events of 1830 brought an entirely new spirit into the foreign policy of both England and France. Miguel, however, had no inclination to adapt his own policy to the change of circumstances; on the contrary, he challenged the hostility of both governments by persisting in a series of wanton attacks upon English and French subjects resident at Lisbon. Satisfaction was demanded, and

Invasion of Portugal by Pedro. July, 1832.

exacted by force. English and French squadrons successively appeared in the Tagus. Lord Palmerston, now Foreign Secretary in the Ministry of Earl Grey, was content with obtaining a pecuniary indemnity for his countrymen, accompanied by a public apology from the Portuguese Government: the French admiral, finding some difficulty in obtaining redress, carried off the best ships of Don Miguel's navy.* A weightier blow was, however, soon to fall upon the usurper. His brother, the Emperor Pedro, threatened with revolution in Brazil, resolved to return to Europe and to enforce the rights of his daughter to the throne of Portugal. Pedro arrived in London in July, 1831, and was permitted by the Government to raise troops and to secure the services of some of the best naval officers of this country. The gathering place of his forces was Terceira, one of the Azore islands, and in the summer of 1832 a sufficiently strong body of troops was collected to undertake the reconquest of Portugal. A landing was made at Oporto, and this city fell into the hands of Don Pedro without resistance. Miguel, however, now marched against his brother, and laid siege to Oporto. For nearly a year no progress was made by either side; at length the arrival of volunteers from various countries, among whom was Captain Charles Napier, enabled Pedro to divide his forces and to make a new attack on Portugal from the south. Napier, in command of the fleet, annihilated the navy of Don Miguel off St. Vincent; his colleague, Villa Flor, landed and

* B. and F. State Papers, xviii. 196. Palmerston, i. 300.

marched on Lisbon. The resistance of the enemy was overcome, and on the 28th of July, 1833, Don Pedro entered the capital. But the war was not yet at an end, for Miguel's cause was as closely identified with the interests of European absolutism as that of his brother was with constitutional right, and assistance both in troops and money continued to arrive at his camp. The struggle threatened to prove a long and obstinate one, when a new turn was given to events in the Peninsula by the death of Ferdinand, King of Spain.

Since the restoration of absolute Government in Spain in 1823, Ferdinand, in spite of his own abject weakness and ignorance, had not given complete satisfaction to the fanatics of the clerical party. Some vestiges of statesmanship, some sense of political necessity, as well as the influence of foreign counsellors, had prevented the Government of Madrid from completely identifying itself with the monks and zealots who had first risen against the constitution of 1820, and who now sought to establish the absolute supremacy of the Church. The Inquisition had not been restored, and this alone was enough to stamp the King as a renegade in the eyes of the ferocious and implacable champions of mediæval bigotry. Under the name of Apostolicals, these reactionaries had at times broken into open rebellion. Their impatience had, however, on the whole been restrained by the knowledge that in the King's brother and heir, Don Carlos, they had an adherent whose devotion to the priestly cause was beyond suspicion, and who might

Death of Ferdinand. Sept, 1833.

be expected soon to ascend the throne. Ferdinand had been thrice married; he was childless; his state of health miserable; and his life likely to be a short one. The succession to the throne of Spain had moreover, since 1713, been governed by the Salic Law, so that even in the event of Ferdinand leaving female issue Don Carlos would nevertheless inherit the crown. These confident hopes were rudely disturbed by a fourth marriage of the King, followed by an edict, known as the Pragmatic Sanction, repealing the Salic Law which had been introduced with the first Bourbon, and restoring the ancient Castilian custom under which women were capable of succeeding to the crown. A daughter was shortly afterwards born to the new Queen, Maria Christina of Naples. On the legality of the Pragmatic Sanction the opinions of publicists differed; it was judged, however, by Europe at large not from the point of view of antiquarian theory, but with direct reference to its immediate effect. The three Eastern Courts emphatically condemned it, as an interference with established monarchical right, and as a blow to the cause of European absolutism through the alliance which it would almost certainly produce between the supplanters of Don Carlos and the Liberals of the Spanish Peninsula.* To the clerical and reactionary party at Madrid, it amounted to nothing less than a sentence of destruction, and the utmost pressure was

* "La Reine Isabelle est la Révolution incarnée dans sa forme la plus dangereuse; Don Carlos représente le principe Monarchique aux prises avec la Révolution pure." Metternich, v. 615. B. and F. State Papers, xviii. 1365; xxii. 1394. Baumgarten, iii. 65.

brought to bear upon the weak and dying King with the object of inducing him to undo the alleged wrong which he had done to his brother. In a moment of prostration Ferdinand revoked the Pragmatic Sanction; but, subsequently, regaining some degree of strength, he re-enacted it, and appointed Christina Regent during the continuance of his illness. Don Carlos, protesting against the violation of his rights, had betaken himself to Portugal, where he made common cause with Miguel. His adherents had no intention of submitting to the change of succession. Their resentment was scarcely restrained during Ferdinand's life-time, and when, in September, 1833, his long-expected death took place, and the child Isabella was declared Queen under the Regency of her mother, open rebellion broke out, and Carlos was proclaimed King in several of the northern provinces.

For the moment the forces of the Regency seemed to be far superior to those of the insurgents, and Don Carlos failed to take advantage of the first outburst of enthusiasm and to place himself at the head of his followers. He remained in Portugal, *The Regency and the Carlists.* while Christina, as had been expected, drew nearer to the Spanish Liberals, and ultimately called to power a Liberal minister, Martinez de la Rosa, under whom a constitution was given to Spain by Royal Statute (April 10, 1834). At the same time negociations were opened with Por- *Quadruple Treaty, April 22, 1834.* tugal and with the Western Powers, in the hope of forming an alliance which should drive both Miguel and

Carlos from the Peninsula. On the 22nd of April, 1834, a Quadruple Treaty was signed at London, in which the Spanish Government undertook to send an army into Portugal against Miguel, the Court of Lisbon pledging itself in return to use all the means in its power to expel Don Carlos from Portuguese territory. England engaged to co-operate by means of its fleet. The assistance of France, if it should be deemed necessary for the attainment of the objects of the Treaty, was to be rendered in such manner as should be settled by common consent. In pursuance of the policy of the Treaty, and even before the formal engagement was signed, a Spanish division under General Rodil crossed the frontier and marched against Miguel. The forces of the usurper were defeated. The appearance of the English fleet and the publication of the Treaty of Quadruple Alliance rendered further resistance hopeless, and on the 22nd of May Miguel made his submission, and in return for a large pension renounced all rights to the crown, and undertook to quit the Peninsula for ever. Don Carlos, refusing similar conditions, went on board an English ship, and was conducted to London.*

<small>Miguel and Carlos removed, May, 1834.</small>

With respect to Portugal, the Quadruple Alliance had completely attained its object; and in so far as the Carlist cause was strengthened by the continuance of civil war in the neighbouring country, this source of strength was no doubt withdrawn from it. But in

---

* Hertslet, Map of Europe, ii. 941. Miraflores, Memorias, i. 39. Guizot, iv. 86. Palmerston, ii. 180.

its effect upon Don Carlos himself the action of the Quadruple Alliance was worse than useless. While fulfilling the letter of the Treaty, which stipulated for the expulsion of the two pretenders from the Peninsula, the English admiral had removed Carlos from Portugal, where he was comparatively harmless, and had taken no effective guarantee that he should not re-appear in Spain itself and enforce his claim by arms. Carlos had not been made a prisoner of war; he had made no promises and incurred no obligations; nor could the British Government, after his arrival in this country, keep him in perpetual restraint. Quitting England after a short residence, he travelled in disguise through France, crossed the Pyrenees, and appeared on the 10th of July, 1834, at the headquarters of the Carlist insurgents in Navarre.

Carlos appears in Spain.

In the country immediately below the western Pyrenees, the so-called Basque Provinces, lay the chief strength of the Carlist rebellion. These provinces, which were among the most thriving and industrious parts of Spain, might seem by their very superiority an unlikely home for a movement which was directed against everything favourable to liberty, tolerance, and progress in the Spanish kingdom. But the identification of the Basques with the Carlist cause was due in fact to local, not to general, causes; and in fighting to impose a bigoted despot upon the Spanish people, they were in truth fighting to protect themselves from a closer

The Basque Provinces.

incorporation with Spain. Down to the year 1812, the Basque provinces had preserved more than half of the essentials of independence. Owing to their position on the French frontier, the Spanish monarchy, while destroying all local independence in the interior of Spain, had uniformly treated the Basques with the same indulgence which the Government of Great Britain had shown to the Channel Islands, and which the French monarchy, though in a less degree, showed to the frontier province of Alsace in the seventeenth and eighteenth centuries. The customs-frontier of the north of Spain was drawn to the south of these districts. The inhabitants imported what they pleased from France without paying any duties; while the heavy import dues levied at the border of the neighbouring Spanish provinces gave them the opportunity of carrying on an easy and lucrative system of smuggling. The local administration remained to a great extent in the hands of the people themselves; each village preserved its active corporate life; and the effect of this survival of a vigorous local freedom was seen in the remarkable contrast described by travellers between the aspect of the Basque districts and that of Spain at large. The Fueros, or local rights, as the Basques considered them, were in reality, when viewed as part of the order of the Spanish State, a series of exceptional privileges; and it was inevitable that the framers of the Constitution of 1812, in their attempt to create a modern administrative and political system doing justice to the whole of the nation, should sweep away the distinctions which had hitherto marked off one group of provinces from the rest of the community. The continuance of war until the return of Ferdinand, and the overthrow of the Constitution, prevented the plans of the Cortes from being at that time carried into effect; but the revolution of 1820 brought them into actual operation, and the Basques found themselves, as a result of the victory of Liberal principles, compelled to pay duties on their imports, robbed of the profits of their smuggling, and supplanted in the management of their local affairs by an army of officials from Madrid. They had gained by the Constitution little that they had not possessed before, and their losses were immediate, tangible, and substantial. The result was, that although the larger towns, like Bilbao, remained true to modern ideas, the country districts, led chiefly by priests, took up arms on behalf of the absolute monarchy, assisted the French in the restoration of despotism in 1823, and remained the permanent enemies of the constitutional cause.* On the death of Ferdinand they declared at once for Don Carlos, and rose in rebellion against the Government of Queen Christina, by which they considered the privileges of the Basque Provinces and the interests of Catholic orthodoxy to be alike threatened.

There was little in the character of Don Carlos to stimulate the loyalty even of his most benighted partizans. Of military and

Carlist victories, 1834–5.

* Essai historique sur les Provinces Basques, p. 58. W. Humboldt Werke iii. 213

political capacity he was totally destitute, and his continued absence in Portugal when the conflict had actually begun proved him to be wanting in the natural impulses of a brave man. It was, however, his fortune to be served by a soldier of extraordinary energy and skill; and the first reverses of the Carlists were speedily repaired, and a system of warfare organised which made an end of the hopes of easy conquest with which the Government of Christina had met the insurrection. Fighting in a worthless cause, and commanding resources scarcely superior to those of a brigand chief, the Carlist leader, Zumalacarregui, inflicted defeat after defeat upon the generals who were sent to destroy him. The mountainous character of the country and the universal hostility of the inhabitants made the exertions of a regular soldiery useless against the alternate flights and surprises of men who knew every mountain track, and who gained information of the enemy's movements from every cottager. Terror was added by Zumalacarregui to all his other methods for demoralising his adversary. In the exercise of reprisals he repeatedly murdered all his prisoners in cold blood, and gave to the war so savage a character that foreign Governments at last felt compelled to urge upon the belligerents some regard for the usages of the civilised world. The appearance of Don Carlos himself in the summer of 1834 raised still higher the confidence already inspired by the victories of his general. It was in vain that the old constitutionalist soldier, Mina, who had won so great a name in these provinces in 1823, returned after long exile to the scene of his exploits. Enfeebled and suffering, he was no longer able to place himself at the head of his troops, and he soon sought to be relieved from a hopeless task. His successor, the War Minister Valdes, took the field announcing his determination to act upon a new system, and to operate with his troops in mass instead of pursuing the enemy's bands with detachments. The result of this change of tactics was a defeat more ruinous and complete than had befallen any of Valdes' predecessors. He with difficulty withdrew the remainder of his army from the insurgent provinces; and the Carlist leader, master of the open country up to the borders of Castile, prepared to cross the Ebro and to march upon Madrid.*

The Ministers of Queen Christina, who had up till this time professed themselves confident in their power to deal with the insurrection, could now no longer conceal the real state of affairs. Valdes himself declared that the rebellion could not be subdued without foreign aid; and after prolonged discussion in the Cabinet it was determined to appeal to France for armed assistance. The flight of Don Carlos from England had already caused an additional article to be added to the Treaty of the Quadruple Alliance, in which France undertook so to watch the frontier of the Pyrenees that no reinforcements or munition of war should reach the Carlists from that side, while England promised to supply the troops of Queen Christina with

<small>Request to France for assistance, May, 1835</small>

---

* Henningson, Campaign with Zumalacarregui, i. 93. Burgos, Analos, ii. 110. Baumgarten, iii. 257.

arms and stores, and, if necessary, to render assistance with a naval force (18th August, 1834). The foreign supplies sent to the Carlists had thus been cut off both by land and sea; but more active assistance seemed indispensable if Madrid was to be saved from falling into the enemy's hands. The request was made to Louis Philippe's Government to occupy the Basque Provinces with a corps of twelve thousand men. Reasons of weight might be addressed to the French Court in favour of direct intervention. The victory of Don Carlos would place upon the throne of Spain a representative of all those reactionary influences throughout Europe which were in secret or in open hostility to the House of Orleans, and definitely mark the failure of that policy which had led France to combine with England in expelling Don Miguel from Portugal. On the other hand, the experience gained from earlier military enterprises in Spain might well deter even bolder politicians than those about Louis Philippe from venturing upon a task whose ultimate issues no man could confidently forecast. Napoleon had wrecked his empire in the struggle beyond the Pyrenees not less than in the march to Moscow: and the expedition of 1823, though free from military difficulties, had exposed France to the humiliating responsibility for every brutal act of a despotism which, in the very moment of its restoration, had scorned the advice of its restorers. The constitutional Government which invoked French assistance might moreover at any moment give place to a democratic faction which already harassed it within the

Cortes, and which, in its alliance with the populace in many of the great cities, threatened to throw Spain into anarchy, or to restore the ill-omened constitution of 1812. But above all, the attitude of the three Eastern Powers bade the ruler of France hesitate before committing himself to a military occupation of Spanish territory. Their sympathies were with Don Carlos, and the active participation of France in the quarrel might possibly call their opposing forces into the field and provoke a general war. In view of the evident dangers arising out of the proposed intervention, the French Government, taking its stand on that clause of the Quadruple Treaty which provided that the assistance of France should be rendered in such manner as might be agreed upon by all the parties to the Treaty, addressed itself to Great Britain, inquiring whether this country would undertake a joint responsibility in the enterprise and share with France the consequences to which it might give birth. Lord Palmerston in reply declined to give the assurance required. He stated that no objection would be raised by the British Government to the entry of French troops into Spain, but that such intervention must be regarded as the work of France alone, and be undertaken by France at its own peril. This answer sufficed for Louis Philippe and his Ministers. The Spanish Government was informed that the grant of military assistance was impossible, and that the entire public opinion of France would condemn so dangerous an undertaking. As a proof of goodwill, permission was given to Queen Christina to enrol volunteers both in England and France. Arms were supplied; and some thousands of needy or adventurous men ultimately made their way from our own country as well as from France, to earn under Colonel De Lacy Evans and other leaders a scanty harvest of profit or renown.

The first result of the rejection of the Spanish demand for the direct intervention of France was the downfall of the Minister by whom this demand had been made. His successor, Toreno, though a well-known patriot, proved unable to stem the tide of revolution that was breaking over the country. City after city set up its own Junta, and acted as if the central government had ceased to exist. Again the appeal for help was made to Louis Philippe, and now, not so much to avert the victory of Don Carlos as to save Spain from anarchy and from the constitution of 1812. Before an answer could arrive, Toreno in his turn had passed away. Mendizabal, a banker who had been entrusted with financial business at London, and who had entered into friendly relations with Lord Palmerston, was called to office, as a politician acceptable to the democratic party, and the advocate of a close connection with England rather than with France. In spite of the confident professions of the Minister, and in spite of some assistance actually rendered by the English fleet, no real progress was made in subduing the Carlists, or in restoring administrative and financial order. The death of Zumalacarregui, who was forced by Don Carlos to turn northwards and besiege Bilbao instead of

Continuance of the war.

marching upon Madrid immediately after his victories, had checked the progress of the rebellion at a critical moment; but the Government, distracted and bankrupt, could not use the opportunity which thus offered itself, and the war soon blazed out anew not only in the Basque Provinces but throughout the north of Spain. For year after year the monotonous struggle continued, while Cortes succeeded Cortes and faction supplanted faction, until there remained scarcely an officer who had not lost his reputation or a politician who was not useless and discredited.

The Queen Regent, who from the necessities of her situation had for a while been the representative of the popular cause, gradually identified herself with the interests opposed to democratic change; and although her name was still treated with some respect, and her policy was habitually attributed to the misleading advice of courtiers, her real position was well understood at Madrid, and her own resistance was known to be the principal obstacle to the restoration of the Constitution of 1812. It was therefore determined to overcome this resistance by force; and on the 13th of August, 1836, a regiment of the garrison of Madrid, won over by the Exaltados, marched upon the palace of La Granja, invaded the Queen's apartments, and compelled her to sign an edict restoring the Constitution of 1812 until the Cortes should establish that or some other. Scenes of riot and murder followed in the capital. Men of moderate opinions, alarmed at the approach of anarchy, prepared to unite with Don Carlos.

Constitution of 1837.

King Louis Philippe, who had just consented to strengthen the French legion by the addition of some thousands of trained soldiers, now broke entirely from the Spanish connection, and dismissed his Ministers who refused to acquiesce in this change of policy. Meanwhile the Eastern Powers and all rational partizans of absolutism besought Don Carlos to give those assurances which would satisfy the wavering mass among his opponents, and place him on the throne without the sacrifice of any right that was worth preserving. It seemed as if the opportunity was too clear to be misunderstood; but the obstinacy and narrowness of Don Carlos were proof against every call of fortune. Refusing to enter into any sort of engagement, he rendered it impossible for men to submit to him who were not willing to accept absolutism pure and simple. On the other hand, a majority of the Cortes, whose eyes were now opened to the dangers around them, accepted such modifications of the Constitution of 1812 that political stability again appeared possible (June, 1837). The danger of a general transference of all moderate elements in the State to the side of Don Carlos was averted; and, although the Carlist armies took up the offensive, menaced the capital, and made incursions into every part of Spain, the darkest period of the war was now over; and when, after undertaking in person the march upon Madrid, Don Carlos swerved aside and ultimately fell back in confusion to the Ebro, the suppression of the rebellion became a certainty. General Espartero, with whom such distinction remained as was to be gathered in this miserable war, forced back the adversary step by step, and carried fire and sword into the Basque Provinces, employing a system of devastation which alone seemed capable of exhausting the endurance of the people. Reduced to the last extremity, the Carlist leaders turned their arms against one another. The priests excommunicated the generals, and the generals shot the priests; and finally, on the 14th September, 1839, after the surrender of almost all his troops to Espartero, Don Carlos crossed the French frontier, and the conflict which during six years had barbarised and disgraced the Spanish nation reached its close. End of the war, Sept., 1839.

The triumph of Queen Christina over her rivals was not of long duration. Confronted by a strong democratic party both in the Cortes and in the country, she endeavoured in vain to govern by the aid of Ministers of her own choice. End of the Regency, Isabella, Queen, Nov., 1843.
Her popularity had vanished away. The scandals of her private life gave just offence to the nation, and fatally weakened her political authority. Forced by insurrection to bestow office on Espartero, as the chief of the Progressist party, she found that the concessions demanded by this general were more than she could grant, and in preference to submitting to them she resigned the Regency and quitted Spain (Oct., 1840). Espartero, after some interval, was himself appointed Regent by the Cortes. For two years he maintained himself in power, then in his turn he fell before the combined attack of his political opponents and the extreme men

of his own party, and passed into exile. There remained in Spain no single person qualified to fill the vacant Regency, and in default of all other expedients the young princess Isabella, who was now in her fourteenth year, was declared of full age, and placed on the throne (Nov., 1843). Christina returned to Madrid. After some rapid changes of Ministry, a more durable Government was formed from the Moderado party under General Narvaez; and in comparison with the period that had just ended, the first few years of the new reign were years of recovery and order.

The withdrawal of Louis Philippe from his engagements after the capitulation of Maria Christina to the soldiery at La Granja in 1836 had diminished the confidence placed in the King by the British Ministry; but it had not destroyed the relations of friendship existing between the two Governments. Far more serious causes of difference arose out of the course of events in the East, and the extension of the power of Mehemet Ali, Viceroy of Egypt. The struggle between Mehemet and his sovereign, long foreseen, broke out in the year 1832. After the establishment of the Hellenic Kingdom, the island of Crete had been given to Mehemet in return for his services to the Ottoman cause by land and sea. This concession, however, was far from satisfying the ambition of the Viceroy, and a quarrel with Abdallah, Pasha of Acre, gave him the opportunity of throwing an army into Palestine without directly rebelling against his sovereign (Nov., 1831). Ibrahim, in command of his

War between Mehemet Ali and the Porte, 1832.

father's forces, laid siege to Acre; and had this fortress at once fallen, it would probably have been allowed by the Sultan to remain in its conqueror's hands as an addition to his own province, since the Turkish army was not ready for war, and it was no uncommon thing in the Ottoman Empire for one provincial governor to possess himself of territory at the expense of another. So obstinate, however, was the defence of Acre that time was given to the Porte to make preparations for war; and in the spring of 1832, after the issue of a proclamation declaring Mehemet and his son to be rebels, a Turkish army led by Hussein Pasha entered Syria.

Ibrahim, while the siege of Acre was proceeding, had overrun the surrounding country. He was now in possession of all the interior of Palestine, and the tribes of Lebanon had joined him in the expectation of gaining relief from the burdens of Turkish misgovernment. The fall of Acre, while the relieving army was still near Antioch, enabled him to throw his full strength against his opponent in the valley of the Orontes. It was the intention of the Turkish general, whose forces, though superior in number, had not the European training of Ibrahim's regiments, to meet the assault of the Egyptians in an entrenched camp near Hama. The commander of the vanguard, however, pushed forward beyond this point, and when far in advance of the main body of the army was suddenly attacked by Ibrahim at Homs. Taken at a moment of complete disorder, the Turks were put to the rout.

Ibrahim conquers Syria and Asia Minor.

Their overthrow and flight so alarmed the general-in-chief that he determined to fall back upon Aleppo, leaving Antioch and all the valley of the Orontes to the enemy. Aleppo was reached, but the governor, won over by Ibrahim, closed the gates of the city against the famishing army, and forced Hussein to continue his retreat to the mountains which form the barrier between Syria and Cilicia. Here, at the pass of Beilan, he was attacked by Ibrahim, outmanœuvred, and forced to retreat with heavy loss (July 29). The pursuit was continued through the province of Cilicia. Hussein's army, now completely demoralised, made its escape to the centre of Asia Minor; the Egyptian, after advancing as far as Mount Taurus and occupying the passes in this range, took up his quarters in the conquered country in order to refresh his army and to await reinforcements. After two months' halt he renewed his march, crossed Mount Taurus and occupied Konieh, the capital of this district. Here the last and decisive blow was struck. A new Turkish army, led by Reschid Pasha, Ibrahim's colleague in the siege of Missolonghi, advanced from the north. Against his own advice, Reschid was compelled by orders from Constantinople to risk everything in an engagement. He attacked Ibrahim at Konieh on the 21st of December, and was completely defeated. Reschid himself was made a prisoner; his army dispersed; the last forces of the Sultan were exhausted, and the road to the Bosphorus lay open before the Egyptian invader.

In this extremity the Sultan looked around for help;

RUSSIAN FLEET IN THE BOSPHORUS.

nor were offers of assistance wanting. The Emperor Nicholas had since the Treaty of Adrianople assumed the part of the magnanimous friend; his belief was that the Ottoman Empire might by judicious management and without further conquest be brought into a state of habitual dependence upon Russia; and before the result of the battle of Konieh was known General Muravieff had arrived at Constantinople bringing the offer of Russian help both by land and sea, and tendering his own personal services in the restoration of peace Mahmud had to some extent been won over by the Czar's politic forbearance in the execution of the Treaty of Adrianople. His hatred of Mehemet Ali was a consuming passion; and in spite of the general conviction both of his people and of his advisers that no possible concession to a rebellious vassal could be so fatal as the protection of the hereditary enemy of Islam, he was disposed to accept the Russian tender of assistance. As a preliminary, Muravieff was sent to Alexandria with permission to cede Acre to Mehemet Ali, if in return the Viceroy would make over his fleet to the Sultan. These were conditions on which no reasonable man could have expected that Mehemet would make peace; and the intention of the Russian Court probably was that Muravieff's mission should fail. The envoy soon returned to Constantinople announcing that his terms were rejected. Mahmud now requested that Russian ships might be sent to the Bosphorus, and to the dismay of the French and English embassies a Russian squadron

Russian aid offered to the Sultan.

appeared before the capital. Admiral Roussin, the French ambassador, addressed a protest to the Sultan and threatened to leave Constantinople. His remonstrances induced Mahmud to consent to some more serious negotiation being opened with Mehemet Ali. A French envoy was authorised to promise the Viceroy the governorship of Tripoli in Syria as well as Acre; his overtures, however, were not more acceptable than those of Muravieff, and Mehemet openly declared that if peace were not concluded on his own terms within six weeks, he should order Ibrahim, who had halted at Kutaya, to continue his march on the Bosphorus. Thoroughly alarmed at this threat, and believing that no Turkish force could keep Ibrahim out of the capital, Mahmud applied to Russia for more ships and also for troops. Again Admiral Roussin urged upon the Sultan that if Syria could be reconquered only by Russian forces it was more than lost to the Porte. His arguments were supported by the Divan, and with such effect that a French diplomatist was sent to Ibrahim with power to negotiate for peace on any terms. Preliminaries were signed at Kutaya under French mediation on the 10th of April, 1833, by which the Sultan made over to his vassal not only the whole of Syria but the province of Adana which lies between Mount Taurus and the Mediterranean. After some delay these Preliminaries were ratified by Mahmud; and Ibrahim, after his dazzling success both in war and in diplomacy, commenced the evacuation of northern Anatolia.

Peace of Kutaya, April, 1833.

For the moment it appeared that French influence had decisively prevailed at Constantinople, and that the troops of the Czar had been summoned from Sebastopol only to be dismissed with the ironical compliments of those who were most anxious to get rid of them. But this was not really the case. Whether the fluctuations in the Sultan's policy had been due to mere fear and irresolution, or whether they had to some extent proceeded from the desire to play off one Power against another, it was to Russia, not France, that his final confidence was given. The soldiers of the Czar were encamped by the side of the Turks on the eastern shore of the Bosphorus; his ships lay below Constantinople. Here on the 8th of July a Treaty was signed at the palace of Unkiar Skelessi,* in which Russia and Turkey entered into a defensive alliance of the most intimate character, each Power pledging itself to render assistance to the other, not only against the attack of an external enemy, but in every event where its peace and security might be endangered. Russia undertook, in cases where its support should be required, to provide whatever amount of troops the Sultan should consider necessary both by sea and land, the Porte being charged with no part of the expense beyond that of the provisioning of the troops. The duration of the Treaty was fixed in the first instance for eight years. A secret article, which,

Treaty of Unkiar Skelessi. July, 1833.

* Rosen, i. 158. Prokesch von Osten, Kleine Schriften, vii. 56. Mehmed Ali, p. 17. Hillebrand, i. 514. Metternich, v. 481. B. and F. State Papers, xx. 1176; xxii. 140.

however, was soon afterwards published, declared that, in order to diminish the burdens of the Porte, the Czar would not demand the material help to which the Treaty entitled him; while, in substitution for such assistance, the Porte undertook, when Russia should be at war, to close the Dardanelles to the war-ships of all nations.

By the Treaty of Unkiar Skelessi, Russia came nearer than it has at any time before or since to that complete ascendency at Constantinople which has been the modern object of its policy. The success of its diplomatists had in fact been too great; for, if the abstract right of the Sultan to choose his own allies had not yet been disputed by Europe at large, the clause in the Treaty which related to the Dardanelles touched the interests of every Power which possessed a naval station in the Mediterranean. By the public law of Europe the Black Sea, which until the eighteenth century was encompassed entirely by the Sultan's territory, formed no part of the open waters of the world, but a Turkish lake to which access was given through the Dardanelles only at the pleasure of the Porte. When, in the eighteenth century, Russia gained a footing on the northern shore of the Euxine, this carried with it no right to send war-ships through the straits into the Mediterranean, nor had any Power at war with Russia the right to send a fleet into the Black Sea otherwise than by the Sultan's consent. The Treaty of Unkiar Skelessi, in making Turkey the ally of Russia against all its enemies, converted the

Effect of this Treaty.

entrance to the Black Sea into a Russian fortified post, from behind which Russia could freely send forth its ships of war into the Mediterranean, while its own ports and arsenals remained secure against attack. England and France, which were the States whose interests were principally affected, protested against the Treaty, and stated they reserved to themselves the right of taking such action in regard to it as occasion might demand. Nor did the opposition rest with the protests of diplomatists. The attention both of the English nation and of its Government was drawn far more than hitherto to the future of the Ottoman Empire. Political writers exposed with unwearied vigour, and not without exaggeration, the designs of the Court of St. Petersburg in Asia as well as in Europe; and to this time, rather than to any earlier period, belongs the first growth of that strong national antagonism to Russia which found its satisfaction in the Crimean War, and which has by no means lost its power at the present day.

In desiring to check the extension of Russia's influence in the Levant, Great Britain and France were at one. The lines of policy, however, followed by these two States were widely divergent. Great Britain sought to maintain the Sultan's power in its integrity; France became in an increasing degree the patron and the friend of Mehemet Ali. Since the expedition of Napoleon to Egypt in 1798, which was itself the execution of a design formed in the reign of Louis XVI., Egypt had largely retained its hold on

France and Mehemet Ali

the imagination of the leading classes in France. Its monuments, its relics of a mighty past, touched a livelier chord among French men of letters and science than India has at any time found among ourselves; and although the hope of national conquest vanished with Napoleon's overthrow, Egypt continued to afford a field of enterprise to many a civil and military adventurer. Mehemet's army and navy were organised by French officers; he was surrounded by French agents and men of business; and after the conquest of Algiers had brought France on to the southern shore of the Mediterranean, the advantages of a close political relation with Egypt did not escape the notice of statesmen who saw in Gibraltar and Malta the most striking evidences of English maritime power. Moreover the personal fame of Mehemet strongly affected French opinion. His brilliant military reforms, his vigorous administration, and his specious achievements in finance created in the minds of those who were too far off to know the effects of his tyranny the belief that at the hands of this man the East might yet awaken to new life. Thus, from a real conviction of the superiority of Mehemet's rule over that of the House of Osman no less than from considerations of purely national policy, the French Government, without any public or official bond of union, gradually became the acknowledged supporters of the Egyptian conqueror, and connected his interests with their own.

Sultan Mahmud had ratified the Preliminaries of Kutaya with wrath in his heart; and from this time all his energies were bent upon the creation of a force which should wrest back the lost provinces and take revenge upon his rebellious vassal. As eager as Mehemet himself to reconstruct his form of government upon the models of the West, though far less capable of impressing upon his work the stamp of a single guiding will, thwarted moreover by the jealous interference of Russia whenever his reforms seemed likely to produce any important result, he nevertheless succeeded in introducing something of European system and discipline into his army under the guidance of foreign soldiers, among whom was a man then little known, but destined long afterwards to fill Europe with his fame, the Prussian staff-officer Moltke. On the other side Mehemet and Ibrahim knew well that the peace was no more than an armed truce, and that what had been won by arms could only be maintained by constant readiness to meet attack. Under pressure of this military necessity, Ibrahim sacrificed whatever sources of strength were open to him in the hatred borne by his new subjects to the Turkish yoke, and in their hopes of relief from oppression under his own rule. Welcomed at first as a deliverer, he soon proved a heavier task-master than any who had gone before him. The conscription was rigorously enforced; taxation became more burdensome; the tribes who had enjoyed a wild independence in the mountains were disarmed and reduced to the level of their fellow-subjects. Thus the discontent which had so greatly facilitated the conquest of the

Rule of Mehemet and Ibrahim.

border-provinces soon turned against the conqueror himself, and one uprising after another shook Ibrahim's hold upon Mount Lebanon and the Syrian desert. The Sultan watched each outbreak against his adversary with grim joy, impatient for the moment when the re-organisation of his own forces should enable him to re-enter the field and strike an overwhelming blow.

With all its characteristics of superior intelligence in the choice of means, the system of Mehemet Ali was in its end that of the genuine Oriental despot. His final object was to convert as many as possible of his subjects into soldiers, and to draw into his treasury the profits of the labour of all the rest. *The commerce of the Levant.* With this aim he gradually ousted from their rights of proprietorship the greater part of the land-owners of Egypt, and finally proclaimed the entire soil to be State-domain, appropriating at prices fixed by himself the whole of its produce. The natural commercial intercourse of his dominions gave place to a system of monopolies carried on by the Government itself. Rapidly as this system, which was introduced into the newly-conquered provinces, filled the coffers of Mehemet Ali, it offered to the Sultan, whose paramount authority was still acknowledged, the means of inflicting a deadly injury upon him by a series of commercial treaties with the European Powers, granting to western traders a free market throughout the Ottoman Empire. Resistance to such a measure would expose Mehemet to the hostility of the whole mercantile interest of Europe; submission to it would involve the loss of a great part of that revenue on which his military power depended. It was probably with this result in view, rather than from any more obvious motive, that in the year 1838 the Sultan concluded a new commercial Treaty with England, which was soon followed by similar agreements with other States.

The import of the Sultan's commercial policy was not lost upon Mehemet, who had already determined to declare himself independent. He saw that war was inevitable, and bade Ibrahim collect his forces in the neighbourhood of Aleppo, while the generals of the Sultan massed on the upper Euphrates the troops that had been successfully employed in subduing the wild tribes of Kurdistan. The storm was seen to be gathering, and the representatives of foreign Powers urged the Sultan, but in vain, to refrain from an enterprise which might shatter his empire. Mahmud was now a dying man. Exhausted by physical excess and by the stress and passion of his long reign, he bore in his heart the same unquenchable hatreds as of old; and while assuring the ambassadors of his intention to maintain the peace, he despatched a letter to his commander-in-chief, without the knowledge of any single person, ordering him to commence hostilities. The Turkish army crossed the frontier on the 23rd of May, 1839. In the operations which followed, the advice and protests of Moltke and the other European officers at head-quarters were persistently disregarded. The Turks were outmanœuvred and cut off from their communications, and on the 24th of June the onslaught

Campaign of Nisib. June, 1839.

of Ibrahim swept them from their position at Nissib in utter rout. The whole of the artillery and stores fell into the hands of the enemy: the army dispersed. Mahmud did not live to hear of the catastrophe. Six days after the battle of Nissib was fought, and while the messenger who bore the news was still in Anatolia, he expired, leaving the throne to his son, Abdul Medjid, a youth of sixteen. Scarcely had the new Sultan been proclaimed when it became known that the Admiral, Achmet Fewzi, who had been instructed to attack the Syrian coast, had sailed into the port of Alexandria, and handed over the Turkish fleet to Mehemet Ali himself.

The very suddenness of these disasters, which left the Ottoman Empire rulerless and without defence by land or sea, contributed ultimately to its preservation, inasmuch as it impelled the Powers to combined action, which, under less urgent pressure, would probably not have been attainable. On the announcement of the exorbitant conditions of peace demanded by Mehemet, the ambassadors addressed a collective note to the Divan, requesting that no answer might be made until the Courts had arrived at some common resolution. Soon afterwards the French and English fleets appeared at the Dardanelles, nominally to protect Constantinople against the attack of the Viceroy, in reality to guard against any sudden movement on the part of Russia. This display of force was, however, not necessary, for the Czar, in spite of some expressions to the contrary, had already convinced himself that it was impossible to act

Relations of the Powers to Mehemet.

upon the Treaty of Unkiar Skelessi and to make the protectorate of Turkey the affair of Russia alone. The tone which had been taken by the English Government during the last preceding years proved that any attempt to exercise exclusive power at Constantinople would have been followed by war with Great Britain, in which most, if not all, of the European Powers would have stood on the side of the latter. Abandoning therefore the hope of attaining sole control, the Russian Government addressed itself to the task of widening as far as possible the existing divergence between England and France. Nor was this difficult. The Cabinet of the Tuileries desired to see Mehemet Ali issue with increased strength from the conflict, or even to establish his dynasty at Constantinople in place of the House of Osman. Lord Palmerston, always jealous and suspicious of Louis Philippe, refused to believe that the growth of Russian power could be checked by dividing the Ottoman Empire, or that any system of Eastern policy could be safely based on the personal qualities of a ruler now past his seventieth year.* He had moreover his own causes of discontent with Mehemet. The possibility of establishing an overland route to India either by way of the Euphrates or of the Red Sea had lately been engaging the attention of the English Government, and Mehemet had not improved his position by raising obstacles to

* Palmerston understood little about the real condition of the Ottoman Empire, and thought that with ten years of peace it might again become a respectable Power. "All that we hear about the decay of the Turkish Empire and its being a dead body or a sapless trunk, and so forth, is pure and unadulterated nonsense." Bulwer's Palmerston, ii. 299.

either line of passage. It was partly in consequence of the hostility of Mehemet, who was now master of a great part of Arabia, and of his known devotion to French interests, that the port of Aden in the Red Sea was at this time occupied by England. If, while Russia accepted the necessity of combined European action and drew nearer to its rival, France persisted in maintaining the claim of the Viceroy to extended dominion, the exclusion of France from the European concert was the only possible result. There was no doubt as to the attitude of the remaining Powers. Metternich, whether from genuine pedantry, or in order to avoid the expression of those fears of Russia which really governed his Eastern policy, repeated his threadbare platitudes on the necessity of supporting legitimate dynasties against rebels, and spoke of the victor of Konieh and Nissib as if he had been a Spanish constitutionalist or a recalcitrant German professor. The Court of Berlin followed in the same general course. In all Europe Mehemet Ali had not a single ally, with the exception of the Government of Louis Philippe.

Under these circumstances it was of little avail to the Viceroy that his army stood on Turkish soil without a foe before it, and that the Sultan's fleet lay within his own harbour of Alexandria. The intrigues by which he hoped to snatch a hasty peace from the inexperience of the young Sultan failed, and he learnt in October that no arrangement which he might make with the Porte without the concurrence of the Powers would be recognised as valid.

<small>Quadruple Treaty without France. July, 1840.</small>

In the meantime Russia was suggesting to the English Government one project after another for joint military action with the object of driving Mehemet from Syria and restoring this province to the Porte; and at the beginning of the following year it was determined on Metternich's proposition that a Conference should forthwith be held in London for the settlement of Eastern affairs. The irreconcilable difference between the intentions of France and those of the other Powers at once became evident. France proposed that all Syria and Egypt should be given in hereditary dominion to Mehemet Ali, with no further obligation towards the Porte than the payment of a yearly tribute. The counter-proposal of England was that Mehemet, recognising the Sultan's authority, should have the hereditary government of Egypt alone, that he should entirely withdraw from all Northern Syria, and hold Palestine only as an ordinary governor appointed by the Porte for his lifetime. To this proposition all the Powers with the exception of France gave their assent. Continued negotiation only brought into stronger relief the obstinacy of Lord Palmerston, and proved the impossibility of attaining complete agreement. At length, when it had been discovered that the French Cabinet was attempting to conduct a separate mediation, the Four Powers, without going through the form of asking for French sanction, signed on the 15th of July a Treaty with the Sultan pledging themselves to enforce upon Mehemet Ali the terms arranged. The Sultan undertook in the first instance to offer Mehemet Egypt in perpetuity and southern Syria for his lifetime. If this offer was not accepted within ten days, Egypt alone was to be offered. If at the end of twenty days Mehemet still remained obstinate, that offer in its turn was to be withdrawn, and the Sultan and the Allies were to take such measures as the interests of the Ottoman Empire might require.*

The publication of this Treaty, excluding France as it did from the concert of Europe, produced a storm of indignation at Paris. Thiers, who more than any man had by his writings stimulated the spirit of aggressive warfare among the French people and revived the worship of Napoleon, was now at the head of the Government. His jealousy for the prestige of France, his comparative indifference to other matters when once the national honour appeared to be committed, his sanguine estimate of the power of his country, rendered him a peculiarly dangerous Minister at the existing crisis. It was not the wrongs or the danger of Mehemet Ali, but the slight offered to France, and the revived League of the Powers which had humbled it in 1814, that excited the passion of the Minister and the nation. Syria was forgotten; the cry was for the recovery of the frontier of the Rhine, and for revenge for Waterloo. New regiments were enrolled, the fleet strengthened, and the long-delayed fortification of Paris begun. Thiers himself probably looked forward

_{Warlike spirit in France. 1840.}

---

* Hertslet, Map of Europe, ii. 1008. Rosen, ii. 3. Guizot, v. 188. Prokesch-Osten, Mehmed-Ali, p. 89. Palmerston, ii. 356. Hillebrand, ii. 357. Greville Memoirs, 2nd part, vol. i. 297.

to a campaign in Italy, anticipating that successfully conducted by Napoleon III. in 1859, rather than to an attack upon Prussia; but the general opinion both in France itself and in other states was that, if war should break out, an invasion of Germany was inevitable. The prospect of this invasion roused in a manner little expected the spirit of the German people. Even in the smaller states, and in the Rhenish provinces themselves, which for twenty years had shared the fortunes of France, and in which the introduction of Prussian rule in 1814 had been decidedly unpopular, a strong national movement carried everything before it; and the year 1840 added to the patriotic minstrelsy of Germany a war-song, written by a Rhenish citizen, not less famous than those of 1813 and 1870.* That there were revolutionary forces smouldering throughout Europe, from which France might in a general war have gained some assistance, the events of 1848 sufficiently proved; but to no single Government would a revolutionary war have been fraught with more imminent peril than to that of France itself, and to no one was this conviction more habitually present than to King Louis Philippe. Relying upon his influence within the Chamber of Deputies, itself a body representing the wealth and the caution rather than the hot spirit of France, the King

---

* "Sie sollen ihn nicht haben
 Den freien Deutschen Rhein."

By Becker; answered by Musset's "Nous l'avons eu, votre Rhin Allemand." The words of the much finer song "Die Wacht am Rhein" were also written at this time—by Schneckenburger, a Würtemberg man; but the music by which they are known was not composed till 1854.

refused to read at the opening of the session in October the speech drawn up for him by Thiers, and accepted the consequent resignation of the Ministry. Guizot, who was ambassador in London, and an advocate for submission to the will of Europe, was called to office, and succeeded after long debate in gaining a vote of confidence from the Chamber. Though preparations for war continued, a policy of peace was now assured. Mehemet Ali was left to his fate; and the stubborn assurance of Lord Palmerston, which had caused so much annoyance to the English Ministry itself, received a striking justification in the face of all Europe.

The operations of the Allies against Mehemet Ali had now begun. While Prussia kept guard on the Rhine, and Russia undertook to protect Constantinople against any forward movement of Ibrahim, an Anglo-Austrian naval squadron combined with a Turkish land-force in attacking the Syrian coast towns. The mountain-tribes of the interior were again in revolt. Arms were supplied to them by the Allies, and the insurrection soon spread over the greater part of Syria. Ibrahim prepared for an obstinate defence, but his dispositions were frustrated by the extension of the area of conflict, and he was unable to prevent the coast-towns from falling one after another into the hands of the Allies. On the capture of Acre by Sir Charles Napier he abandoned all hope of maintaining himself any longer in Syria, and made his way with the wreck of his army towards the Egyptian frontier. Napier had already arrived before Alexandria,

Ibrahim expelled from Syria, Sept.—Nov., 1840.

and there executed a convention with the Viceroy, by which the latter, abandoning all claim upon his other provinces, and undertaking to restore the Turkish fleet, was assured of the hereditary possession of Egypt. The convention was one which the English admiral had no authority to conclude, but it contained substantially the terms which the Allies intended to enforce; and after Mehemet had made a formal act of submission to the Sultan, the hereditary government of Egypt was conferred upon himself and his family by a decree published by the Sultan and sanctioned by the Powers. *Final settlement, Feb., 1841.* This compromise had been proposed by the French Government after the expiry of the twenty days named in the Treaty of July, and immediately before the fall of M. Thiers, but Palmerston would not then listen to any demand made under open or implied threats of war. Since that time a new and pacific Ministry had come into office; it was no part of Palmerston's policy to keep alive the antagonism between England and France; and he readily accepted an arrangement which, while it saved France from witnessing the total destruction of an ally, left Egypt to a ruler who, whatever his faults, had certainly shown a greater capacity for government than any Oriental of that age. It remained for the Powers to place upon record some authoritative statement of the law recognised by Europe with regard to the Bosphorus and Dardanelles. Russia had already virtually consented to the abrogation of the Treaty of Unkiar Skelessi. It now joined with all the other Powers, including France, in a declaration that the ancient rule of the Ottoman Empire which forbade the passage of these straits to the war-ships of all nations, except when the Porte itself should be at war, was accepted by Europe at large. Russia thus surrendered its chance of gaining by any separate arrangement with Turkey the permanent right of sending its fleets from the Black Sea into the Mediterranean, and so becoming a Mediterranean Power. On the other hand, Sebastopol and the arsenals of the Euxine remained safe against the attack of any maritime Power, unless Turkey itself should take up arms against the Czar. Having regard to the great superiority of England over Russia at sea, and to the accessibility and importance of the Euxine coast towns, it is an open question whether the removal of all international restrictions upon the passage of the Bosphorus and Dardanelles would not be more to the advantage of England than of its rival. This opinion, however, had not been urged before the Crimean War, nor has it yet been accepted in our own country.

The Dardanelles.

The conclusion of the struggle of 1840 marked with great definiteness the real position which the Ottoman Empire was henceforth to occupy in its relations to the western world. Rescued by Europe at large from the alternatives of destruction at the hands of Ibrahim or complete vassalage under Russia, the Porte entered upon the condition nominally of an independent European State, really of a State existing under the protection of Europe, and responsible to Europe as well for its domestic government as for its

Turkey after 1840.

alliances and for the conduct of its foreign policy. The necessity of conciliating the public opinion of the West was well understood by the Turkish statesman who had taken the leading part in the negotiations which freed the Porte from dependence upon Russia. Reschid Pasha, the younger, Foreign Minister at the accession of the new Sultan, had gained in an unusual degree the regard and the confidence of the European Ministers with whom, as a diplomatist, he had been brought into contact. As the author of a wide system of reforms, it was his ambition so to purify and renovate the internal administration of the Ottoman Empire that the contrasts which it presented to the civilised order of the West should gradually disappear, and that Turkey should become not only in name but in reality a member of the European world. Stimulated no doubt by the achievements of Mehemet Ali, and anxious to win over to the side of the Porte the interest which Mehemet's partial adoption of European methods and ideas had excited on his behalf, Reschid in his scheme of reform paid an ostentatious homage to the principles of western administration and law, pro- Legislation of Reschid. claiming the security of person and property, prohibiting the irregular infliction of punishment, recognising the civil rights of Christians and Jews, and transferring the collection of taxes from the provincial governors to the officers of the central authority. The friends of the Ottoman State, less experienced then than now in the value of laws made in a society where there exists no power that can enforce them, and where the agents of government are themselves the most lawless of all the public enemies, hailed in Reschid's enlightened legislation the opening of a new epoch in the life of the Christian and Oriental races subject to the Sultan. But the fall of the Minister before a palace-intrigue soon proved on how slight a foundation these hopes were built. Like other Turkish reformers, Reschid had entered upon a hopeless task; and the name of the man who was once honoured as the regenerator of a great Empire is now almost forgotten.

CHAPTER VII.

Europe during the Thirty-years' Peace—Italy and Austria—Mazzini—The House of Savoy—Gioberti—Election of Pius IX.—Reforms expected—Revolution at Palermo—Agitation in Northern Italy—Lombardy—State of the Austrian Empire—Growth of Hungarian National Spirit—The Magyars and Slavs—Transylvania—Parties among the Magyars—Kossuth—The Slavic National Movements in Austria—The Government enters on Reform in Hungary—Policy of the Opposition—The Rural System of Austria—Insurrection in Galicia: the Nobles and the Peasants—Agrarian Edict—Public Opinion in Vienna—Prussia—Accession and Character of King Frederick William IV.—Convocation of the United Diet—Its Debates and Dissolution—France—The Spanish Marriages—Reform Movement—Socialism—Revolution of February—End of the Orleanist Monarchy.

THE characteristic of Continental history during the second quarter of this century is the sense of unrest. The long period of European peace which began in 1815 was not one of internal repose; the very absence of those engrossing and imperious interests which belong to a time of warfare gave freer play to the feelings of discontent and the vague longings for a better political order which remained behind after the convulsions of the revolutionary epoch and the military rule of Napoleon had passed away. During thirty years of peace the breach had been widening between those Governments which still represented the system of 1815, and the peoples over whom they ruled. Ideas of liberty, awakenings of national sense, were far more widely diffused in Europe than at the time of the revolutionary war. The seed then prematurely forced into an atmosphere of storm and reaction had borne its fruit: other growths, fertilised or accelerated by Western Liberalism, but not belonging to the same family, were springing up in unexpected strength, and in regions which had hitherto lain outside the movement of the modern world. New forces antagonistic to Government had come into being, penetrating an area unaffected by the constitutional struggles of the Mediterranean States, or by the weaker political efforts of Germany. In the homes of the Magyar and the Slavic subjects of Austria, so torpid throughout the agitation of an earlier time, the passion of nationality was every hour gaining new might. The older popular causes, vanquished for the moment by one reaction after another, had silently established a far stronger hold on men's minds. Working, some in exile and conspiracy, others through such form of political literature as the jealousy of Governments permitted, the leaders of the democratic movement upon the Continent created a power before which the established order at length succumbed. They had not created, nor was it possible under the circumstances that they should create, an order which was capable of taking its place.

Italy, rather than France, forms the central figure in any retrospect of Europe immediately before 1848 in which the larger forces at work are not obscured by those for the moment more prominent. The failure of the insurrection of 1831 had left Austria more visibly than before master over the Italian people even in those provinces in which Austria was not nominally sovereign. It had become clear that no effort

Italy. 1831—1848.

after reform could be successful either in the Papal States or in the kingdom of Naples so long as Austria held Lombardy and Venice. The expulsion of the foreigner was therefore not merely the task of those who sought to give the Italian race its separate and independent national existence, it was the task of all who would extinguish oppression and misgovernment in any part of the Italian peninsula. Until the power of Austria was broken, it was vain to take up arms against the tyranny of the Duke of Modena or any other contemptible oppressor. Austria itself had twice taught this lesson; and if the restoration of Neapolitan despotism in 1821 could be justified by the disorderly character of the Government then suppressed, the circumstances attending the restoration of the Pope's authority in 1831 had extinguished Austria's claim to any sort of moral respect; for Metternich himself had united with the other European Courts in declaring the necessity for reforms in the Papal Government, and of these reforms, though a single earnest word from Austria would have enforced their execution, not one had been carried into effect. Gradually, but with increasing force as each unhappy year passed by, the conviction gained weight among all men of serious thought that the problem to be faced was nothing less than the destruction of the Austrian yoke. Whether proclaimed as an article of faith, or veiled in diplomatic reserve, this belief formed the common ground among men whose views on the immediate future of Italy differed in almost every other particular.

Three main currents of opinion are to be traced in the ferment of ideas which preceded the Italian revolution of 1848. At a time not rich in intellectual or in moral power, the most striking figure among those who are justly honoured as the founders of Italian independence is perhaps that of Mazzini. Exiled during nearly the whole of his mature life, a conspirator in the eyes of all Governments, a dreamer in the eyes of the world, Mazzini was a prophet or an evangelist among those whom his influence led to devote themselves to the one cause of their country's regeneration. No firmer faith, no nobler disinterestedness, ever animated the saint or the patriot; and if in Mazzini there was also something of the visionary and the fanatic, the force with which he grasped the two vital conditions of Italian revival—the expulsion of the foreigner and the establishment of a single national Government—proves him to have been a thinker of genuine political insight. Laying the foundation of his creed deep in the moral nature of man, and constructing upon this basis a fabric not of rights but of duties, he invested the political union with the immediateness, the sanctity, and the beauty of family life. With him, to live, to think, to hope, was to live, to think, to hope for Italy; and the Italy of his ideal was a Republic embracing every member of the race, purged of the priest-craft and the superstition which had degraded the man to the slave, indebted to itself alone for its independence, and consolidated by the reign of equal law. The rigidity with which Mazzini adhered to his own great

Mazzini.

project in its completeness, and his impatience with any bargaining away of national rights, excluded him from the work of those practical politicians and men of expedients who in 1859 effected with foreign aid the first step towards Italian union; but the influence of his teaching and his organization in preparing his countrymen for independence was immense; and the dynasty which has rendered to United Italy services which Mazzini thought impossible, owes to this great Republican scarcely less than to its ablest friends.

Widely separated from the school of Mazzini in temper and intention was the group of politicians and military men, belonging mostly to Piedmont, who looked to the sovereign and the army of this State as the one hope of Italy in its struggle against foreign rule. *Hopes of Piedmont.* The House of Savoy, though foreign in its origin, was, and had been for centuries, a really national dynasty. It was, moreover, by interest and traditional policy, the rival rather than the friend of Austria in Northern Italy. If the fear of revolution had at times brought the Court of Turin into close alliance with Vienna, the connection had but thinly veiled the lasting antagonism of two States which, as neighbours, had habitually sought expansion each at the other's cost. Lombardy, according to the expression of an older time, was the artichoke which the Kings of Piedmont were destined to devour leaf by leaf. Austria, on the other hand, sought extension towards the Alps: it had in 1799 clearly shown its intention of excluding the House of Savoy altogether from the Italian mainland; and the remembrance of this epoch had led the restored dynasty in 1815 to resist the plans of Metternich for establishing a league of all the princes of Italy under Austria's protection. The sovereign, moreover, who after the failure of the constitutional movement of 1821 had mounted the throne surrounded by Austrian bayonets, was no longer alive. Charles Albert of Carignano, who had at that time played so ambiguous a part, and whom Metternich had subsequently endeavoured to exclude from the succession, was on the throne. He had made his peace with absolutism by fighting in Spain against the Cortes in 1823; and since his accession to the throne he had rigorously suppressed the agitation of Mazzini's partizans within his own dominions. But in spite of strong clerical and reactionary influences around him, he had lately shown an independence of spirit in his dealings with Austria which raised him in the estimation of his subjects; and it was believed that his opinions had been deeply affected by the predominance which the idea of national independence was now gaining over that of merely democratic change. If the earlier career of Charles Albert himself cast some doubt upon his personal sincerity, and much more upon his constancy of purpose, there was at least in Piedmont an army thoroughly national in its sentiment, and capable of taking the lead whenever the opportunity should arise for uniting Italy against the foreigner. In no other Italian State was there an effective military force, or one so little adulterated with foreign elements.

A third current of opinion in these years of hope and of illusion was that represented in the writings of Gioberti, the depicter of a new and glorious Italy, regenerated not by philosophic republicanism or the sword of a temporal monarch, but by the moral force of a reformed and reforming Papacy. *Hopes of the Papacy.* The conception of the Catholic Church as a great Liberal power, strange and fantastic as it now appears, was no dream of an isolated Italian enthusiast; it was an idea which, after the French Revolution of 1830, and the establishment of a government at once anti-clerical and anti-democratic, powerfully influenced some of the best minds in France, and found in Montalembert and Lamennais exponents who commanded the ear of Europe. If the corruption of the Papacy had been at once the spiritual and the political death of Italy, its renovation in purity and in strength would be also the resurrection of the Italian people. Other lands had sought, and sought in vain, to work out their problems under the guidance of leaders antagonistic to the Church, and of popular doctrines divorced from religious faith. To Italy belonged the prerogative of spiritual power. By this power, aroused from the torpor of ages, and speaking, as it had once spoken, to the very conscience of mankind, the gates of a glorious future would be thrown open. Conspirators might fret, and politicians scheme, but the day on which the new life of Italy would begin would be that day when the head of the Church, taking his place as chief of a federation of Italian States, should raise the banner of freedom and national right, and princes and people alike should follow the all-inspiring voice.

A monk, ignorant of everything but cloister lore, benighted, tyrannical, the companion in his private life of a few jolly priests and a gossiping barber, was not an alluring emblem of the Church of the future. But in 1846 Pope Gregory XVI., who for the last five years had been engaged in one incessant struggle against insurgents, conspirators, and reformers, and whose prisons were crowded with the best of his subjects, passed away.* His successor, Mastai Ferretti, Bishop of Imola, was elected under the title of Pius IX., after the candidate favoured by Austria had failed to secure the requisite number of votes (June 17). The choice of this kindly and popular prelate was to some extent a tribute to Italian feeling; and for the next eighteen months it appeared as if Gioberti had really divined the secret of the age. The first act of the new Pope was the publication of a universal amnesty for political offences. The prison doors throughout his dominions were thrown open, and men who had been sentenced to confinement for life returned in exultation to their homes. The act created a profound impression throughout Italy, and each good-humoured utterance of Pius confirmed the belief that great changes were at hand. A wild enthusiasm seized upon Rome. The population abandoned itself to festivals in honour of the Pontiff and of the approaching restoration of Roman liberty. Little was done; not much was actually

<small>Election of Pius IX., June, 1846.</small>

* Farini, i. 153. Azeglio, Corresp. Politique, p. 24; Casi di Romagna, p. 47.

PIUS IX. DRIVING THROUGH THE STREETS OF ROME.

(p. 472.)

promised; everything was believed. The principle of representative government was discerned in the new Council of State now placed by the side of the College of Cardinals; a more serious concession was made to popular feeling in the permission given to the citizens of Rome, and afterwards to those of the provinces, to enrol themselves in a civic guard. But the climax of excitement was reached when, in answer to a threatening movement of Austria, occasioned by the growing agitation throughout Central Italy, the Papal Court protested against the action of its late protector. By the Treaties of Vienna Austria had gained the right to garrison the citadel of Ferrara, though this town lay within the Ecclesiastical States. Placing a new interpretation on the expression used in the Treaties, the Austrian Government occupied the town of Ferrara itself (June 17, 1847). The movement was universally understood to be the preliminary to a new occupation of the Papal States, like that of 1831; and the protests of the Pope against the violation of his territory gave to the controversy a European importance. The English and French fleets appeared at Naples; the King of Sardinia openly announced his intention to take the field against Austria if war should break out. By the efforts of neutral Powers a compromise on the occupation of Ferrara was at length arranged; but the passions which had been excited were not appeased, and the Pope remained in popular imagination the champion of Italian independence against Austria, as well as the apostle of

Reforms expected from Pius.

Ferrara, June, 1847.

constitutional Government and the rights of the people.

In the meantime the agitation begun in Rome was spreading through the north and the south of the peninsula, and beyond the Sicilian Straits.

Revolution at Palermo. Jan., 1848.

The centenary of the expulsion of the Austrians from Genoa in December, 1746, was celebrated throughout central Italy with popular demonstrations which gave Austria warning of the storm about to burst upon it. In the south, however, impatience under domestic tyranny was a far more powerful force than the distant hope of national independence. Sicily had never forgotten the separate rights which it had once enjoyed, and the constitution given to it under the auspices of England in 1812. Communications passed between the Sicilian leaders and the opponents of the Bourbon Government on the mainland, and in the autumn of 1847 simultaneous risings took place in Calabria and at Messina. These were repressed without difficulty; but the fire smouldered far and wide, and on the 13th of January, 1848, the population of Palermo rose in revolt. For fourteen days the conflict between the people and the Neapolitan troops continued. The city was bombarded, but in the end the people were victorious, and a provisional government was formed by the leaders of the insurrection. One Sicilian town after another followed the example of the capital, and expelled its Neapolitan garrison. Threatened by revolution in Naples itself, King Ferdinand II., grandson of the despot of 1821, now imitated the policy of his predecessor, and proclaimed a constitution. A Liberal Ministry was formed, but no word was said as to the autonomy claimed by Sicily, and promised, as it would seem, by the leaders of the popular party on the mainland. After the first excitement of success was past, it became clear that the Sicilians were as widely at variance with the newly-formed Government at Naples as with that which they had overthrown.

The insurrection of Palermo gave a new stimulus and imparted more of revolutionary colour to the popular movement throughout Italy. Constitutions were granted in Piedmont and Tuscany. In the Austrian provinces national exasperation against the rule of the foreigner grew daily more menacing. Radetzky, the Austrian Commander-in-chief, had long foreseen the impending struggle, and had endeavoured, but not with complete success, to impress his own views upon the imperial Government. Verona had been made the centre of a great system of fortifications, and the strength of the army under Radetzky's command had been considerably increased, but it was not until the eleventh hour that Metternich abandoned the hope of tiding over difficulties by his old system of police and spies, and permitted the establishment of undisguised military rule. In order to injure the finances of Austria, a general resolution had been made by the patriotic societies of Upper Italy to abstain from the use of tobacco, from which the Government drew a large part of its revenue. On the first Sunday in 1848 Austrian officers, smoking

Agitation in Austrian Italy.

in the streets of Milan, were attacked by the people. The troops were called to arms: a conflict took place, and enough blood was shed to give to the tumult the importance of an actual revolt. In Padua and elsewhere similar outbreaks followed. Radetzky issued a general order to his troops, declaring that the Emperor was determined to defend his Italian dominion whether against an external or domestic foe. Martial law was proclaimed; and for a moment, although Piedmont gave signs of throwing itself into the Italian movement, the awe of Austria's military power hushed the rising tempest. A few weeks more revealed to an astonished world the secret that the Austrian State, so great and so formidable in the eyes of friend and foe, was itself on the verge of dissolution.

It was to the absence of all stirring public life, not to any real assimilative power or any high intelligence in administration, that the House of Hapsburg owed, during the eighteenth century, the continued union of that motley of nations or races which successive conquests, marriages, and treaties had brought under its dominion. The violence of the attack made by the Emperor Joseph upon all provincial rights first re-awakened the slumbering spirit of Hungary; but the national movement of that time, which excited such strong hopes and alarms, had been succeeded by a long period of stagnation, and during the Napoleonic wars the repression of everything that appealed to any distinctively national spirit had become more avowedly than before the settled principle of the

<small>Austria.</small>

Austrian Court. In 1812 the Hungarian Diet had resisted the financial measures of the Government. The consequence was that, in spite of the law requiring its convocation every three years, the Diet was not again summoned till 1825. During the intermediate period, the Emperor raised taxes and levies by edict alone. Deprived of its constitutional representation, the Hungarian nobility pursued its opposition to the encroachments of the Crown in the Sessions of each county. At these assemblies, to which there existed no parallel in the western and more advanced States of the Continent, each resident landowner who belonged to the very numerous caste of the noblesse was entitled to speak and to vote. Retaining, in addition to the right of free discussion and petition, the appointment of local officials, as well as a considerable share in the actual administration, the Hungarian county-assemblies, handing down a spirit of rough independence from an immemorial past, were probably the hardiest relic of self-government existing in any of the great monarchical States of Europe. Ignorant, often uncouth in their habits, oppressive to their peasantry, and dominated by the spirit of race and caste, the mass of the Magyar nobility had indeed proved as impervious to the humanising influences of the eighteenth century as they had to the solicitations of despotism. The Magnates, or highest order of noblesse, who formed a separate chamber in the Diet, had been to some extent denationalised; they were at once more European in their culture, and more submissive to the Austrian Court.

Affairs in Hungary.

In banishing political discussion from the Diet to the County Sessions, the Emperor's Government had intensified the provincial spirit which it sought to extinguish. Too numerous to be won over by personal inducements, and remote from the imperial agencies which had worked so effectively through the Chamber of Magnates, the lesser nobility of Hungary during these years of absolutism carried the habit of political discussion to their homes, and learnt to baffle the imperial Government by withholding all help and all information from its subordinate agents. Each county-assembly became a little Parliament, and a centre of resistance to the usurpation of the Crown. The stimulus given to the national spirit by this struggle against unconstitutional rule was seen not less in the vigorous attacks made upon the Government on the re-assembling of the Diet in 1825, than in the demand that Magyar, and not Latin as heretofore, should be the language used in recording the proceedings of the Diet, and in which communications should pass between the Upper and the Lower House.

There lay in this demand for the recognition of the national language the germ of a conflict of race against race which was least of all suspected by those by whom the demand was made.

Magyars and Slavs.

Hungary, as a political unity, comprised, besides the Slavic kingdom of Croatia, wide regions in which the inhabitants were of Slavic or Roumanian race, and where the Magyar was known only as a feudal lord. The district in which the population at large belonged to the Magyar stock did not exceed one-half of the kingdom. For the other races of Hungary, who were probably twice as numerous as themselves, the Magyars entertained the utmost contempt, attributing to them the moral qualities of the savage, and denying to them the possession of any nationality whatever. In a country combining so many elements ill-blended with one another, and all alike subject to a German Court at Vienna, Latin, as the language of the Church and formerly the language of international communication, had served well as a neutral means of expression in public affairs. There might be Croatian deputies in the Diet who could not speak Magyar; the Magyars could not understand Croatian; both could understand and could without much effort express themselves in the species of Latin which passed muster at Presburg and at Vienna. Yet no freedom of handling could convert a dead language into a living one; and when the love of country and of ancient right became once more among the Magyars an inspiring passion, it naturally sought a nobler and more spontaneous utterance than dog-latin. Though no law was passed upon the subject in the Parliament in which it was first mooted, speakers in the Diet of 1832 used their mother-tongue; and when the Viennese Government forbade the publication of the debates, reports were circulated in manuscript through the country by Kossuth, a young deputy, who after the dissolution of the Diet in 1836 paid for his defiance of the Emperor by three years' imprisonment.

Hungary now seemed to be entering upon an epoch of varied and rapid national development. The barriers which separated it from the Western world were disappearing. The literature, the ideas, the inventions of Western Europe were penetrating its archaic society, and transforming a movement which in its origin had been conservative and aristocratic into one of far-reaching progress and reform. Alone among the opponents of absolute power on the Continent, the Magyars had based their resistance on positive constitutional right, on prescription, and the settled usage of the past; and throughout the conflict with the Crown between 1812 and 1825 legal right was on the side not of the Emperor but of those whom he attempted to coerce. With excellent judgment the Hungarian leaders had during these years abstained from raising any demand for reforms, appreciating the advantage of a purely defensive position in a combat with a Court pledged in the eyes of all Europe, as Austria was, to the defence of legitimate rights. This policy had gained its end; the Emperor, after thirteen years of conflict, had been forced to re-convoke the Diet, and to abandon the hope of effecting a work in which his uncle, Joseph II., had failed. But, the constitution once saved, that narrow and exclusive body of rights for which the nobility had contended no longer satisfied the needs or the conscience of the time.* Opinion was moving fast;

Hungary after 1830.

---

* Down to 1827 not only was all land inherited by nobles free from taxation, but any taxable land purchased by a noble thereupon became tax-free. The attempt of the Government to abolish this latter injustice evoked a storm of anger in the Diet of 1825, and still more in the county assemblies, some of the latter even resolving that such law, if passed by the Diet, would be null and void.

the claims of the towns and of the rural population were making themselves felt; the agitation that followed the overthrow of the Bourbons in 1830 reached Hungary too, not so much through French influence as through the Polish war of independence, in which the Magyars saw a struggle not unlike their own, enlisting their warmest sympathies for the Polish armies so long as they kept the field, and for the exiles who came among them when the conflict was over. By the side of the old defenders of class-privilege there arose men imbued with the spirit of modern Liberalism. The laws governing the relation of the peasant to his lord, which remained nearly as they had been left by Maria Theresa, were dealt with by the Diet of 1832 in so liberal a spirit that the Austrian Government, formerly far in advance of Hungarian opinion on this subject, refused its assent to many of the measures passed. Great schemes of social and material improvement also aroused the public hopes in these years. The better minds became conscious of the real aspect of Hungarian life in comparison with that of civilised Europe—of its poverty, its inertia, its boorishness. Extraordinary energy was thrown into the work of advance by Count Szóchenyi, a nobleman whose imagination had been fired by the contrast which the busy industry of Great Britain and the practical interests of its higher classes presented to the torpor of his own country. It is to him that Hungary owes the bridge uniting its double capital at Pesth, and that Europe owes the

The Diet of 1832—36.

Széchenyi.

unimpeded navigation of the Danube, which he first rendered possible by the destruction of the rocks known as the Iron Gates at Orsova. Sanguine, lavishly generous, an ardent patriot, Széchenyi endeavoured to arouse men of his own rank, the great and the powerful in Hungary, to the sense of what was due from them to their country as leaders in its industrial development. He was no revolutionist, nor was he an enemy to Austria. A peaceful political future would best have accorded with his own designs for raising Hungary to its due place among nations.

That the Hungarian movement of this time was converted from one of fruitful progress into an embittered political conflict ending in civil war was due, among other causes, to the action of the Austrian Cabinet itself. Wherever constitutional right existed, there Austria saw a natural enemy. The province of Transylvania, containing a mixed population of Magyars, Germans, and Roumanians, had, like Hungary, a Diet of its own, which Diet ought to have been summoned every year. It was, however, not once assembled between 1811 and 1834. In the agitation at length provoked in Transylvania by this disregard of constitutional right, the Magyar element naturally took the lead, and so gained complete ascendancy in the province. When the Diet met in 1834, its language and conduct were defiant in the highest degree. It was speedily dissolved, and the scandal occasioned by its proceedings disturbed the last days of the Emperor Francis, who died in 1835, leaving the throne to his son Ferdinand, an invalid incapable of any serious exertion. It soon appeared that nothing was changed in the principles of the Imperial Government, and that whatever hopes had been formed of the establishment of a freer system under the new reign were delusive. The leader of the Transylvanian Opposition was Count Wesselényi, himself a Magnate in Hungary, who, after the dissolution of the Diet, betook himself to the Sessions of the Hungarian counties, and there delivered speeches against the Court which led to his being arrested and brought to trial for high treason. His cause was taken up by the Hungarian Diet, as one in which the rights of the local assemblies were involved. The plea of privilege was, however, urged in vain, and the sentence of exile which was passed upon Count Wesselényi became a new source of contention between the Crown and the Magyar Estates.*

The enmity of Government was now a sufficient passport to popular favour. On emerging from his prison under a general amnesty in 1840, Kossuth undertook the direction of a Magyar journal at Pesth, which at once gained an immense influence throughout the country. The spokesman of a new generation, Kossuth represented an entirely different order of ideas from those of the orthodox defenders of the Hungarian Constitution. They had been conservative and aristocratic; he was revolutionary: their weapons had

Parties among the Magyars.

---

* Horváth, Fünfundzwangig Jahre, i. 406. Springer, i. 466. Gerando, Esprit Public, 173. Kossuth, Gesammelte Werke, i. 29. Beschwerden und Klagen der Slaven in Ungarn, 89.

been drawn from the storehouse of Hungarian positive law; his inspiration was from the Liberalism of western Europe. Thus within the national party itself there grew up sections in more or less pronounced antagonism to one another, though all were united by a passionate devotion to Hungary and by an unbounded faith in its future. Széchenyi, and those who with him subordinated political to material ends, regarded Kossuth as a dangerous theorist. Between the more impetuous and the more cautious reformers stood the recognised Parliamentary leaders of the Liberals, among whom Deák had already given proof of political capacity of no common order. In Kossuth's journal the national problems of the time were discussed both by his opponents and by his friends. Publicity gave greater range as well as greater animation to the conflict of ideas; and the rapid development of opinion during these years was seen in the large and ambitious measures which occupied the Diet of 1843. Electoral and municipal reform, the creation of a code of criminal law, the introduction of trial by jury, the abolition of the immunity of the nobles from taxation; all these, and similar legislative projects, displayed at once the energy of the time and the influence of western Europe in transforming the political conceptions of the Hungarian nation. Hitherto the forty-three Free Cities had possessed but a single vote in the Diet, as against the sixty-three votes possessed by the Counties. It was now generally admitted that this anomaly could not continue; but inasmuch as civic rights were themselves

The Diet of 1843.

monopolised by small privileged orders among the townsmen, the problem of constitutional reform carried with it that of a reform of the municipalities. Hungary in short was now face to face with the task of converting its ancient system of the representation of the privileged orders into the modern system of a representation of the nation at large. Arduous at every epoch and in every country, this work was one of almost insuperable difficulty in Hungary, through the close connection with the absolute monarchy of Austria; through the existence of a body of poor noblesse, numbered at two hundred thousand, who, though strong in patriotic sentiment, bitterly resented any attack upon their own freedom from taxation; and above all through the variety of races in Hungary, and the attitude assumed by the Magyars, as the dominant nationality, towards the Slavs around them. In proportion as the energy of the Magyars and their confidence in the victory of the national cause mounted high, so rose their disdain of all claims beside their own within the Hungarian kingdom. It was resolved by the Lower Chamber of the Diet of 1843 that no language but Magyar should be permitted in debate, and that at the end of ten years every person not capable of speaking the Magyar language should be excluded from all public employment. The Magnates softened the latter provision by excepting from it the holders of merely local offices in Slavic districts; against the prohibition of Latin in the Diet the Croatians appealed to the Emperor. A rescript arrived from Vienna placing a veto upon the resolution. So violent was the storm excited in the Diet itself by this rescript, and so threatening the language of the national leaders outside, that the Cabinet, after a short interval, revoked its decision, and accepted a compromise which, while establishing Magyar as the official language of the kingdom, and requiring that it should be taught even in Croatian schools, permitted the use of Latin in the Diet for the next six years. In the meantime the Diet had shouted down every speaker who began with the usual Latin formula, and fighting had taken place in Agram, the Croatian capital, between the national and the Magyar factions.

It was in vain that the effort was made at Presburg to resist all claims but those of one race. The same quickening breath which had stirred the Magyar nation to new life had also passed over the branches of the Slavic family within the Austrian dominions far and near.

The Slavic national movements. In Bohemia a revival of interest in the Czech language and literature, which began about 1820, had in the following decade gained a distinctly political character. Societies originally or professedly founded for literary objects had become the centres of a popular movement directed towards the emancipation of the Czech elements in Bohemia from German ascendancy, and the restoration of something of a national character to the institutions of the kingdom. Among the southern Slavs, with whom Hungary was more directly concerned, the national movement first became visible rather later. Its earliest manifestations took, just as in Bohemia, a literary or linguistic form.

Projects for the formation of a common language which, under the name of Illyrian, should draw together all the Slavic populations between the Adriatic and the Black Sea, occupied for a while the fancy of the learned; but the more ambitious part of this design, which had given some umbrage to the Turkish Government, was abandoned in obedience to instructions from Vienna; and the movement first gained political importance when its scope was limited to the Croatian and Slavonic districts of Hungary, and it was endowed with the distinct task of resisting the imposition of Magyar as an official language. In addition to their representation in the Diet of the Kingdom at Presburg, the Croatian landowners had their own Provincial Diet at Agram. In this they possessed not only a common centre of action, but an organ of communication with the Imperial Government at Vienna, which rendered them some support in their resistance to Magyar pretensions. Later events gave currency to the belief that a conflict of races in Hungary was deliberately stimulated by the Austrian Court in its own interest. But the whole temper and principle of Metternich's rule was opposed to the development of national spirit, whether in one race or another; and the patronage which the Croats appeared at this time to receive at Vienna was probably no more than an instinctive act of conservatism, intended to maintain the balance of interests, and to reduce within the narrowest possible limits such changes as might prove inevitable.

Of all the important measures of reform which were

brought before the Hungarian Diet of 1843, one alone had become law. The rest were either rejected by the Chamber of Magnates after passing the Lower House, or were thrown out in the Lower House in spite of the approval of the majority, in consequence of peremptory instructions sent to Presburg by the county-assemblies. The representative of a Hungarian constituency was not free to vote at his discretion; he was the delegate of the body of nobles which sent him, and was legally bound to give his vote in accordance with the instructions which he might from time to time receive. However zealous the Legislature itself, it was therefore liable to be paralysed by external pressure as soon as any question was raised which touched the privileges of the noble caste. This was especially the case with all projects involving the expenditure of public revenue. Until the nobles bore their share of taxation it was impossible that Hungary should emerge from a condition of beggarly need; yet, be the inclination of the Diet what it might, it was controlled by bodies of stubborn squires or yeomen in each county, who fully understood their own power, and stoutly forbade the passing of any measure which imposed a share of the public burdens upon themselves. The impossibility of carrying out reforms under existing conditions had been demonstrated by the failures of 1843. In order to overcome the obstruction as well of the Magnates as of the county-assemblies, it was necessary that an appeal should be made to the country at large, and that a force of public sentiment should be aroused which should both overmaster the existing array of special interests, and give birth to legislation merging them for the future in a comprehensive system of really national institutions. To this task the Liberal Opposition addressed itself; and although large differences existed within the party, and the action of Kossuth, who now exchanged the career of the journalist for that of the orator, was little fettered by the opinions of his colleagues, the general result did not disappoint the hopes that had been formed. Political associations and clubs took vigorous root in the country. The magic of Kossuth's oratory left every hearer a more patriotic, if not a wiser man; and an awakening passion for the public good seemed for a while to throw all private interests into the shade.

It now became plain to all but the blindest that great changes were inevitable; and at the instance of the more intelligent among the Conservative party in Hungary the Imperial Government resolved to enter the lists with a policy of reform, and, if possible, to wrest the helm from the men who were becoming masters of the nation. In order to secure a majority in the Diet, it was deemed requisite by the Government first to gain a predominant influence in the county-assemblies. As a preliminary step, most of the Lieutenants of counties, to whose high dignity no practical functions attached, were removed from their posts, and superseded by paid administrators, appointed from Vienna. Count Apponyi, one of the most vigorous of the conservative and aristocratic

Government Policy of Reform.

reformers, was placed at the head of the Ministry. In due time the proposals of the Government were made public. They comprised the taxation of the nobles, a reform of the municipalities, modifications in the land-system, and a variety of economic measures intended directly to promote the material development of the country. The latter were framed to some extent on the lines laid down by Széchenyi, who now, in bitter antagonism to Kossuth, accepted office under the Government, and gave to it the prestige of his great name. It remained for the Opposition to place their own counter-proposals before the country. Differences within the party were smoothed over, and a manifesto, drawn up by Deák, gave statesmanlike expression to the aims of the national leaders. Embracing every reform included in the policy of the Government, it added to them others which the Government had not ventured to face, and gave to the whole the character of a vindication of its own rights by the nation, in contrast to a scheme of administrative reform worked out by the officers of the Crown. Thus while it enforced the taxation of the nobles, it claimed for the Diet the right of control over every branch of the national expenditure. It demanded increased liberty for the Press, and an unfettered right of political association; and finally, while doing homage to the unity of the Crown, it required that the Government of Hungary should be one in direct accord with the national representation in the Diet, and that the habitual effort of the Court of Vienna to place this kingdom on the same footing as the Emperor's

Programme of the Opposition.

non-constitutional provinces should be abandoned. With the rival programmes of the Government and the Opposition before it, the country proceeded to the elections of 1847. Hopefulness and enthusiasm abounded on every side; and at the close of the year the Diet assembled from which so great a work was expected, and which was destined within so short a time to witness, in storm and revolution, the passing away of the ancient order of Hungarian life.

The directly constitutional problems with which the Diet of Presburg had to deal were peculiar to Hungary itself, and did not exist in the other parts of the Austrian Empire. There were, however, social problems which were not less urgently forcing themselves upon public attention alike in Hungary and in those provinces which enjoyed no constitutional rights. The chief of these was the condition of the peasant-population. In the greater part of the Austrian dominions, though serfage had long been abolished, society was still based upon the manorial system. The peasant held his land subject to the obligation of labouring on his lord's domain for a certain number of days in the year, and of rendering him other customary services: the manor-court, though checked by the neighbourhood of crown-officers, retained its jurisdiction, and its agents frequently performed duties of police. Hence the proposed extinction of the so-called feudal tie, and the conversion of the semi-dependent cultivator into a freeholder bound only to the payment of a fixed money-charge, or rendered free of all

The Rural System of Austria.

obligation by the surrender of a part of his holding, involved in many districts the institution of new public authorities and a general reorganisation of the minor local powers. From this task the Austrian Government had shrunk in mere lethargy, even when, as in 1835, proposals for change had come from the landowners themselves. The work begun by Maria Theresa and Joseph remained untouched, though thirty years of peace had given abundant opportunity for its completion, and the legislation of Hardenberg in 1810 afforded precedents covering at least part of the field.

At length events occurred which roused the drowsiest heads in Vienna from their slumbers. The party of action among the Polish refugees at Paris had determined to strike another blow for the independence of their country. Instead, however, of repeating the insurrection of Warsaw, it was arranged that the revolt should commence in Prussian and Austrian Poland, and the beginning of the year 1846 was fixed for the uprising. In Prussia the Government crushed the conspirators before a blow could be struck. In Austria, though ample warning was given, the precautions taken were insufficient. General Collin occupied the Free City of Cracow, where the revolutionary committee had its headquarters; but the troops under his command were so weak that he was soon compelled to retreat, and to await the arrival of reinforcements. Meanwhile the landowners in the district of Tarnow in northern Galicia raised the standard of insurrection, and sought to arm the country. The Ruthenian peasantry, however, among whom they lived, owed all that was tolerable in their condition to the protection of the Austrian crown-officers, and detested the memory of an independent Poland. Instead of following their lords into the field, they gave information of their movements, and asked instructions from the nearest Austrian authorities. They were bidden to seize upon any persons who instigated them to rebellion, and to bring them into the towns. A war of the peasants against the nobles forthwith broke out. Murder, pillage, and incendiary fires brought both the Polish insurrection and its leaders to a miserable end. The Polish nobles, unwilling to acknowledge the humiliating truth that their own peasants were their bitterest enemies, charged the Austrian Government with having set a price on their heads, and with having instigated the peasants to a communistic revolt. Metternich, disgraced by the spectacle of a Jacquerie raging apparently under his own auspices, insisted, in a circular to the European Courts, that the attack of the peasantry upon the nobles had been purely spontaneous, and occasioned by attempts to press certain villagers into the ranks of the rebellion by brute force. But whatever may have been the measure of responsibility incurred by the agents of the Government, an agrarian revolution was undoubtedly in full course in Galicia, and its effects were soon felt in the rest of the Austrian monarchy. The Arcadian contentment of the rural population, which had been the boast, and in some degree the real strength,

Insurrection in Galicia, Feb., 1846.

of Austria, was at an end. Conscious that the problem which it had so long evaded must at length be faced, the Government of Vienna prepared to deal with the conditions of land-tenure by legislation extending over the whole of the Empire. But the courage which was necessary for an adequate solution of the difficulty nowhere existed within the official world, and the Edict which conveyed the last words of the Imperial Government on this vital question contained nothing more than a series of provisions for facilitating voluntary settlements between the peasants and their lords. In the quality of this enactment the Court of Vienna gave the measure of its own weakness. The opportunity of breaking with traditions of impotence had presented itself and had been lost. Revolution was at the gates; and in the unsatisfied claim of the rural population the Government had handed over to its adversaries a weapon of the greatest power.*

Rural Edict. Dec. 1846.

In the purely German provinces of Austria there lingered whatever of the spirit of tranquillity was still to be found within the Empire. This, however, was not the case in the districts into which the influence of the capital extended. Vienna had of late grown out of its old careless spirit. The home in past years of a population notoriously pleasure-loving, good-humoured, and indifferent to public affairs,

Vienna.

---

* Das Polen-Attentat, 1846, p. 203. Verhältnisse in Galizien, p. 57. Briefe eines Polnischen Edelmannes, p. 31. Metternich, vii. 196. Cracow, which had been made an independent Republic by the Congress of Vienna, was now annexed by Austria with the consent of Russia and Prussia, and against the protests of England and France.

it had now taken something of a more serious character. The death of the Emperor Francis, who to the last generation of Viennese had been as fixed a part of the order of things as the river Danube, was not unconnected with this change in the public tone. So long as the old Emperor lived, all thought that was given to political affairs was energy thrown away. By his death not only had the State lost an ultimate controlling power, if dull, yet practised and tenacious, but this loss was palpable to all the world. The void stood bare and unrelieved before the public eye. The notorious imbecility of the Emperor Ferdinand, the barren and antiquated formalism of Metternich and of that entire system which seemed to be incorporated in him, made Government an object of general satire, and in some quarters of rankling contempt. In proportion as the culture and intelligence of the capital exceeded that of other towns, so much the more galling was the pressure of that part of the general system of tutelage which was especially directed against the independence of the mind. The censorship was exercised with grotesque stupidity. It was still the aim of Government to isolate Austria from the ideas and the speculation of other lands, and to shape the intellectual world of the Emperor's subjects into that precise form which tradition prescribed as suitable for the members of a well-regulated State. In poetry, the works of Lord Byron were excluded from circulation, where custom-house officers and market-inspectors chose to enforce the law; in history and political literature, the leading writers of modern times lay under the same ban. Native production was much more effectively controlled. Whoever wrote in a newspaper, or lectured at a University, or published a work of imagination, was expected to deliver himself of something agreeable to the constituted authorities, or was reduced to silence. Far as Vienna fell short of Northern Germany in intellectual activity, the humiliation inflicted on its best elements by this life-destroying surveillance was keenly felt and bitterly resented. More perhaps by its senile warfare against mental freedom than by any acts of direct political repression, the Government ranged against itself the almost unanimous opinion of the educated classes. Its hold on the affection of the capital was gone. Still quiescent, but ready to unite against the Government when opportunity should arrive, there stood, in addition to the unorganised mass of the middle ranks, certain political associations and students' societies, a vigorous Jewish element, and the usual contingent furnished by poverty and discontent in every great city from among the labouring population. Military force sufficient to keep the capital in subjection was not wanting; but the foresight and the vigour necessary to cope with the first onset of revolution were nowhere to be found among the holders of power.

At Berlin the solid order of Prussian absolutism already shook to its foundation. With King Frederick William III., whose long reign ended in 1840, there departed the half-filial, half-spiritless acquiescence of the nation in the denial of the

Prussia.

liberties which had been so solemnly promised to it at the epoch of Napoleon's fall. The new Sovereign, Frederick William IV., ascended the throne amid high national hopes. The very contrast which his warm, exuberant nature offered to the silent, reserved disposition of his father impressed the public for a while in his favour. In the more shining personal qualities he far excelled all his immediate kindred. His artistic and literary sympathies, his aptitude of mind and readiness of speech, appeared to mark the man of a new age, and encouraged the belief that, in spite of the mediæval dreams and reactionary theories to which, as prince, he had surrendered himself, he would, as King, appreciate the needs of the time, and give to Prussia the free institutions which the nation demanded. The first acts of the new reign were generously conceived. Political offenders were freely pardoned. Men who had suffered for their opinions were restored to their posts in the Universities and the public service, or selected for promotion. But when the King approached the constitutional question, his utterances were unsatisfactory. Though undoubtedly in favour of some reform, he gave no sanction to the idea of a really national representation, but seemed rather to seek occasions to condemn it. Other omens of ill import were not wanting. Allying his Government with a narrow school of theologians, the King offended men of independent mind, and transgressed against the best traditions of Prussian administration. The prestige of the new reign was soon exhausted. Those who had

Frederick William IV., 1840.

believed Frederick William to be a man of genius now denounced him as a vaporous, inflated dilettante; his enthusiasm was seen to indicate nothing in particular; his sonorous commonplaces fell flat on second delivery. Not only in his own kingdom, but in the minor German States, which looked to Prussia as the future leader of a free Germany, the opinion rapidly gained ground that Frederick William IV. was to be numbered among the enemies rather than the friends of the good cause.

In the Edicts by which the last King of Prussia had promised his people a Constitution, it had been laid down that the representative body was to spring from the Provincial Estates, and that it was to possess, in addition to its purely consultative functions in legislation, a real power of control over all State loans and over all proposed additions to taxation. The interdependence of the promised Parliament and the Provincial Estates had been seen at the time to endanger the success of Hardenberg's scheme; nevertheless, it was this conception which King Frederick William IV. made the very centre of his Constitutional policy. A devotee to the distant past, he spoke of the Provincial Estates, which in their present form had existed only since 1823, as if they were a great national and historic institution which had come down unchanged through centuries. His first experiment was the summoning of a Committee from these bodies to consider certain financial projects with which the Government was occupied (1842). The labours of the Committee were insignificant, nor was

United Diet convoked at Berlin, Feb. 3, 1847.

its treatment at the hands of the Crown Ministers of a serious character. Frederick William, however, continued to meditate over his plans, and appointed a Commission to examine the project drawn up at his desire by the Cabinet. The agitation in favour of Parliamentary Government became more and more pressing among the educated classes; and at length, in spite of some opposition from his brother, the Crown Prince, afterwards Emperor of Germany, the King determined to fulfil his father's promise and to convoke a General Assembly at Berlin. On the 3rd of February, 1847, there appeared a Royal Patent, which summoned all the Provincial Estates to the capital, to meet as a United Diet of the Kingdom. The Diet was to be divided into two Chambers, the Upper Chamber including the Royal Princes and highest nobles, the Lower the representatives of the knights, towns, and peasants. The right of legislation was not granted to the Diet; it had, however, the right of presenting petitions on internal affairs. State-loans and new taxes were not, in time of peace, to be raised without its consent. No regular interval was fixed for the future meetings of the Diet, and its financial rights were moreover reduced by other provisions, which enacted that a United Committee from the Provincial Estates was to meet every four years for certain definite objects, and that a special Delegation was to sit each year for the transaction of business relating to the National Debt.*

* Reden des Kœnigs Friedrich Wilhelm IV., p. 17. Ranke's F. W. IV. in Allg. Deutsche Biog. Biedermann, Droissig Jahre, t. 186.

The nature of the General Assembly convoked by this Edict, the functions conferred upon it, and the guarantees offered for Representative Government in the future, so little corresponded with the requirements of the nation, that the question was at once raised in Liberal circles whether the concessions thus tendered by the King ought to be accepted or rejected. The doubt which existed as to the disposition of the monarch himself was increased by the speech from the throne at the opening of the Diet (April 11). In a vigorous harangue extending over half an hour, King Frederick William, while he said much that was appropriate to the occasion, denounced the spirit of revolution that was working in the Prussian Press, warned the Deputies that they had been summoned not to advocate political theories, but to protect each the rights of his own order, and declared that no power on earth should induce him to change his natural relation to his people into a constitutional one, or to permit a written sheet of paper to intervene like a second Providence between Prussia and the Almighty. So vehement was the language of the King, and so uncompromising his tone, that the proposal was forthwith made at a private conference that the Deputies should quit Berlin in a body. This extreme course was not adopted; it was determined instead to present an address to the King, laying before him in respectful language the shortcomings in the Patent of February 3rd. In the debate on this address began the Parliamentary history of Prussia. The Liberal majority in the Lower Chamber, anxious to base their cause on some foundation of positive law, treated the Edicts of Frederick William III. defining the rights of the future Representative Body as actual statutes of the realm, although the late King had never called a Representative Body into existence. From this point of view the functions now given to Committees and Delegations were so much illegally withdrawn from the rights of the Diet. The Government, on the other hand, denied that the Diet possessed any rights or claims whatever beyond those assigned to it by the Patent of February 3rd, to which it owed its origin. In receiving the address of the Chambers, the King, while expressing a desire to see the Constitution further developed, repeated the principle already laid down by his Ministers, and refused to acknowledge any obligation outside those which he had himself created.

When, after a series of debates on the political questions at issue, the actual business of the Session began, the relations between the Government and the Assembly grew worse rather than better. The principal measures submitted were the grant of a State-guarantee to certain land-banks established for the purpose of extinguishing the rent-charges on peasants' holdings, and the issue of a public loan for the construction of railways by the State. Alleging that the former measure was not directly one of taxation, the Government, in laying it before the Diet, declared that they asked only for an opinion, and denied that the Diet possessed any right of decision. Thus challenged, as

Proceedings and Dissolution of the Diet.

it were, to make good its claims, the Diet not only declined to assent to this guarantee, but set its veto on the proposed railway-loan. Both projects were in themselves admitted to be to the advantage of the State; their rejection by the Diet was an emphatic vindication of constitutional rights which the Government seemed indisposed to acknowledge. Opposition grew more and more embittered; and when, as a preliminary to the dissolution of the Diet, the King ordered its members to proceed to the election of the Committees and Delegation named in the Edict of February 3rd, an important group declined to take part in the elections, or consented to do so only under reservations, on the ground that the Diet, and that alone, possessed the constitutional control over finance which the King was about to commit to other bodies. Indignant at this protest, the King absented himself from the ceremony which brought the Diet to a close (June 26th). Amid general irritation and resentment the Assembly broke up. Nothing had resulted from its convocation but a direct exhibition of the antagonism of purpose existing between the Sovereign and the national representatives. Moderate men were alienated by the doctrines promulgated from the Throne; and an experiment which, if more wisely conducted, might possibly at the eleventh hour have saved all Germany from revolution, left the Monarchy discredited and exposed to the attack of the most violent of its foes.

The train was now laid throughout central Europe; it needed but a flash from Paris to kindle the fire far and wide. That the Crown which Louis Philippe owed to one popular outbreak might be wrested from him by another, had been a thought constantly present not only to the King himself but to foreign observers during the earlier years of his reign. The period of comparative peace by which the first Republican movements after 1830 had been succeeded, the busy working of the Parliamentary system, the keen and successful pursuit of wealth which seemed to have mastered all other impulses in France, had made these fears a thing of the past. The Orleanist Monarchy had taken its place among the accredited institutions of Europe; its chief, aged, but vigorous in mind, looked forward to the future of his dynasty, and occupied himself with plans for extending its influence or its sway beyond the limits of France itself. At one time Louis Philippe had hoped to connect his family by marriage with the Courts of Vienna or Berlin; this project had not met with encouragement; so much the more eagerly did the King watch for opportunities in another direction, and devise plans for restoring the family-union between France and Spain which had been established by Louis XIV. and which had so largely influenced the history of Europe down to the overthrow of the Bourbon Monarchy. The Crown of Spain was now held by a young girl; her sister was the next in succession; to make the House of Orleans as powerful at Madrid as it was at Paris seemed under these circumstances no impossible task to a King and a Minister who, in the interests of the dynasty, were prepared to make some sacrifice of honour and good faith.

While the Carlist War was still continuing, Lord Palmerston had convinced himself that Louis Philippe intended to marry the young Queen Isabella, if possible, to one of his sons. Some years later this project was unofficially mentioned by Guizot to the English statesman, who at once caused it to be understood that England would not permit the union. Abandoning this scheme, Louis Philippe then demanded, by a misconstruction of the Treaty of Utrecht, that the Queen's choice of a husband should be limited to the Bourbons of the Spanish or Neapolitan line. To this claim Lord Aberdeen, who had become Foreign Secretary in 1841, declined to give his assent; he stated, however, that no step would be taken by England in antagonism to such marriage, if it should be deemed desirable at Madrid. Louis Philippe now suggested that his youngest son, the Duke of Montpensier, should wed the Infanta Fernanda, sister of the Queen of Spain. On the express understanding that this marriage should not take place until the Queen should herself have been married and have had children, the English Cabinet assented to the proposal. That the marriages should not be simultaneous was treated by both Governments as the very heart and substance of the arrangement, inasmuch as the failure of children by the Queen's marriage would make her sister, or her sister's heir, inheritor of the Throne. This was repeatedly acknowledged by Louis Philippe and his Minister, Guizot, in the course of communications with the British Court which extended over some years.

The Spanish Marriages, October, 1846.

Nevertheless, in 1846, the French Ambassador at Madrid, in conjunction with the Queen's mother, Maria Christina, succeeded in carrying out a plan by which the conditions laid down at London and accepted at Paris were utterly frustrated. Of the Queen's Spanish cousins, there was one, Don Francisco, who was known to be physically unfit for marriage. To this person it was determined by Maria Christina and the French Ambassador that the young Isabella should be united, her sister being simultaneously married to the Duke of Montpensier. So flagrantly was this arrangement in contradiction to the promises made at the Tuileries, that, when intelligence of it arrived at Paris, Louis Philippe declared for a moment that the Ambassador must be disavowed and disgraced. Guizot, however, was of better heart than his master, and asked for delay. In the very crisis of the King's perplexity the return of Lord Palmerston to office, and the mention by him of a Prince of Saxe-Coburg as one of the candidates for the Spanish Queen's hand, afforded Guizot a pretext for declaring that Great Britain had violated its engagements towards the House of Bourbon by promoting the candidature of a Coburg. In reality the British Government had not only taken no part in assisting the candidature of the Coburg Prince, but had directly opposed it. This, however, was urged in vain at the Tuileries. Whatever may have been the original intentions of Louis Philippe or of Guizot, the temptation of securing the probable succession to the Spanish Crown was too strong to be resisted. Preliminaries were pushed forward with the utmost haste, and on the 10th of October, 1846, the marriages of Queen Isabella and her sister, as arranged by the French Ambassador and the Queen-Mother, were simultaneously solemnised at Madrid.*

Few intrigues have been more disgraceful than that of the Spanish Marriages; none more futile. The course of history mocked its ulterior purposes; its immediate results were wholly to the injury of the House of Orleans. The cordial understanding between France and Great Britain, which had been revived after the differences of 1840, was now finally shattered. Louis Philippe stood convicted before his people of sacrificing a valuable alliance to purely dynastic ends; his Minister, the austere and sanctimonious Guizot, had to defend himself against charges which would have covered with shame the most hardened man of the world. Thus stripped of its garb of moral superiority, condemned as at once unscrupulous and unpatriotic, the Orleanist Monarchy had to meet the storm of popular discontent which was gathering over France as well as over neighbouring lands. For the lost friendship of England it was necessary to seek a substitute in the support of some Continental Power. Throwing himself into the reactionary policy of the Court of Vienna, Guizot endeavoured to establish a diplomatic concert from which England should be excluded, as France had been in 1840. There were circumstances

marginal note: Louis Philippe and Guizot, 1847.

---

* Guizot. viii. 101. Palmerston, iii. 194. Parl. Papers, 1847. Martin's Prince Consort, i. 341.

which gave some countenance to the design. The uncompromising vigour with which Lord Palmerston supported the Liberal movement now becoming so formidable in Italy made every absolute Government in Europe his enemy; and had time been granted, the despotic Courts would possibly have united with France in some more or less open combination against the English Minister. But the moments were now numbered; and ere the projected league could take substance, the whirlwind descended before which Louis Philippe and his Minister were the first to fall.

A demand for the reform of the French Parliamentary system had been made when Guizot was entering upon office in the midst of the Oriental crisis of 1840. It had then been silenced and repressed by all the means at the disposal of the Executive; King Louis Philippe being convinced that with a more democratic Chamber the maintenance of his own policy of peace would be impossible. The demand was now raised again with far greater energy. Although the franchise had been lowered after the Revolution of July, it was still so high that not one person in a hundred and fifty possessed a vote, while the property-qualification which was imposed upon the Deputies themselves excluded from the Chamber all but men of substantial wealth. Moreover there existed no law prohibiting the holders of administrative posts under the Government from sitting in the Assembly. The consequence was that more than one-third of the Deputies were either officials who had

Demand for Parliamentary Reform.

secured election, or representatives who since their election had accepted from Government appointments of greater or less value. Though Parliamentary talent abounded, it was impossible that a Chamber so composed could be the representative of the nation at large. The narrowness of the franchise, the wealth of the Deputies themselves, made them, in all questions affecting the social condition of the people, a mere club of capitalists; the influence which the Crown exercised through the bestowal of offices converted those who ought to have been its controllers into its dependents, the more so as its patronage was lavished on nominal opponents even more freely than on avowed friends. Against King Louis Philippe the majority in the Chamber had in fact ceased to possess a will of its own. It represented wealth; it represented to some extent the common sense of France; but on all current matters of dispute it only represented the executive government in another form. So thoroughly had the nation lost all hope in the Assembly during the last years of Louis Philippe, that even the elections had ceased to excite interest. On the other hand, the belief in the general prevalence of corruption was every day receiving new warrant. A series of State-trials disclosed the grossest frauds in every branch of the administration, and proved that political influence was habitually used for purposes of pecuniary gain. Taxed with his tolerance of a system scarcely distinguishable from its abuses, the Minister could only turn to his own nominees in the Chamber and ask them whether they felt themselves corrupted;

invited to consider some measure of Parliamentary reform, he scornfully asserted his policy of resistance. Thus, hopeless of obtaining satisfaction either from the Government or from the Chamber itself, the leaders of the Opposition resolved in 1847 to appeal to the country at large; and an agitation for Parliamentary reform, based on the methods employed by O'Connell in Ireland, soon spread through the principal towns of France.

But there were other ideas and other forces active among the labouring population of Paris than those familiar to the politicians of the Assembly. Theories of Socialism, the property of a few thinkers and readers during the earlier years of Louis Philippe's reign, had now sunk deep among the masses, and become, in a rough and easily apprehended form, the creed of the poor. From the time when Napoleon's fall had restored to France its faculty of thought, and, as it were, turned the soldier's eyes again upon his home, those questionings as to the basis of the social union which had occupied men's minds at an earlier epoch were once more felt and uttered. The problem was still what it had been in the eighteenth century; the answer was that of a later age. Kings, priests, and nobles had been overthrown, but misery still covered the world. In the teaching of Saint-Simon, under the Restoration, religious conceptions blended with a great industrial scheme; in the Utopia of Fourier, produced at the same fruitful period, whatever was valuable belonged to its suggestions in co-operative production. But whether the doctrine propounded was

Socialism.

that of philosopher, or sage, or charlatan, in every case the same leading ideas were visible;—the insufficiency of the individual in isolation, the industrial basis of all social life, the concern of the community, or of its supreme authority, in the organisation of labour. It was naturally in no remote or complex form that the idea of a new social order took possession of the mind of the workman in the faubourgs of Paris. He read in Louis Blanc, the latest and most intelligible of his teachers, of the right to labour, of the duty of the State to provide work for its citizens. This was something actual and tangible. For this he was ready upon occasion to take up arms; not for the purpose of extending the franchise to another handful of the Bourgeoisie, or of shifting the profits of government from one set of place-hunters to another. In antagonism to the ruling Minister the Reformers in the Chamber and the Socialists in the streets might for a moment unite their forces: but their ends were irreconcilable, and the allies of to-day were necessarily the foes of to-morrow.

At the close of the year 1847 the last Parliament of the Orleanist Monarchy assembled. The speech from the Throne, delivered by Louis Philippe himself, denounced in strong terms the agitation for Reform which had been carried on during the preceding months, though this agitation had, on the whole, been the work of the so-called Dynastic Opposition, which, while demanding electoral reform, was sincerely loyal to the Monarchy. The King's words were a challenge; and in the debate on

The February Revolution, 1848.

THE ERECTION OF BARRICADES IN PARIS.

(p. 611.)

the Address, the challenge was taken up by all ranks of Monarchical Liberals as well as by the small Republican section in the Assembly. The Government, however, was still secure of its majority. Defeated in the votes on the Address, the Opposition determined, by way of protest, to attend a banquet to be held in the Champs Elysées on the 22nd of February by the Reform-party in Western Paris. It was at first desired that by some friendly arrangement with the Government, which had declared the banquet illegal, the possibility of recourse to violence should be avoided. Misunderstandings, however, arose, and the Government finally prohibited the banquet, and made preparations for meeting any disturbance with force of arms. The Deputies, anxious to employ none but legal means of resistance, now resolved not to attend the banquet; on the other hand, the Democratic and Socialist leaders welcomed a possible opportunity for revolt. On the morning of the 22nd masses of men poured westwards from the workmen's quarter. The city was in confusion all day, and the erection of barricades began. Troops were posted in the streets; no serious attack, however, was made by either side, and at nightfall quiet returned.

Feb. 22nd.

'On the next morning the National Guard of Paris was called to arms. Throughout the struggle between Louis Philippe and the populace of Paris in the earlier years of his reign, the National Guard, which was drawn principally from the trading classes, had fought steadily for the King. Now, however, it was at one with the Liberal Opposition in the Assembly, and loudly demanded the dismissal of the Ministers. While some of the battalions interposed between the regular troops and the populace and averted a conflict, others proceeded to the Chamber with petitions for Reform. Obstinately as Louis Philippe had hitherto refused all concession, the announcement of the threatened defection of the National Guard at length convinced him that resistance was impossible. He accepted Guizot's resignation, and the Chamber heard from the fallen Minister himself that he had ceased to hold office. Although the King declined for a while to commit the formation of a Ministry to Thiers, the recognised chief of the Opposition, and endeavoured to place a politician more acceptable to himself in office, it was felt that with the fall of Guizot all real resistance to Reform was broken. Nothing more was asked by the Parliamentary Opposition or by the middle-class of Paris. The victory seemed to be won, the crisis at an end. In the western part of the capital congratulation and good-humour succeeded to the fear of conflict. The troops fraternised with the citizens and the National Guard; and when darkness came on, the boulevards were illuminated as if for a national festival.

Feb 23rd.

In the midst, however, of this rejoicing, and while the chiefs of the revolutionary societies, fearing that the opportunity had been lost for striking a blow at the Monarchy, exhorted the defenders of the barricades to maintain their positions, a band of workmen came into conflict, accidentally or of set purpose, with the troops in front of the Foreign Office. A volley was fired, which killed or wounded eighty persons. Placing the dead bodies on a waggon, and carrying them by torchlight through the streets in the workmen's quarter, the insurrectionary leaders called the people to arms. The tocsin sounded throughout the night; on the next morning the populace marched against the Tuileries. In consequence of the fall of the Ministry, and the supposed reconciliation of the King with the People, whatever military dispositions had been begun, had since been abandoned. At isolated points the troops fought bravely; but there was no systematic defence. Shattered by the strain of the previous days, and dismayed by the indifference of the National Guard when he rode out among them, the King, who at every epoch of his long life had shown such conspicuous courage in the presence of danger, now lost all nerve and all faculty of action. He signed an act of abdication in favour of his grandson, the Count of Paris, and fled. Behind him the victorious mob burst into the Tuileries and devastated it from cellar to roof. The Legislative Chamber, where an attempt was made to proclaim the Count of Paris King, was in its turn invaded. In uproar and tumult a Provisional Government was installed at the Hôtel de Ville; and ere the day closed the news went out to Europe that the House of Orleans had ceased to reign, and that the Republic had been proclaimed. It was not over France alone, it was over the Continent at large, that the tide of revolution was breaking.

Feb. 24th.

END OF VOLUME II.

www.ingramcontent.com/pod-product-compliance
Lightning Source LLC
Chambersburg PA
CBHW030300010526
44108CB00038B/649